The Giant Guide to Cocker Spaniels

*The **Giant** Care & Training Manual*

for your Cocker Spaniel

Dr Alex Lloyd

Copyright

This book is written in British English.

Edited, proofread, and formatted by: https://www.onlinebookservices.co.uk/

Table of Contents

1. Greetings from the Cocker Spaniel

'Dogs are small rays of light caught on Earth
a short time to brighten our days.'
~ Unknown ~

The cocker spaniel is a medium-sized dog breed with long ears and a carefree disposition. The cocker part of their name comes from their days of hunting Eurasian woodcock in England, although English cockers have hunted many other breeds of birds too. Their compact size—they grow to about 38 centimetres (15 inches) tall and weigh no more than 13.5 kilograms (30 pounds)—makes them ideal for any size home, from a flat to a family house. They are not a delicate little lapdog, but they are not so big as to have to perform a three-point turn to get round the coffee table, or apt to knock everything off it as they go. Their size, lively temperament, and sweet facial expression endears them to dog lovers worldwide.

English cocker spaniels have medium to long coats, which are flat or slightly wavy with a silky texture. Their legs, chest, and belly are covered with longer hair called feathering, but not as much as their cousin, the American cocker spaniel. Their feathering is more than decorative. It helps to protect the dog's body from scratches or other injuries when they make their way through undergrowth.

Cocker spaniels are described as merry and affectionate with an easy-going temperament. They are playful, trainable, and friendly towards people—although occasionally reserved with strangers—and other dogs. They also bark to let you know someone is approaching, so they are good watchdogs.

They are friendly, fun-loving, and gentle family dogs who do very well with children, especially if they are brought up with them. Adult cockers who are not familiar with children may do best in a home with older children who know how to interact with dogs. Cockers enjoy the company of other dogs and can get along fine with cats, especially if they are introduced at a young age.

Cocker spaniels need early socialisation, i.e., exposure to many different people, sights, sounds, and experiences. Socialisation helps to ensure your cocker puppy grows up to be a well-rounded, happy dog, and the sooner you start, the better.

These dogs are highly adaptable and can even do well living in a flat if they receive adequate daily exercise to keep them in shape. This is a breed with lots of stamina, and certainly enjoy long, brisk walks, games of fetch, or sports such as agility or flyball.

TIP ***This breed has a sensitive spaniel temperament and does not respond well to harshness. Therefore, you should use positive reinforcement techniques such as food rewards, praise, and play.***

Cockers are also fast learners, and if you make training consistent and fun, you will be extremely pleased with your dog's abilities.

History

Spaniels

The spaniel family is one of the oldest breeds of dogs and are the antecedents of the cocker spaniel (pictured).

References to spaniels can be found in the works of many literary masterpieces including Canterbury Tales by Geoffrey Chaucer (1342-1400) and A Midsummer Night's Dream by William Shakespeare (1564-1616). Before England's separation from the Catholic Church, during an audience with Pope Clement VIII, Lord Wiltshire's cocker spaniel bit the Pope on the toe.

It is thought that spaniels may have come to England when Caesar's army invaded in 54-55 BC. It is believed that spaniels originated from Spain and the name is a derivation of Hispania (Spain). Another school of thought is that it comes from the French phrase 'Chiens de l' Espagnol', literally 'Spaniard's dogs'. In his 15th-century work The Master of Game, the 2nd Duke of York describes them as, 'Another kind of hound there is that be called hounds for the hawk and spaniels, for their kind cometh from Spain, notwithstanding that there are many in other countries'.

Originally, spaniels were bred to flush game out of thick undergrowth, and by the late 1600s there were two specific types, water, and land breeds. Now extinct, the English water spaniel retrieved waterfowl shot down with arrows. The land spaniels were further divided into two separate strains. Setting spaniels scented the game, crept forward, and pointed toward their quarry, allowing hunters to ensnare them with nets. Springing spaniels were trained to spring pheasants and partridges for hunting with falcons, or rabbits for greyhound hunting. In the 17th century, Englishmen started to hunt with flintlocks, shooting birds on the wing, which significantly changed the spaniels' role. In

Julia Gasow and Charles S Goodall's 1984 book The New Complete English Springer Spaniel, they describe the spaniel as 'transformed from untrained, wild beaters, to smooth, polished gun dogs'.

FACT ***Springing spaniels are the forebears of modern-day flushing spaniels. In a springer spaniel's single litter, the larger pups were designated springer spaniels, the smaller pups were cocker spaniels, and the medium-sized pups became Sussex spaniels. Size was the only criterion.***

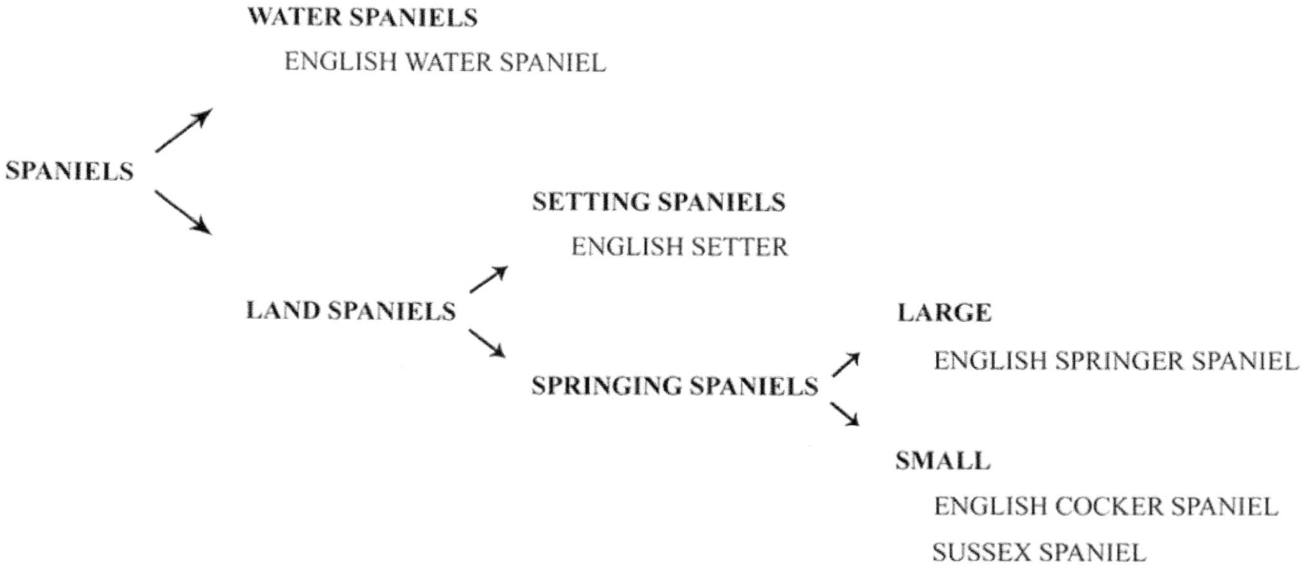

Cocker Spaniels

It wasn't until 1892 that The Kennel Club in the U.K. recognised English cocker spaniels and English springer spaniels as separate breeds. In England, bench shows were confusing as pups were entered as cockers one year and springers the following year as they had grown.

North America imported cocker spaniels from the mid-1800s onwards. Ultimately, some breeding stock returned to the United Kingdom. Unfortunately, the priorities of the breeders either side of the Atlantic differed. 'Most American breeders concentrated on the smaller, elegant solid-coloured cockers blended with the smaller field spaniels. While the British breeders were breeding roan and particoloured springer types with their cocker spaniels to produce a larger, leggier cocker who would hunt and retrieve,' stated Chereen Nawrocki, breeder, and past president of the English Cocker Spaniel Club of America.

By the 1920s, the English and American cockers were noticeably different. Although considered to be the same breed, the American Kennel Club recognised the English cocker spaniel as a distinct variety in 1936. The desire of fanciers was to keep the English strain pure, vowing not to breed them with the American cocker. A decade later, their endeavours were rewarded when the AKC bestowed the status as a separate breed from the American variety on the English cocker spaniel in 1946. Despite this, it took a further 24 years for The Kennel Club in the U.K. to recognise the American cocker spaniel as being separate from the English cocker.

The two modern breeds of cocker spaniels are thought to be sired by two dogs, Obo and Obo II. Obo is deemed

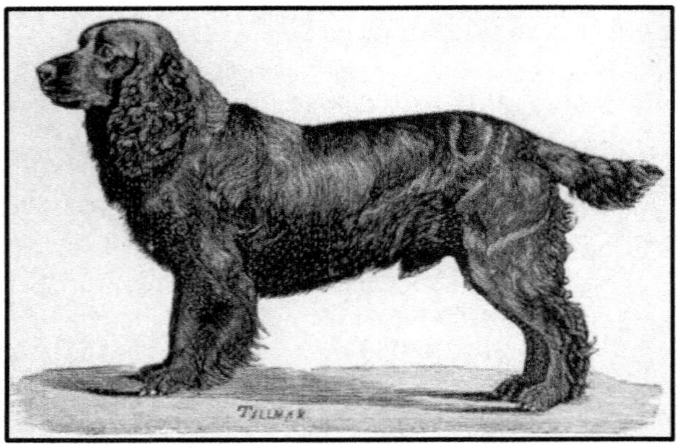

to be the father of the modern English cocker spaniel by breed enthusiasts, and his son, Obo II (pictured) is attributed with the accolade of being the forebear of the American cocker spaniel. In 1879 when Obo was born, size and not ancestry was all that was needed for registration as a cocker. His parents were a Sussex spaniel and a field spaniel. Whilst Obo was an English cocker, Obo II was born in America as his mother was shipped there when pregnant. Throughout his life, advertisements claimed that Obo II was the sire or grandsire of almost every prize-winning American cocker in the United States.

Unlike the English cocker spaniels, its American counterpart was bred for showing rather than hunting. The English cocker spaniels strongly resemble their springer spaniel ancestors.

Tail Docking

Tail docking is a controversial subject and banned in many parts of the world, including the U.K. and Australia. On the other hand, the U.S. does not regulate this procedure at all, meaning it is neither banned nor controlled. Even though New York and Vermont have considered legislation to ban it, neither state has so far. Historically, tail docking was used on cocker spaniels for centuries. Nearly all archived photos and drawings portray the cocker spaniel with a docked tail, having between half and two-thirds of their tail removed. To perform the task, breeders used a sharp pair of shears. The rationale behind docking their tails was that it prevented injury when the dog ran through thick undergrowth as the cocker flushed out game. Today, the practise is unnecessary as cocker spaniels are kept mostly as pets rather than hunters. Furthermore, tail docking influences the dog. Even if a veterinarian performs the procedure, the animal is seldom anaesthetised by local or general anaesthetic because of the risks involved. Not only is it painful, but it also causes stress to the animal. Additionally, the risk of infection and death from the procedure is always a possibility. Other risks include haemorrhaging, meningitis, chronic pain, or loss of sensation. Docking a dog's tail can affect their balance and gait. When its tail is docked, the cocker spaniel adopts a spread stance for balance.

A dog's behaviour can also be altered by tail docking. U.S. psychologist Stanley Coren has observed that dogs with docked tails appear to be victims of aggressive encounters with other dogs. When communicating with one another, dogs use their tails as part of their body language. If the tail is docked, the dog can inadvertently send out mixed messages to other dogs that result in hostile confrontations.

Emerging Fame

American cocker spaniels initially captured the hearts of the world in the early 1900s. The first time an American cocker spaniel won 'Best in Show' at the Westminster Kennel Club Dog Show was in 1921. If you have ever owned an American cocker spaniel, you would clearly understand why. With their soulful eyes, gentle disposition, easy-going and affectionate attitude, and liveliness they are irresistible. The public were so enamoured with the American cocker that it held the number one position for 25 years between 1936 and 1952 in the American Kennel Club registrations. This is an accomplishment no other breed has achieved.

With seven 'Best in Show' wins since the prize was first awarded in 1928, the English cocker spaniel is the most successful breed at the prestigious Crufts dog show in the United Kingdom. The English cocker was the 3rd most popular dog breed in the U.K. in 2021, while the American cocker ranked 30th in the U.S.

Cocker Spaniel Breed Standards

United Kingdom Breed Standard

The breed standard describes the ideal temperament, characteristics, and appearance including the correct colour of a breed to ensure the breed is fit for function. Absolute compliance is essential. At all times, both breeders and judges should avoid any deviations that would be detrimental in any way to the health, welfare, or soundness of the breed. Occasionally, certain conditions or exaggerations can be thought to have the potential to adversely affect dogs in some breeds and can be found in the breed watch section of the United Kingdom's Kennel Club website: www.the-kennel-club.org.uk. Below are the current standards for the English cocker spaniel (pictured):

General Appearance. Merry, sturdy, sporting; well-balanced; compact; measuring approximately the same from withers to ground as from withers to root of tail.

Characteristics. Merry nature with ever-wagging tail shows a typical bustling movement, particularly when following scent, fearless of heavy cover.

Temperament. Gentle and affectionate, yet full of life and exuberance.

Head & Skull. Square muzzle, with distinct stop set midway between tip of nose and occiput. Skull well developed, cleanly chiselled, neither too fine nor too coarse. Cheek bones not prominent. Nose sufficiently wide for acute scenting power.

Eyes. Full, but not prominent. Dark brown or brown, never light, but in the case of liver, liver roan and liver and white, dark hazel to harmonise with coat; with expression of intelligence and gentleness but wide awake, bright, and merry; rims tight.

Ears. Lobular, set low on a level with eyes. Fine leathers extending to nose tip. Well clothed with long, straight silky hair.

Mouth. Jaws strong with a perfect, regular, and complete scissor bite, i.e., upper teeth closely overlapping lower teeth and set square to the jaws.

Neck. Moderate in length, muscular. Set neatly into fine sloping shoulders. Clean throat.

Forequarters. Shoulders sloping and fine. Legs well boned, straight, sufficiently short for concentrated power. Not too short to interfere with tremendous exertions expected from this grand, sporting dog.

Body. Strong, compact. Chest well developed and brisket deep, neither too wide nor too narrow in front. Ribs well sprung. Loin short, wide with firm, level topline gently sloping downwards to tail from end of loin to set on of tail.

Hindquarters. Wide, well rounded, very muscular. Legs well boned, good bend of stifle, short below hock allowing for plenty of drive.

Feet. Firm, thickly padded, cat-like.

Tail. Set on slightly lower than line of back. Must be merry in action and carried level, never cocked up. Previously customarily docked.

- Docked: Never too short to hide, nor too long to interfere with, the incessant merry action when working. *
- Undocked: Slightly curved, of moderate length, proportionate to size of body giving an overall balanced appearance; ideally not reaching below the hock. Strong at the root and tapering to a fine tip; well feathered in keeping with the coat. Lively in action, carried on a plane not higher than level of back and never so low as to indicate timidity.

Gait/Movement. True through action with great drive covering ground well.

Coat. Flat, silky in texture, never wiry or wavy, not too profuse, and never curly. Well feathered forelegs, body and hindlegs above hocks.

Colour.

Solid Colours: Black; red; golden (pictured); liver (chocolate); black and tan; liver and tan; No white allowed except a small amount on chest.

Particolours: Bicolour: Black and white; orange and white; liver and white; lemon and white; All with or without ticking. Tricolours: Black, white, and tan; liver, white and tan. Roans: Blue roan; orange roan; lemon roan; liver roan; blue roan and tan; liver roan and tan.

Any colour or marking other than the above is undesirable.

Size. Height approximately: dogs: 39-41 centimetres (15.5-16 inches); bitches: 38-39 centimetres (15-15.5 inches). Weight approximately: 13-14.5 kilograms (28-32 pounds).

Faults. Any departure from the foregoing points should be considered a fault and the seriousness with which the fault should be regarded should be in exact proportion to its degree and its effect upon the health and welfare of the dog, and on the dog's ability to perform its traditional work.

Note: Male animals should have two apparently normal testicles fully descended into the scrotum.

N.B. * Docking is banned in many countries (see History section above).

American Breed Standard

The official breed standards for the American cocker spaniel, as specified by the American Kennel Club, vary slightly from those for the English cocker spaniel (pictured) and are listed below. Any dogs not conforming to these set standards will be disqualified when presented for show in an AKC sanctioned event:

General Appearance. The cocker spaniel has a sturdy and compact body, and a cleanly chiselled and refined head, with the overall dog in complete balance and of ideal size. They stand well up at the shoulder on straight forelegs with a topline sloping slightly towards strong, moderately bent, muscular quarters. This is a dog capable of considerable speed, combined with great endurance.

Adult Height and Weight. The following height and weight measurements are the ideal breed standard measurements for an adult cocker spaniel:

- Height: when measured at the withers (the highest point of the shoulder blades), 34-39 centimetres (13.5-15.5 inches).
- Weight: 9-13.5 kilograms (20-30 pounds).

Proportion. The measurement from the breastbone to the back of the thigh is slightly longer than the measurement from the highest point of the withers to the ground. The body must be of sufficient length to permit a straight and free stride; the dog never appears low and long.

Head, Expression. A well-proportioned head, which must be in balance with the rest of the dog. The expression is intelligent, alert, soft, and appealing.

Eyes. The eyeballs are round and full and look directly forwards. The shape of the eye rims gives a slightly almond-shaped appearance, the eye is not weak or goggled. The colour of the iris is mahogany brown and the darker the better. Disqualifications: Eye(s) blue, blue marbled, blue flecked.

Ears. The ears are lobular, long, of fine leather, well feathered, and placed no higher than a line to the lower part of the eye.

Neck. The neck is sufficiently long to allow for the nose to reach the ground easily, muscular, and free from pendulous 'throatiness'. It rises strongly from the shoulders and arches slightly as it tapers to join the head.

Body and Legs. The cocker has a strong, muscular neck, a deep chest that extends no lower than the dog's elbows and a strong back, that slopes downward slightly towards the tail. The legs are straight, strong, and muscular and the feet are large, round, and compact.

Forequarter. The shoulders are well laid back forming an angle with the upper arm of around 90 degrees, which permits the dog to move the forelegs in an easy manner with forward reach. Shoulders are clean-cut and sloping without any protrusion and so set that the upper points of the withers are at an angle that permits a wide spring of rib. When viewed from the side with the forelegs vertical, the elbows are directly below the highest point of the shoulder blades. The forelegs are parallel, straight, strongly boned, and muscular and set close to the body under the scapulae. The pasterns are short and strong. Dewclaws on forelegs may be removed. The feet are compact, large, round and firm with horny pads; they turn neither in nor out.

Hindquarters. The hips are wide and quarters well rounded and muscular. When viewed from behind, the hind legs are parallel when in motion and at rest. The hind legs are strongly boned and muscled with moderate angulation at the stifle and powerful thighs. The stifle is strong and there is no slippage of it in motion or when standing. The hocks are strong and well let down. The dewclaws on hind legs may be removed.

Coat Colours and Features. The silky cocker spaniel coat may be slightly wavy (pictured) or flat, fine, and short on the head and medium length on the body with longer feathering on the chest, legs, and abdomen. The following are acceptable breed standard coat colours and markings:

- Black – solid jet black or black with tan-coloured points, with a small amount of white permitted on the chest or throat.
- Any Solid Colour – these colours should be of a uniform shade throughout the body, with lighter colouring permissible on the feathering. Colours may range from the lightest cream, including brown and brown with tan points, to the darkest red.
- Parti-Colours – a parti-coloured coat is a coat existing of two or more solid or broken colours, so long as one of the colours is white (i.e., black and white, red and white).
- Tan Points – the tan points or markings may vary in shade from the lightest cream colour to the darkest red colour and breed standards specify that the percentage of the markings is restricted to 10%. The markings are permitted in the following locations: over each eye, the sides of the muzzle, on the cheeks, underside of the ears, on all feet or legs, under the tail, on the chest.

Intelligence

TIP ***If you really want to rate your cocker spaniel's intelligence, there is a book titled The Intelligence of Dogs, which has become the standard for rating the intelligence of different canine breeds.***

Though every dog is different, even within the same breed the cocker spaniel is quite an intelligent breed.

It is written by psychology professor Stanley Coren, a researcher and writer on the intelligence, mental abilities, and history of dogs. Coren's criteria for judging canine intelligence are based on the following three categories:

- Instinctive Intelligence – a dog's ability to carry out tasks it was bred to perform, such as guarding, herding, hunting, pointing, retrieving, or supplying companionship.
- Adaptive Intelligence – how well a dog can solve problems on their own.
- Working/Obedience Intelligence – how quickly a dog can learn from humans.

In the case of the cocker spaniel, Coren places this breed in the 'Excellent Working Dogs' category. This means the spaniel is undoubtedly a highly intelligent companion with the ability to understand new commands after 5 to 15 repetitions, and when properly trained can obey first commands 85% of the time or more.

English Cocker: working vs show

The modern-day English cocker spaniels are classed as either a show-type or working-type. Although there are some major differences between them, the Kennel Club does not distinguish between the two varieties.

A working cocker has its ears set higher and is shorter and slimmer. Usually, they have a longer and narrower muzzle, and the top of their skull is flatter than the show cocker's. Their ears are markedly smaller and set higher than their eyes. The show spaniel's long, low ears would be impractical for hunting and other field work.

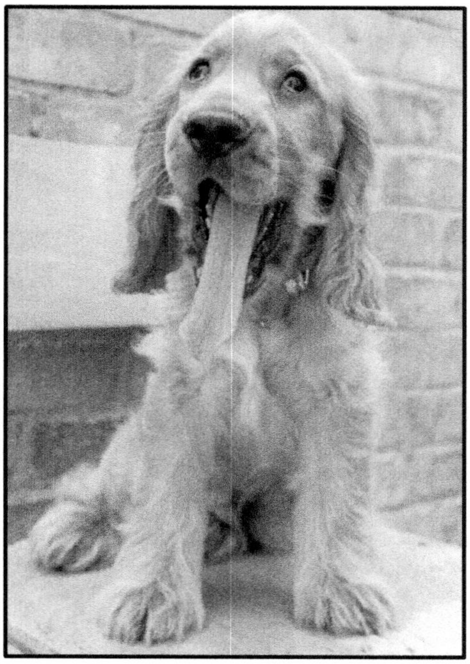

The show cocker spaniel has a longer, more abundant coat than the working cocker whose coat is fine, shorter, and has less feathering. To conform to the breed standards, show cocker spaniels must have specific coat colours, with no white allowed apart from 'a small amount on the chest'. However, for working spaniels there is no such requirement and they come in a variety of colours, including mostly white.

Technically, both strains are working dogs, so whether you choose a working or show cocker, expect a lively, energetic dog with a kind-hearted disposition. Although a show cocker spaniel needs approximately an hour of exercise per day, the working cocker frequently requires significantly more. Having been bred for increased stamina, working cocker spaniels are far harder to tire out than show dogs.

While working cockers are great family pets, it is essential to remember that they will become frustrated and behave badly if you do not give them sufficient opportunities to use their pent-up energy. To keep their dog contented and physically and mentally stimulated, many working cocker spaniel owners participate in gundog, scent-work, and agility classes.

English vs American Cocker Spaniel

Not long ago, it became evident that cocker spaniels in the U.K. were different from those in the U.S.—as specified in the breed standards—and the decision was made to classify them as separate breeds.

The key differences are:

Size. English cocker spaniels are larger and taller than their American counterparts.

Coat. American cockers have a longer and more lustrous coat.

Head. The American's skull is quite distinctly dome-shaped, whereas the English cocker's is flatter (pictured).

Face. Both breeds have a different eye placement. The American cocker's eyes are a bit wider and set farther forwards than the English cocker's. The English cocker has a long muzzle compared to the American's, which is shorter, with a droopy mouth. English cockers also sport longer ears that reach the tip of their nose when pulled forwards.

Hunting skills. The American breed has long been used as a companion dog, unlike the English, which is still considered a sporting breed. Therefore, English cockers tend to be more active when they find themselves outdoors, loving to chase birds and other game. The American cockers, though excellent sporting dogs themselves, have not retained their hunting skills over the years.

Activity levels. Staying close to their primary purpose, English cocker spaniels have more intensive exercise routines than their American cousins. The English breed enjoy running and frolicking in a garden or park, whereas the American cockers love to accompany their owners on long walks.

Temperament. Although this point is highly debatable, it has been observed that the American cocker tends to be a tad too sensitive compared to the English cocker. Both breeds have several similarities regarding their temperament: they're cheerful, family-oriented, and affectionate. But the American is known to be prone to displaying mood swings, although it is unfair to generalise.

Pet Quality versus Show Quality

The difference between a show and a pet dog is the degree to which each meets the standard for the breed. Knowing which type of dog you are interested in and understanding the standards is crucial. Some standards have disqualifications that prevent such dogs from entering the show ring.

FACT ***Pet-quality and show-quality are labels breeders attach to their puppies, but they can be quite fluid. Experienced breeders spend many years grading, selecting, and following puppies. This helps them learn their growth patterns and develop a baseline for predicting how they will turn out.***

In many cases, the differences are so small that only a qualified breeder or dog show judge would be able to recognise any of these minor flaws.

Most cocker spaniel owners are more concerned about their dog's health and temperament, before considering whether the puppy has what it takes to win first place at the local dog show. Some traits or considerations designate 'pet-quality' because they display faults that are not in line with the written standard for the breed:

- Underbite.
- Overbite.
- Eye colouration.
- Coat colour, texture, or markings.
- Height.

- Weight.
- Sold on limited registration—cannot participate in conformation.

Whether your cocker is considered 'show-quality' largely depends on how closely they adhere to the breed standards. When deciding if you should choose a cocker puppy of 'show-quality' there are many aspects to consider, including:

- Long waiting list to get one.
- Higher cost.
- The breeder might ask you to sign a contract that you agree to show.
- Health clearances are required.
- The breeder could retain partial ownership or breeding rights.
- Show dogs must remain intact (no neutering or spaying).
- Conformation classes to learn how to be a show dog.
- Standard structure (how the dog is built).
- Standard temperament (personality, character).
- The breeder can require owners to hire a professional handler.

20 Cocker Spaniel Secrets

The following are interesting facts, trivia, and secrets about the cocker spaniel breed:

1. During the 19th century, the name cocker spaniel was given to any type of small field spaniel that weighed less than 11 kilograms (25 pounds).
2. While the true origins of this breed are not definitively known, dogs referred to as 'spaynels' are noted in writings as long ago as the 14th century.
3. George Clooney adopted Einstein, a cocker spaniel, from a shelter when the dog was five years old and within days of being put down. Because Clooney and his wife had such a positive experience with the rescue, they adopted two more older shelter dogs.
4. Oprah Winfrey referred to her cocker, Sophie, as 'the true love of my life'. Sophie was Oprah's constant companion for 14 years, along with Solomon, whom Oprah called 'one of a kind'.
5. While Elton John has owned many dogs over the years, Arthur, the cocker spaniel, held a special place in his heart. Besides making red carpet appearances with his owner, Arthur served as 'best man' at Sir Elton's wedding to David Furness in 2005.
6. The first spaniel came across to North America on the Mayflower in 1620 but the breed was not registered with the American Kennel Club until 258 years later, in 1878.
7. At the Westminster Kennel Club Dog Show, the American cocker spaniel has won 'Best in Show' four times.
8. A female American cocker spaniel called 'Lady' is featured in the well-loved, 1955 Walt Disney film Lady and the Tramp.

9. There is a cocker spaniel depicted on the 'Coppertone' sunscreen bottle.
10. The 35th president of the United States (John F Kennedy) had a cocker spaniel called 'Shannon' and the 37th president (Richard Nixon) owned a cocker spaniel called 'Checkers'.
11. With seven wins, the English cocker spaniel has been the most successful breed at Crufts since 'Best in Show' was introduced. Six of those wins were by Mr H S Lloyd who won with 'Luckystar of Ware' in 1930 and 1931. In 1938 and 1939, his dog, 'Exquisite Model of Ware', took the title, with two further wins in 1948 and 1950 for his other dog, 'Tracey Witch of Ware'.

12. A cocker spaniel called 'Prince' was the inspiration for the successful 'Sperry Topsiders' worn by boat enthusiasts for sure-footed grip in slippery and wet conditions. The patented 'Razor-siping' soles were designed after the wave-like grooves found on the pads of the feet of the cocker spaniel that give them great stability when running on slippery surfaces.
13. The cockapoo, a hybrid breed comprised of crossing a cocker with a poodle, beats all the pedigree spaniel breeds in the popularity rankings, being the U.K.'s most popular dog breed overall.
14. The cocker spaniel is highly intelligent, and one dog called 'Bella Boo' could perform over 250 tricks.
15. During a weekend of intense competition, a cocker spaniel called 'Striker' beat nearly 5 000 dogs to earn a $50 000 cash prize, a sparkling, paw print diamond pendant, and the title 'Best in Show' at the 2017 American Kennel Club National Championship in Orlando, Florida.
16. A male American cocker spaniel called 'My Own Brucie' won 'Best in Show' at the Westminster Kennel Club Dog Show two years in a row, in 1940 and 1941.
17. The Duke and Duchess of Cambridge—William and Catherine—owned a cocker spaniel called 'Lupo' before he died, in November 2020, of unknown causes.
18. According to behavioural experts, cocker spaniels are the 18th most intelligent species of dog. In 2015 a four-year-old cocker spaniel called 'Ginger from Strone', near Dunoon in Scotland, took Gaelic classes with her owner, mastering basic commands such as suidh (sit) and fuirich (stay) in just three weeks.
19. In 2004 researchers successfully showed that dogs could identify cancer by scent alone. The English study used six dogs and a cocker spaniel called 'Tangle' had the best success rate. After training, 'Tangle' correctly identified cancer 80 percent of the time.
20. Cocker spaniels were sometimes used during World War II as mine detectors in the field.

There is no doubt that the highly intelligent, beautiful, and loving cocker spaniel is a very popular choice amongst the dog-loving population. Now that you have grasped the basics of this heart-warming breed, please read on to find out how to take best care of your new family member and help them become a well-rounded, happy dog!

2. Before You Welcome Your Puppy

'Properly trained, a man

can be dog's best friend.'

~ Corey Ford ~

Before buying your cocker spaniel puppy there are many relevant points you should consider that might not initially come to mind but could influence your decision. For those first timers, beyond the initial price of purchasing a puppy, the following pages provide a more complete picture of what's really involved in dog ownership.

To be fair to yourself, your family, and the puppy, it can be very helpful to take a serious look at your life, both as it is today and what you envision it being in the next ten to fifteen years. During this process, you need to ask yourself a few important, personal questions before making the commitment to a puppy:

- Do you have the time and patience necessary to devote to a puppy that will grow into a dog who needs a great deal of attention, training, and devotion?
- Do you lead a physically active, medium, or low intensity life? For instance, are you out jogging the streets daily or climbing mountains, or would you rather spend my leisure time engaged in more sedate pursuits?
- Do you like to travel frequently? A dog small enough to travel in the plane cabin with you is a consideration.

- Are you a super tidy person? A low or non-shedding breed might make more sense.
- Do you have allergies? Some breeds are more compatible with those who suffer from allergies.
- Do you have a young, growing family that takes up all your spare time? A dog takes a lot of time and attention.

- Are your children old enough to carefully handle a puppy?
- Are you physically fit and healthy enough to be out walking a dog two to three times a day, every day, come rain or shine?
- Are you able to afford the extra expenses that are part of being a conscientious dog owner?
- Is the decision to bring a puppy into your life a family decision, or just for the children, who might quickly lose interest?
- Have you thoroughly researched the cocker spaniel breed you are interested in?
- If you do not already have experience with raising a dog, is there someone who can help you with this?
- If you plan to travel where the dog cannot go, can you afford to hire a dog sitter while you are away?
- Is the dog compatible with your lifestyle or you considering this breed because you had a similar dog when you were a child, or just because you like the way it looks?
- What is the number one reason you want a dog in your life?

Once you ask yourself these important questions, you will have a much better understanding whether making the decision to add a puppy or dog to your family is going to enhance everyone's life. Once you are sure, it is time to discover what the true costs of dog ownership might be. While bringing home your four-legged canine friend is super exciting, it is easy to become distracted and quickly skim over the reality of true expenses, so let us take a closer look.

FACT ***The Pet Industry is BIG Business. You might be shocked to discover that according to Pet Industry Market Size and Ownership Statistics, dog owners worldwide spent approximately £168 billion ($232 billion) on their pets in the year 2021 and it is estimated that this figure will increase to £254 billion ($350 billion) by 2027.***

Basic supplies, food and clothing may vary in price depending on what you have access to where you live. In general, estimates have shown that while appropriate yearly canine upkeep can be as low as £2 310 ($3 180), it could also be much more than you ever imagined.

To gain a more accurate estimate of what the true cost of owning a cocker may entail, and whether this is an affordable proposition, it might be helpful to break down expenses into 'one-time', 'monthly' and 'annual'.

Please note that the following cost estimates suggested here are based on average pricing and exchange rates as noted at the time of writing, and they may change over time.

Also keep in mind that many of the noted expenses may vary in price depending upon where you live, what is available to you, the age and size of your dog, and that some are entirely optional. For instance, canine clothing is quite pricey, however, an individual may be able to sew their own doggy fashions.

One-Time Cost of Ownership

Initial cocker puppy purchase varies depending on whether the choice is to rescue or search out a reputable breeder. Even between breeders, the cost of purchasing the chosen puppy may differ immensely depending on the breeder's reputation and experience.

Beyond breeder fees, there are numerous hidden costs and expenses that aren't always obvious at first glance when initially deciding if adding a dog to your life is an affordable option. Listing average one-time costs helps to provide a more realistic picture, and would include:

- Cocker spaniel breeder fee: Average £2 230 ($3 000).
- Rescue fee: £135 to £200 ($180 to $270).
- Potty-training supplies: £15 to £220 ($20 to $300).
- Lead, collar, ID tags: £87 ($120).
- Bed and crate: £18 to £180 ($25 to $250).
- Food and water bowls: £7 to £36+ ($10 to $50+).
- First vaccinations: £30 to £60 ($40 to $80).
- Microchipping: £11 to £30 ($15 to $40).
- Neutering/spaying: £110 to £365 ($150 to $495).
- Obedience training (optional): £70 to £435+ ($100 to $600+).

Estimated Total One-Time Costs: £1 265 to £2 540 ($1 740 to $3 500).

Monthly and Annual Cost of Ownership

Monthly costs of dog ownership fluctuate significantly between those who choose to purchase the latest in canine couture, and the meat and potatoes person who is only interested in the solid basics. However, even if you do not need any of the optional products or services, there are still many monthly costs to consider.

With the first-year expenses averaging about £1 900 ($2 530) subsequent years will cost £960 ($1 330/year) or £80 ($111/month) after that. Through your dog's lifetime, the average cost of owning a cocker spaniel is £13 000 ($17 160) including purchasing and set-up costs.

This covers all the essential costs. Additional, optional costs including medical expenses and other services such as dog walking, dog boarding, and pet insurance can increase the overall cost of ownership.

To put this into perspective, if you hire a dog walker five times a week for 50 weeks and use a boarding service for one week every year, the total cost of owning a cocker spaniel could climb to £43 465 in the United Kingdom and between $59 900 and $116 840, with an average of $86 675 in the United States.

Of course, the above are average estimates and the actual costs may be more, or less depending on which *optional* items are included.

Choosing a Breeder

When you have finally made your decision to add a cocker to your family, the next step is to locate a reputable breeder, and there are several ways to determine whether you have made the right choice.

The internet is a valuable resource when beginning to look for a breeder and researching their reputation. You can post on most forums discussing breeders to quickly find out what you need to know from those who have first-hand experience.

Conduct as much research as possible about the specific breeder you are considering before making your initial contact with them. The more information you have gathered about the breeder, and the more the breeder knows about you, the more successful the match will be. In the United Kingdom, it is advisable to contact your nearest regional cocker spaniel breed club.

Contact details for all these clubs available at: https://www.thecockerspanielclub.co.uk/breedclubs.htm

There is an online puppy sales list on The Kennel Club website listing breeders who have litters available at: https://www.thekennelclub.org.uk/search/find-a-puppy/. Please note that The Kennel Club does not guarantee that breeders appearing on the list are reputable so would-be buyers should bear this in mind and check the breeders out for themselves.

For the United States, a list of cocker spaniel breeders is available through the American Spaniel Club, at: https://americanspanielclub.org/find-a-cocker/list-of-breeders/. The club states that these breeder names are furnished to you for your information only and you must inquire and satisfy yourself as to the background, quality, health, and condition of any dogs being offered for sale.

FACT ***Your puppy's personality or temperament is a combination of what they experience in the early days of their environment when they are in the breeder's care, the genes inherited from both parents, and how their new owners train and socialise them.***

Make an appointment to meet the breeder, either in person, or through a video session as this is the best way to get a feeling about the cleanliness of the premises and the breeder's commitment to raising healthy puppies. Meeting the mother and father of your potential new puppy can tell you a great deal about what the likely temperament and demeanour of your puppy will be when they grow into adulthood.

Visiting the breeder several times, observing the parents, interacting with the puppies, and asking plenty of questions will help you to get a true feeling for the sincerity of the breeder. Here are some questions you can ask the breeder:

- Why did they decide to breed cocker spaniels?
- How long have they been breeding?
- Do they ever show their dogs?
- What does the breeder look for in a home for their puppies?
- Will they permit you to visit them and tour their facility?

- Do they own both breeding parents? If not, have they worked closely with both parents?
- How often do they permit the females and males to breed?
- Will they let you see the other dogs in the kennel?
- Can you to observe the dogs and puppies socialising together?
- Are they registered with a local or national breed organisation?
- How old must the puppies be before they can go to their new home? If the answer is anything less than 8-10 weeks (and 10 is better), they are probably more interested in making a profit than in the health of their puppies.
- Do they offer a return policy?
- Will they take a puppy back if it does not work out?
- Do they provide the puppy's pedigree documentation? Be wary of breeders who ask for an extra fee for papers or those who offer to provide them later via mail.
- Will they give you testimonials from past clients?
- What is the procedure for picking up the puppy when old enough to go to their new forever home?

How a breeder answers these questions can tell you if they are genuinely concerned about the health and welfare of their puppies. If you find the breeder is patient when answering your questions and eager to provide you with all the information you request, this might be a breeder to consider.

Once you are satisfied you have located the right breeder and visited their facility, pay attention to whether the breeder limits the amount of time you are permitted to handle the puppies. A reputable breeder will be concerned for the safety and health of their puppies and only permit serious buyers to hold them.

Also, be prepared to answer questions the breeder might have for you. A responsible breeder will want to ask a prospective buyer their own questions to satisfy themselves that you are going to be a good caretaker for their puppy and can provide them with a loving, forever home.

Health and Medical Questions to Ask

Even a good breeder cannot guarantee the lifelong health of any puppy.

However, they should easily be able to guide a prospective owner and provide plenty of information about the health of the puppy's parents. The breeder should be willing to provide medical information and answer the following health questions:

- What health conditions typically affect the cocker breed? Beware if the breeder says there are no health conditions that typically affect the breed.

- What health tests have been carried out on the parents?
- Have the parents been tested for hip, thyroid, eye, or any other health problems?
- Do the parents or grandparents have any congenital problems?
- Have there been any premature deaths?
- Has the veterinarian seen the puppies?
- Who is the breeder's veterinarian?
- Have the puppies been wormed?
- Have the puppies received any vaccinations?
- Can they provide the veterinarian's report on the puppies?

TIP ***Always ask the breeder what shots the puppy has received, when they were last de-wormed, and for the name of the breeder's veterinarian. If you discover the breeder has not carried out any of these procedures or they are unable to tell you when the last shot or de-worming was carried out, you might be best advised to look elsewhere.***

Also ask to see the breeder's veterinarian report on the health of the puppy you are interested in, and if they cannot produce this report, again, it may be best to look elsewhere.

Temperament Questions to Ask

When you are ready to choose a puppy from the litter, your breeder should be able to provide valuable insight concerning each puppy's unique personality. The breeder is ideally suited to help you make the right selection based on your energy and lifestyle, and the following questions could help you choose:

- What is the temperament and personality of the parents?
- Which puppies are friendly, easy going and congenial?
- Which puppies are timid?
- Which puppies are more outgoing or independent?
- What have they done to socialise the puppies?
- Have they been introduced to children or other dogs?
- Have they been introduced to other animals?

Return Contract

A reputable breeder will want you to call them should a problem arise at any time during the life of your puppy. In addition, a good breeder will want you to return a puppy or dog to them if, for some reason, you are unable to continue to care for it, rather than seeing your cocker go to a shelter or rescue facility. If the breeder you are considering does not offer this type of return policy, beware, as no ethical breeder would ever permit a puppy from one of their litters to end up in a shelter.

Reliable breeders offer return contracts, as they want to protect their reputation and make sure any puppy they have sold who might display a genetic defect will not have the opportunity to breed and continue to spread the defect, which could weaken the entire breed.

Many breeders also offer return contracts because purchasing a puppy can be an expensive proposition, and if you find the puppy has a worrisome, genetic defect, this could cost you a great deal in unexpected veterinarian care. In such cases, most honest and reputable breeders offer a return policy, and are happy to give you another puppy.

A good breeder has nothing to hide and should be more than willing to provide you with testimonials from previous clients, as their best recommendation is a happy customer. If you are able to contact some of the breeder's past clients or ask to have them contact you, this is a good way to ask about their experience with the breeder and the health and temperament of their dog.

TIP ***Always be certain to ask if the puppy you are interested in has displayed any signs of aggression or fear, because if this is happening at such an early age, you might experience behavioural problems when the puppy gets older.***

How to Avoid Puppy Mills

Often, when a breed of dog becomes popular, they are particularly susceptible to being bred by disreputable, high-profit puppy mills (pictured) or commercial breeding farms. Frequently, a specific dog breed quickly gains popularity due to what is referred to as the Lassie effect, which occurs when a dog is featured in a popular movie and shortly afterward is highly sought after.

Puppy mill breeding is especially prevalent with cute, smaller breeds, such as the cocker spaniel, as it takes less space to mass-produce smaller dogs. This inhumane and cruel world of canine pregnancy for profit occurs all over the world, and if you are not incredibly careful about where and how you purchase your puppy, it is possible to unknowingly end up promoting this disreputable practise.

FACT ***Puppy mills seriously contribute to overpopulation and produce diseases and genetically flawed puppies who might suffer with behavioural and/or health related problems. These issues cost their owners immensely in terms of grief and stress and the unexpected financial burden associated with veterinarian costs, while the puppy's life may be prematurely cut short.***

These dogs suffer in ways most of us could never imagine. For instance, the majority of these poor breeding dogs have never walked on solid ground or felt grass, as they are housed in cramped, wire cages. Females are bred continuously until they can no longer produce puppies, at which time they are sold to laboratories for experiments, killed, or dumped on the side of the road. Pet stores are the main source for selling these unfortunate puppies, who are taken away from their mothers far too young—at 4 to 5 weeks old—and sold to brokers, who pack them into crates to ship them off to pet stores. Many innocent puppies die during transportation.

Just like the drug trade, it is difficult to shut down these mass-producing farming operations because it is business on a large and lucrative scale. Although puppy mill puppies are sold in a variety of different venues, there are certain locations to be suspicious of, including:

- Pet stores.
- Flea markets.
- Roadside.
- Beaches.
- Back gardens.
- Newspaper ads.
- Fancy websites.
- Internet classifieds.

Almost all puppies sold in pet stores—whether the employees working there are aware of it—are the result of inhumane, puppy mill breeding.

Every time someone buys a cocker spaniel puppy from a pet store that was obtained from a puppy mill, the store invariably orders more from the same source. As far as the pet store is concerned, the puppies are simply inventory, like bags of dog food, and when one item drops off the inventory list, another is purchased to replace it.

The only way to put these shameful, commercial businesses out of business is by never buying a cocker puppy from a pet store, or any other advertising medium, unless they have first been thoroughly checked out by visiting the facility in person.

It is always wise to be wary when answering an advertisement for a low-priced puppy for sale, especially if the person selling offers to deliver the puppy to you. These could easily be signs that you are about to be involved in an illegal cocker spaniel puppy mill operation. Educating yourself and spreading the word to others about puppy mills is the first step towards ensuring that you and everyone you know is never unknowingly involved in the suffering that is forced upon the breeding dogs and puppies trapped in a puppy mill or mass farming operation.

TIP ***Consider visiting a shelter or rescue centre, or a responsible pet store that hosts animals from shelters/rescues for adoption to find your next cocker spaniel.***

Since October 1, 2018, amendments to the United Kingdom Animal Welfare Act have introduced long needed changes regarding strict compliance for anyone selling dogs. For instance, the sale of three or more litters within the same year requires a licence and the keeping of clear, detailed records as well as strict rules for advertising dogs for sale, which must include the breeder's licence. All these changes are a very strong deterrent for back garden and puppy mill breeders, and for those illegally importing dogs across borders.

How to Choose a Puppy

Choosing the right cocker puppy for your family and your lifestyle is more important than you might imagine and deserves some serious thought before making the final decision to bring one home. Although your breeder can often help to select the right puppy for you and your family, you might feel especially drawn to one puppy over another. However, while there are other considerations, how you feel towards a particular dog in a litter is an important part of deciding which one to bring home.

Apart from your feelings, considering the following basic guidelines will help improve the odds of having a positive relationship with your new cocker spaniel puppy:

- Be objective when evaluating each puppy in the litter—try not to let personal feelings get in the way.
- Do not be overly emotional as this could make you choose a puppy who displays extreme behavioural issues—overly shy, overly aggressive.
- Be aware that while extreme behaviour can sometimes be corrected, often it cannot.
- Be careful not to choose a puppy simply because you feel sorry for them as they might have obvious health or emotional issues—they are the runt of the litter, and afraid of everything.

Choosing the Right Temperament

Some people become very emotional when choosing their cocker puppy and are attracted to those who display extremes in behaviour because they want to 'save' them. However, it isn't a particularly good idea to choose a puppy who shows signs of being very shy, frightened, or aggressive in the hope that they might grow into a happy, well-behaved dog.

It is certainly wonderful that people have the capacity to raise and care for puppies who might be afflicted with health or behavioural problems. However, it is important that these decisions are not undertaken lightly, as such challenges can lead you down a path that could be an emotional rollercoaster of highs and lows, creating emotional and financial problems for both canine and human alike.

Of course, many minor behavioural problems can be modified with early training. Although, you should be aware that the time and effort needed to do so can be difficult to predict and 'rescuing' a dog who could grow up to have behavioural problems can require the services of a professional dog trainer or psychologist.

Male or Female?

Everyone you ask will have an opinion about whether you should choose a male or a female cocker. If you are a first-time dog owner, there are a few considerations that could help you make a more informed decision regarding the gender:

- Male dogs tend to want to mark or pee on anything upright—trees, telegraph poles, tall grass, a stranger's leg—wherever they are out walking far more than females. However, a dominant female will also pee to mark territory.
- Some breeders will not sell you a female puppy unless you sign a contract promising to have them spayed.

- Neutering a male dog is a less invasive medical procedure, as opposed to spaying a female.
- A male dog, even a house-trained one, can try to lift their leg on furniture when visiting a home where other dogs are present.
- Some people choose their spaniel based on sex alone, because they have a strong desire to attribute human characteristics to their chosen dog. A potential owner might believe a female dog will have a sweeter temperament, or a male dog could be more independent. Bear in mind that it can be harmful to project human emotions onto your cocker or imagine they will act like humans just because we are human.

One or Two?

TIP ***Adding two puppies to your family at the same time could be twice the fun, but it usually requires twice the work. This means being doubly alert and patient and losing even more sleep than you bargained for during the toilet-training phase.***

Every puppy needs constant attention and guidance. Therefore, before taking the plunge and committing to two, ask yourself the following questions:

- Do you have the time and energy to provide constant attention and guidance for two little cocker puppies who could be running in opposite directions?
- Why do you think two puppies are a good idea?

You need to be careful that deciding on two puppies (pictured) is not because you think they will always have someone to play with, or that one puppy would never be alone while you are at work all day. Yes, while having two puppies can be double the fun, there may be considerations for choosing just one that make more sense. Some things a prospective new owner might not be aware of include:

- Two puppies can often be too much work for the average family.
- When they grow up, there might be continual sibling rivalry. As each puppy vies for attention from their owners, they might not get along with each other as well as they did when they were young puppies.
- Two puppies who spend all their time together do not always socialise as well with people and other animals as they have each other.
- Each puppy requires individual attention during toilet training and basic training and having two cocker puppies can make it difficult for them to concentrate or focus on the job at hand. For instance, teaching puppy No. 1 to '***Sit***' while puppy No. 2 is trying to bite the tail of puppy No. 1 is going to be far more challenging.

- When two puppies grow up together, one will always have the more dominant personality, and this could mean neither puppy fully develops their individual personality.
- Two puppies in the home can focus much more on one another and bond far less with their owners, which can make it more difficult to train or convince either that the owners are the actual leaders.

TIP ***Most professional trainers or psychologists advise that if you want two puppies, not to get them at the same time, or from the same litter. Therefore, you can house train and teach basic commands to one puppy before you bring another one into the home.***

Which Puppy in the Litter?

When choosing a stable and well-balanced cocker spaniel puppy from a litter, consider the following tips and cues:

- Look for one who is friendly and outgoing, rather than one who is overly aggressive or fearful.
- Take note of the puppy's social skills when they are still with their littermates. Puppies who demonstrate good social skills with their littermates are far more likely to develop into easy-going, happy adults who play well with other dogs.
- When the puppies are playing, see which ones are comfortable both on top and on the bottom when play fighting and wresting with their littermates, and which puppies seem to only like being on top. Puppies who do not mind being on the bottom or who appear fine with either position usually play well with other dogs when they become adults.

- If the puppies have toys to play with, observe which puppies try to keep the toys away from the other puppies and which puppies share. Those who want to hoard the toys and keep all other puppies away might be more aggressive with other dogs over food or treats, or in play where toys are involved as they become older.
- Notice which puppies seem to like the company of the other pups and which ones seem to be loners. Puppies who like the company of their littermates are more likely to be interested in the company of other dogs as they mature.
- Observe the reaction of puppies who get yelped at when they bite or roughhouse too hard with another puppy. Puppies who ease up when another puppy yelps or cries are more likely to respond appropriately when they play too roughly as adults.
- Check if the puppy you are considering is sociable with people. If they will not come to you, or display fear of strangers, this could be a problem when they become adults.
- Notice if the puppy you are considering is relaxed about being handled. If not, they could become difficult with adults and children during daily interactions, grooming, or visits to the vet.

How to Check if a Puppy is Healthy

Of course, you need to check if the cocker puppy you are considering taking home is not just emotionally healthy, but also physically healthy.

First, ask to see veterinarian reports from the breeder to satisfy yourself that the puppy is as healthy as possible. Then, once you make your decision to share your life with a particular puppy, you should make an appointment with your own vet for a complete examination. However, before you get to this stage, here are the general signs of good health to be aware of that can help you choose a healthy puppy from a litter:

Ears – Check redness and if the ears are clean, because dirty ears can mean mites or infection. A healthy puppy with good hearing should react if you clap your hands or snap your fingers behind their head.

Eyes – A healthy cocker puppy has bright, clear eyes without crust or discharge, and they should notice if a ball is rolled past them within their field of vision.

Nose – A healthy puppy breathes quietly, without coughing or sneezing, and has no crusting or discharge around their nostrils.

Body – They look round and well fed, with an obvious layer of fat over their ribcage. The body should be strong, with good muscle definition and no protruding belly that could indicate worms or other health issues.

Skin – Part the puppy's fur and check to see if their skin is clean and smooth, and not showing redness from scratching or flea bites.

Coat – A healthy cocker spaniel puppy has a clean, full, soft coat with no dandruff, dullness, greasiness, or bald spots.

Genitals – There should not be any sort of discharge visible in or around their genital or anal regions and constant licking might indicate a problem.

Poos – If possible, check whether the puppy's stools are firm, as loose stools can indicate diarrhoea from sickness.

Energy – A well-rested puppy is alert and energetic and wants to play.

Mobility – A healthy cocker puppy walks and runs normally without wobbling, limping, or appearing to be weak, stiff, or sore.

Considerations for Allergy Sufferers

In the United Kingdom it has been found that ten percent of pet owners suffer from allergies. Since the Asthma and Allergy Foundation of America has noted that 'as many as 30 percent of Americans have pet allergy', it is understandable that many people are allergic to the pet dander found in cats and dogs. The good news is those who find owning a dog challenging because it might trigger sneezing, wheezing, and watery eyes, or even hives in more severe cases, could still be able to know the joy of sharing their lives with a cocker by taking a few precautions.

FACT ***The first thing to bear in mind is no dog is 100% allergy-free, despite the confusing and conflicting claims made by some.***

It is common knowledge that breeds with non-shedding coats produce less allergy-causing dander. Therefore, choosing a dog with a non-shedding coat and being vigilant about regularly hoovering and keeping them well-groomed can reduce the amount of dander to an acceptable level.

Canine breeds have quite different coats, and for anyone suffering from allergies the type of coat a particular breed has could have a significant effect on the severity of any allergies. For instance:

- Curly, woolly coats: tend to shed minimally—Bedlington terrier.
- Shorthaired, thin-coats: easy to keep clean—Italian greyhound.
- Soft, curly hair: sheds minimally and tends to produce less allergens—poodle, and hybrids mixed with poodle.
- Hard, wiry coats: tend to shed much less—wire fox terrier.
- Straight, silky hair: less likely to produce high amounts of allergens—Yorkshire terrier.
- Water-repellent coats: dogs who swim regularly, such as the Labrador retriever, have been shown to have lower allergen levels and less allergen concentrations in their hair.

For those individuals who suffer from allergies but still want to share their lives with a furry canine friend, there are many purebred terriers and other breeds of various sizes known to produce less dander. While some are hairless or have coats that shed minimally, there are many breeds that fall into the category of being 'allergy-friendly'. The following is a list of some of the most common allergy-friendly breeds:

- American hairless terrier.
- Australian terrier.
- Bichon frisé.
- Bolognese.
- Border terrier.
- Brussels griffon.
- Cesky terrier.
- Havanese.
- Irish terrier.
- Irish water spaniel.
- Maltese.
- Norwich terrier.
- Poodle.
- Schnauzer.
- Scottish terrier.
- Shih tzu.
- Tibetan terrier.
- Welsh terrier.
- Wire fox terrier.
- Yorkshire terrier.

FACT ***While some hybrid dogs are also considered to be 'allergy friendly', they are not listed above because it is more difficult to predict the type of coat or amount of dander that might be produced when mixing two or more breeds together.***

If you are uncertain whether you have dog allergies, an allergist can evaluate and provide proper diagnosis. A skin-prick test is the most common way for diagnosing a dog allergy. During this test, a small amount of an extract of dog allergen is put on your skin, which is then pricked with a small, sterile probe that allows the liquid to seep under your skin's surface. Then, you are monitored for swelling and redness or other signs of a reaction, signalling an allergy. Typically, results are available within 15 to 20 minutes. Even if you are sure your symptoms are caused by your dog, it is always a good idea to be tested, since the symptoms can also be the result of another environmental exposure.

TIP ***If you have severe allergies, the best way to find out their triggers is to take the specialised medical tests as well as immunisation therapy.***

How to Choose a Puppy That is Better for Allergy Sufferers

How someone who has allergies to pet hair and dander reacts around a specific dog can vary greatly. For instance, an individual who has a violent, allergic reaction to a Maltese may show no such reaction to a Yorkshire terrier. Every dog is different, as is how a particular person suffering from allergies reacts to a particular dog.

When considering a breed, only personal interaction is the deciding factor. It is helpful when searching for the right match to make a shortlist of the allergy-friendly breeds you are interested in, then test each of them to establish which one produces less of an allergic reaction.

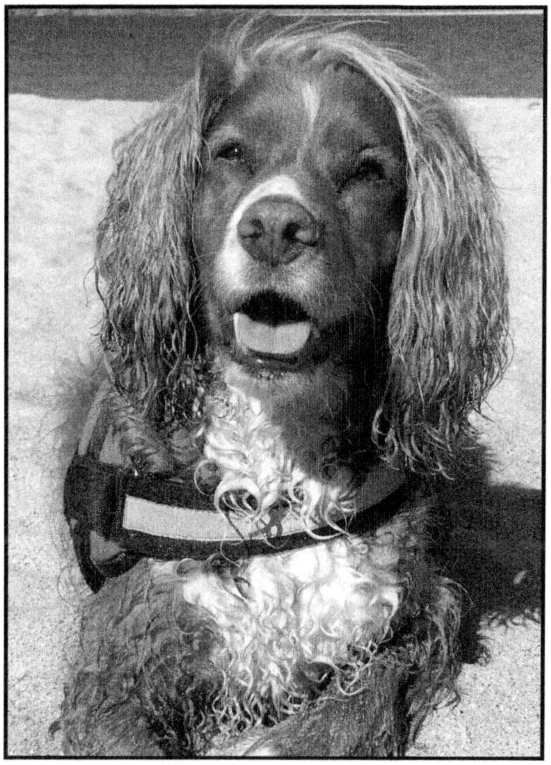

If you are suffering from allergies, before bringing home your cocker puppy, it is important to search for the right match. This means physical interaction by petting and being near the dog to determine how much they trigger your allergy. For example, if you have a friend who owns a cocker spaniel, try to visit them as often as possible and spend time with their dog. Play with the dog, rub their body, and touch your face multiple times. Then, observe whether you get any type of allergic reaction over the following days.

Another good idea is to try to see the litter when you visit your breeder. Again, touch and play with your chosen puppy and then rub your hands on your face as much as possible. Take an old T-shirt, rub it over the puppy's body and then wear it for a few hours when you get home. If you do not see any allergic reaction over the next couple of days, then this is the puppy for you.

Before committing to your cocker puppy, a responsible breeder or shelter should allow you to return the dog if they set off allergies. Many shelters let you spend one-on-one time before going through with the adoption of a four-legged friend.

Can I Have a Cocker Spaniel Without Suffering?

Whether you can share your home with a cocker spaniel without suffering depends on how severe your allergic reaction is to the breed.

The cocker spaniel is not considered to be a hypoallergenic breed. It is interesting to note that cockers have participated in allergen research with studies revealing that their saliva has a greater potential to trigger an allergic reaction than their dander. In fact, when it comes to finding the best hypoallergenic dogs regarding dander, the cocker spaniel has very little protein in theirs. This means the dander on cockers is unlikely to cause allergic reactions in most people. Still, they cannot be considered hypoallergenic, but they might not be bad for someone who is allergic to dander.

Now you know the cocker spaniel is not hypoallergenic, you want to know more about their shedding. They have a double coat, which is long and silky. They also have an undercoat. While not all cocker spaniels lose the same amount of hair, they do shed moderately. If you are not going to show your cocker spaniel, you can trim their coat, but even if you do, they are still going to shed. During the shedding seasons—autumn and spring—they shed more than normal.

If you have your heart set on this beautiful spaniel, there are things you can do to determine whether this is a viable proposition. First, you need to evaluate the severity of your allergy. When you place yourself in close, physical contact with the cocker spaniel, you will find out how quickly or severely your allergy is triggered. Next, should the degree of symptoms be manageable, taking steps to reduce pet allergens, as noted below, should make it possible for you to enjoy sharing your life with this lovely dog.

Reducing Pet Allergens

While many believe it is the dog's hair that people are allergic to, it is the dander—dead flakes of skin—and the saliva that cause most of the allergic reaction. People with highly sensitive immune systems can react in various ways when their allergies are triggered, including:

- Sneezing.
- Postnasal drip.
- Coughing.
- Chest tightness.
- Difficulty breathing.
- Red, itchy eyes.
- Stuffy, itchy, runny nose.
- Itchy skin.
- Rash on face, neck, or chest.
- Hives.

TIP ***If you brush your cocker spaniel every day, this will get rid of the extra hair they would otherwise shed throughout your house.***

All our furry friends shed dander, and a combination of dead skin cells and hair can trigger asthma attacks. However, there are many steps that can be taken to diminish pet allergens at home. Implementing the following suggestions could make adding a non-hypoallergenic cocker spaniel to your life a viable option:

HEPA Air Purifier – A HEPA filter is a specific type of high-quality air filter that meets the HEPA filter standard, which is to remove at least 99.97% of particles from the air down to at least 0.3 microns in size. HEPA filters are a common component found in air purifiers which filter the air to clean it. A HEPA air purifier (pictured) traps pet dander rather than allowing it to circulate throughout the home.

HEPA Vacuum Cleaner – A regular vacuum cleaner filter is not designed to trap and hold the allergens and will circulate them back into the air. Instead, use a HEPA filter vacuum cleaner.

Closing Air Vents – In a home that has air conditioning or forced-air heating vents, closing these can reduce the amount of animal hair and dander circulating through your home. If it is not possible to close all the vents, closing those located in rooms where you spend most of your time—especially bedrooms—will help.

Dusting – Something as simple as being fanatical about dusting as often as possible, helps keep dander, hair, dust mites, and other allergens to a minimum.

No Dogs in the Bedroom – It makes sense to ban your dog from sleeping close to you if you have asthma or are allergic to pet dander.

No Dogs on Furniture – Training your cocker to sleep in their own doggy bed, rather than on soft, upholstered sofas, chairs, or beds can reduce exposure to dander.

No Dogs in the Car – The inside of most vehicles is quite a small space. Therefore, having your dog inside your vehicle if you have pet allergies could trigger a reaction. Keeping pets out of vehicles altogether, or at least restricting them to non-upholstered areas where they are farthest from the allergy sufferer will help considerably.

Hard Floors Instead of Carpets – Replacing wall-to-wall carpets that trap and hold hair, dander, and other unwanted debris with wood or other hard flooring makes it easier to remove hair, dust, and dander.

Frequent Washing of Pet Materials – Frequently hoovering and washing your dog's bed, pillows, blankets, or rugs they regularly walk or lay on will reduce allergens.

Personal Hygiene – Simply changing your clothes after a play session with your cocker spaniel or washing your hands after petting your furry companion certainly helps to reduce allergic reactions.

Pet Bathing – A study reported in the Journal of Allergy and Clinical Immunology compared levels of allergens found in dog dander before and after a five-minute bath and discovered the bath 'reduced the dog's allergen levels by about 85%'. Unfortunately, allergen levels return quite quickly—in about three days. While most would agree that bathing your dog twice a week is excessive, if you choose a mild shampoo that does not dry out their skin and coat, once a week will help significantly.

Pet Saliva – Some people who aren't allergic to dog dander could still be highly allergic to your dog's saliva. If this is the case, simply teaching your dog not to lick people will prevent an allergic reaction.

Clothing – For those who know they have allergic reactions to pet dander, and their desire to share their life with a dog still outweighs their allergic response, they might want to consider canine clothing, such as a T-shirt or Lycra body suit. Clothing a dog makes their skin less accessible, while also containing shedding hair and dander.

Antihistamines, Decongestants, Nasal Steroids – Dog allergies can be treated with all these common drugs that block the effects or reduce swelling and calm inflammation.

Allerpet – You can try using Allerpet dog dander remover (pictured). This is a liquid damp-wipe product that you apply on your dog and offers an easy way to remove allergens without the trouble of bathing your dog with shampoo to remove dander. In addition, this treatment softens your dog's skin, unlike bathing with shampoo, which can dry it out or irritate it.

Allergy Shots – While a course of treatment will help some who suffer from pet dander, allergy shots might not work for everyone and could take a long time to become effective.

As you can see, being allergic does not necessarily mean that you cannot have a cocker spaniel or that you need to give up one you already have. Learning about minimising pet-related allergens and making some minor adjustments can help to solve your problems.

FACT ***It is often possible for allergic people to live comfortably with a dog if they make an honest effort and commitment to care for their dog and home environment on a regular basis.***

3. Bringing Your Puppy Home

'If I could be half the person my dog is,

I'd be twice the human I am.'

~ Charles Yu ~

Taking your new puppy home is an extremely exciting time. You have probably been planning the arrival of your new, furry friend for months—or even longer—or you might have fallen in love with an adorable stray pup who is suddenly joining your household. But regardless of the circumstances of the new arrival, the first weeks with your cocker spaniel puppy is a time of changes for everyone involved.

TIP ***Moving to a new home with a new family can cause stress for your cocker puppy, and it can certainly be stressful for you, too. You can make the transition easier on both of you by doing a little advanced planning and preparation.***

When owners bring their new puppy home, they often consider dog insurance. Puppies are curious and can get into trouble. It is comforting to know that, in the event of an accident or illness, you will not be on the hook for large medical bills, so you can stay focused on making sure your cocker puppy feels better. Research your dog insurance options and find out what is and is not covered before you buy a policy (see more about insuring your puppy in Keeping Your Dog Safe, Chapter 16.

Essential Puppy Supplies

There are many essential supplies every new puppy requires. The best way to get ready for their arrival is to get your shopping list in order and head off to the pet store before the exciting day when you bring them home. That way, you can relax as you will already have everything your puppy needs in place.

The following list will help to ensure the essentials are not missed:

- **Pee pads** – no matter what type of house-training routine you plan to follow, it is always a good idea to have a package of pee pads on hand while your new puppy is learning where their toilet is.
- **Food** – most breeders send the new owner home with a couple of weeks' supply of the food the puppy has been eating while in their care. If you plan to change your cocker puppy's food, you need to do it gradually over the course of 5 to 7 days, so you do not cause them any stomach upsets. Begin by feeding a ratio of 25% new food with 75% old food on day 1. On the 3rd day, increase the ratio to 50% new with 50% old, then in on day 5 change to 75% new and 25% old. Finally, by day 7, your puppy can transition to 100% new food.
- **Food and water bowls** – always make sure your cocker spaniel's food and water bowls are small enough for them to get close enough so they can comfortably eat and drink.
- **Treats** – every puppy enjoys special treats, and they are an important part of helping to solidify good behaviour during house-training or when teaching commands or tricks. The best treats are those with a single ingredient, such as chicken or liver. Also, freeze-dried ones are easier for your puppy to chew.
- **Crate or Sherpa** – every cocker puppy or dog should have their own hard-sided crate, as this is their quiet space where they can go to get out of the middle of a busy home or have a nap. It is also a good idea to purchase a soft 'Sherpa' bag for transporting your puppy. Any dog who is 7 kilograms—15 pounds—or less can easily be trained to enjoy travel inside a Sherpa bag (pictured).

- **Collar and lead** – you will have to purchase several new collars for your puppy until they grow to full adult size. However, you will only need to purchase one lead, so make sure it fits comfortably in your hand, has a light weight, and an easy-to-operate clip on the end that attaches to your puppy's collar.
- **Soft beds** – while your cocker puppy always has a hard-sided crate to nap in, it is a good idea to also offer them a soft bed or two for other areas of your home where they might be spending time near you (pictured).

- **Blanket** – when puppies are young, they can get cold and often appreciate the comfort of a little more warmth inside their crate, Sherpa, or bed when transported in a vehicle, or snuggling with their owners. A small, soft blanket that is easy to launder is a marvellous addition to your puppy's list of essential items.
- **Soft toys and a ball** – your puppy will love a couple of soft toys to play with and snuggle up to in their bed or crate (pictured). Most puppies enjoy the fun game of chasing a ball or favourite toy.

- **Canine shampoo and conditioner** – your puppy will need to accept the routine of a cleansing bath every month. Getting them used to this procedure early on means buying shampoo and conditioner that is specially formulated with the correct pH for your cocker's skin. Be sure not to make the bath water too hot—test it on your wrist—and keep it just above warm.
- **Non-slip mat** – because having a bath might not be your spaniel's most favourite pastime, it is especially important when getting them used to this as a puppy that you do everything to make the process as easy for them as possible. Sinks and bathtubs are very slippery surfaces when wet, therefore, putting down a non-slip mat will help to keep your puppy's feet stable and make them feel less nervous.
- **Drying towels** – just as we need bath towels to dry ourselves after a bath, your puppy needs their towels, too. A good supply includes at least two small hand towels and a couple of larger towels to squeeze out excess water and rub your puppy as dry as possible before using a hairdryer to finish the job.
- **Hairdryer** – if there is not a hairdryer in your home, it is essential to buy one for drying your puppy. Puppies and older dogs often get cold very quickly after their bath and begin to shiver. So, thoroughly dry their fur immediately after their bath with the hairdryer to prevent this. Keep the temperature moderate and do not blow air into their ears or directly into their face. When your puppy gets used to the hairdryer early in life, they will grow to enjoy it, and might even come running to ask you to share some of that warm air when they hear you drying your own hair.
- **Soft bristle brush** – brushing is a normal part of keeping your cocker's coat in good condition. Beginning the brushing routine with your puppy when they are young will condition them to enjoy the process.
- **Daily moist wipes** – (pictured) these are specifically made with the correct pH balance for your dog and are a great way to wipe off the dust and debris of the day before bedtime or to freshen their face and eyes in the morning.

- **Nail scissors** – it is important to trim your cocker's nails every two to four weeks and starting this routine when your dog is a young puppy helps to ensure that they accept nail trimming as a normal part of their life. A simple way to introduce your puppy to nail trimming is by buying an easy-to-use pair of nail scissors, as all you need to do is snip off the curved tip of each nail. Once your puppy is a few months old and their nails are much stronger, it is time to buy a pair of medium-sized, plier type nail clippers.

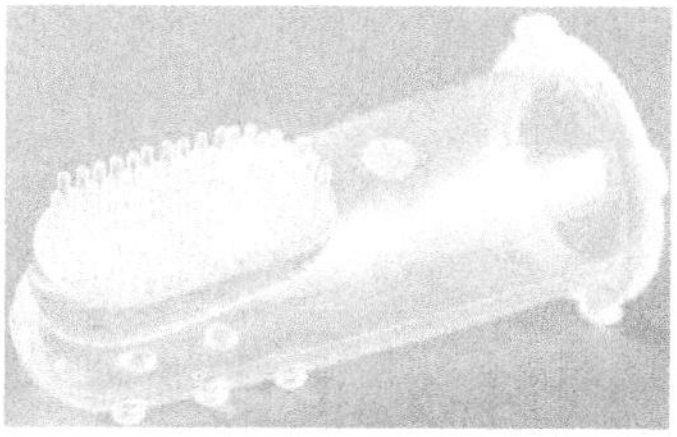

- **Finger toothbrush** – (pictured) dental health is extremely important for every dog, and just like trimming their nails, getting your puppy used to the procedure when they are very young helps them to calmly accept the necessary tooth brushing throughout their life. Begin with a soft, rubber finger toothbrush that fits over your finger to get them accustomed to having your fingers in their mouth, while you rub their teeth and gums. Once their adult teeth have pushed through—at approximately 28 weeks—you can graduate to a soft, child's toothbrush, and then, for the best clean, to a child-size electric brush.

Dogs and the law in the U.K.

Owning and caring for your cocker spaniel can be great fun and rewarding in many ways but it is important for you to understand the relevant dog laws to protect yourself, your dog, and others. This guide explains what your responsibilities are.

Animal Welfare

If you own, or are responsible for a dog, even on a temporary basis, by law you must care for it properly and take reasonable steps to ensure its well-being. One aspect of the Animal Welfare Act 2006 is that owners must provide their animals with a suitable environment, a proper diet, the ability to exhibit normal behaviour patterns, protection from suffering pain, injury, or disease and their need to be housed with, or apart from, other animals.

Taking your dog out

Transport – The U.K. Highway Code states that dogs must be properly restrained when in a vehicle so they cannot distract you while you are driving or injure you, or themselves, if you stop quickly. Ensure that you have a seatbelt harness or other suitable method for restraining your cocker in your car, such as a dog guard or crate.

Dogs in hot cars – Never leave your spaniel alone in your car on a warm day. Dogs pant to keep cool. In hot, stuffy cars they cannot cool themselves down. Opening a window or having a sunshield on your windscreen will not be enough to keep your dog cool. Leaving your dog in your hot car could be considered an offence under the Animal Welfare Act 2006. Every year, dogs die in hot cars.

Keeping them on a lead – On all motorways and designated roads, it is an offence to have your dog off their lead. To remain within the law and in the interests of your cocker's safety, it is recommended that you keep your dog on a lead at all times when on a road. Several local authorities have made it a requirement for dogs to be kept on their leads in certain areas such as public gardens and parks. For more information in your area, contact your local council.

Cleaning up – In England and Wales there are laws that require you to clean up after your dog. Failure to do so could result in a fine. Do not be caught out, make certain you have plenty of poo bags whenever you and your cocker spaniel are out and ensure you dispose of the bags properly.

Identification

Collar and tag – The Control of Dogs Order 1992 states that your dog must wear a collar and tag when in public. The tag must have your name and address on it. Your telephone number is optional but could also be helpful. Without a collar it is possible your dog could be caught and treated as a stray. You should always keep your contact details on the tag up-to-date and failure to do so can result in a fine. That means if you move home or change your telephone number you need to update those details.

Stray dogs – If your cocker spaniel goes missing, your local authority should be your first point of contact. They are responsible for strays and might charge a fee to reclaim your dog. If your dog is not claimed within 7 days, the local authority has the right to rehome or euthanise them. Up-to-date identification makes it easier for your cocker to be reunited with you.

Microchip – Since 2015 in Wales and 2016 in England, by law it is compulsory for all owners to have their dogs microchipped—if they are over 8 weeks old.

Control of dogs

Livestock worrying – Your cocker must never worry livestock—the owner, or whoever is responsible for your dog at the time, is committing an offence if your dog chases, attacks, or causes suffering to livestock. A police officer can seize your dog if they are suspected of worrying livestock. If convicted of an offence under the Act, the person might be liable to a maximum fine of £1 000. Please note that a farmer could shoot any dog worrying their livestock if there are no other reasonable means for stopping the dog from doing this. To avoid this, keep your dog on their lead whenever livestock are around.

Dangerously out of control – Under the Dangerous Dog Act 1991, it is a criminal offence to allow your cocker spaniel to be 'dangerously out of control' either in a public place or on private property, such as your home. A 'dangerously out of control' dog is defined as a dog who has injured somebody or who a person has grounds to reasonably believe might injure someone. Ensure your cocker is always under control, as something as simple as your dog chasing, barking at, or jumping up at an adult or child could result in an investigation. If your spaniel injures someone, they could be seized, and if convicted you could face a lengthy prison sentence and/or a fine. Also, your dog could be euthanised—unless you can convince the courts that your cocker is not a danger to the public, in which case it might be subject to a control order. Under the same law, if your dog attacks an assistance dog it is a criminal offence.

Dogs and the law in the U.S.

In Germany, dog ownership is taxed, rather than requiring licence and breeds deemed to be 'dangerous' attract higher taxes.

Most American states and municipalities have licensing laws in place. Dogs living in Australia, Canada, Ireland, and New Zealand also require a licence. Legal regulations in the U.S. vary between states and many fines are levied for violating the legal regulations relating to:

- Transporting dogs.
- Behaviour in public.
- Ensuring they are securely confined behind an escape-proof fence.
- Providing safe access to your front door.

- Wearing a collar and lead in public.
- Safely controlling your dog in public.
- Mistreatment, cruelty, or failure to properly care for your dog.
- Tail or ear cropping.
- Not picking up after your dog.
- Wearing a muzzle if your dog is dangerous.
- Owning a banned breed.
- Excessive barking.
- Chasing livestock or wildlife.
- Destroying property.

You can check the local dog laws for the state you live in on this page from the Michigan State University website: https://www.animallaw.info/content/state-dog-laws.

Puppy Proofing

Most puppies are a curious bundle of bouncing energy, eager to explore, which means they quickly find their way into everything within their reach. Therefore, even before your cocker puppy arrives at their new home, it is time to consider how safe their new environment is.

Watching out for the well-being of your new puppy means taking a serious look around your home not just from the human eye level, but also from that of a curious puppy.

TIP ***A young puppy has a much lower vantage point than their owners when standing. Therefore, there could be items in their unfamiliar environment that are potentially harmful to them, which you might not immediately notice unless you get down on the floor and take a good look.***

So, you need to crawl around at floor-level to eliminate any sources of danger, like the precautions you would take for an inquisitive toddler. This can be a fun exercise to ask children to help with.

For example, power cables can be found in about every room in the home, and to a curious, teething spaniel puppy, these look like irresistible, fun chew toys. It is a good idea to tuck all electrical leads securely out of your puppy's reach or enclose them inside a chew-proof PVC tube.

Puppies and dogs become familiar with their environment through sniffing, touching, or tasting things. Your young cocker spaniel has much to learn and will want to touch, sniff, taste, chew, investigate, and closely inspect every electric cable, closet, shoe, nook and cranny, dust bunny under the bed, and everything that might have been left lying about on the floor. There may be hidden dangers for an inquisitive young puppy that could cause choking hazards.

Initially, you can choose to close off some rooms in a larger home to let your small puppy slowly get used to their new space.

Kitchen – first, there are many human foods that are harmful to dogs, therefore, your kitchen should always be strictly off-limits to your puppy any time you are preparing food. Calmly send them out of the kitchen any time you are in there, and they will quickly get the idea that this area is off-limits to them.

Bathroom – bathroom cupboards and drawers, or the side of a bathtub where you might leave your shaving supplies can hold many dangers for your cocker puppy. Tissues, cotton swabs, cotton buds, toilet paper, razors, pills, soap, or other materials left within your puppy's reach are an easy target that could result in an emergency visit to your veterinarian. Family members need to put shampoos, soap, facial products, make-up, and accessories out of reach or safely inside a cabinet or drawer.

Bedroom – if you do not keep your shoes, slippers, and clothing safely behind doors, you could find that your puppy has claimed them for their new chew toys. Be vigilant about keeping everything safely in containers or drawers, including jewellery, hair ties, bank notes, coins, and other items small enough for them to swallow.

TIP ***Especially when your cocker spaniel puppy is going through their teething stage, if you have children, make sure they understand they must keep their bedroom tidy and leave nothing that could cause a choking problem to your puppy lying about on the floor or within their reach.***

Living Room – we tend to spend many hours in our cosy gathering places watching movies or playing games. Often, the living areas of our homes have many items that are very enticing for a nosey and teething puppy, such as books, magazines, pillows, tablets, mobiles, TV remotes, and more.

Office – if you spend a great deal of time in your home office, your puppy will want to be there too, and they will be interested in all the items an office has to offer, such as papers, books, magazines, and USB cables. Although your puppy might think that elastic bands or paperclips are fun to play with, leaving these items within their reach could end up being a fatal mistake if your puppy swallows them.

Plants – plants can be a very tempting target for your puppy's teeth, so keep them well out of their reach. If you have floor plants, you need to move them to a shelf or worktop or placed behind a closed door until your furry friend grows out of the habit of putting everything in their mouth. Also, bear in mind that many common houseplants are poisonous to dogs (see Toxic Foods, Plants and Products, Chapter 15)

Garage and Garden – there are obvious and subtle dangers that could seriously harm your cocker puppy, which can often be found in your garage or garden. Some of these include antifreeze, petrol, fertilisers, rat poison, weed killer, paint, cleaners and solvents, grass seed, bark mulch, and various insecticides.

If you are storing any of these toxic substances in your garage or garden shed, make certain you keep all such products inside a locked cabinet, or stored on high shelves your cocker puppy cannot reach. Even better, choose not to use toxic chemicals anywhere in your home or garden.

Take time to walk through your home and try to view it through your puppy's eyes to identify potential dangers. Here are some additional tips when puppy-proofing your home:

- Store cleaning products where your cocker spaniel puppy cannot reach them or put them in a locked cabinet.
- Put all rubbish in a bin with a tight-fitting lid or keep it secured in a cupboard.
- Store open food containers in a larder or cupboard—anything left out needs a lid.
- Pick small objects off the floor—they are a choking hazard for your adventurous spaniel.
- Cover open bodies of water—such as the toilet, bathtub, outdoor ponds, swimming pools, etc.
- Put all medications and other toiletries out of reach, such as in the medicine cabinet
- Keep windows and external doors securely closed when your puppy is roaming around.
- Use baby gates or pet gates to keep them away from out of bounds areas (pictured).

- If there is a cat, keep their litter box where your puppy cannot reach it, so they do not eat the poo.
- Dispose of all food waste properly so your puppy cannot get it—this is especially important for chicken bones and food that can be harmful to your cocker.
- Store all lawn and garden tools where your puppy cannot get to them, making sure they will not fall over if your spaniel bumps into them.
- If you have a garden, consider adding a fence to keep your puppy in.
- Never leave them alone in your back garden. Even a fenced garden is little deterrent to a motivated or inquisitive puppy who could be smart enough to figure out how to escape.
- Avoid the use of toxic chemical fertilisers, pesticides, or herbicides anywhere your puppy could be exposed to—this includes toxic carpet and floor cleaning products.
- While your puppy is very young and you cannot closely watch them—for example, when taking a shower—closer confinement, such as placing them in their crate would be sensible.

Naming Your Puppy

You might have decided on a name for your new cocker spaniel puppy even before you bring them home.

However, if you have not yet found a name, this is one of the things you need to address straight away so you can get them used to responding to it.

While choosing a name can be a fun process involving the entire family, you might want to consider what the puppy will look like when they are fully grown, rather than letting the children choose to name them 'SpongeBob' after their favourite childhood cartoon.

Once you get to know your puppy better, certain traits begin to emerge as their personality starts to reveal itself. For example, they might show a preference for running as fast as possible up and down the hallway. In which case, a good name could be 'Racer'.

Of course, their name is going to be around for a long while, so be careful not to choose one they will grow out of. For instance, calling them 'Nipper' when they are going through their teething stage, or 'Fluffy' when they are still in their fluffy, puppy coat would not be appropriate.

Introducing Your Cocker Spaniel to Your Home and Children

FACT ***Understandably, your spaniel puppy will be nervous about new and unfamiliar faces, smells, and surroundings, and will be missing their mother, other siblings, and everything in their environment they have grown used to during their first 8 to 10 weeks of life.***

You should not overwhelm your new puppy with too much all at once. For instance, closing off rooms that they do not need access to and encouraging your puppy to follow you as you wander about in a smaller space is less stressful for them.

Even before your cocker puppy has arrived at their new home, you can help make introductions go smoothly by taking a few minutes to sit with your children and explain to them that they must be calm, quiet, and approach slowly until the puppy gets used to them.

If your children are very young, they will instinctively want to pick up your little puppy and carry them around like a stuffed toy, and for the safety of your cocker puppy this must be discouraged.

Toddlers can sometimes squeeze a puppy too tightly or drop them. They might also scream loudly in excitement, which can scare your puppy and make them afraid of children. When introducing your small puppy, close supervision and limiting exposure to very young toddlers is recommended.

Introducing Your Puppy to an Older Cat or Dog

TIP ***When introducing your young puppy to an older cat or dog, go slowly and be ready to protect them from sharp cat claws or a much bigger dog who might feel jealous.***

Most puppies are extremely excited when greeting another animal and can be too rambunctious at first. For example, a cat who has never seen a puppy before, or just does not appreciate your puppy's bouncing approach, could retaliate with hissing and sharp claws. This is where you need to be the careful mediator and make sure nobody gets upset or suffers an injury.

Introducing your small cocker spaniel puppy to an older dog also requires a slow and steady approach until you can clearly see the puppy has been accepted into the pack and they are not in any danger. Often, it is the new puppy who is overly excited to see another dog, and if the older dog has little tolerance for an energetic puppy, they might respond with a growl or a snap if your puppy gets too close (see more tips on how to introduce your pup to another cat or dog in Chapter 6).

The First 24 Hours

Before you go to the breeder to pick up your cocker puppy, there are a few last-minute suggestions to bear in mind:

- Hoover your floors.
- Carry out a final check of every room in the home to make certain everything that could be a puppy hazard is carefully tucked away out of sight, and nothing is left on the floor or low down on shelves where your inquisitive puppy might get into trouble.

- Close most of the doors inside your home, so there are just one or two rooms your puppy has access to. You need to keep it this way for the first few days while your cocker is getting used to their new home.
- You have already been shopping and have everything you need, so get out a puppy pee pad and have it at the ready when you bring your new furry friend home.
- Also, have your cocker's soft bed in an area where you spend most of your time and where your puppy can easily find it.
- Take your puppy's first toy with you when you go to pick them up.
- You need your hard-sided crate or your soft-sided 'Sherpa' travel bag—lined with pee pads—with you when going to collect your puppy. Securely fasten it to the seat of your vehicle with the seatbelt restraint system. Even though you will no doubt be tempted to hold your new puppy in your lap on the drive home, it is a dangerous place for them to be in case of an accident and is illegal in the U.K. and other countries.
- Ask a friend to drive for you, so you can sit beside your puppy in the backseat. If your puppy cries on the way home, remind them they are not alone by speaking in a soft, soothing voice.
- Before bringing your cocker puppy inside your home, take them to the place where you want them to relieve themselves and try to wait long enough for them to at least wee. Praise them if they do.
- Once back home with your new little cocker spaniel, the following routine will help them to get used to their unfamiliar surroundings:

- Introduce them to where their food and water bowls are in case they are hungry or thirsty.
- Let them wander around sniffing and checking out their new surroundings and encourage them to follow you where you go.
- Show them where the puppy pee pad is located and place it near the door you will use to take them outside to pee or poo or near their indoor toilet. Many pee pads are scented to encourage a puppy to pee.
- Show them where their hard-sided crate is and put them inside with the door open while you sit on the floor in front of it and quietly encourage them to relax in it. Depending on the time of day you bring your puppy home for the first time, practise the above crate exercise several times throughout the day. If they have a little treat each time you entice them to go inside their crate, this will help to further encourage them to go inside.
- Take a break from exploring and sit quietly with them. This is a good time to allow your children to slowly approach and gently greet your puppy. They will be exhausted by then, so let them go to sleep.

After they have had their evening meal, take them outside approximately 20 minutes later to go to the toilet, and when they do, make sure you are very enthusiastic with your praise and even give them a small treat.

Sleep time – Before it is time for bed, again take your puppy outside for a short walk to the same place where they last went to the toilet and make sure they wee before bringing them back inside. Before bed, prepare a hot water bottle for your cocker puppy and wrap it in a towel so it is not too hot for them and place it inside their crate. Remember, they are used to sleeping with their warm mother and other puppies so the water bottle might help them to fall asleep. You can also make their crate even cosier with a soft lining or blanket and a toy.

Turn the lights down low and encourage them to go inside their crate. Let them walk into the crate under their own steam, and when they do, give them a little treat, and persuade them to snuggle down while you sit on the floor in front of their crate. Once they have settled down, close the door, go to bed, and turn all the lights off. It might help your puppy to sleep during their first night home if you can play quiet, soothing music in the background.

If they cry or whine, stay calm and have compassion as this is the first time in their young life when they no longer have the comfort of their mother and siblings and are alone. Do not immediately let them out of the crate if they cry, instead, simply reassure them with calm, soothing words so they know you are with them, and hopefully, they will fall asleep.

TIP ***Unless you want them to sleep on your bed when they are fully grown, even when they have wet or dirty feet, now is the time to exercise a little tough love and keep them in the crate, though they would prefer sleeping next to you.***

Another alternative is to place their crate on your bed if space allows. This would help your puppy sleep soundly as they are next to you but still safe inside their crate. As they grow, they will become used to their crate and not mind that it is sitting on the floor.

BEWARE: If there is any danger of the crate falling off the bed during the night, do NOT do this as you will traumatise your puppy and make them afraid of their crate.

How Can I Help My Scared Puppy?

It is understandable that sometimes your cocker spaniel puppy might seem afraid or nervous of their new surroundings when you first bring them home. If everyone remains calm, this usually passes quickly. In the meantime, there are a few things you can do to help your frightened puppy overcome this initial stage:

- Talk soothingly.
- Engage them with a distracting game or toy.
- Keep them close to you until they begin to relax.
- Play relaxing music.
- No screaming at home or sudden, loud noises to frighten them.
- Keep interaction with other animals and people to a minimum until they begin to settle down.

The First Week

The first week with your new cocker spaniel puppy is the time for establishing a routine that works well for both you and your puppy. It involves getting used to your puppy's needs as they become accustomed to your usual schedule.

TIP ***Be as consistent as possible with your waking and sleeping routine. Getting up and going to bed at the same time each day makes it easier for your puppy to get into the routine of their new life.***

First thing in the morning, remove your puppy from their crate and take them outside to relieve themselves at the place where they last peed. This should be done quickly, as they might not be able to hold it for very long after waking up. Of course, if you are training them to have an indoor toilet, take them there.

If you are teaching them to ring a bell to go outside, lift their paw to ring it before you go out the door with them, whether you are carrying them, or they are walking out on their own.

When you bring them back inside, let them follow you so they get used to their new lead and/or harness arrangement. Be careful not to drag your puppy if they stop or pull back on the lead. It takes a little while before they are used to being on a lead. Now is the time for their first feed of the day. After they have finished eating, keep an eye on the clock as you need to take them outside or to their indoor toilet to relieve themselves after about 20 minutes.

When your cocker puppy is not eating or sleeping, they will want to explore and have little play sessions with you. These times will help you bond with your puppy more each day. As their new owner, it is your responsibility to keep a close eye on them throughout the day, so you know when they need to relieve themselves.

You also need to ensure they are eating and drinking enough, so set regular feeding times four times a day. Also, set specific times in the day when you take your puppy out for a little walk on its lead or harness. Then they are not only going outside when they need to relieve themselves, but also learn to explore their neighbourhood and become familiar with new scents.

When your puppy is still very young, you must not walk them for long as they easily tire. Similarly, too much exercise when they are young can stress joints or bones that are still growing. You need to keep your walks to no more than 15 or 20 minutes during the first week, and if they seem tired or cold, you can simply pick them up and carry them home.

The First Few Weeks

Within the first few weeks, you will begin to really notice how much your cocker puppy has grown, how well they have become adapted to their new routine, and how much you have already accomplished together.

For example, they might have had their first visit to the vet, experienced their first bath and teeth brushing, happily sleep in their crate at night, and rung the bell to let you know when they want to go outside.

Dealing with Whining and Crying

FACT ***Whining and crying are your puppy's natural ways to communicate that they need something or are unhappy about something.***

Patience, compassion, understanding and working out the root cause of the crying and then solving the problem is the best way to help them. For example, there could be many reasons why they are whining or crying, including:

- They need time to adjust to being taken away from their mother.
- They are lonely.
- They do not want to be locked in their crate.
- They are afraid or nervous.

- They are hungry or thirsty.
- They want affection.
- They want a walk or playtime.
- They want a toy.
- They need to go to the toilet.
- They are bored.
- They do not feel well.

It will take time for your spaniel puppy to adjust to their surroundings and learn the new rules and what is expected of them. While their crying or whining noise can be hard on the ears, yelling or becoming frustrated will only make matters worse. The good news is puppy whining and crying does not usually last long s dogs are fast learners and really want to please their owners. Having patience and understanding during this early stage is the beginning of developing a strong bond between you and your cocker spaniel.

During the next few weeks, there will be many new things you need to introduce them to, including:

- New sounds, such as the doorbell, telephone, hairdryer, vacuum cleaner, music, etc., need to be a positive experience. Introduce new sounds slowly, play with your puppy so they will not be frightened, and offer a treat reward when they do not run away.
- Stairs and other terrains can be difficult for your cocker spaniel puppy. Carefully entice them to work out how to traverse obstacles without injuring themselves.
- At first, travelling in a vehicle can be a scary experience for your young puppy. So, get them used to being inside their crate in the car before you go anywhere. Then just start the engine and leave your car running for a while. Next, take a short trip around the neighbourhood and home again until you are certain they are placidly accepting the experience.
- Grooming is something every puppy needs to become acquainted with early in their life, so they learn to accept the process. Get them used to the bathtub, being brushed, having their teeth rubbed with a finger brush, their feet and toenails touched, and the curved tip of their nails snipped off with a pair of scissors.
- Getting your puppy accustomed to being handled is important because they need to be taught to placidly accept being picked up and handled when it is grooming time or when they go for a check-up at the vet's. Get them used to being up on a table or worktop early on, so they will not be afraid when these necessary procedures must be done.

- Bonding with family members is also important during the first few weeks of your cocker puppy's life. Each family member should try to spend time socialising with your puppy and being involved in various daily tasks.

4. Crate Training & House-training

'Dogs do speak, but only to
those who know how to listen.'
~ Orhan Pamuk ~

A dog crate is an enclosure with a door, made from metal, wire, plastic, or fabric where a dog can be kept for protection or transportation. Dog crates are designed to resemble your dog's natural den and provide a safe place for them in their home or when travelling.

Although, we sometimes feel guilty for crate training our canine friend, enclosed spaces form a haven for your cocker spaniel to relax and rest in. Most dogs instinctively seek small spaces to create protective shelters for themselves. Crates are useful training tools for puppies, safe refuges for senior dogs, and lifesavers for many emergencies.

FACT ***Most vets, dog trainers, and breeders recommend crate training cocker spaniels from about 8-10 weeks old.***

Crate training is an essential part of house-training your puppy, as dogs do not like to soil their sleeping quarters. They learn to hold their bladder while they are in the crate, so you will not have to clean up their mess. Therefore, when your puppy has learnt to accept sleeping in their own crate at night-time, this can help accelerate their toilet-training procedure.

Contrary to what some people believe, a crate is not a canine jail cell. When conditioning steps are correctly implemented, a crate will provide your puppy or dog with a calm, secure and relaxing space where they can feel safe and comfortable, like that special chair or place where humans go to relax.

Crate training is always a good idea for any puppy early in their education, as it can be utilised in different situations. The benefits for both owner and puppy are many because a crate can be:

- A refuge from noise or a busy home.
- A secure place for sleep at night-time.
- Required for safe aeroplane transportation.
- A calm space for a relaxing, daytime nap.
- Protection from possible injury when home alone.
- A secure space while travelling in a vehicle.
- A familiar home away from home.
- A safe space for post-surgery convalescence.
- Easy to move from room to room. A helpful tool for house-training.

Choosing a Dog Walker or Day-care

Although we love our dogs, sometimes we must be apart from them such as when we go to work. If you need to regularly leave your cocker spaniel alone for more than 4 hours at a time, and do not a friend or family member to help you, your dog should have a dog walker to break up their day. Alternatively, you could leave them at a dog day-care.

The dog walker will come to your house, take your dog out for a walk, and then bring them home again. They usually have a key to let themselves in and out of your home at the agreed time(s).

A dog walker allows your cocker to get out and go to the toilet, get some fresh air and exercise, and then come back home where they will have company again in the evening.

If you are looking for a dog walker, ask for recommendations from other dog owners in your area. Here is a checklist of things to ask a potential dog walker, and for you to consider:

- First, check whether the walker is independent or part of a company.
- Ask for proof of insurance, and ideally a qualification, such as dog first-aid.
- Ask for references or reviews from other clients. If the walker or organisation has a website, you can usually find reviews there.
- What do they use to transport the dogs if they need to? Check these are clean, secure, well-ventilated and each dog has a separate section.
- Ask what contingencies they have in place should they be unable to walk your dog, or the weather is bad, for example, extremely hot or cold.
- Check how the dog walker plans to safeguard your keys and home security.
- Introduce your dog one on one to the walker. It is important for your cocker spaniel to trust the walker and they are familiar with how your dog usually acts.

- You should also establish whether your dog needs to be walked alone or would benefit from being walked with either a couple of dogs or a large group of dogs.
- If the latter is the case, check if the other dogs being walked alongside your dog are vaccinated and up to date with flea and worming treatment.

If you enrol your cocker spaniel in a day-care centre your dog might receive less one-to-one human attention but will interact with other dogs and certainly will not be bored. If they are already familiar with other dogs who attend the day-care it can help with their introduction to the environment. Here is a checklist of questions to ask a potential dog day-care, and things to consider:

- When considering services online or by word of mouth, make sure to look at reviews and do not be afraid to ask for references.
- By law, in the United Kingdom, as of 2018, dog day-care providers must be licensed by their local authority. This guarantees they are trained to a minimum of an OFQUAL regulated level 2 qualification in a relevant subject, such as canine behaviour, or have clear evidence of knowledge and experience.

- Visit the day-care and look at their facilities. Is it spacious, clean, and well-organised? Do they have water readily available? There should be separate play and rest areas, so your dog does not become over-tired. If there are any dogs there, they should appear contented and upbeat.
- Ask whether all the dogs who attend are checked for up-to-date vaccinations and insurance.
- Similarly, the day-care centre should ask you about your dog's behaviour. For example, how does your cocker spaniel interact with other dogs and new people.
- Choose a day-care with a warm and friendly service. A love of dogs is important.

In the event of a dog fight, you should check what measures the staff have in place. With several dogs playing together, it is inevitable a squabble will break out now and again, so they should be happy to let you know their procedure.

Crate Training

There are different sizes, styles, materials, and types of crates. If you are into interior decorating, you could integrate a custom dog crate into the design of your home, i.e., underneath a staircase, or any type of built-in cupboard or cabinet.

Dog crates are available in a variety of sizes, with the most common being 60, 75, 90, 100, and 120 centimetres, (24, 30, 36, 42, and 48 inches). Some brands offer slightly different sizes, but most will offer these most common options.

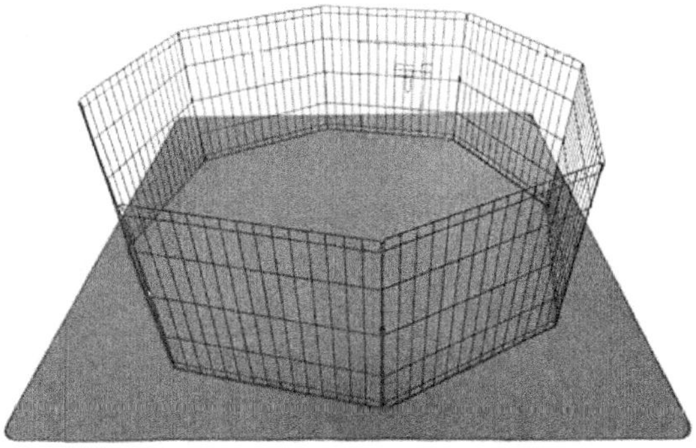

The best type of crate for use at home is a wire crate. It is easy to store as it is collapsible, provides great puppy visibility, and typically comes with a metal divider allowing you to adjust the crate size to fit your puppy as they grow. Once you have the crate, you need to proceed slowly as rushing the crate training process could create trauma or puppy anxiety that will take a long time to overcome. The following steps will help train your new cocker puppy to view their crate as a place where they want to be:

- Choose the right sized crate where your puppy can stand up and easily turn around inside or lie down with outstretched legs when they are fully grown. For a cocker spaniel, a 90-centimetre (36-inch) one would probably be most suitable. Note that placing your tiny puppy in a very large crate could encourage them to simply go to the farthest reaches to do their business. If the crate is large enough to accommodate your puppy when they are an adult, simply block off the back half of the crate until they need the extra space.
- Place the crate in a quiet place away from high traffic, heating vents, direct sunlight, and cables or plants.
- Place a vet bed at the bottom of the crate and put soft bedding on top of it. Vet beds are tough and durable mats vets use in their post-surgery recovery and treatment rooms. These are made from double-strength polyester and their construction allows extra warmth and increased airflow around your dog to avoid over-heating and discomfort.
- Place a favourite chew toy in the crate.
- Sit with the puppy on the floor beside the open crate door.
- Leave the door open and place a treat just inside to encourage them to go inside—you can also hold a toy in your hand to entice them to enter the crate.
- Praise them when they venture inside the crate on their own and encourage them to step inside to get another treat—praise them again.
- Feed your puppy their meals inside the crate—if they are nervous about entering, begin with their food bowl close to the door and then gradually move it farther and farther inside the crate.

- When your cocker puppy is comfortable with eating their meals inside the crate, close the door while they are eating, and open it when they have finished.
- Increase the time for your puppy to be inside their crate with the door closed—place a treat or toy or food puzzle in the crate and close the door for about 15 to 20 seconds.
- If there is no stress—crying, whimpering—and she seems happy with her toy or puzzle, increase to 30 seconds, and slowly build up to 1 minute, 5 minutes, 10 minutes. Always stop if your puppy seems anxious and be where they can see you.

- When you open the door to let your puppy out, rather than allowing them to rush out of the crate, ask them to stop and sit at the entrance so they relax before slowly emerging.
- Once your puppy is content with being inside their crate for several minutes, you can begin to move yourself farther from it, with the goal being to go to another room for a few seconds before returning to where they can see you.
- If they do not make a fuss and begin to whine or bark, when you return, open the door, and offer your puppy a treat.
- Slowly increase the time when you are out of sight while your puppy remains calm, quiet, and comfortable behind the closed door of their crate.
- Further increase the time when your puppy is calm and quiet in their closed crate, with the goal to increase to 15 minutes, then 30 minutes, and eventually 60 minutes.
- Always remove collars, clothing, and anything that could possibly be a choking hazard before putting your puppy in the crate, so there is no possibility of them becoming getting caught on anything that might cause discomfort or fear.
- When your dog is used to spending time in their crate, you can use it for longer periods, such as overnight or while you are away. Provide them with an enrichment feeder or a safe toy to keep them occupied. This will prevent boredom from setting in. However, you should not leave your cocker alone in their crate for more than four to five hours at a time during the day.
- Avoid emotional and prolonged departures. Give your spaniel praise and a treat for entering their crate, then leave quietly. If your dog is acting excited when you return home, do not reward them by responding enthusiastically. Arrivals should be kept low key.
- If you are on a budget and want to buy only one crate, buy one which is big enough for an adult dog, and reduce the size for your puppy by using crate dividers or by placing a box in the crate. As your dog grows up, you can re-adjust the size of the crate.
- Your cocker puppy can safely be left in the crate for a certain amount of time depending on their age. Consult your veterinarian for specific recommendations, but these timeframes can be used as a guide:

Age of the Puppy	Maximum Time in Closed Crate
9 – 10 weeks	30 to 60 minutes
11 – 14 weeks	1 to 3 hours
15 – 16 weeks	3 to 4 hours
17 + weeks	4 to 6 hours

A crate is not a magical solution. If used incorrectly, your cocker spaniel could feel trapped and frustrated. For example, if your dog is left in the crate all day while you are at work and then again all night, they are spending too much time in a confined space. If you need to use a dog crate for your puppy or dog during the

8 or so hours you are at work, try to go home for visits or consider hiring a dog walker. Other arrangements should be made to accommodate their physical and emotional needs.

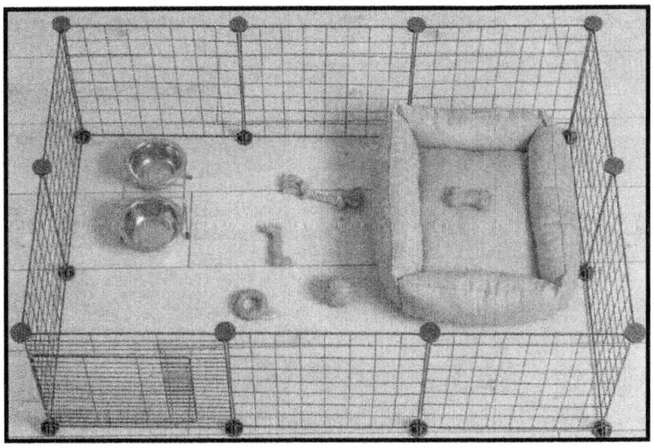

You should practise after your cocker has been exercised and is tired, so they are ready to relax and even go to sleep inside their comfy crate. By now, you should see them visibly unwind, knowing they are in a safe place where good things happen. They might even choose to rest there of their own accord if you make them feel so happy in there.

Give your dog tough, rubber toys that can be filled with food they can take slowly lick out, or long-lasting tasty chews, inside their crate while the door is closed, to give them different reasons to enjoy spending more time in their crate.

The more you practise, you will be free to attend to other household activities while your dog is inside their crate. It is important for them to still feel comfortable inside when you are busy outside. This is useful when you have visitors who are worried about dogs, and you need to pop your cocker inside their crate while they are there.

It is also important never to use their crate as punishment. Your cocker spaniel will not understand the reason for this and might resent being in their crate, excluded from the fun they were having moments earlier.

House-training

Whether you call it 'toilet training', or 'house-training', teaching your cocker spaniel not to do their business inside the house is the first step in their education. When you first bring them home, they will rely on the guidance of their new human family to teach them what they need to learn. When their humans are kind and understanding, puppies are capable of learning at a very early age. House-training is all about establishing a regular routine, and as with any new experience, it takes time and patience. Remember to exercise plenty of calm, compassionate understanding while your cocker puppy learns their new toilet rules.

House-training your puppy requires diligent supervision, and the more vigilant you are, the quicker your puppy will learn what is expected of them and where you want them to go to the toilet. Though it would be nice to have all family members involved in recognising your cocker's 'must go' body language, younger children are often easily distracted and not the best candidates for the task.

Some people prefer not to confine their puppy to one or two rooms in their home and instead allow them to freely roam wherever they wish during the day. This is called free training, which is not recommended. Far more attentiveness is required when free training your puppy. If they are not closely watched throughout the day, the chances are high they will have an accident when first learning their toilet routine.

While it would be wonderful if you could wait until your puppy 'tells' you they need to go to the toilet, this does not usually happen until they have already learnt exactly where their toilet is. Until your spaniel puppy can ring a bell or bark and scratch at the door to let you know they need to go out, it is up to you to watch for the following signs and take them outside for regular toilet breaks:

- Sniffing around.
- Circling.
- Looking at or approaching the door.
- Whining, crying, or barking.
- Scratching at the door.
- Acting agitated.

TIP ***Remember, puppies are puppies, and yours is bound to have some accidents, such as peeing on the nice, hardwood floor or soft, Persian rug. Though this might be upsetting, it is never a good idea to become cross or scold your puppy for having an accident inside your home.***

This could result in teaching your puppy to be frightened of you or sneaky and only relieve themselves in dark, hidden, or secret places when nobody is watching. All that is required when catching your puppy making a toilet mistake, is to stay calm, firmly say, '***No***', scoop them up and take them to their designated toilet area.

Puppies are particularly sensitive when first introduced to their new home environment, and any type of loud voice when they make a toilet mistake will be very upsetting. They will sense something is wrong and could become afraid and more difficult to train. It is important to have compassion during this house-training time in your young cocker spaniel's life, so their education is as stress-free as possible.

Do not forget, leaving your puppy confined in a locked crate for too many hours in the day can derail both the crate and house-training processes. As comfortable as the crate might be for your puppy, if they are in there for too long, it is possible they will become nervous, anxious, or depressed and do their business inside their crate.

It is also important to pay attention to the signs that mean your puppy needs to wee. This will minimise the possibility of a toilet mistake in the first place.

How Often?

As your cocker puppy grows, they can usually 'hold it' for about one hour for every month of their age.

For example, if your two-month-old puppy has been quietly snoozing for two hours, once they wake up, they will need to relieve themselves.

Paying close attention to your puppy's sleeping, eating, drinking, and playing habits also helps to predict when they will need to relieve themselves. Your cocker will normally perform their duties at regular times during the day:

- Immediately after they wake up.
- After being in their crate.
- After intense and exciting situations—with dogs, people, or toys.
- Approximately 20 minutes after a meal or drink.
- After a play session.
- Before bedtime.

How often your cocker spaniel puppy needs to go will vary from puppy to puppy. While the number of toilet breaks each puppy requires diminishes as they grow, on average you can expect your puppy to relieve themselves eight or more times daily, until they are six to seven months old. At six months old, your puppy's bladder and bowel control will be much greater, and they are able to wait longer before needing to relieve themselves.

Indoors or Outdoors

The difference between indoor training and outdoor training is simply a choice of location convenience. For instance, someone living in a 40-floor high-rise building might prefer to house train their dog inside rather than take the lift 8 or 10 times a day to get their puppy outside for toilet breaks. On the other hand, someone living in a house with a garden, or easy access to the street will usually prefer to train their puppy to go to the toilet outside from the start.

Indoor Instructions

Toilet training your puppy can be difficult if you do not know what to do, but there are several aids you can use for indoor training. Pee pads, potty patches, and litter box arrangements can all be used to train your puppy to use an indoor toilet.

Pee pads (potty pads or training pads). These square or rectangular pads are comprised of layers of material that readily absorb any sort of puppy mess. Whilst there are numerous different kinds of toilet training pads, the most basic is a leak-proof paper pee pad (pictured). There are also washable fabric pads and pheromone infused ones.

Litter Box. While it is true that most people associate litter boxes (pictured) with indoor toilets for cats, there is no reason why your puppy cannot be trained to use them in the same way.

FACT ***Remember, when your puppy is small, they might need a ramp or step to help them get into the box. Also, the box needs to be at least 7.5 centimetres (3 inches) deep, and large enough for the puppy to comfortably turn around inside it.***

For anyone considering a litter box doggy toilet you need to decide on which litter to put in it. Puppies eat anything, which means it is not a good idea to leave them unsupervised in a box full of litter crystals they might decide to eat. A better choice of litter for a puppy might be natural, paper fibre litter infused with a pheromone attractant to help entice your puppy to use the box.

Potty Patches. There are various potty patch-type systems available for house-training your puppy, such as:

- Basic synthetic turf with mat and tray (pictured).
- Synthetic turf with removable waste bin.
- Natural grass in a tray.
- Plastic grate in a tray.

While more substantial than pads and designed to mimic the feel and smell of being outside in a grassy area, these patches can be used in much the same way as pee pads.

If this is going to be their permanent toilet, much like choosing the right size crate, the litter box needs to be large enough to accommodate your cocker when they are fully grown.

You can choose any of the above three options to house train your puppy indoors. Here are the steps you need to follow if you select to use a potty patch:

- First, decide where your puppy's indoor toilet will be. It should be somewhere easy for your puppy to get to. Perhaps this could be in a spare room, or the bathroom. If at all possible, choose a room that has a hard surface, such as tiles, linoleum, or hardwood, which is easier to clean if they miss the mark.
- Place the potty patch in this area and disperse pee pads or newspapers all around it.
- Keep some tasty treats in your pocket or close at hand, so you can reward good performance when your puppy uses the designated area for their toilet.

TIP ***Positive reinforcement using treats can work wonders with a cocker spaniel. Originally bred as hunting dogs, spaniels are eager to please their owner and take to positive, reward-based training very quickly.***

- The moment you see your puppy telling you they need to go—or at their regular times during the day as mentioned—pick them up and take them to their toilet area. Encourage them to relieve themselves by saying, 'hurry up', or something similar. Helping them by using a voice cue reminds your easily distracted cocker puppy why they are there.

- The second they have done their business, give them a treat and praise them so they begin to associate using their toilet location with receiving a reward for good behaviour.
- After they have used their toilet for the first time, their scent will still be there and the next time it will be easier for them to associate the toilet area as the right place to relieve themselves.
- Do not allow them to play in their toilet space as they are there for one specific purpose.
- If they wee on a pee pad near their toilet area, simply move the soiled pee pad closer to further help them identify the familiar toilet scent they left previously.
- Soon, your cocker puppy will learn that when they feel an urge, they must take themselves to the toilet area and do their business on the potty patch. This is time for celebration because you no longer have to be so attentive about looking for the 'signs' or cover the entire floor with pee pads or newspaper, as your spaniel has now learnt where to go.

NOTE: The same positive reinforcement training process outlined above for teaching them to use their toilet area applies when teaching your cocker to use pee pads or a litter box. The only difference is instead of placing a potty patch in the designated area, you would use pee pads or the litter box.

Depending on how well your puppy sleeps when they are young, some might not be able to hold it all night long, but others will. Therefore, for night-time, you have the following options:

Option 1: You can set the alarm and get up at 3:00 in the morning to take them outside.

Option 2: You could section off part of the room where they sleep and lay a plastic sheet in one corner of that area with a pee pad laid on top. Soaking a tissue in your puppy's pee and placing it in the centre of the pee pad will encourage them to go where you want them to. This is the preferred option as it will be less disruptive to your sleep pattern.

Outdoor Instructions

Once you become familiar with the signs your dog typically exhibits when they feel the urge to go, as discussed earlier, most cocker puppies are not difficult to house train. The following steps will get your cocker off to a good start when starting to use their outdoor toilet:

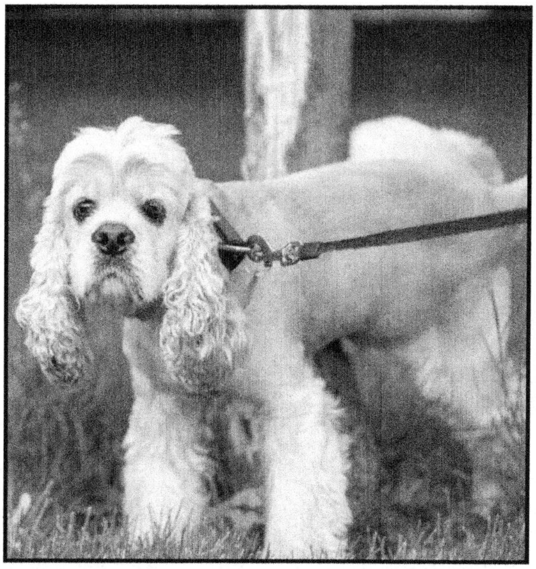

- To be on the safe side, place several pee pads on the floor near the door the puppy usually uses when going outdoors.
- Always use the same door when taking them outside, so they quickly learn to associate the door with their need to urinate or defecate.
- When they begin showing the signs that they are looking for a place to go, or it is their regular time, quickly put on their collar and lead and take them outside.
- Present them with familiar scents by taking them to the same spot in the garden or the same street corner where they last did their business or where some other dog might have peed before.

- Let your puppy walk up and down or run about and sniff the area—both exercise and sniffing help stimulate going to the loo. It is better to let your puppy out in the garden without a lead on as it is too restrictive. However, if your puppy needs to be on their lead when in the garden for whatever reason, an extendable one is a good solution as this gives them the freedom they need to go to the toilet.
- Say, '***Good boy/girl***' and give them a treat immediately after they have done their business. This helps reinforce the message that when they perform their duty outside it is a happy occasion. You can further help to strengthen their good performance by giving a life reward—your happy praise, a chest rub or scratch behind the ears—every time they do it in the right place.
- Do not let them become distracted from the task at hand when they are taken out for a toilet break—in other words, this is not a play session. If they seem distracted, help them to concentrate by moving them along to areas that potentially contain scents encouraging them to pee—a corner with a pole or tree, a patch of grass—and keep using your chosen voice cue to remind them why they are outside.
- Once they have used their outdoor toilet, bring them back inside rather than allowing them to play or greet other people or dogs. This helps them understand they were outside for the sole purpose of a toilet break.
- Being consistent with the voice cue during this early training teaches them to go on command, which can be very helpful when time is short, or on dark, rainy nights when everybody wants to get back inside quickly.
- Once they are regularly using their outdoor toilet, the treat incentive can slowly be removed and replaced by a life reward, or simply waiting to give them a treat after returning home.

Doggy Doors

Anyone living in a home with a securely fenced back garden might like to consider installing a doggy door—or pet flap—as this can speed up the house-training process. Once the doggy door has been installed, it is time to teach your cocker how to use it to get to their outdoor toilet. Place a pee pad beneath the doggy door until they get used to exiting and entering on their own and use the following steps:

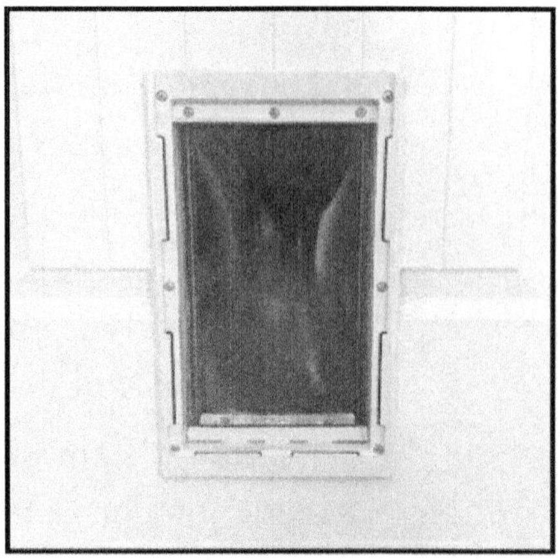

- Show your puppy the door (pictured) and open it to the outside with your hand, so they can smell the interesting outdoor scents that will entice them to want to investigate. Two people are useful when getting your puppy used to their new door.
- Have one person on the outside of the doggy door and the other on the inside. The person on the outside could hold a treat in their hand as an extra incentive and reward for your cocker once they push their nose through to the outside.
- It might help if you put your puppy's lead on and have the outside assistant draw it through to provide a gentle tug towards the outdoors. At the same time, the inside person uses their hand to guide your puppy through the flap.

It is important not to hurry this process, especially if your puppy is at all nervous about the door. They must feel confident enough to go through the door under their own steam, rather than being forced.

When the doggy door training is approached with a relaxed and fun attitude, it can become an entertaining game, which your cocker puppy will soon learn to enjoy, especially when there is praise from you and tasty treat rewards involved. Once your puppy is a little older and fully house-trained, they will be able to go outside—and back inside again—without needing your assistance.

Bell Training

To introduce your cocker spaniel puppy to house-training, give them a convenient method to let you know they 'have to go'. Teaching them to ring a bell whenever they need to go outside is a handy alert system for both you and your puppy and can prevent toilet accidents. It is also fun and easy to teach.

There are many types and styles of commercially manufactured bells for you to choose from. These range from the elegant '***Poochie Bells***' that hang on a leather or nylon strap from a doorknob (pictured), the simple '***Tell Bell***', reminiscent of an old school desk bell that sits on the floor. Or there are various high-tech door chime systems that function much like a doggy intercom system where your cocker puppy can push a pad with their paw to ring a bell.

Of course, you might prefer to craft a bell system yourself. This can easily be done by taking a trip to your local store and buying a bell with a loud ring. Attach the bell to a piece of ribbon or string and hang it from the door handle on the door you use to take your puppy out. The string needs to be long enough so your puppy can reach the bell with their nose or paw.

Okay, so how do you get your puppy to ring the bell when they need to go out to the toilet? This is what you need to do:

- Every time you take your puppy out, say, '***Out***' and proceed to the door where their bell is.
- Lift their paw and knock it against the bell to make it ring. If you have chosen the type that sits on the floor, press their paw on it to ring it.
- Praise them for this 'trick' and say, '***Out***' again while you immediately open the door and go outside.
- Once outside, say your cue word, and when they go, reward them with praise and a treat.
- Go back inside straight away so they associate ringing their bell with the act of going outside to the toilet—as opposed to going outside just to play or explore.
- If they ring their bell just because they are bored and want to go for a walk, you will still have to take them outside.

When you consistently use this method, your smart cocker puppy will soon be ringing their toilet bell by themselves.

Tips for Working Dog Owners

Cocker spaniels are social animals who they love to be in a pack, which includes their humans. So, if you work full-time, you will need to juggle your workday schedule around your dog to make it all work. If your dog has separation anxiety, they will get into all sorts of destructive behaviour that needs to be addressed before it becomes a problem. If you unable to hire a dog walker or use a day-care facility, here are some tips to smooth the process of leaving your cocker alone at home:

- Before you leave in the morning, take your dog out for a walk. Make sure they have enough exercise before you go to work. Perhaps, include a game of fetch if you can squeeze it in. If you exercise your cocker it will keep them happy. The adage that a tired dog is a happy dog rings true.
- Dogs are creatures of habit and routine. Try to maintain a workday routine. Leave at the same time and try not to stay late at work as consistency is key. The more regular you are the more your cocker spaniel will become used to the time of day and hours you will be away from them.
- To keep them from becoming bored, cockers need stimulation. Before setting off in the morning, have some interaction time with you dog, and leave them their favourite chew toy or stuffed toy.
- When you leave, ensure there is a soothing ambience around. Some research suggests soft jazz or classical music will relax your dog. So, should try leaving some soft music on.
- Keep your home temperature regulated and make certain there is enough daylight coming in.
- If you choose to let your cocker run free around the house, you need to puppy-proof your home. Dogs will chew or get into things they are not supposed to when bored or feeling separation anxiety.
- Some companies allow their workers to take their dog to work with them. The theory being that having pets around improves productivity and overall wellness of their employees.
- Unfortunately, barking is something that is unavoidable. To reduce the chances of your neighbours hearing your cocker, put your dog in a confined space in the innermost part of your home away from shared walls or the front door.
- These days, it is often possible to have a flexible working policy where you can either work from home or take an extended lunch break to drop in on your dog.
- To help build their mindset where they do not feel as if every time you leave they are being abandoned, pop in and out of sight while your cocker is in the other room for a minute or two. They will soon learn it is okay for you to be out of sight every now and then as you will come back.
- If possible, consider opting for drop-in services. Maybe you have a retired parent or a friend who works from home who can drop in and check on your pup. There are also paid-for drop-in services available.
- Finally, it is not necessary to beat yourself up over having to work full-time and deciding to have a cocker spaniel. They are wonderful life companions who reduce your stress levels, increase your exercise time, and can be great bundles of fun. Everyone has to work, and it is entirely possible to have both a spaniel and work full-time. So, put your mind at ease and do not feel guilty.

Dealing with Accidents

Despite your best intentions, and your puppy's, 'accidents' will happen along the way. In some ways, puppies are like human babies.

When dealing with puppy accidents, the following tips will help gradually reduce their frequency:

- Always stay calm because your puppy has no agenda or desire to upset you, but simply does not have a fully developed bladder or bowels, or the muscles that control them, and has yet to learn their toilet rules.
- Remain compassionate and remember your puppy does not understand that doing their business anywhere they like is unacceptable behaviour.
- Remember they are young and need to be taught by you, and one of the rules is where their toilet is located.
- If they are caught whilst having an accident, simply use a firm tone and say something like, '***Uh-oh***', or '***Oops***', followed by a firm, '***No***'. Then take them directly to the place where they should go to the toilet.
- If they have an accident that is not immediately observed, and a puddle is discovered some hours later, there is no need to take them to their toilet location. It is too late for them to associate this with having made a mistake they have no doubt long since forgotten about—just thoroughly clean it up and forget about it.

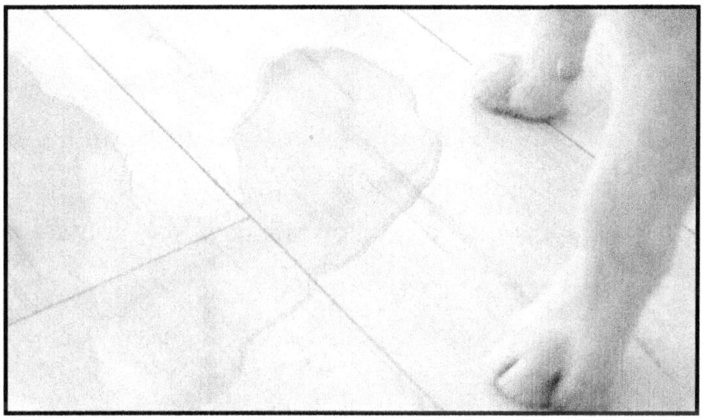

- It is never a good idea to yell, scare, or punish your cocker spaniel puppy for having a toilet accident. This only frightens them and might teach them to avoid going to the toilet in front of you.

FACT ***You might have heard it is a good idea to rub your cocker's nose in any mess or take them over to the scene of the crime and admonish them. Unfortunately, such training methods are extremely damaging and perplexing for your puppy and are best avoided.***

For puppies to be quickly toilet-trained, they need to be calmly told when a mistake is made and praised when they get it right.

It can be confusing and frustrating when your puppy continues to use the wrong place in the home for their toilet, especially after the area has been thoroughly cleaned. Any leftover smells will attract your cocker to return to the same spot repeatedly to relieve themselves and therefore a proper clean-up is essential.

Your spaniel's sense of smell is as much as 2 000 times more sensitive than yours. In other words, the accident that was just cleaned up might look and smell clean to you but might still retain an odour that will attract your puppy to the same spot.

Proper Clean-up. Finding a product that effectively and completely removes all smells from house-training accidents can be challenging, as many products that are supposed to remove smells and stains are not effective enough. **Choose a professional grade oxy-charged, enzyme cleaner (pictured).** This does not simply mask one scent with another but completely removes odours and stains. These contain professional-strength odour neutralisers and urine digesters that bind to and completely absorb odours on any surface.

Marking

There can be many reasons why dogs use their urine for 'marking territory' or 'scent marking'. Though marking is more often carried out by male dogs who lift their leg to pee on the corner of a sofa or chair, females occasionally mark their territory.

Dogs are famous for marking territory when out on a walk, with trees, corners of buildings, tufts of tall grass, and other upright objects usually receiving the most attention.

Dogs have a deeply ingrained evolutionary urge to mark things in their territory with their own scent, and the best way to do this is to pee on it. Dogs do not begin to engage in marking behaviour until they reach adulthood.

When your cocker spaniel smells a urine mark left by another dog, they might feel compelled to 'overmark' or place their urine scent on top of what was left by the previous dog. This leaves a dominance message that the previous dog who peed there is now subordinate to the one who peed last. Some reasons why a dog marks their territory in the home include:

- A female dog might pee inside the home when coming into heat.
- A dog entering a home where there are—or have been—other dogs present can often mark furniture to display dominance over the smell of the other dogs.
- Dogs might begin marking when a new animal or person is introduced to the home or when something has changed—e.g., new, unfamiliar furniture, carpet, curtains, painted walls.
- Visiting guests have the scent of another dog on them.

To avoid the problem, always keep a watchful eye when their environment changes or other dogs visit, and quickly interrupt this undesirable behaviour. Keeping a visiting dog on a lead and a loud '***No***' or a hand clap could be all that is required to get your cocker to desist from marking. For those dogs who persist with marking territory inside the home, there are several ways to help prevent this unwelcome activity, including:

- Spay or neuter your cocker spaniel—50 to 60% of males stop marking once they are neutered.
- Thoroughly clean previously marked areas with an enzymatic cleaner to eliminate their scent, otherwise, it might attract your dog to pee there again.
- Use bitter sprays on furniture or other areas they are attracted to weeing on.
- Play calming music.
- Use a diffuser with calming, essential oils, such as lavender.

- Have your dog wear a belly band. It wraps around your cocker's midsection and has a removable, absorbent inner liner. It can also be used when toilet-training or if an older dog becomes incontinent.

Excitement Urination

As with other breeds, many cocker spaniels tend to urinate when excited, especially when they are puppies. When overly excited, because their young muscles cannot hold the flow of urine back, puppies pee. Just the joy of seeing their owner is often enough to make them lose control of their bladder. As your puppy will not be aware of what they have done, as it is purely reflexive, punishment will confuse them and is totally inappropriate. Normally, your cocker will outgrow the problem as they mature and gain command of their bladder. Rarely, a cocker spaniel never outgrows this problem.

Never scold or punish your dog for excitement urination as it will only make the situation worse as your puppy will then start to pee out of fear. If you become angry with your cocker puppy for excitement urination, it can easily turn into submissive urination.

If the issue does not diminish as your puppy gets older, the following steps will help:

- Ask visitors not to approach your puppy with enthusiastic energy.
- Keep your voice soft and non-threatening when greeting.
- Ignore an overly enthusiastic puppy until they learn to settle down.
- Try a new greeting routine—ask your cocker puppy to sit and wait for a treat.
- Make sure there is no bladder infection or other medical issue.

Submissive Urination

When in a scary situation, even if your cocker spaniel is house-trained, they could succumb to submissive urination. This is commonly seen in cocker puppies who roll on their back when approached by a larger or more dominant dog or person they are feeling nervous around.

If you are too dominant and strict, it will reinforce submissive urinating. So, stay calm and be gentle and kind to your cocker spaniel. Keep your temper under control. Never scold or punish your cocker for submissive urination. Your dog will not understand why you are angry, and in their mind, peeing is their attempt to calm and appease you.

FACT ***In most cases, submissive urination is an instinctive reaction to another dog or person who they find intimating and is typically a behaviour they grow out of as they mature.***

Nevertheless, your cocker spaniel puppy might continue to be nervous or overly timid into adulthood. If this is the case, it could become an issue in the home. There are other signs of submissive behaviour such as tail tucking, crouching, and rolling over. There can be many reasons why your dog engages in submissive urination, such as:

- A naturally shy or timid nature.
- A history of being punished inappropriately.
- They could have been treated harshly or yelled at.
- They might be unsure of the rules.
- They are trying to avoid punishment.
- Strangers approaching them make them nervous.
- Uncertainty about how to behave when being greeted.
- There is a loud noise or disturbance.
- They may not have been properly socialised.

If your cocker spaniel exhibits this behaviour, there are many steps you can take to boost their confidence that will eventually lead to a cessation of submissive urination:

- Thoroughly socialise with different people, dogs, and situations.
- Never yell at your nervous cocker.
- Keep any greetings low-key.
- Keep their home environment calm and quiet.
- Teach commands using positive reinforcement and rewards.
- Make new experiences happy and positive—play games, give treats.
- Never approach your timid or apprehensive cocker spaniel with a loud voice or dominant posture.
- Let your nervous dog come to you and sniff the back of your hand.
- Avoid direct eye contact and keep your body language calm.
- Spend time sitting together while your cocker spaniel is on their lead.
- Encourage them to respond to simple commands that reap a treat reward—'***Sit***', '***Stay***'.
- Do not pat the top of your dog's head—rub them under the chin instead.
- Avoid placing your cocker into loud, noisy, or unpredictable situations that you cannot control until they begin to gain confidence.

Helping your cocker gain confidence requires patience, as it will take time for them to overcome their fears.

Excitement or submissive urination is instinctual rather than behavioural in the cocker spaniel breed. They do not do this to be disobedient or punish you. They can be excited, frightened, or show submissiveness to a person or animal they perceive to be dominant.

5. Puppy Care

'Dogs are not our whole life,

but they make our lives whole.'

~ Roger Caras ~

Whether you are getting your first cocker spaniel or just need a refresher course, here is what you need to know to get your puppy on the right track to adulthood, starting with the many development stages they go through before they are fully grown adults:

Neonatal Stage: Birth to 2 weeks – The neonatal stage is the 'new-born' time between birth and two weeks of age when puppies have the senses of touch and taste but are still blind and deaf. At this age, a puppy is only capable of a slow crawl and entirely dependent on their mother for food and grooming.

Transitional Stage: 2 to 4 weeks – The transitional stage is between the ages of two and four weeks when the puppy's eyes open, their hearing begins to develop, and their milk teeth emerge. During this time, puppies start to walk, wag their tails, and make those cute, little barking noises.

Weaning Stage: 5 to 8 weeks – At the end of four weeks, puppies can urinate and defecate without receiving stimulation from their mother, and they will play and wrestle with their littermates and are ready to start on solid food.

When they are eight weeks old, they should have transitioned to solid food and no longer need to nurse. Near the end of this period, a puppy is emotionally mature enough to form strong bonds with their new human family.

New Home Stage: 8 to 10 weeks – This stage is known as the 'fear period' as this is when a puppy is extremely impressionable. It is important to make new experiences with people, places, and other animals fun and positive. It is helpful to treat events that might not be the most pleasant—such as vaccines—like a game with abundant praise.

First Learning Stage: 8 to 16 weeks – This is when your cocker puppy will have a fervent desire to be near their owner, and many people enrol their puppy in their first training class. There they can experience other puppies in a fun, group setting. During these weeks, it is imperative to get them out in their new world. Every puppy needs to be where they can meet and greet new people of all ages, ethnicities, and experience different situations in a positive way.

Pre-Adolescent Stage: 4 to 6 months – During this stage, you will see a gradual increase in confidence and independence in your puppy as their curiosity motivates them to explore farther afield. This is a good time to step up training routines and make sure they have learnt their basic commands.

TIP ***When your cocker puppy can go everywhere with you, which broadens their horizons and helps cement a strong bond of trust and respect between owner and puppy. This is helpful during more advanced training sessions. Also, nearing the end of this timeframe is when you should consider whether you wish to have your puppy neutered or spayed.***

Adolescent Stage: 6 to 12 months – This 'terrible teens' time in your young cocker's life is when they have attained sexual maturity and begin to test the boundaries of their environment. This is also a high-energy time when your puppy might become bored. Their need for mental and physical stimulation can display itself through lapses in obedience as their personality asserts itself and they test to see what they can get away with.

While it might seem that the obedient puppy you once knew has all but disappeared, when you continue to exercise patience, find ways to engage them in vigorous play and exercise, and do not expect perfection, you will both make it safely through this stage.

Emotional Maturity Stage: 12-18 months – When your cocker spaniel is approaching emotional maturity, any inclination towards dominance or wanting to assert themselves within their human household might begin to show itself. When your dog begins to exhibit a desire to exercise dominance within the family, you need to increase your own energy level and time spent training so they understand they must remain a follower. Should this behaviour manifest itself as aggression, it might be time to consult a behaviourist.

Weight Table – It can be helpful to understand how your cocker puppy might grow and how long it could be before they attain their adult weight. Your cocker's weight could vary as certain factors influence their adult size, such as:

- Parental size—you can usually tell the size a puppy will grow to when you see their parents.
- Gender—male dogs are usually larger than females.
- Time of spaying or neutering—when spaying or neutering, the chemical signals that tell the bones to stop growing are cancelled, which means dogs neutered earlier in life tend to be taller.

Regardless of the above factors, the following weight table can be used as a generic guideline. It outlines the expected variances in weight from 1 to 12 weeks for a cocker spaniel puppy:

Age (Months)	Male Expected Weight (kgs)	Female Expected Weight (kgs)
1	1.4	1.3
2	3.0	2.7
3	4.9	4.4
5	8.0	7.0
6	9.2	8.2
7	9.6	8.6
12	11.9	10.5

Bonding with Your Puppy

Bonding with your cocker spaniel puppy begins the moment you bring them home from the breeder. This is the time for calmly and gently introducing them to their new home.

TIP ***At this stage, you need to take on the role of guiding them and making sure they stay safe. While they get used to their new surroundings, you need to be extra patient, kind and gentle with them as they learn all about their human family who are now the centre of their universe.***

Daily interactions during disciplined exercises that include going for walks on a loose lead, teaching commands, tricks, and routines (see Training Chapter 11), are all wonderful bonding opportunities. There are endless ways to strengthen the bond with your puppy and the best times usually occur during teaching your puppy new things.

Playtime is a fantastic time to bond with your puppy. Some puppies want to play the second they step inside your home. Others might need time to adjust to their new environment, so having their favourite doggy treats to hand can entice them into playing with you. Games such as 'hide and seek' and 'find it' offer both training and fun quality time for you and your puppy.

TIP ***Cuddle sessions are also important and provide your puppy with a sense of safety and comfort they long for. When they are sleepy is the ideal time to snuggle up with your cocker puppy.***

To encourage your spaniel puppy to relax with you, have some food or treats in your hand to coax them, and use it to reward them when they settle beside you. Gradually eliminate the food over time and replace it with your love and affection. Cuddling, massaging, and just hanging out together is another good way to get your puppy to unwind at the end of the day and gets them used to having their paws, muzzle, ears, tummy, etc. handled. You can also use this time for some light grooming practise such as brushing their fur or cleaning their eyes. By working these sessions into your puppy's daily routine every evening teaches them this time of the day is when they should be settling down.

Teething and Play Biting

How to Help with Teething – When your puppy is teething, they naturally want to chew on everything within reach to try to alleviate the pain of their new teeth pushing through their gums. Thankfully, there are many simple things to help your cocker puppy through the teething stage, such as:

- Have compassion—teething is painful.
- Keep items you do not want chewed safely out of reach.
- Have plenty of chewable items to hand—chew toys and treats, rope toys, stuffed and frozen Kong, hard rubber toys, cold carrots, a knotted tea towel soaked in water and placed in the freezer.
- Chicken broth ice cubes—messy, so should be given outside or somewhere you can easily clean.
- Rub their sore gums with your finger—a good time to introduce the beginning of your spaniel's teeth brushing routine.
- Buy them teething toys that are designed to be frozen.

Every puppy is different when it comes to teething and some are more upset or bothered than others. For example, it is not unusual for a puppy to lose their appetite or even have a low-grade fever when their new molars are pushing through. If they are feeling reluctant to eat, feed them warm, soft foods that are easier on their sore gums.

How to Stop Play Biting – Sometimes, puppies get into the habit of biting and nipping at human fingers or other body parts when they are young. This is their way to play with their littermates and your cocker puppy might try to do the same with you.

While there are many things you can do to discourage this type of behaviour, it would be better not to encourage it in the first place. This means not engaging in play that is too rough, which includes tussling with your puppy and sliding them across the floor. It might be entertaining to see them scramble and run back for more, but this type of behaviour can teach them to bite at people. The following simple steps can help stop your young cocker from play biting:

- Loudly say, '***Ow!***' in a high-pitched voice, so your puppy knows they are getting over-excited and biting too hard.
- Do not shout—as this can create more excitement—instead, firmly say, '***No***'.
- If they are biting your fingers, make a fist and firmly say, '***No***'.
- Give a light tap with a finger on the end of your puppy's nose.
- A further light tap on their nose, with a firm '***No***' if they continue to bite your fingers or toes.
- Exchange your fingers for a doggy chew toy.
- Praise your puppy when they choose the chew toy.
- Stop the play session so they know there is no reward for biting.

Puppies need to learn how to moderate the force of their bite so when they are playing or biting out of excitement or pain, they will not harm anyone.

Common Mistakes to Avoid

It is easy to make a mistake that could have been avoided when first bringing home your adorable new cocker spaniel puppy. We are so excited to have a new, furry family member to share our lives with that we might not consider how today's actions might result in future unwanted consequences. While every owner and canine must inevitably choose their own path, the following section outlines some of these common mistakes for you to consider as an owner.

Sleeping in Your Bed

It is often tempting to allow your crying puppy to sleep with you in your bed. Whether this is a good idea depends on your dog and what sort of relationship there is between you. Of course, while this can help to calm and comfort your new cocker puppy when first bringing them home, this might not be the best idea:

- It can set a precedent that results in behavioural problems later in their life—if they believe they are the boss.
- While sleeping, your body could easily crush your small puppy.
- Your puppy could injure themselves if they fall off the bed during the night.
- It might aggravate allergies.
- If your puppy suffers from separation anxiety, it could make them feel even worse when left alone.
- It might encourage your puppy to grow up to be overly clingy.
- Sharing a bed with your puppy could be inviting hair, biting critters, and anything your pup has encountered into your bed.
- Your squirming puppy can interrupt your sleep cycle, especially if they are a restless sleeper, barks at every little noise they hear, snores, or has wind.

- Your puppy could accidentally wee in your bed.
- They might start to growl when you move, or your partner comes to bed because they believe this is their domain. If they are already a bossy dog, this can make things worse.
- Once your puppy has been permitted to sleep in your bed for some time, it will be difficult to discourage the habit.

TIP ***As much as it might pull on your heart strings to hear your new puppy crying the first couple of nights in their crate, a little tough love at the beginning will keep them safely confined while helping them to learn to both love and respect you.***

Picking Up a Puppy at the Wrong Time

There can often be a strong urge to pick your puppy up when they are displaying nervousness, fear, or aggression—such as growling or barking—at an object, person, other dog, or animal. This is easy to do when they are still young, and indeed, while picking them up can help relieve their anxiety or stop them barking, this might not be the best course of action for the following reasons:

- Picking up your puppy or dog is a reward for unbalanced behaviour.
- It teaches them that the behaviour they just displayed is acceptable to you and they could learn to continue to do it.
- It teaches your puppy that they are in charge.

Anyone concerned about teaching their puppy to be a balanced follower, who will default to their owner's rules any time they react inappropriately, will want to gently correct their unbalanced behaviour. This is easily accomplished with a firm, '***No***' followed by standing in front of them—between your puppy and the dog or person they growled at—so their attention is now focused on you, their owner. They need to learn to listen to you and not react to new people, dogs, or situations with fear or aggression.

Armpit Alligators

When your cocker spaniel puppy or dog is small, many owners get into the habit of carrying them far too much. Sometimes, it is necessary to pick your puppy up to help them, such as getting them into their crate inside your car. However, you should try to keep your pup on the ground walking on their own most of the time, so:

- They are not placed in the 'top dog' position.
- They can properly meet and greet other dogs.
- They do not get the idea they are the leader.
- They do not become an armpit alligator (see below).

TIP ***Depending on your dog and the control you have over them, carrying your small puppy or dog can create an 'armpit alligator' situation. This happens when your cocker becomes overly possessive of you as you carry them everywhere. As a result, when another adult, child, or dog sees your cute little dog and approaches to say hello, your cocker spaniel, who has come to believe they are the boss, might then lunge, snap, and/or growl.***

Even dogs who are friendly or not naturally wary or suspicious of strangers can learn to become intolerant of other people and pets if they do not receive adequate socialisation. This means it is always possible to allow them to become protective or possessive of their owners. The recommendation is to help your puppy when needed, but not to overdo it by carrying them all the time.

Playing Too Hard, Too Long, Too Often

FACT ***The average puppy sleeps between 16 and 20 hours a day. While this may seem like a long time, it is essential for the healthy growth and development of their muscles, brain, central nervous system, and immune system.***

Puppies are naturally playful and bouncy and always seem to be up for a game. However, sometimes people play too much, too long, or too roughly with their young puppy. As much fun as it is to play with your adorable little furry friend, it is important to remember your young cocker tires easily and needs their rest. Just like setting regular eating and toilet times for your new puppy, they also need to have regular resting times when they are still growing and developing.

It is perfectly normal for your puppy to take time out for a nap approximately every hour. New puppies burn a lot of energy when they are awake because it is tiring experiencing all the new places, people, sights, and sensations, plus learning the new rules.

The world is a stimulating and exciting place for your young cocker, and they might not always know when it is time to take a break. Thankfully, there are a few simple steps you can take to create a routine that allows your puppy to get enough rest throughout their exciting day:

- Establish a routine where play sessions or walk times are followed by a rest period.
- Make sure they know where their comfortable crate or bed is located, and if they seem tired, encourage them to go to bed.
- Make sure they are left undisturbed—children need to learn to leave the puppy alone when they are sleeping.

Puppy Play and Rest Routine – The following is an example of an appropriate routine to ensure your puppy receives the regular rest they need:

Morning Routine

- Upon waking, take them out for a toilet break.
- Feed them their breakfast.

- Take them out for another toilet break shortly after eating.
- Playtime, or a walk and a little socialising until they tire.
- Rest time—puppies tire easily and can sleep up to 16-18 hours a day.
- Take them out for a toilet break as soon as they wake up.
- Give them their lunch.

Afternoon Routine

- After lunch, take them out for another toilet break.
- Indoor playing or exploring until they are ready to lay back down.
- Rest time.
- Take them out for a toilet break when they wake up.
- Training or a walk.
- Rest time again.

Evening Routine

- Feed them their dinner.
- Take them out for a toilet break and short walk.
- Let them spend time playing and interacting with family.
- Take them out for a toilet break before bedtime.
- Settle them into their crate with their favourite toy for their night-time sleep.

Free Feeding

Free feeding is usually associated with how most people feed their cat, as most cats know when to stop and do not overeat. However, the same is often not true of dogs who tend to eat whatever is in their bowl.

FACT ***If there is food in your cocker puppy's bowl 24/7 so they can eat any time of the day or night, whenever they feel like it, they will almost certainly eat too much.***

As cockers love food and are an exceedingly food-oriented breed, free feeding is not recommended for them. When training, their love of food is advantageous as they are highly motivated to work for it. Frequently, their waistlines suffer, as they would eat until they burst if given the chance.

Treating them Like a Human Child

FACT ***Often, we get into the habit of treating our dogs more like small, furry humans than dogs. This is called 'anthropomorphism' and this tendency usually begins when they are an adorable, young puppy who we must supervise and protect from harm.***

Like doting parents, the list of worries and questions we ask ourselves when considering the wellbeing of our children is similar for our puppies, as follows:

- Are they getting too much or too little exercise?
- Are they warm enough?
- Are they eating and drinking enough?
- Are they sleeping enough?
- Are they feeling okay?

While you want to do your best for your cocker spaniel, remember, no matter how much you wish to act as if they are a small, fur-covered human, your relationship will be better if you handle them like the amazing dog they are. By not doing so, you can create confusion that leads to behavioural problems.

It is very human of us to evaluate our canine counterparts based on human emotions and the belief that our dogs think and reason the same way we do. When you combine this way of thinking with your cocker's awesome ability to read human cues and adjust themselves and their way of life to integrate with ours, it seems our dogs really do think like us.

We should not blame ourselves for attributing to our dogs our human ability to feel, reason, and think, as this popularised notion was taught to us as children. We were indoctrinated into this mostly misguided view of canine psychology through popular children's books about talking rabbits and bears. There were also cartoon series that featured loveable dog characters, such as Pluto, Goofy, and Lady. Then, how dogs were portrayed in popular, blockbuster Hollywood films starring well-trained dogs such as Lassie, Rin Tin Tin, and Benji encouraged us to delve even further into anthropomorphism.

As entertaining as it might be to believe our dogs can think and reason like we do, truly expecting your dog to live up to the standards of human understanding can cause difficulties in the relationship, such as:

- Expecting you cocker to 'know better' or 'feel guilty' when they peed on the floor.
- Blurring the line and creating confusion about who is the leader in the relationship.
- Overfeeding or feeding them an unhealthy diet.
- Making them uncomfortable—e.g., insisting they wear unnecessary human clothing(pictured).
- Causing them to feel anxious or stressed when they do not react in the way you want them to.
- Curtailing their need and desire for exercise—e.g., being overprotective by carrying them or putting them in pushchairs and wheeling them around like a baby.

Even though our dogs certainly have their own set of emotions, they do not show them or understand them in the same way we do. Ascribing our human emotions and feelings to our dog is often a disservice to our canine companions.

Perhaps a more accurate description of why dogs are so good at appearing to understand us and do what we ask of them is that they have learnt how to be expert opportunists. You could say dogs do what works best for them, so they get what they want. The priorities for most dogs include:

- An owner who will guide them.
- A predictable, standard schedule.
- Consistent rules, boundaries, and praise.
- Being at their owner's side.
- Learning routines and tricks.
- A regular feeding programme.
- The occasional treat.
- Plenty of daily exercise.
- A chest rub or neck massage.
- Time to check 'pee-mail'.
- Opportunity to play with their toys.
- Socialising with new friends.
- A quiet, comfortable place to sleep.

Waiting Too Long Before Socialising

When first bringing home your adorable cocker puppy, you will want to let them enjoy their playtime and have as much free rein as possible. However, sometimes you can have so much fun you forget your puppy needs to be socialised.

Part of the socialising process is interaction with other dogs early on. Nevertheless, it is advised not to introduce your cocker spaniel to other dogs until they have been fully vaccinated, which is about 13 weeks old. The problem is between 3 and 16 weeks of age is considered the critical time for canine socialisation.

One option is to attend a puppy class, but this involves the risk of your puppy catching a virus from the other pups. While there might only be a minimal risk of your puppy contracting a deadly virus, as most will have had at least one vaccination, you should weigh the benefits of early interaction against health risks.

Meanwhile, focus on things you can do at home to make your puppy as confident, inquisitive, and brave as they can be. This should give your puppy a great head start, ready for when they are able to learn even more about the outside world. The idea is to expose them to as many everyday things within the confines of your home, garden, or garage.

TIP ***Once your puppy is fully vaccinated, you should typically wait two weeks before giving them full access to the outdoors. When visiting new places where they might be nervous, you could take treats to reward them for not displaying anxiousness, or a favourite toy to distract them and make the new experience a pleasant one.***

There are detailed instructions about socialising your puppy later in the book (see Socialisation, Chapter 10).

Waiting Too Long Before Establishing Basic Manners

You need to start shaping your cocker spaniel's behaviour from the moment you bring them home. Teaching them basic manners, phrases, and commands is the cornerstone for your well-behaved companion and make them a joy to be around. If you wait too long, it is possible for you to end up going down the long road of re-training undesirable behaviour.

Rather than being faced with fixing the problem, it is much easier and less stressful to help teach your young cocker puppy before they are five months old, which is when they are most impressionable. As soon as your puppy's paws cross the threshold of their new home, even at the age of 8 weeks, they are ready to start learning. With just 5 or 10 minutes a day, by the age of 4 to 5 months they will already know the following basics (see Training, Chapter 11 for details on how to teach these commands):

- Come.
- Sit.
- Stay.
- Down.
- Ring a bell to go outside.
- Loose lead walking without pulling.

Many puppies are ready to learn far more than just a few basic commands long before six months of age. If your cocker spaniel puppy seems eager to learn more, perhaps begin with some simple tricks—shake a paw, roll over, sit up—or begin teaching them a fun canine sport.

Keeping Your Pup Healthy

Choosing an appropriate veterinary clinic is very similar to choosing the right doctor or health care clinic for your personal health. Caring owners want to ensure that their cocker spaniel receives the quality care they deserve, and this means taking time to find a suitable vet.

This is one of the most critical decisions you will ever make for your puppy to keep them healthy. **Your vet plays an important part in making sure your cocker lives a long and healthy life**. When choosing, you must think about the issues that are essential to you, such as their hours and location. Word of mouth is by far the best way to find a vet. Ask your friends and family for any recommendations. Online reviews can also be helpful, but suggestions from people you know and trust are even better.

Preferably, you will have found a veterinarian before you get your puppy. Within a few days of taking your new pup home, you must take them to your vet for a general exam. Over the course of your pup's first six months, you will see a lot of your vet. This starts with puppy vaccinations and leads to spaying or neutering if you decide to do that, which should be done after they are six months old.

Your vet can help identify any potential health problems early on and advise you about caring for your dog long-term. The initial visit also opens the door to communication between you and your vet.

Puppy's First Vet Visit

It is always a good idea to have your new cocker puppy checked over by your vet as soon as you buy or adopt them. It is recommended that you do this as part of the buying process and agree with the breeder that you can take the pup back within a set time, usually 24-48 hours.

FACT ***Some veterinary clinics specialise in caring for smaller pets, others in larger animal care, while some have a wide range of expertise and care for all animals, including livestock and reptiles.***

Your vet will give your puppy a thorough examination to ensure they are in good condition. This includes checking for signs of worms and fleas and weighing them. If your cocker puppy has not already had their first vaccinations to protect them from serious infectious diseases, these will also be done during their first vet visit. Not only will this benefit your puppy, but it will give you peace of mind that your cocker spaniel is healthy.

Beyond the above procedures, the vet will usually discuss your puppy's history, such as the name of the breeder, any prior treatments that might have been initiated by the breeder and confirm your puppy's birthdate. This is when you should review future vaccination plans, ask questions about feeding or other future care, and even talk about pet insurance.

Vaccinations

Puppies – Puppies must be vaccinated to provide them with protection against four common and serious diseases. These diseases are parvovirus, canine distemper, leptospirosis, and infectious canine hepatitis. If your puppy has not been vaccinated and encounters a virus, they might quickly become sick. Even when treated, there is no guarantee they will survive. Therefore, vaccination is the best form of prevention.

TIP ***The Royal Veterinary College in London recommends that dogs should be vaccinated from nine weeks old onwards with a second vaccination given four weeks later. Approximately one week after your cocker puppy has completed all their vaccinations—called 'core' vaccines—they are fully protected from those specific diseases.***

Adults – It is common practise to vaccinate adult dogs every 1 to 3 years. If your veterinarian is adamant about a yearly vaccination for your dog, ask them why, because 'over vaccinating' has the potential to cause other health problems. Rather than getting unnecessary vaccinations or boosters, you could ask the vet to give your cocker a blood test first, because this is a straightforward way to determine whether they need a booster (see Titre Testing below).

An adult dog might require non-core vaccines—'lifestyle vaccines'—which are optional and often depend on your spaniel's lifestyle and where they live. Besides their general health, when considering boosters or non-core vaccines, the vet might bear the following factors in mind:

- Whether your cocker attends a day-care facility, boarding kennel, or groomer.
- The risk of certain diseases known to be present in the area where you live.

- Whether your spaniel's lifestyle includes travelling across borders, hiking through heavily wooded areas, or regularly swimming in bodies of water.

Non-core vaccines offer protection from the following viruses/diseases:

- Bordetella bronchiseptica.
- Canine influenza H3N2 virus and H3N8 virus.
- Lyme disease.
- Parainfluenza.
- Rabies.

Titre Testing – Titre testing is an easy way to minimise the possible side effects inherent in multiple vaccinations by foregoing unnecessary boosters. A titre test is a blood test that measures antibodies in a blood sample. This simple test can indicate whether a previous vaccine is still producing antibodies and protecting your cocker spaniel's immune system.

For instance, some dogs are protected for their entire lifetime with just their initial puppy series of vaccinations and the one-year booster. In other words, why give a dog a booster if they do not need one? That aside, if you are travelling internationally between countries, such as bringing your cocker spaniel to the United Kingdom, be certain to check that your dog is up to date with their vaccinations and conforms to the country's requirements.

The People's Dispensary for Sick Animals (PDSA) has reported that 'side effects from vaccines' can vary widely, and include:

- Allergic reactions.
- Autoimmune problems.
- Lethargy.
- Mild swelling around the vaccine site that disappears in two to six weeks.
- Lack of appetite.
- Fever—high temperature.

While we certainly need to protect our dogs from harmful diseases, it is well known that giving a vaccine when it is not needed can expose dogs to unnecessary hazards that could have been avoided.

Worming

Worms are a common parasite in dogs and live mainly in their intestines and respiratory system. Every puppy has a susceptibility to worms, some species of which they get through their mother's milk or placenta. The most prevalent worms that affect cocker puppies are roundworms, tapeworms, lungworms, and hookworms.

Roundworms are intestinal parasites found in the gut and look like spaghetti. They can cause diarrhoea and intestinal irritation. Puppies are affected more than adult dogs. The microscopic roundworm eggs are frequently passed in apparently normal faeces. The worms infect the puppy through their mother's placenta, which is why many cocker puppies have contracted worms at birth.

The tapeworm is another kind of intestinal worm. The tapeworm's lifecycle relies on an intermediate host, which is usually eaten by your cocker for it to infect them. Fleas are the intermediate host for the most common tapeworm in dogs. Dogs get tapeworms when nibbling or grooming, often in response to a flea bite, thereby ingesting the tapeworm infected flea.

As their name implies, lungworms reside in your spaniel's respiratory system. Like the tapeworm, the lungworm's lifecycle requires an intermediate host, in this case, normally slugs and snails. Dogs tend to contract lungworm through eating slugs, snails, or grass with snail trails on them. They can also acquire it through playing with toys that have been in contact with snails.

Dogs can also be infected with hookworms, whipworms, and heartworms. Hookworms are dangerous as they rob your puppy of nutrients, which can lead to anaemia. If there is a heavy infestation, they can also spread to the lungs. The heartworm is not indigenous to the United Kingdom but can be contracted when travelling abroad.

As worms are common in puppies, knowing how to treat them is crucial. Puppy worming should be done at five, eight, and twelve weeks old, and then at least every three months for the rest of their lives to ensure they do not pick up worms.

Most worming products stay in the body for no more than 48 hours as the liver metabolises them. What they do is to kill and remove any worms present in your cocker's system during that period. Therefore, your dog can become re-infected soon afterwards. It is not uncommon for dogs to be re-infected with worms within a month of being treated.

If your cocker spaniel puppy has come from a reputable breeder or rescue centre, they should be worm free as they will be wormed prior to you taking them home. Make sure any paperwork is safe so you can monitor your puppy's worming treatment.

As fleas are frequently the cause of worms in puppies, you need to ensure your cocker is regularly checked and treated for any flea infestations.

Although it is rare, worm-related disease do pose a risk to humans. The tiny roundworm eggs can be picked up on children's hands when playing in soil and sandpits and cause infections. The worms migrate from the intestine and travel around the body, damaging organs such as the liver, heart, brain, and eyes. Should this happen, seek immediate medical treatment.

Using a veterinary prescribed prescription-only product is the best way to treat worms. These come in the form of tablets, spot-on treatments, and palatable chews. If you suspect your cocker spaniel puppy has worms, contact your vet straight away. They will recommend the best course of treatment and wormer to treat multiple species of worm to ensure your dog does not suffer from any nasty side effects. You can also buy conventional and natural worming treatments available off the shelf

Should you wish to limit the amount of worming products your cocker spaniel is exposed to, a new method called Faecal Egg Count provides an evaluation of the number of worm eggs in your dog's faeces. This indicates the number of adult female worms in your cocker's gut. Having identified each species of worm egg present, where appropriate, they are quantified to give an indication of the level of infestation.

Every 3 months, you send in a sample of your dog's poo. If worm infestation is found, you need to de-worm your dog, otherwise no treatment is required. If you are in the United Kingdom, there are diagnostic vet labs such as Wormcount: https://www.wormcount.com/. There are similar services in the United States as well, including: https://zeroeggcount.com.

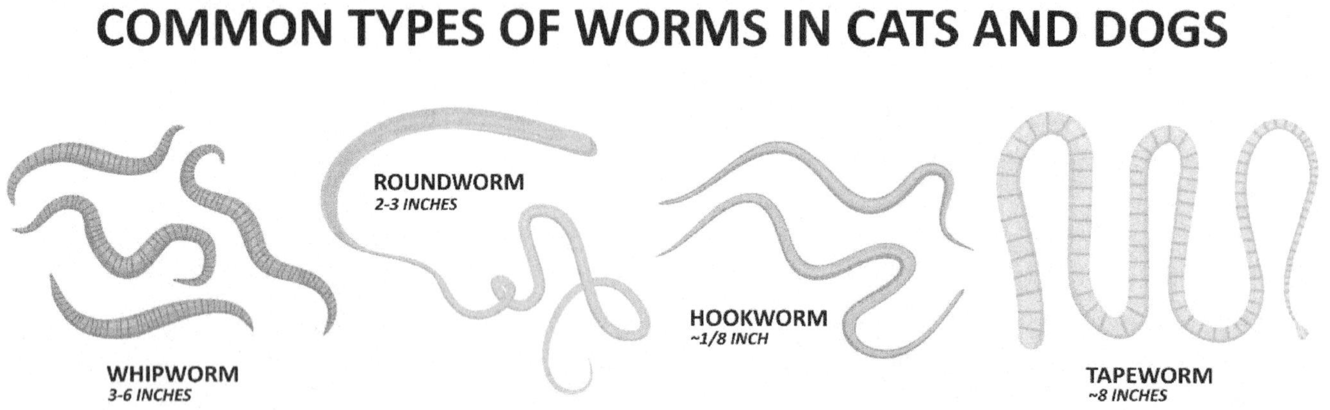

As you can see, there are many types of worms that can cause a variety of health issues for puppies, and just as many deworming products designed to eliminate those infestations. Therefore, it is vital for them to be treated with a suitable de-wormer as soon as possible. Your vet will advise what products are licensed for use at each puppy age, how much to give, and how often.

Worm Prevention – Thankfully, there are effective de-worming medications, and many natural remedies for treating and preventing worms. While various chemical medications are quite harsh, the belief is the pesticides kill the worms and if given to your dog in small enough quantities the poison will not be fatal for your cocker spaniel.

Conventional Worming Medications – There are many chemical or pesticide-based products that are conventionally used to eliminate or prevent worms. Some of these common preparations include:

PRO-Wormer 2, Nemex-2 – The active ingredient in these products is 'Pyrantel Pamoate' (paralysing agent). These medications treat roundworms and hookworms in puppies and adult dogs. They are recommended for small dogs and approved for use on pregnant females. They can be administered directly or mixed with your dog's food.

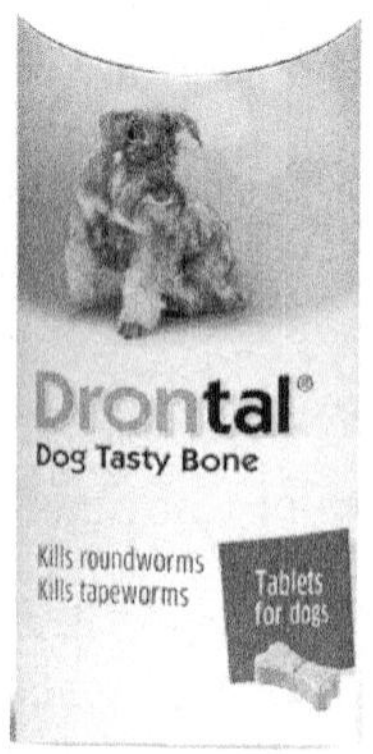

Panacur and Safe-Guard – The active ingredient in these deworming medications is 'Fenbendazole' (anti-parasitic). These drugs provide an effective treatment for dogs to eliminate several gastrointestinal worms, including roundworm, tapeworm, and lungworm.

Droncit, Drontal (pictured) – These are highly effective treatments against all common species of tapeworm that infect dogs. They are developed with praziquantel as the main active ingredient, and target both the immature and mature forms of tapeworm by impairing their normal functions.

Natural Worming Products – Those who are concerned about the possible side effects of conventional worming products will be relieved to know there are many natural alternatives to treat and prevent parasites from invading your cocker's body, such as:

Pumpkin Seeds contain an amino acid that paralyses the worms and easily eliminates them. Just one teaspoon of raw seeds per 4.5 kilograms (10 pounds) of body weight twice a day is very effective.

Carrots, when coarsely chopped and added to your puppy's dinner, scrape the walls of the stomach during digestion, removing mucus and any parasites contained within it. Since carrots are a source of vitamin A, they also boost the immune system.

Coconut is a 'vermifuge' or agent that destroys or expels parasitic worms. When dried and sprinkled on your cocker's dinner, coconut can easily kill off any worms that are present and helps to prevent further invasive parasitic infections. A recommended daily dosage depends on your dog's weight, as follows:

- Puppies and small dogs: ½ to 1 teaspoon.
- Medium-sized dogs: 2 teaspoons.
- Large dogs: 1 tablespoon.

Also, coconut oil, besides having other beneficial properties—shiny coat, eliminating bacteria, improving digestion, reducing inflammation—when given regularly can rid your spaniel of internal parasites.

Turmeric (pictured) is an antibacterial, anti-fungal, anti-inflammatory super food that, besides boosting the immune system, contains four compounds to help eliminate worms. It also assists in repairing any damage the parasites have caused to the intestine. It is suggested to combine turmeric with coconut oil to make it easier for your puppy to absorb.

Cider Vinegar can also work effectively as a worm treatment. This fermented vinegar increases the alkaline levels in the intestines making it an inhospitable environment for the parasites. You should add ¼ to 1 teaspoon of raw organic vinegar to your dog's water bowl.

Diatomaceous Earth (pictured) is the remains of microscopic, one-celled plants—phytoplankton—that at one time lived in the oceans and lakes and are now mined from underwater beds or the bottom of ancient, dried lakes that are thousands of years old. Under a microscope, these crushed particles look like tiny shards of broken glass. When the sharp particles touch a parasite, they pierce the protective coating making the pest quickly dehydrate and die.

FACT ***Diatomaceous earth is full of many beneficial minerals—calcium, copper, magnesium, iron, phosphorous, potassium, selenium, silicon, sodium, zinc—making it an effective nutritional supplement.***

Food grade diatomaceous earth is inexpensive, easy to use and deadly to any parasite, yet completely harmless to animals, and a natural way to eliminate all intestinal worms and parasites in both dogs and humans. The recommended daily dosage to sprinkle on your cocker's dinner depends on their weight. For a cocker spaniel puppy, the suggested dose is ½ teaspoon.

6. Behaviour of the Cocker Spaniel

'Don't make the mistake of treating your dogs like humans, or they'll treat you like dogs.'

~ Martha Scott ~

What is interesting about our dogs is that they must learn the language of an entirely new species so they can communicate with us and try to understand how we think better than we understand how they think.

Our dogs are highly accomplished at observing behaviour and understanding subtle differences, and while we try to communicate with them as if they are human, they do not try to communicate with us like we are dogs. They only understand that the differences between the species are huge, so they learn ways to communicate we can understand. Cocker spaniels know there are some things they cannot easily accomplish in the human world, such as reaching the top shelf where the treats are, or opening the door to the back garden, so they devise clever ways to get their unmistakeable messages across to their owners. For example, how many times have you seen a dog sit at a door and bark or sit in front of the cupboard where their favourite treat is kept? While no human words are spoken, there is no question what your spaniel is asking for.

Since cockers will never learn how to master human speech, they communicate what they are thinking through their body language and behaviour. If you are observant, you will soon develop an unspoken communication with your cocker spaniel. For instance, if your dog wants to play, they will signal this message with their 'play bow' body language (see Energy and Body Language, Chapter 7).

While the dog brain is smaller, it is much like the human brain in that the left hemisphere is associated with language for both dogs and humans. Scientists have established that the dog brain is capable of:

- Vocabulary recognition of a pre-school child.
- Memory skills—they can remember familiar people, places, and animals.
- Sensing danger.
- Learning search patterns.
- Learning to discriminate smells, signals, and sounds.
- Establishing routines.
- Anticipating habits of people.
- Solving problems.
- Reading human behaviour.

Though our canine counterparts are indeed accomplished, there is a greater difference between how dogs and humans think in the part of the frontal cortex associated with higher-level reasoning.

Okay, so perhaps our dogs cannot do our tax returns for us. However, dogs are an entirely different species from humans and are capable of so much more than we give them credit for.

Canine Emotions

For millennia, dogs have been considered 'man's best friend'. Today that embraces canine companions in much the same way as any human family member. There is ample opportunity for learning how to be 'dog's best friend' and this includes being aware of canine emotions.

FACT ***Even though understanding canine emotions remains a point of controversy, science has proven that both dogs and humans have the same hormones and undergo the same chemical responses during various emotional states.***

Did you know that dogs also produce the hormone 'oxytocin' that elicits feelings of affection and love for others in humans? Since both species possess similar brains, neurology, and chemical reactions, logic would seem to suggest that the ability to experience emotions is similar for both humans and dogs.

However, before we go overboard with this comparison, recent scientific evidence shows the dog's mind is not as fully developed as that of an adult human. It is believed the dog's mind is approximately equivalent to the mind of a 2 to 2 ½-year-old child. This suggests your cocker's mind is certainly capable of experiencing emotions like a young child who has not yet developed a full complement of emotions. So, the emotions our dogs experience could be limited.

Certainly, cocker spaniels pass through their developmental stages quicker than humans, reaching their emotional maturity at around four to six months old. Therefore, the emotions your dog is capable of expressing are basic ones, such as:

- Anger.
- Anticipation.
- Anxiety.
- Contentment.
- Disgust.
- Excitement.
- Fear.
- Frustration.
- Joy.
- Love.

FACT ***Current research leans towards the idea that the more complex emotions, such as feelings of shame (for having peed on the floor), pride (for having won a blue ribbon) or guilt (for stealing a biscuit from the coffee table) will simply not exist in the mind of our canine companions.***

As much as we might wish our dogs were capable of all the same complicated emotions we humans have, the feelings our dogs express are truly remarkable, and we are blessed that they are sharing their lives with us.

Emotion and the Senses

Your cocker's nose dominates their brain as the part dedicated to scent is forty times greater in a dog than in a human. Built around the information it gets from scent and smell, their brain is loosely linked to their emotions. The evidence suggests your cocker spaniel's emotional experiences might be even greater than we ever imagined.

Has something you smelt ever evoked a memory? When you or your cocker inhale, scent molecules stimulate chemical messages, bypassing other areas of the brain and going straight to the amygdala, the brain's emotional centre. This passes emotional judgments to other structures that collate memories that are passed on to the cortex. Emotionally appropriate hormones that affect mood are then released into the body. Because your dog's dominant sense is smell and a large portion of the brain is dedicated to processing scent, it is further evidence that dogs might be even more driven by their emotions than humans.

The Food/Brain Relationship

This knowledge provides us with crucial data not only about how the brain functions, but how we can use the information to help dogs learn and modify behavioural states such as anxiety and fear. For example, by stimulating your spaniel's sense of smell with food, it will not only motivate your dog to learn, but is a valuable tool in changing the way their brain works.

Many people think using food as a reward is tantamount to bribery. What they do not understand is how powerful food is as a motivator, as food is incompatible with fear.

When your cocker is frightened, several changes happen in their body. Their heart beats faster, blood pressure rises, and blood flow is diverted to muscles prepared for fight or flight. If food is offered before your spaniel reaches a high level of stress, a positive emotional response can take place from the presentation or anticipation of the food.

Some circuits in your dog's brain encourage seeking or hunting behaviour, while others elicit the fear response. By giving your cocker spaniel a tasty treat or a toy filled with food, it will turn on their seeker system and shut off their fear. That encourages them to play a game in the presence of something they are afraid of.

Therefore, activities such as scent work is so valuable for frightened dogs. Through turning on your cocker's thinking brain it deactivates their emotional brain, enhancing your dog's attention with positive motivation. It allows your dog to move into a calmer state where learning can take place. This is one reason why most canine trainers advocate positive reinforcement with treats as the most effective training method (see Training, Chapter 11).

Canine Personalities

Cocker spaniels are full of personality, and every dog has their own unique traits, but did you know there are five basic personality types? These different types are:

1. Shy or timid.
2. Confident.
3. Independent.
4. Adaptable.
5. Happy, laidback.

While most puppies fit into one or more of the categories listed above, a large factor in influencing how your cocker spaniel's personality develops is usually related to the people, places, and situations they experience during their first six months. Considering what personality type is more dominant in a puppy provides insight into how they view their world and offers valuable clues about the best way to raise and train them.

The Shy or Timid Personality

Some cocker puppies can be naturally timid, nervous, or shy, especially when meeting new people and dogs, or becoming acquainted with new places or situations. Introducing a shy puppy to new experiences requires a patient, slow, and careful approach so they do not feel uncomfortable. When they are learning about their new world, it is important not to force them into situations that could frighten them because they could learn to mistrust you.

Your shy or nervous puppy will learn best at a slow pace that includes treats and enthusiastic encouragement. If your puppy has a naturally timid and sensitive personality and does not enjoy loud or chaotic environments, they will flourish better in a calm home where there is harmony between family members.

The Confident Personality

A confident cocker spaniel is one who has no worries when venturing out into their new world. Though this puppy can take charge of a situation and display dominance towards another dog, if the need arises. They are also happy to be a team player. This puppy does well at the side of an equally confident owner who trains with positive reinforcement, and they could be a great candidate for learning many canine sports.

The Independent Personality

The independent puppy is usually the type of cocker spaniel who has been bred to work alongside humans or in isolation for hundreds of years and had to think on their own. These dogs were valuable companions who could hunt, herd, and protect livestock, family, and property.

A cocker with an independent personality is a one-person dog who is often standoffish with strangers and does best with an owner who is able to provide firm leadership. This dog might be a challenge to train because they prefer to think for themselves. However, if the owner has experience, understands the independent mind, and there is a relationship of trust and respect, there is no end to what such a team might accomplish together.

The Adaptable Personality

The adaptable puppy easily fits themselves into any type of situation, as they are willing to do whatever their owner asks of them. A puppy who has a naturally strong desire to please is easy to train and usually a friendly—yet not overly exuberant—spaniel who will get along well with everyone while paying attention to their owner. This type of loving and calm personality will often be the perfect therapy dog.

The Happy, Laidback Personality

The happy, laidback cocker is the one with the ever-wagging tail who loves everybody, whether human or animal. They will gleefully invite all the robbers in the neighbourhood inside and help them carry their ill-gotten booty to the get-away vehicle.

FACT ***The cocker spaniel's personality usually falls under the happy category. However, every dog is always unique, and therefore your cocker might easily have traits from the other personality types too.***

They are a highly enthusiastic greeter who just cannot resist bouncing and jumping all over everyone in their excitement to make a new friend. Though easy to train, if they are larger, take care to teach them to be calm around toddlers or unsteady seniors who they could accidentally bowl over.

Common Cocker Spaniel Traits

While every breed has traits common to the canine world, each individual breed has characteristics that are associated with them. Cocker spaniels have some very breed-specific and unique personality traits all their own, and as you are considering owning one, or already do, it is important to know all about these:

- They are quite open and welcoming to strangers. They also enjoy being petted by people who they have only just met.

- These dogs have a strong reputation for being kind and tolerant with children. They will often bond strongly with your children and share many of their interests when it comes to playing and raiding the biscuit jar. You need to make sure your children are taught the correct way to handle and play with them and know when to leave them alone.
- These dogs tend to be very receptive and trusting of their owner once they know what is happening around them. They take new challenges and situations in their stride without excessive levels of fear.
- Cocker spaniels can sometimes become overly clingy if they are not used to spending time alone and have not been trained to be calm and quiet when left. They can also manifest serious separation anxiety when something throws them off their normal daily routine. It is important to start training your cocker from a young age to willingly use a crate or go to their bed to chill out, as they cannot be around people all the time. The cocker is a real people pleaser and typically works hard to achieve what you ask them to do when training.
- The cocker is typically very tolerant and forgiving of children's mistakes, but when pushed too far, they will eventually growl or snap.
- These dogs are intelligent enough to learn quickly and repeat commands reliably. They will thoroughly enjoy working one-to-one with you and picking up new skills.
- Cocker spaniels easily learn to perform tricks as well as a range of higher-level commands. They work well on the praise and reward structure of positive reinforcement training, while being given treats they like for successful responses.
- Calm and kind handling that is firm but encouraging is what is required for the cocker spaniel to thrive. Their lively natures, high intelligence, and willingness to make you smile will make training them a very pleasant experience.
- As a working dog breed, the cocker was traditionally confident, bold, and calm in most situation s when faced with the unknown. However, today these dogs are far more commonly kept as pets at home than as working animals, and this trait has somewhat weakened within the breed. Therefore, some spaniels may have a predisposition for being quite shy or wary of situations they are not familiar with.
- If your cocker spaniel is het up or suspicious of something, such as taking a bath or having their nails trimmed, occasionally they might become snappy and react quickly. It is critical that you are familiar with your dog's body language and recognise their triggers and warning signs of potential aggression.
- Historically, as a working breed, they would have spent most of their day outside running around and utilising both body and mind. These dogs are tenacious and can be good hunters, but they can

also be trained to supress their natural hunting instinct when this is inappropriate. They are lively, active dogs who must be walked several times per day and are certainly not one of the more sedentary breeds.

- You should provide lots of play, stimulation, and exercise to keep your cocker happy within the family home.
- Cocker spaniels are very affectionate dogs who will never shy away from a cuddle.

20 Ways to Avoid Unwanted Behaviour

Of course, it is always best to avoid unwanted behaviour, rather than having to work out how to correct something that has already happened. For example, it is easy to get into the habit of distracting your misbehaving dog by picking them up or giving them a treat. However, any sort of reward—treats, picking them up, talking soothingly, petting them, giving undivided attention—given to your dog when they display unwanted behaviour is likely to send an unspoken 'message' to your cocker spaniel that they can repeat this behaviour.

Now and then, an owner inadvertently blurs the lines of communication between themselves and their dog. An example might be when at the park playing a game of fetch. If your cocker is excited to chase the ball, when they bark at you to throw it, you will most likely toss the ball immediately. Your spaniel has just learnt to associate their loud barking with them getting what they want, which is to chase the ball.

TIP ***How dogs learn is mainly through associating an action with a result. For instance, a dog quickly learns to associate picking up their lead with going out for a walk.***

To be preventive and avoid unwanted behaviour from your cocker spaniel before it occurs, you can try the following:

1. Never give a treat or life reward—picking them up, petting, talking soothingly—as distraction for unwanted behaviour—i.e., barking, growling, lunging. No matter what your cocker's bad behaviour, it is important for you to stay calm. Even if you shout or gesture because you are angry or upset, your excitement could be interpreted as play or encouragement, which is something your dog will misunderstand. Instead, keep your gestures slow and deliberate, your voice low and level, and all your actions placatory to help calm your cocker.
2. Extensively socialise them so they learn not to overreact when meeting new people and dogs or being introduced to new situations.
3. If they become overly excited in any situation—i.e., meeting new dogs or people—remove them from the source of excitement so they learn being overly excited is unacceptable.
4. Be assertive if they display unwanted behaviour of any sort by firmly saying, 'No', they must learn from you what is acceptable.

5. Teach patience by not giving your cocker what they want, for instance, because they barked for the ball or pulled harder to get to the park. Slow down so they begin to understand being impatient does not get them what they want. It can be helpful to have an interrupt command your spaniel is trained to obey when they do something bad. You could use 'Stop', 'No', 'Drop it', or 'Leave it', to get your dog's attention and let them know their behaviour is unacceptable. A harsh, loud tone of voice helps reinforce the meaning of your command and teaches your cocker to cease and desist.

6. Praise them for good behaviour. If they are excited to greet strangers, teach them to sit when meeting new people and then treat and/or praise them for being good.
7. Increase their exercise, as a bored and/or under-exercised dog is more likely to act up than a tired dog. Certain bad behaviour, such as digging or chasing, could be the result of pent-up energy. By giving your cocker more exercise, it will help burn off their energy. They are then less likely to misbehave. It also reinforces your bond with your dog, so they are more likely to pay attention to you and obey your commands.
8. Give them mental exercises. Teaching them a trick, command, or routine as mental exercise is even more tiring than physical exercise.
9. Teach rules and boundaries so they learn to respect you and follow their commands.
10. Teach basic commands before they are 4-months old so there is already a relationship of trust and respect established (see Training, Chapter 11).
11. Desensitise them if going for a walk makes them overly excited. For example, put them on their lead and do not go out until they are calm and listening to you.
12. Teach them to be quiet when someone knocks on the door. Have them sit and wait at least 3 metres from the door and ask visitors to ignore them until they are calm.
13. Teach them not to pull on their lead when out walking. The second the lead is tight because they are not beside you, stop walking so they learn that feeling tension on the lead means no forward momentum.
14. Teach them to bark—speak—on command if they bark too much. Often, training your dog to bark with hand signals stops excessive barking as they will wait for the command.
15. Make a list of all the things they love, and then use those things as rewards for their good behaviour.
16. Teach them hand signals for all their commands. Hand signals make them more attentive as they must pay attention to you to know what they are being asked to do (see Training, Chapter 11).
17. Ensure your cocker has their own space at home, where family members and guests know not to disturb them. Give them a quiet place they can escape to whenever they need it. This will help them

feel safe, even if they use it infrequently. Having the option to get away will often make your spaniel feel more comfortable and less likely to misbehave.

18. Consistency is the key. Even if you do not feed your dog treats from the table but your spouse or children secretly do, they will soon learn to beg. Or if you prevent your cocker from jumping on you, but others allow them to and pet them when they do, inevitably, they will think this is permissible. It is important that everyone follows the rules to set the standards for your spaniel's behaviour.
19. In extreme cases, it can be necessary to work with a trainer to try to curb your cocker spaniel's bad behaviour. A good trainer will offer you several options for controlling unwanted behaviour. They will also help identify what will work best for your cocker to stop their unwelcome actions.
20. Some instinctual behaviour, such as chewing and digging might be impossible to completely stop. Instead, redirect your cocker to more appropriate choices, like providing safe chew toys or allowing digging in one specific spot to spare the rest of your garden from unwanted attention.

Many types of bad behaviour are purely attention seeking, such as jumping up, barking, or begging. If you ignore their behaviour, your cocker spaniel will not receive the attention they are seeking, and their behaviour will eventually change. This includes not shouting or punishing your spaniel's actions, as even negative attention is still attention your dog craves.

Behaviour with Children

Teaching children the proper way to interact with your cocker spaniel puppy or dog varies, depending on the age of the children. Toddlers might not understand how easily a small puppy can be injured during rough play, while older children will already know they must be careful.

TIP ***When introducing your cocker puppy to younger children, keep a watchful eye on both children and puppy so everyone remains safe. There are some situations that can potentially create problems with a new canine family member, such as when a child squeezes your puppy or pulls their ears.***

We all love our children and dogs unconditionally and want them to live in harmony within their family environment. The best way to avoid problems between younger children and your cocker puppy is to teach children the difference between an inanimate, stuffed toy and a live puppy. Children can easily be taught to interact with the puppy politely and kindly, so your spaniel is not afraid and does not feel the urge to protect themselves with a growl or a nip. It is sensible to provide a safe and secure refuge for your puppy, such as their crate, so they can get away from children when they want to. There are many fun activities children can play with your cocker spaniel without any rough play, such as:

- Games of fetch.
- Gentle playing with puppy toys.
- Simple tricks with treat rewards.
- Playing hide-and-seek.
- Going for a walk.
- Giving the puppy their dinner.

Always be extra safe and vigilantly supervise when there are young children around your puppy, as accidents can happen quickly that might not be anyone's fault.

How to Keep a Baby Safe

Even though most adult dogs are far more tolerant of babies as they can recognise they are young infants, the same is not true of puppies who might have no prior experience. Puppies can learn to both love and are afraid of babies, which is why properly introducing your puppy to the baby will help them become friends. The following suggestions will make your cocker's introduction to the baby a positive experience:

- Allow your puppy to see, sniff, and gently touch the baby, so they understand there is nothing to fear.
- Always associate something good with the baby—give your spaniel a treat to reward them when they calmly approach for a sniff.
- Do not make a big fuss as you want your puppy to think the baby is just a normal part of their day.
- Always closely supervise any interactions between baby and puppy.
- Do not force your puppy to approach the baby—especially if they are crying.

How to Keep a Toddler Safe

The best way to keep toddlers safe around puppies and older dogs is to teach them the proper way to safely interact with the dog, whether it is the family puppy or a dog they meet in the neighbourhood. Here are a few things to teach your toddler:

- Never run up to a strange puppy or dog as this might startle or scare them.
- To never approach a strange dog without permission from their parents and the dog's owner.
- Always approach slowly and quietly.
- Let the dog approach and sniff the back of the child's hand.
- Tell them not to put their hands on the dog's head—it is better to stroke them under the chin or the chest.

- If the dog appears nervous of the child, do not force a meeting.
- Never approach a dog that has a treat or a toy.
- Never approach a puppy or dog when they are eating.
- Never approach or try to interact with a sleeping puppy or dog.
- Never pull on a puppy's ears, tail, or feet.
- Do not hug puppies or dogs—this usually makes them uncomfortable.
- No yelling, screaming, or running around a puppy or dog.
- Do not pick up a young puppy—most toddlers will want to—as they could accidentally squeeze too tight or drop the puppy.
- They must eat their food where the puppy cannot reach it, because puppies can be tempted to grab food that is easily within reach, and this could scare a child.

Never expect all dogs to like or accept children, especially those who have never experienced them before.

Behaviour with other pets

A cocker spaniel puppy will not usually harbour any ill intentions towards other household pets and is curious and excited to meet them. Your puppy might not have previous experience of other dogs, cats, birds, or other pets, and will not understand how to meet and greet in a safe way that does not upset anyone.

Introducing an Older Dog

Some older dogs will welcome a new puppy, others can feel that their turf is being invaded and could react with growling. Of course, much of how an already established canine member reacts to your puppy will depend on how respectful or boisterous your cocker spaniel is when meeting the older dog.

Here are several steps to take that can make their first meeting less traumatic and more pleasant:

- Let them meet outside your home on neutral ground and/or with a fence between them.
- Take the puppy and the older dog walking side by side.
- Go to a local park and allow both to be off lead.
- Allow them to sniff each other.
- Give them each a treat as a reward for calm behaviour.
- If they decide to play together, do not let it get too wild.
- Let everybody walk home together.
- Stop in the garden and let them sniff about.
- Offer them both treats again for calm behaviour.
- Have the older dog enter the home first.

Once these two new friends have spent some time together in an unthreatening space, it should be much easier to integrate your new cocker spaniel in the home environment. However, until you are certain your puppy and older dog have learnt to be considerate of each other's space, always keep a close eye on both.

Introducing a Cat

Many cocker spaniels love their cat friends. However, it can take some careful planning to make sure your cocker puppy does not end up with a scratch and the cat is not overly stressed during first encounters. The following steps will help keep everyone safe:

- Place the cat in another room behind a closed door.
- Place a blanket with your puppy's scent on it next to the cat.
- Place a cat-scented blanket where your puppy can find it.
- Encourage your spaniel to sniff under the door where the cat is.
- Let them hear and smell each other without direct contact.
- Place the cat in their secure carrier.
- Place the cat carrier in the middle of the room.
- Allow your puppy to walk around and sniff at the carrier.
- Place your puppy on its lead and open the carrier door.
- Let the cat come out of their carrier.

At this point, if the cat slinks out of its carrier, they may want to quickly run away from your puppy and hide or gain higher ground by jumping up on a worktop or sofa. Keep a grip on your puppy's lead, as they will undoubtedly be curious and might wish to immediately chase after the cat.

TIP ***If the cat does not completely disappear and seems to want to get a little closer to check out your puppy, let them slowly greet. The moment it seems your puppy is going to become too excited, or the cat hisses, put some space between them so the cat does not become scared, and your cocker learns to be calm around them.***

Once it is clear the cat is not terribly worried about the other member of your household, you can let the puppy off their lead. However, always keep a close eye on them both, so you can step in to create some space if anyone gets too aggressive.

Introducing a Pet Bird

Most dogs naturally view birds as prey, especially breeds like the cocker spaniel that were bred for hunting birds. Even so, if they are introduced slowly and carefully, it is possible for them to learn to get along. Thankfully, most pet birds usually live in a secure cage well out of reach of a puppy, where they spend most of their time. When the bird is in its cage, simply let them hear and observe one another. If the bird is occasionally allowed outside its cage, the following steps will help to make them comfortable together:

- Place the bird's cage closer to your cocker puppy.

- Let them calmly observe one another.
- When they are calm, give them both a treat.
- Move the bird's cage even closer to your puppy.
- When both remain calm, give each another treat.
- Place the bird's cage on the floor and let them be eye to eye.
- If they both remain calm, give each another treat.

Practise this type of exercise every day for several days, observing the excitement level of both the bird and your cocker puppy. Your goal could be to eventually remove the bird from its cage and allow it to sit on your hand or shoulder while your puppy is nearby.

You can never predict how your puppy will react to a bird, especially if the bird suddenly squawks or flaps its wings. No matter how carefully the two are placed in one another's company, remember cocker spaniels retain an instinct to hunt birds. Despite how friendly you think they have become, to prevent accidents they must always be supervised.

Introducing a Pet Rodent

There are many smaller pets that are rodents, including rats, mice, gerbils, hamsters, and guinea pigs. When introducing a rodent to your cocker, even when they are small puppies, you should be extra careful, as most spaniels are hard-wired to seek and destroy these small creatures.

FACT ***Prey drive, which is the urge to hunt and dispatch small creatures, will usually be strongest in breeds that have a working history of being hunters such as the cocker spaniel.***

Therefore, encouraging your cocker to make friends with a pet rodent could be expecting too much, and it might not be possible to completely trust the two to get along. If you decide to go for it and introduce a rodent to your cocker puppy, the following steps might come in handy:

- Place them in their cages with a metre or two between them and let them observe one another and get used to how they both smell.
- If both remain calm, give each of them a reward.
- Move the cages closer together.
- If they remain calm, give another treat to both.
- Keep your cocker spaniel puppy on lead and/or have them wear a muzzle.
- Open the rodent's cage and let them out.
- Keep a tight grip on your puppy's lead.
- Allow the rodent and puppy to come close to other another.
- If your puppy tries to nip or becomes aggressive, take them away.
- If the rodent is agitated, fluffs up its hair, chomps its teeth, or tries to bite, immediately place it back in its cage.

While rodents and cockers can learn to become friends—depending on the dog and the rodent—and even enjoy playing together, closely observing any interaction is essential.

Common Behaviour Issues

There are many canine behaviour issues that are common occurrences between owners and their furry companions. The 10th PDSA Animal Wellbeing (PAW) report in 2020 reveals that 75% of dog owners would like to change their dog's behaviour. So, without doubt, you are not alone if you feel the same way. Dogs pick up bad habits in the same way humans do, which can create problems for their owners.

Such things as jumping up and pulling on the lead are both annoying and frustrating behaviour. However hard it is not to become annoyed when your dog does things you do not want it to, one should bear in mind that every dog has its imperfections. If you would like to change some of your cocker's habits, it is imperative that you remain calm and teach your dog a better way to behave. I am sure you would not want to swap your canine friend for anything! Read on to see how to eliminate these bad habits.

Excessive Barking

Barking is your dog's natural way of communicating what they think. Depending on the breed and history of what they were originally bred to do, some dogs are more prone to vocalise than others. The cocker spaniel can be quite a notorious barker and may bark for a wide variety of reasons, such as:

- Warning you about intruders.
- When excited or happy to meet another dog or person.
- Bored or anxious when left alone.
- Protecting property or family.
- Herding a flock.
- Eager to go for a walk.
- Playing with other dogs or children.
- When playing games of fetch.
- Feeling dominant.
- Seeking attention.
- Feeling afraid.

When your cocker becomes a member of their human family, excessive barking is not going to be appropriate behaviour. Once the reason for their excessive barking has been determined, stopping the unwanted behaviour will involve communicating to them that this is not acceptable to you. There are three simple steps to make your cocker spaniel to stop barking:

- Firmly say, '***No***' and tell them to '***Sit***' whenever they bark.
- Remove them from whatever is making them bark.
- Let them see what it was that made them bark.

By following these steps, your dog will view this as you are taking charge of the situation as; (1) they were given a command and their attention was redirected back to you; (2) space was created between them and the reason for their barking; and (3) they were allowed to see it was nothing to get upset about. You can read more about canine barking in Chapter 7, Energy and Body Language.

Destructive Chewing

FACT ***Chewing objects is natural, normal, and necessary for a puppy or older dog, because it is how they explore their world. Cocker spaniels are not known to be especially prone to chewing compared to other breeds.***

A young puppy will chew everything in sight to relieve the pain of teething and to help their adult teeth push through (pictured). An older dog also needs to chew and their reasons for doing so include:

- To relieve boredom.
- To offset mild anxiety.
- It helps to keep their teeth clean and jaws strong.
- They are hungry

When your cocker spaniel is chewing to relieve boredom, this means they are not receiving enough attention. As soon as more time is spent engaging in outdoor adventures, training, socialising, and involving them in more physical and mental activities, this type of chewing usually disappears.

If your dog is chewing relieve themselves from mild anxiety, this usually occurs when they are left alone and feel frustrated and upset and might be accompanied by whining, barking, or escape attempts. If your spaniel is chewing inappropriate items when left alone, this is their way of saying they are unhappy to spend so much time on their own. There are several ways to alleviate this type of mild anxiety:

- Vigorously exercise them before they are left alone, so they are tired and more likely to sleep.
- Re-visit crate training methods until you determine the length of time they are comfortable with.
- Find ways to keep them occupied while you are away—provide interesting chew toys, food puzzles.
- Play soothing, calm music while you are away.
- Take them with you when you go out.
- Shorten the length of time you leave them alone.
- Have someone stay with them when you must be away.

Dogs need to chew to keep their teeth clean and jaws strong. If they do not have chew toys that satisfy this natural chewing urge, they may turn to shoes, the corner of a carpet, or the wooden leg of a coffee table.

Each dog is different with respect to what they like to chew, and how gentle or tough a chewer they are. This often means a little experimentation before finding the right chew toys.

For instance, if your cocker spaniel has a strong bite, giving them a chew toy designed for a soft chewer could mean they devour it, or ingest some. Chew toys are identified according to whether they are for soft, medium, or heavy chewers, and here are some examples:

- Firm, rubber toys—these can be in any shape.
- Rope toys—usually for tug-of-war games.
- Balls or durable, stuffed toys—for fetch games.
- Interactive toys—usually used for games of fetch.
- Treat dispenser or puzzle toys.
- Self-amusement toys—they can play with them when alone.
- Comfort toys— normally soft, plush toys your cocker likes to sleep with.
- Synthetic bones—there are many types, sizes, and strengths.
- Real bones—choose organic and avoid cooking, as this can cause shards to break off.
- Antler pieces—if they are not processed with chemicals and additives, these will usually satisfy the heavy chewer.

From time to time, your cocker spaniel might begin to chew on unacceptable things about the home, because they are hungry. If your dog is regularly not being fed enough, or they are on a restricted calorie diet, they could begin to chew objects to add more sustenance to their diet. If this is the case, there are a few steps to take:

- Weigh your cocker to determine if they are the right weight for their age and size.
- Take them to the vet for a complete check-up—they could have worms that are eating their food before it is digested.
- If they are receiving plenty of daily exercise and are not overweight, feed them more.

When your spaniel is engaging in destructive chewing behaviour, resolving this problem can be as simple as teaching them what they ARE and what they ARE NOT permitted to chew. The following tips will help:

- Dog-proof the home—place items your cocker might chew out of reach and off the floor.
- Provide your dog with plenty of things they ARE allowed to chew and praise them when they choose one.
- Use deterrent spray on objects that cannot be removed—i.e., furniture.

- Make a note of when they are more likely to want to chew and provide an interesting chew toy, treat puzzle, or walk to keep them occupied during those periods.
- Do not give your puppy an old shoe, pair of socks, or other article of clothing to play with as they will not know the difference between an old trainer and your new pair of expensive shoes.
- Often, destructive chewing is a direct result of your cocker spaniel's frustration and boredom from lack of exercise or mental stimulation appropriate to their age and activity level.

Digging

Digging is a primal urge for almost every dog, whether large or small, just like barking is part of being a dog. Also, some breeds are more prone to dig as they were bred for their ability to dig and search for their prey in underground dens. Cockers have an instinct to dig and many dig simply because they enjoy it, while others do it due to relieve boredom, anxiety, and more (see below).

FACT ***The instinctual need to dig the carpet or the cushions on the sofa before settling down is likely a throwback to the times when wild dogs roamed the Earth. When it was time to settle down for the night, they would often circle and dig as a means of disguising their scent.***

Today, there are other reasons why your dog might dig, including:

- Seeking rodents tunnelling just under the surface.
- Hiding a bone they want to eat later.
- To find cooler ground on a hot day.
- When pregnant, as part of the denning instinct.
- Digging under a fence to escape captivity.
- To relieve boredom or anxiety.
- Just because it is fun.

Although it can be difficult to curtail your cocker's urge to dig, especially as the breed has a particularly strong instinct for this activity, there are ways to control it, so the back garden does not end up looking like the face of the moon.

First, think about the reasons why your spaniel is digging, Next, ask yourself if they are getting enough exercise or interesting mental stimulation throughout their day. If they are not, they could simply be digging to relieve boredom. An easy fix for that would be to provide them with opportunities for more walks or setting aside time to teach them a new trick or command. Other things that can minimise the destruction of a perfectly landscaped garden, might be:

- Always supervise your dog when they are in the back garden.
- Provide interesting puzzle toys in the back garden.
- Section off an area for a sandbox and bury toys in it, to make it the most fun place to dig.
- Play games of fetch in the back garden.
- Set up an agility course in the back garden.

- Place rocks along fence lines.

Ground Scratching

Many dogs, including the cocker spaniel, engage in this type of scratching activity where they scrape the ground with their hind legs after peeing or pooing. While this is a natural and healthy activity, it can really rip up a nicely manicured lawn.

The reason cockers do this is deeply ingrained and instinctual. Just like peeing on trees to mark their territory, when they scratch the ground after their toilet routine, it is another way to mark their territory. There are scent glands located on their paws, and when they paw at the ground not only does it leave a visible warning scar to other passing dogs, but also the long-lasting scent from the paw glands is transferred to the ground. Although it is difficult to completely curb this ground scratching instinct, there are several things you can do to minimise the activity:

- In the back garden, immediately interrupt your dog with a favourite toy before the scraping begins.
- As soon as they finish their toilet routine, call them towards you to get a treat.
- Section off a corner of your garden for your cocker spaniel's toilet, so the entire garden is not scraped up.
- Take them for on lead toilet walks outside the home, so if they begin to scratch the ground you can easily interrupt them.

When your dog is engaging in an activity that is simply part of their genetics, while you can redirect this behaviour by interrupting them, you need to be patient and reasonable about what you can really expect.

Separation Anxiety (Separation distress)

Many cocker puppies and dogs suffer from separation anxiety when they become hyper-attached to their owners. Some sensitive breeds that have been bred for the purpose of close companionship tend to be more prone to developing this type of anxiety than others.

FACT ***Cocker spaniels frequently suffer from separation anxiety, as they do not like to be left on their own and tend to become anxious or stressed when their owner leaves the house. Occasionally, just seeing you putting your coat on or picking up your keys could trigger your cocker's anxiety.***

Fortunately, there are ways to treat your spaniel's separation anxiety and minimise any stress they feel. When raising your puppy, if time has not been taken to crate train or gradually get them used to spending brief times alone, it can be more difficult to eradicate this stressful situation when your puppy is older. If your cocker puppy is suffering from the stress of separation anxiety there are many behavioural issues they may engage in, such as:

- Whining.
- Chewing.
- Howling (pictured).
- Barking.
- Crying.
- Pacing.
- Trembling.
- Drooling.
- Panting.
- Digging—around windows or doors.
- Escape attempts.
- Pooing or peeing in the house.

If your cocker puppy feels extreme stress, they can appear terrified, as if the end of the world is at hand, as they are so worried the person they rely upon might never return. The only way to help your puppy if they have not previously learnt to tolerate moments alone is to teach them as soon as possible that no harm will come to them if they are on their own for a while. Here are some tips that can help your spaniel feel far more relaxed about their alone time:

Exercise – The first thing to do when having to leave your puppy by themselves for a while is to take them out for an energetic walk, so they are tired when you leave them alone. Also, a good mental workout is just as taxing, so perhaps teach them a new trick or command. A tired puppy will always be less stressed and could simply fall asleep.

Haven – Your cocker spaniel should have a safe place set up somewhere where they can settle and relax when at home. Think about things that might interrupt your dog when creating this area. If your cocker feels frustrated, it makes sense to set this up in a room that does not overlook the garden or roads. Apprehensive or anxious dogs frequently prefer a crate covered with a blanket. Your spaniel should always have free access in and out of their safe area, so if you use a crate always leave the door open.

Mental stimulation – When you leave your cocker, make sure they have different things to keep them occupied and provide them with mental stimulation. Give this to your dog in the room where you will leave them and make sure they are interested and engaged with it before you go.

Low-key departures – Avoid making too much fuss when leaving your home. Leaving should be a normal, everyday occurrence and let your cocker it is not something they need to be stressed about.

Low key arrivals – When you arrive home, greet your cocker spaniel with gentle, verbal praise and encourage calm behaviour where possible. Try not to over-excite your dog, as you do not want to encourage any more stressful behaviour.

Step-by-step – Gradually increase the amount of time your cocker is alone. You should do this slowly over a period of a few weeks. Closely watch your dog for signs of stress as you increase the time and go back to shorter lengths of time if your spaniel is starting to show signs of being unsettled.

Baby gates – If you can, instal baby gates throughout the house to allow you to move from room to room without your cocker always following you. This will help train your dog to stay relaxed when you are not nearby. Scattering a few morsels of your dog's daily allowance of dry food on the floor when you leave a room will provide them with a distraction.

Teaching to settle down – If your cocker spaniel is especially anxious and is struggling with you being away from them even for a short time, you can practise teaching them to settle on their own. This will help your cocker become more independent and will improve further training in the future. To achieve this, fill a food toy such as a Kong and place it by your feet while watching television. Do this regularly over a few weeks and gradually place it farther away from you each time. This teaches your cocker to settle down and engage in activities without you. While your dog is occupied with the food, go in and out of the room as normal.

Reward independency – Reward any independent behaviour from your dog with gentle praise if they choose to settle down somewhere away from you.

Training – If your cocker spaniel is frightened or anxious when left alone, it could be to do with their confidence. Just like humans, the more you reward your dog and boost their confidence, the more relaxed and content they are to do things on their own. Another way to help your dog to be less anxious about being left alone is by engaging in some basic training they already know to increase their self-confidence.

Calming Aids – There are many calming aids on the market that help reduce the stress of separation anxiety, including:

- Calming sonic collars.
- Calming chews.
- Thundershirts.
- Calming sprays, essential oils, and diffusers.
- Pheromone products (DAP).
- White noise calming music.
- ZenCrates.
- DogTV.
- Edibles.

Shirts – There are several sorts of shirts that can help a dog suffering from separation anxiety. The premise behind these shirts is they provide your cocker puppy with a hugging sensation that helps them feel safer and more secure.

Collars – Species-specific sonic collars are designed to play calming music at the perfect sound frequency to relax your stressed puppy or dog. There has been a large amount of research carried out recently in this relatively new field of sound behaviour, and clinical studies prove sound therapy is an effective method to reduce your spaniel's stress levels.

ZenCrates – This can be an interesting solution for puppies and dogs who are stressed or anxious about loud noises or being left alone. Every dog needs to feel they have a safe place to retreat to and this is even more important when your cocker puppy is nervous. Although this safe place could easily be your puppy's crate, the 'ZenCrate' (pictured) takes the haven concept several steps further. When your puppy enters the crate, motion sensors automatically play soothing music with a gentle airflow, while also blocking noise from outside sources, all of which helps to relax them.

Calming, white noise music played in the home has also shown to help reduce stress, especially for dogs who are nervous when hearing loud, booming noises, such as thunder, or sirens.

DAP Products – There are many pet calming products—sprays, collars — designed to calm your overstressed cocker puppy or dog using dog appeasing pheromones (DAP). These products (pictured) contain a synthetic pheromone designed to reduce stress and anxiety by mimicking the 'feel good' pheromone released after a mother dog gives birth. Some dogs find these DAP products calming, while others only experience marginal relief.

DogTV – This is the first cable television network made specifically for dogs. It has 24/7 television programmes providing entertainment for dogs and is available in both the U.K. and U.S. With the help of dog behaviour trainers and specialists it has been colour-adjusted to appeal to canines. The 3 6-minute segments are designed to relax, stimulate, and expose your dog to scenes of everyday life, such as doorbells or riding in a car. If you have ever noticed certain programmes seem to be attractive to your dog and catch their attention, this could be a viable solution.

Essential Oils – It is known that aromatherapy has a profoundly calming effect on humans, as the molecules react with compounds in our bodies, and the same is true for dogs. Essential oils can be mixed into a spray for spritzing bedding or kennels, you can spray your hands and give your spaniel puppy a relaxing massage, apply them directly to your puppy's ears or tummy with a roll-on, or diffuse them through the air so your dog can inhale the calming scents. Some of the most popular essential oils (pictured) for calming your stressed dog include:

- Bergamot – anti-depressant.
- Cedar –reduces and grounds panic, repels pests.
- Chamomile – deep, calming, soothing pain relief.
- Cypress – soothes frazzled emotions.
- Frankincense – quietens anxiety.
- Lavender – classically calming.
- Peppermint – mood booster, flea repellent.
- Rock Rose – relieves terror and panic.
- Star of Bethlehem – relieves shock or trauma.
- Sweet marjoram – calming, stress relief.
- Tangerine – soothes the nervous system.
- Vetiver – stress relieving.
- Ylang-ylang – anti-depressant, skin soothing.

Although many essential oils are safe to use with puppies and dogs, they should always be diluted with a neutral carrier oil—such as coconut or olive oil—so they are not too strong. If you mix your own, the dilution ratio for dogs should be no higher than 1%. For example, 3 drops of pure essential oil mixed into 30 ml (1 oz) of carrier oil.

It is important to be aware there are also many essential oils that are NOT suitable for use on pets, as they might be either irritating or toxic if eaten, such as anise or birch. Before using essential oils on your dog, always make sure they are safe to use.

Edibles – There are many chews, bites, and treats designed to calm your dog if they are suffering from anxiety. These contain a wide variety of calming ingredients, such as hemp, chamomile, passionflower, and valerian root. These edible products (pictured) work for some dogs but not others.

Medications – There are many medications your vet can prescribe for your cocker if they are suffering from the effects of separation anxiety. However, you should do all you can to modify the behaviour in a more natural way, especially since medications are often not effective until they have been treated for approximately 30 days. The following medications are commonly prescribed for the treatment of canine separation anxiety:

- Alprazolam—Xanax.
- Amitriptyline.
- Buspirone.
- Clomipramine hydrochloride—Clomicalm (pictured).
- Dexmedetomidine—Sileo.
- Diazepam—Valium.
- Fluoxetine—reconcile or Prozac.
- Lorazepam—Ativan.
- Paroxetine—Paxil.
- Sertraline—Zoloft.

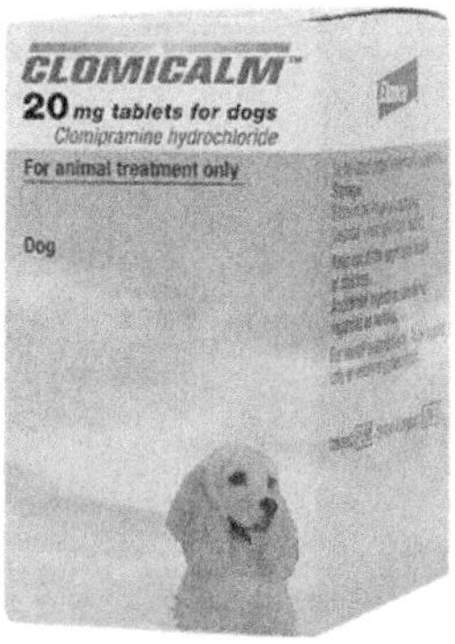

As with any medication that must be prescribed by a health professional, there can be side effects, such as weakness or vomiting.

Despite your best efforts, some dogs are so strongly attached to their owners they might never truly be able to relax and get over their feelings of anxiety when they are left alone. In these cases, you are faced with doing your very best to leave them alone only when you absolutely must, or perhaps, consider having someone stay with them or leave them at a day-care facility.

Begging

Dogs are programmed to find food wherever they can—even if they are not hungry—and when their owners are eating, it is only natural for many dogs to see this as an opportunity to add to their own food intake. Begging is a biological, instinctive behaviour for all dogs who have no idea that, in the human world, it is considered rude.

Being highly food motivated cockers are prone to beg while you are eating. It is hard to refuse them anything when your sweet cocker stares up at you with those loving eyes. However, unless you are careful, giving in to their begging will soon have your intelligent puppy opening cupboards and stealing from the rubbish bin. It is important to stop the habit before it becomes a problem.

FACT ***Most dogs do not realise that eating everything in sight may not be a good idea causing stomach-ache or diarrhoea. Therefore, many dogs appear to be hungry 24/7 and simply do not know when to stop eating.***

Also, we humans are often guilty of creating the begging behaviour in the first place. It is easy to do because a begging cocker is usually quite comical and difficult to resist. They might dance about, perform tricks without being asked, closely watch your every bite with an intense stare and 'talk' to you with cute little growls. Those pleading eyes are so endearing you will often feel the desire to share food with your canine companion who so clearly craves it.

The reality is your cocker spaniel begs for food because you probably unwittingly reinforced the behaviour. When your cocker wants food, you might only need to give in once to reinforce their begging behaviour. However, when your dog has become skilled at begging, there are several things you can do to diminish or even eliminate the behaviour, if you do not give in:

- Have your dog sit and stay at least 2-3 metres away from where people are eating.
- Send them to their crate when it is time for you to eat.
- Give them a puzzle toy to occupy them while you eat.
- Feed them in their normal place at the same time.
- Ignore whining, growling, or any cute acrobatics.
- Feed your puppy on a regular schedule.
- Do not give in, because if it worked once they will persist.
- Ask visitors to not feed your cocker from the table as this will undo all your previous work to curb their begging.
- Remember, your dog is not really starving.
- Teach yourself not to equate food with loving your dog.
- Give your dog a treat to reward them for not begging.

When you find yourself falling prey to those manipulative doggy eyes, perhaps it would help to consider that over 50% of dogs are overweight and over-feeding your dog can contribute to shortening their life.

Chasing

Chasing is an instinct for cockers. There are many chasing activities dogs might engage in that might be just for fun or dangerous.

FACT ***Some breeds, such as the cocker, are more prone to engage in chasing activities because they were originally working dogs who were bred to chase.***

Most dogs like to chase a ball (pictured), toy, or Frisbee, as the fast movement is exciting to them and ignites their urge to chase after the object and catch or retrieve it, known as 'prey drive'.

The intensity of prey drive varies between extremely high in some breeds to almost non-existent in others. For example, some dogs only occasionally enjoy the fun of chasing their tail, while others with a strong prey drive might engage in dangerous activities, such as chasing moving vehicles. If your puppy is simply enjoying a game of fetch, there is nothing to worry about. However, if your puppy begins to show a desire to chase or herd other moving objects, such as vehicles, bicycles, joggers, children, skateboards, squirrels, cats, etc., to keep everyone safe, this behaviour needs to be stopped.

How long it takes to teach your cocker control their impulse to chase depends on how strong their instinct is. Following are some steps and suggestions for curbing the chasing behaviour and safely channelling the urge into other areas.

- Put your cocker on their lead and go out for a walk.
- Have some treats in your pocket.
- When your dog tries to chase a bird, squirrel, or skateboard firmly say, '***No***' and when they switch their attention to you, give them a treat to reward their positive behaviour.
- You can also carry a small, squeaky toy that you squeak whenever your dog lunges forwards to chase.
- Reward them every time they control their impulse to chase.

Once your spaniel has learnt impulse control and understands what they are and are not allowed to do when out on a walk, it is time to work on re-directing their desire to chase into a fun game, such as fetch, tug-of-war, or hide-and-seek inside the home. Also, there are several canine sports that appeal to dogs with a strong desire to chase, such as:

- Herding trials—herding sheep.
- Disc dog—chasing and catching a Frisbee.
- Flyball—racing and retrieving a ball.
- Lure coursing—pursuit of a mechanical lure—a plastic bag attached to a line that moves at speed on a track to simulate a hunt.

Jumping on People

There are different reasons why dogs jump on people, the most common one being that they are excited to greet and want to get closer so they can receive the attention they desire. Cockers are sociable canines who enjoy company and meeting new people. They can also be extremely enthusiastic when you return home or have visitors and often jump up. Although it is nice to know your puppy is happy to see you, there are several reasons why trying to control this jumping behaviour is a good idea:

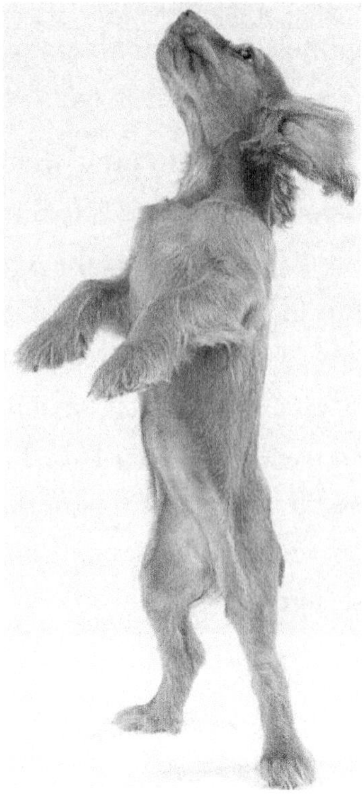

- They might knock over toddlers or unstable seniors.
- This behaviour can frighten young children.
- They might bruise or scratch the person.
- They could have muddy feet, which most people will not appreciate.
- It encourages overly exuberant behaviour.

Instead of using any sort of negative rebuttal your cocker needs to learn a more polite way of greeting people. The following suggestions will help teach an overly boisterous jumper (pictured) to keep their paws on the ground:

- Remain calm and keep it low-key when greeting your dog.
- Withhold attention when they are excited, to let them understand they need to be calm if they want to receive attention from people.
- Do not make a fuss, talk to them, or act excited in any way.
- If they jump up, walk towards them so they must move away.
- When they calmly greet you with all four paws on the ground, give them a treat to help reinforce their good behaviour.

TIP ***Teaching your puppy to keep their feet on the ground requires patience, consistency, and help from other family members and friends. It is best to also 'train' all other members of your family as well as visitors, so everyone is aware of the new, polite way to greet. Otherwise, they only learn to not jump on you, while everyone else remains fair game.***

Excessive Excitement

An over-excited puppy can seem adorable, and most people will read this as your cocker being happy. However, if they are learning to be overly eager, this can have a negative effect on their health. When they become hyper-aroused by someone or something that makes them excessively enthusiastic, it releases a rush of dopamine that can become addictive. When you are unable to control their over-excitement, it has the potential to lead to future behavioural issues.

For instance, an over-stimulated dog usually has a difficult time listening to their owner. When your cocker spaniel becomes used to a rush of dopamine in their system, this lack of self-control can result in future negative reactions to other dogs or people when out walking. The problem is owners often do not know how to identify when their puppy is being overly zealous, or accidentally encourage the behaviour.

While knowing the difference between play, high-energy and being overly rambunctious can be tricky to spot, there are certain signs to watch for, including:

- Uncontrollable running in circles or back and forth.
- Jumping up, nipping, and mouthing at people's hands.
- Barking and spinning in circles.

- Wildly running through the house and bouncing off furniture.

Once their overwrought behaviour has been identified, the following steps can help calm your puppy and teach them to control themselves:

- Do not encourage their behaviour by giving them your attention and reacting with equally excited energy as this can teach them to behave this way even more.
- Re-direct their energy towards something more structured or controlled, such as a toy, puzzle, or game of fetch.
- Do not believe the misconception that they will soon 'grow out of it', as this is not simply puppy energy and can continue into adulthood.
- Always reward your cocker's calm behaviour by giving a special treat, together with calm attention.
- Always remain placid and when talking to your puppy, do so in a slow, gentle voice.

Worktop Surfing

Checking the kitchen worktops for food (pictured) might not be something to worry about when your puppy is too small to get up there. Nonetheless, it is still a good idea to watch out for this activity as some puppies, despite their size, can be amazingly acrobatic when the strong allure of food is the goal.

Puppies and dogs are natural opportunists when it comes to scavenging for food. Whether it is kitchen worktop surfing or the family's dining table, it is still a natural cocker spaniel behaviour. Unfortunately, if your dog got away with it once they will remember, and it is only natural for them to look for a chance to score again.

FACT ***Pilfering human food right off the table is certainly annoying for owners, and it can also be harmful for the dog should they scarf down something that is toxic to them.***

Thankfully, there are steps that can help prevent these 'worktop surfing' activities:

- Make sure all worktops and tabletops are kept clear of any food.
- Thoroughly clean all worktops and tabletops with cleaner to remove any crumbs or enticing scent.
- Keep a closed door or gate between the kitchen and your cocker.
- Teach them to stay out of the kitchen.

- Train them to ignore a food item that has less scent than chicken or roast beef—such as a carrot—and when they ignore it, reward them.
- Slowly 'up the ante' by placing more difficult to disregard food items on a table or worktop, and when they ignore them, give them a reward, and praise them.
- Teach them to prefer a treat when, for example, they sit and patiently wait, or go to their bed or crate instead of jumping up at the worktop.

Never punish your cocker for stealing food from the worktop, as they might have already forgotten about it or learnt to be sneaky, and only do it when nobody is around. Plus, if they are still young, a little leniency could be in order, as they might not have yet learnt this is unacceptable behaviour.

Stealing Items

Although most puppies will steal food that is within reach, which is perfectly normal, they might also steal other not so normal items. Your cocker puppy will be curious while they get used to their new environment and steal anything they can get to. This includes such things as socks, underwear, sponges, tea towels, tissues, or anything they might find on the floor.

The first step to controlling stealing habits is to make sure there is nothing left within their reach that might be too tempting to ignore. What often happens is that a puppy steals something they are not supposed to have, and the result is a chase to try to pry it out of their mouth. Most puppies love a good chase, and this will seem like a fun game to them. Therefore, you should resist your instinct to give chase—unless it is something harmful they have in their mouth—as doing so will teach your puppy that stealing things is fun.

Normally, cocker spaniels steal socks as they want to chew or play with them. There are two schools of thought on the subject. One is people believe spaniels love socks because it offers them a sense of comfort, while others say it is because they smell like their owners. Being notorious hoarders, cocker spaniels will take things back to their bed or crate, including any socks you leave lying around.

Once your puppy has discovered an interesting activity that gets them attention and involves chasing, they might start looking for things they can grab that can result in them getting the results they desire. This is especially true when they are feeling bored or under-exercised. Therefore, making sure they get enough exercise and mental activities should also help counter this type of behaviour.

Patience and consistency will teach your curious cocker spaniel puppy not to steal people's belongings. Also, once your puppy grows out of their mischievous first year, they are usually no longer interested in the things that attracted their younger self.

Not Coming When Called

There are several reasons why your puppy refuses to come when called, with the most common ones being:

- They may think they are in trouble.
- They might not understand what the word means—using too many words for the same thing can create confusion, such as '***Come here***', '***Come now***', '***Come right now***', etc.
- They do not want to end their fun play session with their friends.
- They think your request to '***Come***' is not as much fun as what they are enjoying now.

- The '***Come***' command has not been taught correctly (see Training, Chapter 11).
- If the '***Come***' command is always used to end a fun play session, your cocker might learn to ignore or associate the command with something unpleasant, so offer a treat reward so they get something better for having to leave their play session.

TIP ***Never use a frustrated or angry tone when asking your puppy to 'Come'. If they learn to associate the command with getting into trouble, they will soon learn that responding is not in their best interests. If this has already happened, you should start to teach the recall command again, but this time use a different word that means 'Come', so they connect the new word with a positive outcome.***

Expecting an easily distracted puppy to '***Come***' when their recall is not yet 100% reliable could be asking too much. When they are in the middle of an exciting activity, such as a wrestling play session with another furry friend or pursuing a chattering squirrel up a tree, this is a huge distraction.

The only way to ensure your puppy always comes to you when called is to make certain the '***Come***' command is always a positive experience.

Pulling and refusing to walk on lead

Contrary to what people believe, it is NOT natural for your spaniel to be tethered to you, and as it is unnatural, time must be spent teaching them how to properly walk without pulling. It IS natural for cockers to be exploratory, curious, playful, and social. If they discover straining on their lead will get them to a particularly interesting scent sooner, you can bet they will pull (pictured). It is a simple equation in your dog's mind. If they have already learnt pulling gets them what they want, why would they not pull?

Sometimes, you can encourage pulling on the lead without even realising you are teaching this behaviour. For example, when your cocker puppy tugs on their lead and you continue to move forwards, they have just been rewarded for pulling. Thankfully, even if your puppy has already learnt this habit, there are some things you can implement to return everyone to a comfortable, loose lead walking habit, including:

- Stop moving forwards when your puppy pulls.
- If they pull, stop, and tell them to sit.
- Change direction when your puppy pulls.
- Walk in a circle or figure of eight.

When you first put their collar and lead on your puppy, it is only natural that this new, and often disturbing sensation of restraint, might cause several unexpected reactions, such as:

- Biting at the lead.
- Trying to get their collar off.
- Standing still and refusing to move.
- Lying down.

- Rolling on the ground.
- Bucking.
- Squealing or screaming.
- Pulling backwards.

When starting out, always remember to be patient and understanding, and above all else, never drag your puppy. See Training, Chapter 11, to learn how to train your puppy to walk on a loose lead and teach them to associate pleasant experiences with wearing their lead and collar.

Running Away

There are many reasons why your cocker puppy or dog could get into the habit of running away. What we might not realise is it is in the DNA of every canine companion to be an energetic explorer. As a species, dogs are active, curious, and built to roam. A recent survey commissioned by Blue Cross found Labrador retrievers are the most likely breed of dogs to run away, with the cocker spaniel and Jack Russell also in the top three. The pet charity's researchers compiled their list from the experiences of 2 000 British dog owners. When they become part of your human family, it is your responsibility to ensure opportunities for setting out on an exploring adventure are easily found. Some of the reasons why your cocker spaniel might make running away their top priority, include:

- High prey drive—they cannot resist chasing a bird, squirrel, cat, etc.
- Easy escape route and no human supervision—a low fence, a chain-link fence that is easy to climb, a hole in the fence, a lock on a gate that can be opened, an open window.
- Strong urges to mate when not neutered or spayed.
- Boredom and lack of exercise.
- Frightening sounds—loud, sudden noises, thunder, car alarms, sirens.

Most of these reasons can easily be prevented by never leaving your cocker alone or unsupervised. Bear in mind the following tips:

- Giving your puppy more opportunities for exercise and fun activities will relieve boredom.
- If your spaniel has a high prey drive, keeping them on their lead when outside the home will prevent your puppy from chasing unsuspecting prey.
- Regularly checking the back garden fence for holes and making sure gate latches are dog-proof, and windows are closed—when you leave them alone in the house—will eliminate possible escape routes.
- If your cocker spaniel has been desensitised to frightening noises, they will no longer feel the need to run away from those sounds (see Socialisation, Chapter10).

Aggression

Even dogs who are naturally friendly and loveable, such as the cocker, have the potential to become aggressive when they are not socialised and taught how to interact politely in the human world. Also, some dogs are more prone to developing aggressive tendencies than others, such as when they have been:

- Bred from parents who have aggressive histories.
- Abused or mistreated.

- Bred for protection work.
- Bred from a long line of fighting breeds.

Whatever the reason, it is simply unacceptable for any dog who is going to be part of a human family to display signs of aggression, such as biting, snapping, snarling, baring teeth, growling, or lunging. The following sections will discuss the common kinds of aggression and how to correct this behaviour.

Fear Aggression

As the name suggests, this type of aggression is the result of fear. The reason dogs react with aggression when they are afraid is usually because their senses tell them they are in a dangerous situation they cannot escape from. If your cocker feels trapped or unable to remove themselves from a situation that feels dangerous, panic sets in and they might be forced to defend themselves. This is usually when aggression comes into play. For example, if your senses they have no way out of an uncomfortable situation, they might growl or bare their teeth.

TIP ***If you find yourself confronted by an aggressive dog, the easiest and safest way to defuse the situation is to back away from them so they no longer feel afraid. When you give the dog space, they no longer have the need to protect themselves, and a tense situation that could have resulted in a bite can be avoided.***

Dominance Aggression

When your cocker spaniel is displaying dominance aggression (pictured) it is usually for one of two reasons. Firstly, it might be directed towards another dog merely as a behaviour to show they have a lower standing in the pack. Secondly, dominance aggression can be displayed to demonstrate your dog is in control of their owner and the other dog should not come close.

Either reason could have developed because your puppy's early training was not soon enough or firm enough and they have learnt to be their own boss. Accomplishing the desired results when correcting this type of behaviour can take some time. To gain control of the situation, you must increase your command energy and be more dominant than your cocker spaniel.

If you have been too soft on your dog and have not yet begun teaching basic commands or establish any house rules and boundaries, you might have to create a relationship of trust and respect between you. Should this happen, your cocker could believe they are in charge. The following steps will help to turn this situation around:

- Teach them basic 'Come', 'Sit', and 'Stay', commands (see Training, Chapter 11).
- Teach house rules and boundaries.
- Firmly tell them 'No' when they display aggressive tendencies.

- When they greet politely, reward them with a treat.

When you begin to teach commands, rules and boundaries strongly control your cocker spaniel's actions, this change in energy will usually 'tell' them you are now in charge, and they no longer need to react with dominance.

Territorial Aggression

FACT ***All dogs, no matter their size, are naturally territorial to some degree. When you consider their long history, it makes sense that in a dog's mind they want to protect resources—food, water, shelter—from those who might steal them.***

Territorial or protective aggression might be exhibited towards people or other animals who approach your cocker's property. Unfamiliar or unusual people and other animals your dog encounters are the most likely targets for territorial aggression.

Protective territorial displays can range in their level of aggression from growling and barking to lunging, chasing, snapping, or biting. They can exhibit this behaviour at windows, doors, behind fences, and in the car. When out, some dogs have been known to claim territory and show similar behaviour at picnic areas, park benches, etc.

Dogs who are frustrated as they are physically restricted from gaining access to the stimulus, by a barricade or lead, might suffer from heightened aggression. They could also develop displacement behaviour—spinning, circling, self-mutilation—or redirected behaviour where they turn their aggression towards their owner when you attempt to reach for or grab your spaniel.

Even when the person who is the cause of their behaviour has entered the territory or home, they can continue their aggression, which could result in biting and severe injury. Due to the high arousal level of the dog, in some cases, an element of frustration might present itself and lead to redirected behaviour towards objects, other animals, or people.

There are steps to help eradicate this type of aggression:

- Give a solid foundation of obedience training as this teaches your dog to control excited energy and defer to your directions.
- Teach the '***Leave it***' command (see Training, Chapter 11) to distract their attention and tell them to leave what is exciting them.
- Reward them for calm behaviour.
- Tire them out through daily exercise, as they will be less likely to spend their time being mega watchful.
- Close the curtains to restrict their access to the window to stop them barking at anyone walking by.
- Go outside and stand between them and the fence, door, or gate they are patrolling, and firmly tell them, '***Go***' as you point away.

- If they bark at people walking past, let them know you do not want them to, by firmly telling them, '*No*' and making them sit.
- Exercise their brain by teaching your cocker tricks or canine sports as this will tire them out
- Always remember to reward good behaviour, for example, when they remain calm when seeing a person walking by but do not bark or ignores them.

While it is difficult to eliminate a strong, territorial instinct, when time is taken to interrupt the unwanted behaviour, teach your dog what is acceptable through positive reinforcement, it is certainly possible to effectively manage the situation.

Possessive Aggression

When your dog is possessive, their instinct is to growl, bare their teeth, snap, or furiously bark to tell another dog, animal, child, or adult not to get too close. Guarding resources is an instinct for dogs and depending on the dog and what they are being possessive about, the instinct can vary in intensity. It makes sense when you consider the canine's history when survival meant learning how to fend for themselves in the wild.

Some dogs only display aggressive tendencies over a particularly prized object, such as a favourite toy or their dinner bowl. Others guard anything they find around the house, such as an old, rubber bone, a pair of shoes, or a tissue they pulled out of the rubbish bin. Furthermore, some dogs display possessive outbursts over a favourite person. Many cockers have issues with resource guarding and show control-dominant behaviour. In other words, it depends on the dog and the value they place on each object they are being possessive about. Signs to be aware of include:

- Lowered head and intense stare.
- Curling their lip.
- Low growling.
- Baring teeth.
- Snapping or biting.
- Protecting an item by pulling it near to them.
- Running away with an item.

As well as the guarding instinct, there are several other reasons why your dog might display possessive aggression, such as:

- Competition from other dogs or family members.
- The addition of another dog in the home.
- Prolonged time in a shelter that encourages competition for limited resources.
- Guarding can be a behaviour learnt from their mother or littermates.

FACT ***Possessive aggression, also known as resource guarding, simply means your cocker spaniel is being possessive of their toys, food bowl, treats, or other objects they value.***

When your dog is guarding an object, young children should be kept away as your cocker might not hesitate to bite. Rather than forcing them to give up their prized possession, they need to understand giving it up voluntarily results in them receiving something better. They must learn to trust people when they are around their treasured objects. The following steps can help:

- Reinforce the '***Leave it***' command (see Training, Chapter 11), so they will voluntarily drop the object.
- Offer them something they consider to be of higher value than whatever they are guarding—special treat or toy.
- After they receive the higher value reward, give them back the item they were guarding, so they comprehend there was no need to protect it.
- If they are seriously trying to bite and the above steps are not helping, consider asking for help from a trainer or behaviourist.

Patience and a careful approach, plus the above behavioural modification exercises are very effective in teaching your cocker spaniel they no longer need to guard their resources.

Frustration Aggression

Frustration aggression occurs when your cocker is being continually restrained or prevented from getting what they want. For some dogs living in their human controlled environment, this can be a large part of their day. Frustration aggression is more common in higher energy dogs. Here are some reasons why your cocker spaniel might feel frustrated:

- They are always restrained when they are on their lead.
- They are in their locked crate for too long.
- They are behind closed doors inside the home.
- They have been left inside a closed vehicle.
- They have been left inside a closed vehicle.
- They saw a squirrel through the window but are unable to get to it.
- They are tied up in the back garden.
- They saw a cat walking by but cannot chase it.
- There is a dog across the street, but the fenced garden stops them from visiting.

Depending on your dog, their circumstances, and the degree of frustration, if they have not learnt how to safely deal with it, frustration can erupt into destructive behaviour. This could include ripping the curtains, destroying their crate, or even snapping at their owner. It might help your cocker spaniel improve their impulse control and frustration tolerance if you can teach them patience. This includes instructing them to sit and wait at the door before entering/exiting, or before they are given their food bowl.

Instead of immediately giving in when they whine or cry, only give them what they want after they stop making a fuss.

Illness or Pain Aggression

Since, for the most part, your cocker is unable to tell your when they are ill or feeling pain (pictured), if your normally friendly puppy suddenly starts to act aggressively by growling, biting, or snapping when you move them or pick them up, they might be telling you something is medically wrong. There are many signs to be aware of that can indicate your dog is sick and experiencing pain, such as:

- Sudden change in usual habits.
- Refusing to go on a walk.
- Lack of energy.
- Avoiding other dogs.
- Not wanting to play games they previously enjoyed.
- Declining to eat.
- Being unusually clingy.
- Yelping, whining, growling, leaping, pulling away when touched.

TIP ***Pain can be a common cause of aggression and a careful approach is needed to avoid being bitten. Usually, if your dog bites because something is hurting them, it is not because they want to harm you, but are simply biting as a reaction to feeling pain.***

If your cocker spaniel has been injured or is ill, they need to be taken to the vet's where a professional can determine the best course of action. If moving them makes them aggressive, where gloves to protect your hands, be as gentle as possible, and wrap them in a blanket for easier transport. Being aware of your puppy's usual behaviour can help to identify signs and seek medical assistance before the problem becomes worse.

Rage Syndrome

Also known as sudden onset aggression (SOA), or avalanche of rage syndrome, rage syndrome is a serious behavioural problem that has been reported most frequently in the English springer spaniel. Although it can affect a variety of other dog breeds. Reports show within the cocker spaniel breed, it is more common in full coloured dogs, such as the red, golden/blonde, or black cockers than any other colour. This has a lot to do with their specific breed lines. It has been found that, if the breed line included dogs with rage syndrome it tends to have a higher occurrence. The solid-coloured cocker spaniels are at greater risk than their multi-coloured counterparts, with darker colours being most affected.

Often, it is confused with other forms of aggression and can be misdiagnosed by veterinarians and behaviourists. This condition can be inherited and is believed to be genetic in origin.

Dr Roger A Mugford, an animal behaviour consultant is attributed with introducing the term rage syndrome. If your cocker suffers from rage syndrome, they will suddenly act aggressively to anyone or anything nearby (pictured), but within minutes will become calm and normal again.

A dog who has the syndrome does not seem to remember what has taken place and can act friendly to the person they previously attacked. Unfortunately, such attacks as these will never be controlled through training as the condition is one your dog is unable to consciously control. These attacks will happen without any cause or apparent reason and often with no warning signs.

However, if you observe your cocker shortly prior to any attack, their eyes will glaze over and go hard. This is followed by your dog becoming exceedingly alert before finally attacking. To any outsider with no prior knowledge of the condition, it will appear to be an exaggerated form of aggression. What makes it all the harder to control is the absence of any trigger or pattern to these attacks.

During his research, Dr Mugford identified the problem as starting during the adolescent stage, at around seven and a half months old, on average. There are a variety of treatments for affected dogs, including antiepileptic tablets, which have been reported to be effective. Sadly, not every treatment works, and in many cases, euthanasia is the only solution left.

The Unruly Adolescent

FACT ***The transition from being a juvenile to becoming an adult occurs in adolescence. It can start between the ages of 6 and 12 months, and finish between 18 and 24 months. During this time, your cocker spaniel's brain undergoes a reorganisation and dramatic hormonal changes happen.***

The hormonal changes in adolescent dogs can make them appear less obedient. Although, this is more of an increase in motivation for exploring, interacting, and running, and a need to interact with the environment and people around them. Adolescent cockers have the energy and motivation to do more, just like human teenagers. While they play, explore, and interact with their friends—human and non-human—they do not possess the necessary knowledge and experience to think about and manage their actions and reactions.

No matter how friendly, any cocker spaniel can develop obnoxious levels of barking, digging, and other undesirable behaviour when bored, untrained, or unsupervised. During adolescence such behaviour is more prevalent, making your dog a trial to live with. With the cocker, the 'teen' years start at about 6 months and continue until they are approximately a year old.

Due to teenage cockers' highly energetic nature, they often feel conflicted when told to stop what they are doing, or simply to calm down, even in situations where they were previously 'obedient'. Dog owners often interpret these changes as their dog being stubborn or trying to assert their dominance rather than appreciating they are having difficulty controlling their impulsiveness. During adolescence, you might experience changes in your spaniel's personality that you are displeased about. For example, your young cocker might:

- Bark or whine when left alone.
- Not be as friendly with strangers.
- Begin to show their aggressive side to other dogs.
- Begin to be possessive of their owner.
- Start to bark at unknown people and dogs.
- Decide to excavate the back garden.
- Become possessive of their toys or food bowl.
- Look for opportunities to chase the neighbour's cat.
- Begin to show their stubborn side.
- Ignore their owner when called.
- Appear to have suddenly gone deaf.
- Ignore the commands they have already learnt.
- Start to relieve themselves inside again.
- Begin to mark.
- Attempt to escape from the back garden.

Welcome to the world of canine adolescence, where it appears all the previous socialising and training work has flown out the window and the adolescent puppy has turned into some sort of monster.

Too often, cocker spaniel owners become frustrated and impatient and give up on their dogs during the time when they change from being the cute, cuddly, and mostly obedient little puppy into all kinds of madness. Nevertheless, with consistency, understanding, endless patience, and perseverance, you and your furry friend can emerge out the other side of this adolescent period with a much stronger bond.

FACT ***It is important to note that not all dogs go through an intensely crazy adolescent period. For some dogs, the adolescent period can pass unnoticed.***

Remember, you have already lived through toilet-training, teething, socialising, and basic rules and boundaries with your cocker spaniel puppy and can feel proud of all the progress you have achieved over the last several months. Also, bear in mind you will eventually be able to enjoy the joyous rewards all those months of diligent puppy training have brought to your relationship. Here are some top tips to help you through the teenage years:

Keep your dog stimulated – Having trouble getting your attention can also be exasperating for your adolescent cocker spaniel, but predictability is a good way to avoid frustration. Try to include more interactive games in your dog's routine, such as playing with a ball or Frisbee, or hiding something for them to find.

Remember to give cues as to when the play session begins and concludes. You can tell your dog '***Playtime***' or show them a toy when you want to start and then let them know when you are through. You can either say,

'***Finish***' and throw the toy away from them or remove the toy and give your cocker spaniel something else to do. This helps minimise their feelings of frustration at the end of a pleasant activity. Additionally, you can scatter some treats or give your dog something to chew on.

Do not tell your cocker off – If your dog used to play with other dogs, but started to become too aggressive or boisterous, telling them off will only worsen the situation. You should use a cheerful voice, instead of reprimanding your spaniel, to distract them from the situation and to take them out of it.

It could be safer to continue socialising your cocker with dogs they already know and minimise their exposure to other dogs to prevent the problem from worsening.

Keep up activity levels – Dogs in adolescence are energetic. They can benefit from longer walks in quiet environments, plenty of exploration and just letting them use their nose. During this time, the best way to ride the storm is to stick to the rules and continue to be a firm, yet fair leader while increasing training time to keep your cocker's body exercised and their mind occupied.

Adolescent dogs can become more panicky and anxious, which might make them not follow your instructions, behave in destructive ways, soil your house, or start barking excessively. If frustration is getting the upper hand, rather than letting things deteriorate, consider hiring a professional who can provide valuable assistance to help you get through this stage of your cocker spaniel's development.

Fear Issues

Although there are many reasons why your cocker spaniel can develop fear issues, this is often the result of inadequate socialisation when they were a puppy. A dog who has not been adequately socialised and learnt to calmly accept many different situations, places, people, dogs, and other animals might learn to be fearful of them.

Cockers tend to be apprehensive, even with proper early socialisation. Their sensitive personality means you should never use harsh training methods. To prevent your cocker spaniel from becoming afraid, use consistent and gentle training methods to obtain the results you are looking for.

When your dog is frightened, they can react in several ways. For example, they might try to run away or hide, they may shake, tremble, whine, or bark. If they are extremely scared, they could even become aggressive.

It is useful to identify some of the common situations that can possibly make your dog feel scared:

- Other dogs.
- Strangers.
- Other animals.
- Young children.
- Being left alone.
- Bath time.
- Visits to the vet.
- Changes in their environment.

- Vehicle travel.
- Air travel.
- Stairs.
- Bridges.
- Water.
- Mirrors.
- Shiny surfaces.
- Loud noises

Helping your nervous or stressed dog learn to overcome their insecurities may require behaviour modification. The term 'behaviour modification' simply means a systematic approach designed to change or 'modify' your cocker spaniel's behaviour with a view to decreasing their unwanted habit. In this case, it refers to changing your dog's attitude, emotional response, or reaction to the trigger that causes fear.

Changing your cocker's emotional response when they are afraid depends on how frightened your dog is (pictured). Apart from extensive socialisation when young, which helps to prevent nervousness and fear responses, there are several positive steps that can improve confidence and reduce fear issues:

- Revisit their basic obedience training (see Training, Chapter 11).
- Be careful not to reinforce fearful behaviour by saying words they associate with stress, such as, '***It's okay***'.
- Being careful not to accidentally reward fearful behaviour by saying, '***Good Boy***' or trying to offer a treat.
- Forward plan so you can utilise potential fear triggers as a socialisation or training opportunities.
- When your puppy is afraid, remaining calm and distracting them by asking them to do something they have already learnt.

It is possible to help your cocker puppy work through their fear of just about anything if they can focus on your commands. The best approach is to slow the process down and break their exercise into patient, little steps that are reinforced along the way. Using the example of being afraid to cross a bridge:

- Make sure they are securely on their lead.
- Ask them to '***Sit***' and watch them until they calm down.
- Do not force them to move closer to the bridge until they are calm.
- Quietly stay there and let them know you are relaxed and confident about the bridge.
- Ask a friend with a dog who is not afraid of bridges to join you.
- If there are other people and dogs happily crossing the bridge, even better—they will learn by observing and might even decide to follow another dog.
- Give them a treat for positive reinforcement and take one step closer.
- Give a gentle, forward tug on the lead and offer another treat.

- If they take the treat, this means their fear level has decreased.
- Continue steadily moving forwards and rewarding them for staying calm.
- If they are beginning to show signs of agitation, end the session and come back the next day.

Depending on your dog, their level of anxiety or fear, the sort of relationship they have with you, and how well they have learnt to trust and follow your lead will affect the time needed to make it across the bridge.

Other Curious Behaviour

Sometimes, our canine companions can seem to have some curious behaviour. While all dogs are unique and act in different ways, the following few pages outline some of these behavioural issues and offer suggestions why they might have occurred and what you can do.

Being Clingy

FACT ***Initially, when your cocker puppy is clingy and wants to follow you everywhere, this is often simply the result of not yet feeling comfortable in their new surroundings. Once they are used to their living arrangements, depending on the natural confidence level of your dog, this will often subside.***

Of course, every puppy is unlike any other, and their experiences and how they were raised is different from what their siblings in the litter might have experienced. In other words, their life experiences and how you interact with them will contribute to how clingy your puppy grows up to be.

Many of the more sensitive breeds tend to be naturally clingier than others. If they are bored, do not exercise enough to burn their excess energy, or get away with clingy behaviour, cocker spaniels often have needy and attention-seeking attitudes.

When your puppy receives constant attention from their human family during their early developmental months, they can grow to be nervous of being alone. As your puppy becomes used to their new environment and continues to demonstrate clingy behaviour, this is typically a learnt behaviour they have been taught. For example, giving them a reward or treat every time they follow you. Some other reasons why your cocker might become clingy are:

- Advancing senior years with loss of hearing or vision.
- Illness.

- Boredom.
- When sensing your stress or anxiety.

Some owners might not mind when their dog follows them from room to room, but if this becomes a less than desirable habit, here is what you can do:

- Increase the amount of daily physical exercise—if tired, they are less likely to follow you everywhere.
- Desensitise them to actions they have learnt to associate with specific results—e.g., pick up your keys but do not go out the door, go to the kitchen but do not get food, go to the bathroom but do not take a shower or spend any time there—all of this will teach them these are boring activities and do not warrant their attention.

- Train them to go to their special, relaxing bed, crate, or place where they have access to their favourite chew toy whenever you need to do something such as take a shower. Say, '***Relax***' and when they go to their special bed, reinforce this behaviour by giving them a reward. Ask them to '***Stay***' and when you return, if they have indeed stayed, praise them. You can start with just a minute of them 'staying' and increase it over several days and weeks, until they always stay in their relaxing space until you return

When your dog is visibly shaking this could simply be because they are afraid of something, such as a loud noise they do not understand. Other reasons why your dog might be shivering, or trembling include the following:

- They are excited that you have arrived home.
- They have just had a bath and being wet is making them feel cold.
- They just came in from a walk in the rain or snow and are wet and cold.
- They are seeking attention—some dogs quickly learn that shivering elicits a sympathetic response and lots of attention from their owner.
- They are in pain—from injury or illness.
- They are not fully vaccinated—the distemper virus can cause tremors.
- They are feeling nauseous from motion sickness or eating too much too fast.
- Advancing years have weakened their muscles.
- Old age has caused arthritis or joint pain.
- They could have White shaker disease syndrome—also known as generalised tremor syndrome.

TIP ***If they receive a fright from a sudden, loud noise, this trembling will soon pass, and even quicker if you can show them the source of the noise. If they are just cold, warm them with a hairdryer or wrap them in a warm blanket until the shivering stops.***

Shivering from excitement or happiness will subside on its own when they have calmed down. If they are trembling from eating too much too fast, simply feed them smaller portions and buy a slow feeder bowl so they are unable to consume their food so quickly.

As your cocker advances into their senior years, their muscles might start to weaken, or they could suffer from arthritis and joint pain, any of which can make them develop tremors. If there is a medical reason for the trembling, such as generalised tremor syndrome or arthritis, they need to be diagnosed by a qualified veterinarian who will prescribe the proper treatment.

Burying Items & Bones

Burying objects, especially bones, is an instinct that is a throwback to a time before dogs became domesticated members of the human family. At that time, they lived in the wild and had to make do with a 'feast or famine' diet. This meant when they were lucky enough to find food, anything they unable to eat needed to be protected, hidden, and preserved in a buried stash they could return to in times when hunting was scarce.

FACT ***When your dog buries bones and carcasses in the earth this creates a natural refrigerator that keeps it cooler while also hiding it from view and disguising the scent to protect it from other predators who might catch the scent and pilfer their bounty.***

Even though most of our domesticated dogs do not need to worry about where their next meal is coming from, some of them still retain a very strong instinct to bury bones or other prized things. Also, rather than burying them in the back garden, they may have learnt to use the sofa cushions or the bottom of the laundry basket as prime locations for squirreling away items for future use.

If your cocker is constantly burying or hiding food, treats, toys, or your favourite pair of socks, this is not your dog being naughty, but instead a natural survival instinct to preserve their treasured objects in a place where they can find them later. If there are other pets in the home, your dog might also hide their prized items to prevent what they view as competition from stealing them. The following points can help diminish this type of behaviour:

- If they are stashing human items, move them out of reach.
- Question how many toys or treats they are receiving. If it is too many, rather than refusing them, they could be trying to save them for later.

Another crime that only CSI could solve.

- Give them more exercise and teach them interesting tricks so they are not bored.
- Rather than giving them ten toys, give them just two at a time and rotate them.

The bottom line is it is totally normal for your cocker spaniel to have the urge to bury things, whether in the back garden, or under a convenient blanket or cushion.

Eating Faeces

The one thing you need to know about canine coprophagy—the proper scientific term to describes the act of your dog eating their own faeces—is it is far more common than you might think. According to studies conducted in 2008 and 2018, somewhere between 16 to 49% of all dogs will eat their own poop.

Eating faeces can result from several factors, such as:

- Your dog is young and will taste everything at least once—puppies usually grow out of the habit of eating poo.
- Dogs are natural scavengers who seek their food through smell—they think poo smells great.
- Their diet may be lacking in nutrients, minerals, and calories.
- They could have an enzyme deficiency.
- They might have parasites, which means they have to compete for nutrients.
- They may have diabetes or thyroid issues, which can make them feel hungry enough to eat stools.
- Nursing females eat the poo of their young to keep the den clean.
- Your puppy might smell faecal odours on their mother's breath after they have cleaned them and learn to associate the smell with a food source.
- The poo of other animals may taste good to a dog—many dogs like goose poo and cat poo.
- Puppy mill dogs are more likely to develop this habit because of poor nutrition and stressful, over-crowded living conditions.
- They might not be feeling well or could have an illness.
- They may not be properly absorbing nutrients in their food.
- Perhaps they are not be getting enough food in their daily diet.
- Attention seeking—if they have learnt that this gets them the attention they desire, they may do it more.

If your puppy continues to eat poo on a regular basis after they have grown out of the tasting everything stage of their development, here is what you can do to control this unsavoury habit:

- Immediately clean up their poo as soon as it happens.
- Prevent them from getting anywhere near the cat's litter box.
- Keep them on their lead in areas where they might discover another dog's poo.
- Feed them a well-balanced, nutritious diet that contains all the enzymes, minerals, and calories they need.
- When feeding a cooked diet, add digestive enzymes.

- If suspecting a key nutrient is absent from their diet, add supplements.
- Screen them for parasites.
- Keep their body and brain healthy by developing an exercise and mental stimulation routine.

Medically, there is little risk to a dog who eats their own faeces. However, if your cocker spaniel eats the poo of other animals, they can pick up parasites and bacteria that cause vomiting, diarrhoea, decreased appetite, and tiredness.

Eating Grass

The most common assumption about why dogs eat grass is because they have an upset stomach and want to throw up, but research has proven this belief is flawed. Based on statistics, most grass-eating dogs are not previously sick, and less than 25% of dogs throw up after eating grass.

A look back to a time when dogs roamed the wild and ate a balanced diet by consuming what they hunted could offer an explanation to this grass-eating curiosity. Although we often think of dogs as being strictly carnivores—meat eaters—this is not entirely true, and they are also not strictly omnivores—meat and plant eaters—either. Consider when dogs had to fend for themselves, they would often eat an entire animal. This consisted of a balance of meat, bones, and organs, as well as the stomach contents that contained the plants and grass—fibre—consumed by their prey. Back then, dogs were scavengers who literally consumed anything that would fulfil their dietary requirements. Interestingly, the examination of stool samples taken from wild wolves has shown as many as 47% of wolves eat grass. Therefore, it stands to reason many domesticated dogs have retained the urge to eat grass.

In addition to their historically based urge, many puppies and adult dogs today eat grass as they have learnt to like it. Some dogs become grass-eating connoisseurs whose refined tastes only lead them to eating the new, tender grass that emerges during the springtime growing season, while others eat grass all year long.

Being scavengers, they navigate their world through scent and touch and are always on the lookout for something to eat. If the grass is healthy and has not been sprayed with toxic chemicals, a little grass eating should not be a concern for your cocker spaniel.

Eating from the Cat's Litter Box

As disgusting as this sounds to us mere humans, raiding the cat's litter box is a totally natural behaviour for dogs who are born to scavenge. Many dogs find cat poo especially tasty, as it smells like the cat food they are never allowed to eat. Even though this habit is not likely to seriously harm your dog, they can ingest parasites and bacteria that can cause vomiting or diarrhoea.

Furthermore, if they eat a large quantity of cat litter, it could produce a harmful blockage that leads to difficulty with their bowel movements. If they seem to have a problem and you know they were just in the cat's litter box, it is time for a visit to the vet. To prevent your cocker spaniel from eating cat poo, try the following:

- Keep the cat's litter box well out of reach of your dog—such as behind a closed door.
- Put up a baby gate, so they cannot get to the litter box.
- Invest in a closed top or dog-proof litter box.

If neighbourhood cats are pooing in your back garden and it is hard to keep a close watch on your cocker spaniel puppy to ensure they do not eat it, regular visits to the vet to check for internal parasites might be in order.

Licking People

Instinctually, cocker spaniels lick. It can be soothing and therapeutic as it releases endorphins. To show their dominance, your cocker spaniel might try to lick other dogs, and they could lick you because they like the taste of salt on your skin. Furthermore, your cocker spaniel could be licking people for the following reasons:

- To show submission—indicates to other dogs they mean no harm.
- As a welcome home greeting.
- As a learnt habit.
- To be noticed—licking gets your attention.
- For a reward—we often pet or praise them.
- For taste—your skin may contain food residue.
- Communication—licking can identify where you have been.

In the wild, a wolf puppy will lick their mother's face to encourage them to regurgitate food. Is this what your cocker spaniel is hoping for when they lick your face? While the jury is still out concerning any definitive answer about why dogs like to lick people, this is mostly an affectionate form of self-expression rather than a reason for worry.

Licking and Chewing their Paws

Most dogs occasionally engage in licking and/or chewing their paws, this is natural. If this behaviour is excessive, occurs suddenly, or is accompanied by limping, swelling, redness, or bleeding, this is usually a sign of injury, pain, or infection requiring diagnosis and treatment at the vet's.

TIP ***You can tell if a white or light-coated dog has been persistently licking at their paws, as the saliva in their tongue will turn their feet a rusty, pink colour.***

There can be many factors that result in your dog licking or chewing their paws:

- A burn or cut. Arthritic pain.
- Arthritic pain.
- A fur ball between their pads.
- They are under-exercised and bored.

- A puncture wound.
- An allergic skin disease.
- A broken or fractured claw.
- They are simply grooming wet or dirty paws.
- A corn, cyst, or tumour.
- A disease of the pads or nail beds.
- A food allergy.
- A foreign object lodged between their pads—burr, spear grass, splinter, etc

If your cocker is licking their paws as part of their grooming regimen this is not a problem. Also, if they are licking or chewing simply because they are bored and need more exercise or mental stimulation, this is easily remedied by providing opportunities for more outdoor excursions and teaching fun tricks that exercise their brain. For other possible medical reasons, unless you can clearly see what is causing the licking and are able to remove it—such as something stuck between their pads—it would be wise to seek professional help at the vet's.

Rubbing Their Face

Dogs rub their faces on a wide variety of substances, from the grass in the back garden to the cushions on the sofa, and here is why they do it most often:

- It just feels good—different fabrics or textures feel better than others.
- To relieve an itch they cannot quite scratch—often a coarse carpet will find that elusive spot.
- Marking territory—rubbing leaves invisible pheromones to signal ownership other dogs can smell.
- They like how it smells.
- To alleviate an eye irritation or dental pain.
- To clean or dry their face—this is a common occurrence, and many dogs rub their face on a chair, carpet, pillow, or other surface after a meal or drink.
- To relieve collar irritation—if it is too tight, has a sharp edge, or is making their hair mat and pull on their skin.
- To relieve the itching caused by biting bugs.
- Allergies—skin irritation leads to rubbing.

If any of the rubbing sessions are the result of a medical issue, and you can see red, irritated skin, it is wise to take your cocker the vet for a professional analysis and treatment protocol.

Bottom Scooting

Bottom scooting—also known as the bottom crawl—is usually conducted on a nice, plush surface, preferably at a friend's house with pristine, white carpets, and most often is an attempt to relieve an itchy rear end. The exact reasons why your dog might practise this embarrassing behaviour include:

- Anal gland issues—overfull, infected, or cancer.

- Allergies–an allergic reaction to something in the environment or food causes itching.
- Dingleberries—dogs with long hair often get poo stuck in the fur around the anus, which causes irritation.
- Diarrhoea—prevents the anal glands from emptying and can also irritate the anal skin.
- Parasites—tapeworms can cause anal irritation.
- Attention seeking—if your cocker spaniel learns this behaviour makes you fuss over them or creates attention of any sort, they may learn to do it more often.

FACT ***Located on either side of your dog's anus, the anal glands are approximately the size of a small grape. Whenever your dog poos, the anal sphincter squeezes against these glands, which then release a super smelly secretion—much more aromatic than the poo itself—that is specific to each dog. This anal sac secretion leaves a 'message' to other dogs identifying who was there before them.***

Infrequently, dogs have anal gland issues requiring regular help from a qualified individual who knows how to express them—such as a groomer or veterinary technician—when the glands are overfull. Should the glands become infected, impacted, or cancerous, or bottom scooting is an allergic response or the result of a parasitic infestation, these are situations requiring the assistance of your veterinarian.

Again, if your cocker is experiencing bouts of diarrhoea, this type of loose stool prevents the natural expression of the anal glands. If the situation is chronic, it is important to seek the advice of a qualified veterinarian.

Howling at Sirens

The most popular belief as to why some dogs howl at sirens is that it is simply a throwback to their instinctual, wild wolf-like ancestry when wolves howled as a means of communication to locate their pack. Perhaps, some dogs howl and others do not because the pitch of a siren needs to be within the perfect range that tickles the dog's primal urge to respond. In this case, perhaps they believe the sound of the siren is another dog howling in the distance. The strong connection with working in a breed such as the cocker spaniel, might encourage a strong drive to howl and verbally communicate.

In some cases, howling can also have a contagious element, just like when one dog starts barking, and then another joins in. Often, your cocker's howling (pictured) might start a chorus of wailing neighbourhood dogs. Additionally, some dogs howl like wolves to communicate their displeasure when their owners leave them alone in the house. Howling is nothing to worry about, as it is a completely natural behaviour and usually does not last very long. However, if the howling becomes excessive, here are a few things you can do:

- Interrupt your cocker with a toy or treat when they throw back their head to begin howling.

- Whenever they hear a siren and do not react, praise them, and give them a reward.
- Get a recording of a siren that you can play and practise the above steps.

Once your cocker learns that forgetting about howling will reap the benefits of a reward, they will usually choose the latter.

Depression

As cocker spaniels are a highly sociable dog breed who love to be with their human companions, insufficient time with their human family can lead to the blues, as can major life changes and events (pictured). Any time your cocker's behaviour changes significantly, signs of depression can mask illness, therefore a vet check-up is essential. Some of the signs indicating your dog is feeling depressed are as follows:

- Sudden changes in mood or behaviour.
- Change in appetite.
- Change in sleeping patterns.
- Antisocial behaviour or hiding.

Depending on how well you know your cocker's normal behaviour and facial expressions, you might only need to look at their face to know they are not feeling themselves. Some spaniels are more sensitive than others with respect to what could make them sad or depressed. However, there are some common events that could make your dog depressed, such as:

- Moving to a new town or house.
- Renovating the home.
- A change in their usual daily schedule.
- A new pet or baby in the home.
- Loss of a family member.
- You have gone on holiday.
- They are physically unwell.
- Sudden loss of a close animal companion.
- You are feeling depressed.

If your cocker is depressed because they are missing a companion pet, when the time is right, filling the void with another animal will usually help. If you travel for work or are away on holiday and cannot take your spaniel with you, it will take a while for them to get used to being cared for by a new person. But your dog will usually settle down within 3 or 4 days and start to relax again.

FACT ***Dogs are very sensitive to emotions around them, and if you are feeling depressed, your dog might also succumb to a feeling of sadness or depression.***

Thankfully, it is not usually too difficult to reorientate your dog if they are feeling down in the dumps. Here is what to do:

- Increase the amount of time spent with them.
- Take them to different parks, trails, or walks.
- Teach them some fun new tricks.

- Enrol them in an exciting canine sport.
- Take them for a check-up to make sure they are well.

If you take the time to engage your dog in new, interesting tasks and adventures, it will normally improve their mood. If all the above suggestions seem to make little change and there is nothing physically wrong, the vet may suggest a natural remedy or prescription medication to help elevate their mood.

7. Energy and Body Language

'The dog lives for the day,
the hour, even the moment.'
~ Robert Scott ~

Good communication between owner and canine is not just about the words you speak. Perhaps, even more important than your words are your human energy and body language when delivering messages to your cocker spaniel. While your dog can learn many human words, their natural way to communicate with their world is much more about feeling the energy and reading the body language of other animals and people around them. For example, when your cocker senses energy from you that is not confident enough to provide them with a feeling of security so they can relax, this uncertain energy can create confusion in your dog's mind and may often be the beginning of behavioural issues.

Because cockers are pack animals, they cannot function as well as they might unless they have a leader to follow. When your dog becomes a member of your human family, for them to be a relaxed and well-behaved family member who follows directions, they need to feel that you are a confident leader who is always in charge. You might ask, '***What is a confident leader?***' The dictionary definition of the word 'confident' describes it as '***being certain of your abilities or having trust in people, plans, or the future***'. Therefore, in a dog/owner relationship a confident leader would feel sure about their success when they interact with their dog.

TIP ***When walking your cocker spaniel, remember the moment they sense you are no longer completely in control, they will take this unspoken 'message' as being in charge has now defaulted to them.***

On the other hand, if you are focused on your dog, firmly in charge of the walk, and aware of your own energy and body language, the likelihood of your dog misbehaving or acting up in a loud or aggressive manner towards others will usually be very slim.

What is Energy?

Every living creature generates an energy field. Perhaps, the most profound communication difference between humans and their dogs is humans do not consciously consider energy when interacting, while dogs sense energy as a central part of how they communicate in their world.

When connecting with our canine counterparts, it is very important for you to convey the right energy to your dog. For example, when you have difficulties getting a message across to your puppy, it may be because the energy level your cocker spaniel is 'reading' is either too mellow or too forceful. Just like the nursery story about Goldilocks and the Three Bears, the human energy needs to be 'just right' for your puppy to learn to trust, respect, and eagerly follow you.

Weak Energy

When your dog senses your energy level is too mellow, gentle, or weak, they might not feel confident in your ability to lead them, and the following may occur:

- Your dog becomes confused.
- They do not listen to commands.
- They become nervous or timid.
- They are unsure where they fit in the hierarchy of their human family.
- Your naturally assertive dog can become more dominant.
- They pull you when on a walk.
- They become protective and bark at everyone when walking.
- They are territorial and bark at neighbours.
- They become protective of food, toys, treats.
- They show aggression towards other dogs and people.

If it appears the desired results when interacting with your dog are not happening, it is possible you need to implement some of the following energy exercises when communicating with your dog:

- Stand up straight.
- Square your shoulders.
- Expand your chest.
- Breathe deeply.
- Hold your head high.
- Make eye contact with your dog.
- Speak in a firm, yet calm voice.
- Be focused and without distractions.
- Recall a time when you felt powerful.
- Check commands do not have a questioning tone—there is a big difference between, '***Sit?***' and '***Sit***'

- when expecting your dog to obey a command.
- Imagine being a real or fictitious person who is a confident, no-nonsense leader.
- Visualise a successful outcome.
- Believe you have what you need.
- Never doubt—just do it.

Forceful Energy

On the other side of the coin, when your cocker senses your energy is too forceful, or sounds angry or frustrated when communicating with them, this is counterproductive, and the following may occur:

- Your spaniel becomes confused.
- They are nervous or afraid.
- Your naturally timid dog can become neurotic and unstable.
- They engage in fear peeing.
- They stop listening to commands.
- They hide or run away.
- They cower or shake nervously.
- If your cocker is very sensitive they might throw up.
- They shut down completely.
- They learn to fight back out of fear.

TIP ***Sometimes, when you interact with your dog during training or ask them to perform specific commands, you might use a tone that conveys overly forceful energy and almost borders on anger. Typically, almost all dogs respond best to firm, yet calm energy.***

While some dogs react better to firm energy, those who are more sensitive usually respond better with a softer approach. If firm energy is not getting the desired results, the following exercises will help adjust an overly forceful energy to find the right balance:

- Take a deep, relaxing breath and slow down.
- Do not let your frustration get the better of you.
- Make a conscious change in mindset—trying a different approach could produce the desired results
- Ask yourself if you are feeling calm— if not, take a deep breath, calm down, and try again.
- Try using a softer tone with your cocker.
- Notice how your dog is responding to you—when you change something, does this improve your dog's response?

Just the Right Energy

It can take personal awareness and a little time to discover what 'just the right' energy balance is when communicating with your cocker spaniel, as every human and dog is individual, when putting the two together there are many different family dynamics that come into play.

When you bring your cocker puppy home, they could be timid and uncertain as everything is new to them. Furthermore, without the support of their mother or siblings, they will need time to adapt to the energy of their new family.

However, as your new puppy becomes familiar with their home and gains more confidence, their true personality will slowly begin to emerge. By the time they are entering adolescence they will have already worked out many of the house rules and who is really in charge.

As your puppy begins to mature, you will see whether the rules are being followed, and if your cocker listens when given a command. This is the time when paying closer attention to your human energy comes into play.

For instance, if your commands are largely ignored by your puppy, this implies your energy is not confident enough for your cocker spaniel to respect or pay attention to you.

Increasing the energy in your voice does not mean starting to yell at them but feeling more confident and in command of the situation by implementing some of the suggestions above and really meaning it when giving your puppy a command. As the energy in your voice gradually increases, it will become clear when the perfect energy balance has been achieved, as your cocker will start to pay attention and do what is asked of them. On the other hand, when communicating with energy too forceful for your dog, slowly tone it down until the desired balance has been achieved.

TIP ***Once you are used to using the right energy when asking your puppy to perform various commands, it will soon be second nature. After a certain point, you will not even realise you are adjusting your energy level to get your message across to your dog.***

Canine Sounds

Apart from finding just the right energy when communicating with your spaniel, it is also time well spent making yourself familiar with basic canine body language and the sounds they make. This includes their body and tail positioning, face, eyes, posture, barking, and growling noises.

Frequently, gestures or actions people assume mean one thing could be the dog saying the exact opposite. For example, determining what that wagging tail or barking really means can sometimes be the difference between a tummy rub and a bite. Knowing the difference can help prevent an unwanted encounter during a visit to the local park.

The following are common canine sounds and postures and what they really are conveying to other dogs and people around them.

Barking

Since the very first canine, they have communicated over long distances by barking or howling to one another, and when in closer proximity, barking or growling to warn off other dogs approaching what they consider to be their territory. Dogs also bark and whine in excitement or happiness when greeting another returning member of their pack.

These days, domesticated dogs have learnt to bark for a wide variety of reasons, such as when they sense danger or are alerting their humans to someone approaching the home. Barking is an effective way to get the attention of their owners, as it is a loud and difficult noise to ignore. While it can mostly be easy to interpret what your cocker spaniel's bark is 'saying', there are some circumstances that might not be so easily understood and require more explanation.

When your dog barks for unknown reasons, the first step is to calmly assess the situation rather than immediately become annoyed or upset with your cocker spaniel. As your dog's sense of smell, hearing, and often their eyesight is far more acute than yours, they must rely upon you to teach them what they are permitted to bark at.

FACT ***While it is true any dog, no matter their size, can learn to be a big barker, how they react to various circumstances largely depends on how they are raised.***

If your dog seems to be overly eager to bark at everything, they need to be taught what is acceptable.

Attention – Most dogs bark to get your attention as they are bored or want to be taken for a walk or chase a ball. Some reasons dogs bark for attention are:

- You are on the phone or computer.
- You are having a conversation with someone.
- You are watching a movie.
- They want to play a game.
- They want a treat.
- It is dinner time.
- They need to go to the toilet.
- They want to go for a walk.
- Their water bowl is empty.

Danger – Many dogs bark to alert you to visitors or intruders, and part of training your cocker puppy includes teaching the difference between what they perceive as danger and what is truly dangerous. In other words, your puppy might bark because they are not yet familiar with the noises the neighbour's children make when returning home from school, or the sound the washing machine makes during the spin cycle, or the sound of neighbours walking down the hall in a shared living situation. You want your cocker to alert you to when there is real, imminent danger, and should the danger involve an unwanted intruder, you want them to bark loudly to possibly scare the threat away.

Boredom – Dogs get bored, just like their owners. Often, when they have had enough of just quietly lazing around the home, are tired of playing with their toys or chewing on a bone and want to get outside for a change of scenery and some exercise, they might bark to let you know they would like to get moving.

Separation Anxiety – Dogs are naturally pack animals, which means it is not normal for them to spend long periods of time in lonely isolation. Although dogs would never choose to be left alone, when introduced to it with kindness and compassion, they can learn to quietly accept short periods of solitude.

Unfamiliar Noises – When introducing your puppy to their new home, it can take time before they learn what noises are part of their new daily life and are to simply be ignored. You can help your cocker puppy to understand unfamiliar sounds they do not need to bark at by letting them see what caused it.

Excitement – Many puppies and dogs bark excitedly for a plethora of reasons, such as jubilation when you arrive home, seeing other dogs at the park, in anticipation of going for a car ride or a walk outside, or when getting wound up during a game. Depending on your living situation, excitement barking might be relatively acceptable. For instance, dogs living in a multi-complex situation, such as a block of flats, should be discouraged from loud barking activities that could potentially disturb the neighbours.

On the other hand, if you live on a farm or smallholding where there is considerable space between neighbours, excitement barking will not be a worrisome or disturbing problem, and the sound of your cocker spaniel barking could be the type of security system that might discourage unwanted trespassers.

An Interesting Scent – Some dogs are more naturally prone to barking or howling when they smell an interesting scent on the wind. Often, this can be the scent of another animal that has crossed through the garden, such as a rabbit or hedgehog, and depending on how strong your cocker's sense of smell is they may simply vigorously sniff about or start to bark incestuously.

Food or Toys – Cocker puppies and dogs can be understandably excited in anticipation of receiving a treat, their food bowl, or a prized toy. If they have not yet learnt to control their enthusiasm, it can often erupt into a bark. If they bark intensely, simply ask them to '***Sit***' but do not give the treat, food bowl, or toy until they are quiet.

TIP ***If your dog is barking, they are being too demanding of you. Therefore, your dog needs to learn to be patient and less insistent before you capitulate.***

Knocking at the Door or Ringing the Doorbell – Some dogs bark loudly whenever someone knocks at the front door or rings the doorbell. At that point, they are simply letting you know someone is at the door, which is acceptable. What might not be acceptable though is persistent barking. It is up to you to firmly tell your cocker when to stop barking, by saying, '***No***', and asking them to '***Sit***' and be calm.

Fear – A dog will bark when they are afraid, nervous, or uncertain about something. There may be a new object in the neighbour's garden they have not seen before, so they bark at it. Or they might bark if they are uncertain about an unknown dog they encounter when out on a walk, or when hearing thunder or a car alarm. If this is something you do not want your dog to bark at, you must teach them not to bark by saying, '***No***' and slowly approach and let them see it is nothing scary.

Pain – Another reason for your dog barking is when they are in pain. Usually, this bark sounds quite different from all the others, and is often a combination of a bark and a whine, or a yelping noise. This is a bark you will want to pay close attention to, so you can quickly respond and offer the assistance your cocker spaniel needs.

Territorial – Dogs bark at other dogs and people if they feel they must protect their property and/or people. Normally, this happens when your dog is not receiving a strong enough lead from you. If you become more confident, your cocker will typically learn they no longer need to protect you or be territorial. When this happens, your dog can relax and let you take control, which will result in the barking stopping.

If your cocker has learnt to randomly bark at every new person or dog they encounter when out on a walk, they will need to be told by you that this behaviour is unacceptable by firmly saying, '***No***'.

Manipulation – When your cocker spaniel learns to become the centre of attention, they will not be so eager to accept that you could be interrupted by other people or various communication devices, such as the telephone. If your dog is used to getting all the attention, they might bark in impatient protest if they feel they are no longer the centre of your world. If this is the case, your cocker needs to learn patience, so tell your dog to '***Sit***' or '***Wait***'.

If loud barking worked once, they never forget. When a ball or other object they desire appears, they understand they can take charge with just some loud barking. If your dog becomes excited about chasing their ball, they could bark, rather than immediately throwing it for them, you should say, '***No***', tell your dog to '***Sit***' and '***Wait***', and make eye contact with them before you throw the ball for them.

Whining

Whining is often the pre-cursor to full-blown barking. The first time you will probably hear your cocker spaniel puppy whine is when they think they have been left on their own and are feeling the panic of loneliness. Other reasons why your dog might whine include:

- They are unhappy with being confined in their crate.
- They are trying to tell you they want or need something.
- They are hungry or thirsty.
- Their new surroundings are making them nervous.
- They need to go to the toilet.

During house-training, your puppy learns their toilet is in a specific place, such as the back garden. They might whine to get your attention when they need to go outside. Initially, your new puppy could whine at night when they are expected to sleep in their crate, as this is a lonely routine compared with their previous one of cuddling next to their littermates.

Talking

FACT ***Some dogs are naturally vocal and seem to be talking to you. If only we could learn to speak 'dog'. This can be for any number of reasons, or just because your dog likes to produce those noises and has learnt that when they make their growling, 'talking' noises, it might appear to please you, which usually results in attention being switched to them.***

Dogs are very adept at reading their people and quickly learn what sounds get them what they are looking for. When your dog makes a noise that sounds as if they are trying to talk to you, the result can often be that you mimic the sound back to them. Then, if there is also a reward that reinforces your dog making that sound, bingo, they have just learnt how to 'growl talk' with you. Now, your smart dog can use their voice to ask you to do many things, such as:

- Take them out for a walk.
- Open the door where the treats are located.
- Fill their water bowl.
- Give them a pet or a scratch behind the ears.
- Play a game.
- Plus, any number of other sorts of interaction.

Cockers are often quite a vocal breed. When they become excited, they like to 'talk'. When their vocalisation starts, you will have to work on rewarding their quiet times to avoid it becoming an out-of-control habit.

Growling

Growling is just another form of canine communication frequently used when more subtle forms have not had the desired effect. When your cocker is upset, afraid, nervous, or aggressive, they sometimes growl. More specifically, your dog could growl as a pre-cursor to a full-blown bark.

Also, cocker spaniels often growl noisily when play fighting with other dogs or even their owners. In this case, the growling does not mean they are being aggressive, unless the play session gets too rough, and one dog begins to become more threatening. This is easily defused if you are watchful and step in when you notice their play is beginning to get out of hand.

You will not usually have any difficulty recognising the difference between playful growling noises and the much louder and more intense sound when two dogs are seriously fighting with one another.

Finally, there are other happy growls your cocker spaniel will use when communicating with you, which usually sound quite different from the rest. These growls are typically a lower sound that your dog affectionately makes when being petted, having a tummy rub or wanting your attention.

Howling

Howling is a deeply ingrained form of primal, canine communication. Some breeds are naturally more prone to engage in howling—such as hunting hounds, like the beagle—as this is their way to tell their owners they have found the scent. Depending on the breed and the circumstances, howling can occur for much the same reasons as barking.

TIP ***Whatever the reason for your dog howling, this behavioural trait does not normally require any formal training to teach them not to howl, as this noise is likely to be quite infrequent and short-lived. If your dog has an insistent howling problem, the best way to eliminate it is mostly through redirecting their attention and rewarding them when they stop.***

Body Language Messages

The following are other subtle, body language messages our furry, canine friends use to convey messages to their owners. These may not be as easy to interpret as those previously mentioned, but with a little practise, they will soon make sense.

Stalking Stance

FACT › ***A stalking stance, often accompanied by raised hackles—hair along the back—is when your cocker spaniel lowers their head and shoulders, crouches, and slowly creeps forwards with an intense stare. Typically, this happens just before a serious attack.***

When your dog approaches with raised hackles, this is an indication they are feeling dominant or aggressive. Likewise, it can be an indication they are excited, fearful, startled, nervous, or overly timid.

In any of these circumstances, keep a respectful distance and place your cocker behind you until it becomes apparent what is really going on, because any dog who is nervous, anxious, or fearful can quickly turn into a reactive, biting dog.

Staring

Cocker spaniels can stare at you for many reasons, and even more so if you are a confident leader who your dog has learnt to trust, respect, and obediently follow. For example, some of the reasons why your cocker might stare at you include:

- Manipulation to get them something they want.
- They need to be let out for a toilet break.
- They want to go for a walk.
- They want their dinner.
- They need their water bowl filled.
- They are watching you eat, eager to get what is left over.
- They are guarding a toy or food.
- They are waiting for instructions.
- They are reading your energy.
- They find what you are doing fascinating.
- They are expressing affection.

Usually, your clever spaniel will have learnt the act of staring at you is a way of communicating that will eventually get them something they want (pictured).

Play Stance

Also called the 'Play bow', looks like the 'Stalking' stance, and without careful scrutiny it can be difficult to identify the difference between the two. Whenever your cocker spaniel wants to play with you or another dog, the following will occur:

- They bring their chest low to the ground.
- They lean on their front elbows.

- They stretch out their front legs.

This bowing posture is your cocker's way of inviting another dog or human to play and is normally accompanied by an excited bark that, in the doggy world, undoubtedly declares, '*Come on, let's play*'.

Ear Movements

The many ear movements your cocker makes are especially subtle and challenging to interpret. All dog breeds, even those with long, hanging ears, such as the cocker, are still able to move their ears forwards and back as they display different emotions. When your dog is feeling relaxed, their ears are typically held slightly back or out to the sides. As your cocker spaniel becomes curious, more alert, or paying closer attention, their ears move farther to the front or towards what has caught their interest.

TIP ***When dogs are feeling afraid, they flatten their ears against their head. They also do this when they feel aggressive, in combination with menacing facial gestures such as barking or baring teeth and growling.***

Lip Licking

Of course, some dogs lick their lips in anticipation of a tasty treat or when they are about to be given their dinner. However, when there is no food involved, lip licking can be an indication that your dog is feeling worried or threatened by something going on around them. Dogs also lick their lips as an 'appeasement' or submissive gesture to signal to a more dominant dog they are not interested in fighting.

During training sessions, a confused dog might lick their lips when feeling stressed about having difficulties understanding what it is they need to do. Should this happen, ask your dog to perform a simple task they have already learnt, and then offer the reward of a treat and end the session on a high note.

Finally, dogs can lick their lips if they are not feeling well or are experiencing pain as the result of a tooth or mouth problem.

Crotch Sniffing

Dogs sniff the privates of other dogs to try to get to know them, and the same is true when a dog rushes in to sniff an unfamiliar person's crotch. It is their natural way of gathering information about who the person is.

The reason your dog will sniff the groin area of people is because the groin and armpit areas contain the highest concentrations of apocrine or sweat glands, which produce pheromones. This means sniffing these areas will provide the most social information to your cocker.

Head Tilting

There are several different views and hypotheses from various researchers and scientists concerning why your cocker might tilt their head (pictured) when listening to your various voice inflections, including:

- It makes you smile and often results in praise for your dog.
- It allows your dog to determine the direction of the sound.
- It helps your spaniel understand what the noise is.
- A higher pitched sound might be appealing to your dog's ear.
- It improves or better focuses your dog's vision.
- The word or phrase is familiar to your cocker.
- Persistent head tilting is due to an ear infection.

Whether we really understand why dogs tilt their heads at different sounds, words, or phrases we direct towards them, there is no doubt this head tilting makes us smile.

Yawning

When your dog yawns, they are sending several different messages, including:

- Indifference about a situation.
- They feel stressed and might yawn in rapid succession.
- When a dog comes face to face with a more dominant dog, they might yawn to 'tell' the aggressor they are neither willing to be submissive nor interested in challenging.
- Sometimes, the yawn is a calming signal and a way to avoid conflict. It might be enough to defuse the aggressive approach of another dog.

What is interesting about yawning is just like the 'contagious' aspect of yawning between people, the same thing happens between dogs, or humans and dogs who know one another well. Therefore, while a yawn may indicate stress, it can also be a normal part of life and a sign your dog is closely bonded with you.

Tail Vocabulary

While people enjoy various forms of vocabulary inherent in their different cultures, the vocabulary of dogs includes a tail language common to all canines.

FACT ***Tail language is an important dimension in understanding the emotional state of your canine companion. For example, the position and speed of your cocker spaniel's wagging tail functions much the same way as a smile or frown on the face of a human when greeting others.***

Tail Positions

Your well socialised dog will happily wag their tail when greeting others. However, it can be a mistake to automatically assume if a dog is wagging their tail, they are friendly. When determining a dog's true intent or demeanour, it is important to take into consideration all the different messages a dog's tail can convey. It is entirely possible they are wagging their tail just before they decide to take an aggressive lunge towards a person or another dog.

More important in determining the emotional state of most dogs is the height or positioning of their tail. Here are the possible positions and what each of these can mean.

Stiffly Vertical – A stiffly held tail pointing to the sky could mean your dog is feeling aggressive and dominant and about to challenge or threaten another less dominant dog. It might also mean your cocker is very excited. Some breeds—such as terriers—naturally hold their tails in a vertical position. A long tail held stiffly and slowly sweeping is frequently an aggressive communication.

In Line with the Back – A tail held parallel to your dog's back usually suggests they are feeling alert and attentive and gathering information about what's going on around them with neutral energy and possible interest in exploring their surroundings.

Held Much Lower – When your dog holds their tail much lower than in line with their back, it can mean they are feeling stressed, afraid, submissive, or unwell. In which case, keep a close eye on your cocker to determine if they were simply upset by a particular situation or unknown dog, or if they might be unwell and need to be checked out by their vet.

Tucked Underneath the Body – When your dog tucks their tail under their body between the back legs, this is commonly a submissive sign they are feeling highly stressed, nervous, fearful, or threatened by an older or more dominant dog, person, or unfamiliar situation.

The Speed of the Wag

How quickly your dog's tail is moving also offers an idea of their mental state. The speed of the wag usually signifies how happy or excited your dog is but can also mean they are feeling aggressive.

Slow Low Slightly Swinging Tail – A stiffly held tail that is low and reminiscent of a broom sweeping the floor frequently means your cocker is feeling anxious, unsure, or tentative about greeting another dog. This is more of a questioning type of wag that might become aggressive. If there is also a raised paw, your dog is questioning.

Fast-Moving Tail – Typically, the faster the wag, the higher your spaniel's level of excitement. Also, the stroke of the tail sends different messages. Smaller strokes of the tail can indicate your dog is becoming more nervous or uncertain about a meeting. On the other hand, when the strokes are broader, this can mean your spaniel is feeling happier about a situation.

The Circle Wag – This type of tail wag, often also referred to as the '***propeller***' or '***helicopter***' wag, almost always indicates a happy, friendly dog who is overjoyed to see someone they know, someone they wish to meet or someone they have missed.

Tail Wagging to the Left – When your dog wags their tail to the left (pictured), it could indicate they are feeling more wary or dominant because they are coming near a dog or person they have not met before.

Tail Wagging to the Right – When your dog wags their tail to the right, this usually means they are pleased about meeting or greeting someone they already know.

8. Feeding

'I feel sorry for people who don't have dogs.

I hear they have to pick up food they drop on the floor.'

~ Unknown ~

A dog fed wholesome food is a healthy, content, and longer-lived companion. We are what we eat, and the same is true for our dogs.

Mostly, the domestic dogs' diet consists of meat, but they also consume grains, fruits, and vegetables. Non-meat foods do more than serve as fillers, they provide a range of essential vitamins, minerals, and fibre. Quality dog food includes meat, vegetables, grains, and fruit. High-quality versions of these ingredients are used in the best dog foods that are safe for your cocker's digestive system.

It is important to try to choose a high-quality dog food, instead of shopping by price alone. The problem with choosing lower priced food is the cheaper dog food is frequently less nutritious. Inexpensive dog food brands can include low-quality fillers such as wheat, corn, soy, and other unnecessary ingredients to add bulk to the product, rather than providing any nutritional benefit. It is worth noting that dogs cannot efficiently digest corn or wheat.

TIP ***Whilst you might pay a little more for a better-quality diet for your cocker spaniel, their improved health is well worth it, but there is an additional payback. You will probably find that you need to visit the vet less often, as your dog's immune system is strong and their general health much better too.***

Canine Teeth and Jaws – All your cocker's teeth are sharp and pointed as they are designed to rip, shred, and tear into animal meat and bone. On average, an adult dog has a third more teeth than their human owner.

Adult canines have 42 permanent teeth compared to a person's 32—without the wisdom teeth. On average, puppies have 28 baby teeth or 'milk teeth', while human babies have 20 baby teeth.

Puppies begin to lose their sharp, baby teeth at approximately 12 to 16 weeks old. Aged four months, almost all your cocker puppy's milk teeth will have been shed and replaced by their permanent, adult teeth (pictured).

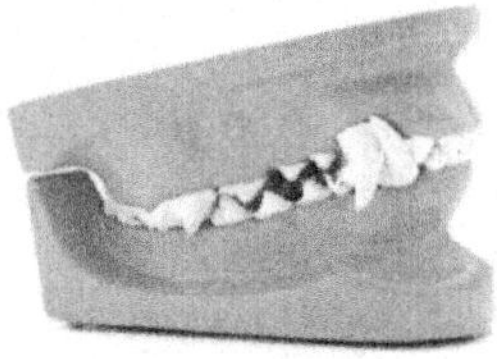

Every dog is born equipped with powerful jaws and neck muscles for the specific purpose of being able to pull down and tear apart their hunted prey. The jaw of every canine opens wide to hold large pieces of meat and bone, while the mechanics of the jaw permit only vertical—up and down—movement designed for crushing.

Getting into the habit of **carefully reading the food labels** can go a long way towards avoiding over-processed foods that contain fillers, such as corn meal or wheat gluten, which are inappropriate for a healthy canine diet.

Throughout their lives, dogs have different dietary needs. A puppy's nutritional requirements are different from those of an adult or senior dog. **Most dog food companies offer specifically formulated foods for dogs at various life stages. They are commonly labelled as Puppy, Adult, and Senior.** There are even some companies that have products explicitly for the adolescent phase, identified on the label as 'Junior'. It is important to choose the right food for your cocker's stage of life.

If you are concerned about what is the best food for your spaniel's life stage, you should consult your veterinarian to determine what is appropriate for your cocker.

In the United Kingdom, the Pet Food Manufacturers' Association (PFMA) standards state that 'all information given on a pet food label must be truthful and not misleading about the nature and quality of the product'. Also, 'the law requires a statutory statement to be put on every label or package, which must contain certain obligatory declarations.'

These must state:

- Whether the product is complete or complementary.
- The species for which the product is intended.
- Directions for use/feeding instructions.

An ideal, nutritional diet for your cocker spaniel contains protein, carbohydrates, fats, fibre, vitamins, and minerals to be certain your dog has all the nourishment they need. Maintaining a healthy, well-balanced diet will not only keep your best friend trim, but it will also help them live a longer, healthier, and happier life.

Emerging, but inconclusive, scientific evidence suggests a dog could do very well on a 'plant-based' diet. These studies argue that available meat sources today are often polluted with wheat, chemicals, drugs, and other products that would not be part of a wild dog's natural diet. Note that one of the world's longest living canines was a highly energetic border collie who was fed a clean, organic, plant-based diet, and lived to be over 25 years old, even though the average for the breed is 14. It is highly likely that feeding a clean, organic diet to a dog will increase their lifespan.

Top Food Tips

As responsible owners, we should be actively involved in what we are feeding our dogs and look for ways to improve their diet. Hopefully, the following tips will make it easier for you to choose the best food possible for your cocker spaniel:

1. Carefully examine what is really in the dog food.
2. Be careful not to choose food based upon entertaining ads whose job is to make even the worst foods look appealing and healthy. Beware of clever marketing, simply because it IS very clever.
3. Realise that, just because the vet is selling food, it does not mean it is necessarily the best choice for your dog.
4. Avoid feeding food that states a shelf life of 12 to 24 months. This means there are many preservatives that may not be a healthy choice.
5. Add fresh whole foods to your cocker's diet.
6. Puree vegetables and fruits for maximum absorption.
7. Add foods that are high in antioxidants to help reduce inflammation—blueberries, blackberries, squash, sweet potatoes, etc.
8. Choose organic fruits and vegetables whenever possible.
9. If organic is difficult to find, scrub toxins from fruit and vegetables. You can do this by soaking them in four parts water, one-part cider vinegar and gently brushing with a soft bristle brush.
10. Gluten is harmless, but it can create long-lasting and occasionally irreparable damage for the small percentage of dogs suffering from gluten intolerance or celiac disease.
11. Stay away from genetically modified foods (GMO) often found in pet food.
12. Consider CBD oil to help improve appetite, reduce anxiety and inflammation, and for pain relief of sore or arthritic joints.
13. Clean dog bowls and dishes daily with white vinegar that disinfects and is odourless when dry. Some dogs are allergic or sensitive to commercial soaps and cleaners.
14. Practise a controlled feeding timetable and feed at the same time each day.
15. If your cocker seems bored, feed their mind when you feed their body by giving them meals in a food puzzle.
16. Become familiar with what foods are dangerous for dogs (see Toxic Food, Plants, and Products, Chapter 15).
17. Discard opened canned or wet food within two days of opening.
18. Dogs are always interested in food. However, it does not mean they are hungry or need more food. Constantly giving them food can lead to unwanted behaviour problems, such as 'begging for food' and hyperactivity whenever they see people eating. Dogs are hard-wired to constantly forage and look for food. No matter how much you feed them, they will still ask for more. You can prevent obesity by sticking to your dog's regular feeding schedule.
19. Choose organic, single ingredient treats.

20. When your cocker begins to show signs of aging—between 8 and 9 years old—their feeding schedule might need to be adjusted to help them maintain their ideal weight. Some senior cockers prefer to be fed only once a day.
21. When you are out and a kind person offers to give your dog a treat, thankfully decline and explain that they are on a special diet, so your dog will not be eating treats that might not be a good choice.
22. You can help your cocker maintain optimum health throughout their life by keeping an open mind, questioning everything, and feeding based on their specific nutritional requirements. Remember to consider age, size, and activity level, as this will change over time and is different for every dog.
23. The most important thing to bear in mind when feeding your cocker spaniel is to ensure they eat a complete and balanced diet.
24. Keep an eye on the condition of their body and coat. If your dog appears to be thriving on their food and they have a glossy coat, plenty of energy, and a fit appearance, clearly, their food agrees with them. It is possible the way the food has been processed or the ingredients it contains could prevent your cocker from absorbing all the needed nutrients. If your dog has a dull coat and lacks energy, try changing to another kind of food.

25. Also, check the back garden for other signs of trouble, such as an abundance of faeces, which might indicate a problem with digestibility. If this is the case, you should reconsider your dog's diet.
26. Assess your cocker's activity level. If your cocker is active and exercises outdoors, they might need 20% to 40% more food. Working dogs usually need a food designed for working or performance dogs. Such foods have a higher fat content to provide extra calories.
27. Serious illness, pregnancy, or nursing can increase your cocker's energy requirements. Ask your vet about adjusting the quantity or type of food.
28. The feeding charts on pet food labels are a useful guide. Begin by checking the amount recommended for your dog's weight range. If your cocker is on the lower end of the scale, feed the lower recommended amount. Dogs who are on the heavier end could require more food.

FACT ***Many of the common diseases affecting the canine population have a direct correlation with over-feeding and/or feeding poor quality foods.***

Dog Food Types

Dog food has significantly changed since 1785, when the English Sportsman's Dictionary described the best diet for a dog's health in an article entitled 'Dog'. This article indicated that the best food for a dog was something called 'Greaves', described as 'the sediment of melted tallow made into cakes for dogs' food'.

From these meagre beginnings, commercially manufactured dog food has become a massively lucrative industry that has only recently evolved beyond feeding our dogs the dregs of human leftovers, as it was cheap and convenient to do so. Even today, most dog foods have far more to do with their convenience for people to store and serve than being a nutritionally balanced, healthy food choice for our canine companions.

Thankfully, there is always new research coming to the forefront, and we can help ourselves to be well informed by talking to experts and reading everything published about canine food. Educating yourself about what is available, plus considering the requirements of your cocker spaniel, such as their age, energy, and activity levels are key factors when choosing the appropriate food.

Knowing our dogs also suffer from many of the same life-threatening diseases commonly found in human society, such as heart disease, cancer, diabetes, and obesity helps us make better food choices.

There is no doubt that choosing the best food for your cocker spaniel can mean the difference between a shortened lifespan or a long life with few health issues. Unfortunately, there is no simple answer to the 'What should I feed' question, due to the endless variety of food products on the market and the uniqueness of every dog. Read on to learn about the different diet choices, how to read the food labels and what your cocker's nutritional needs are. With this information, you can make educated and healthy food choices for your furry friend.

The Raw Diet

Raw feeding has grown in popularity over the past few years. Even popular pet shops stock commercially prepared raw food. Although, there are numerous confusing arguments both for and against raw feeding that can prove to be a real minefield. Frequently, it is hard to know how to do the right thing for your cocker, as you will often find strong arguments both for and against raw feeding.

Raw feeding is exactly what it sounds like—feeding your spaniel raw ingredients, instead of traditional cooked food that is more commonly available. The usual ingredients in a raw diet include organ meats, muscle meat, whole or ground bone, raw eggs, and dog-safe fresh fruits and vegetables. The raw meals for dogs can be homemade, store-bought, freeze-dried, frozen, or fresh.

Advocates of raw feeding believe the ideal diet is one that is like what a dog living in the wild would have access to while hunting or foraging. It is claimed that raw food is packed full of all the essential nutrients required for a balanced diet. Often, these canine purists are opposed to feeding their dog any sort of commercially manufactured dog foods, as they consider them to be poor substitutes, and claim the following potential benefits:

- Healthier, shiny coats.

- Less shedding.
- Fewer allergy problems.
- Healthier skin.
- Fresher breath.
- Cleaner teeth.
- Improved energy levels.
- Better digestion.
- Smaller stools.
- A strengthened immune system.
- Increased mobility in arthritic dogs.
- Overall improvement in health.

Conversely, critics of the raw diet report the following cons:

- There are larger fragments of bones in raw dog food that might be difficult for dogs to eat.
- It could lead to infections and gastrointestinal inflammation.
- Dogs who suffer from kidney or liver diseases should not be given raw food as it has high levels of protein that are difficult for dogs to digest.
- Preparing the meals at home is very time-consuming. Plus, it is relatively more expensive than cooked dog food readily available in the market.
- The bacteria and parasites in raw bones and meat presents a significant contagion risk. Whilst some of these bacteria are unlikely to have negative effects on health, others can have serious consequences. For example, it has been discovered that between 20-44 percent of commercial raw meat diets are contaminated with salmonella. These harmful bacteria are of particular concern to those who have children or elderly people at home—or for those who have a compromised immune system.
- Diarrhoea and bowel constructions can be triggered in dogs through eating raw dog food.
- Raw dog food—especially homemade—is often nutrient deficient for dogs and can create health problems. You should consult your vet if you decide to feed homemade raw food to your cocker, to make sure the nutritional value of their meal meets their requirements.
- As they are more susceptible to bacteria, many experts advise that raw dog food should not be given to dogs suffering from cancer or other such diseases.

Although raw diets might provide some benefits, the cost—financial, time, and contagion risk—is relatively high. If your cocker spaniel has certain medical issues or allergies, switching to raw food might be worth a try. However, for most families, a cooked, manufactured dog food diet is a better choice.

Even if traditional dog food is giving your cocker stomach problems, you should try a homemade, cooked diet before committing to raw. There are many other changes you can make to help your spaniel if they have digestive issues. Just changing to a different kind of kibble or protein source could be the fix your dog needs.

Maybe, instead of feeding your dog a raw diet, consider adding wet food or supplements, such as fish oil to your cocker's kibble. These adjustments are far more feasible for most owners and can provide many of the benefits that are associated with a raw diet.

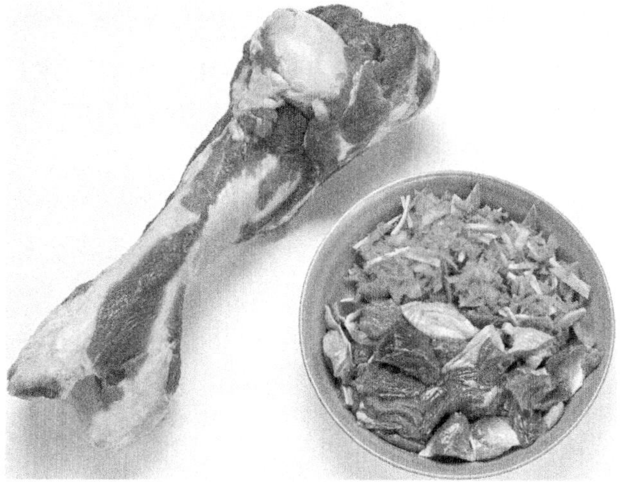

You need to ensure the food you choose is good enough for your dog if you do decide to try the raw diet. In the United Kingdom, vets and owners can easily source frozen raw meals that are readily prepared and formulated to the same European standards as the other pet foods found in our supermarkets and veterinary surgeries.

Always try to source your raw foods from Defra-registered producers. These products are governed by bacteriological rules more stringent than even human-grade raw meat products. They are supplied in clean, hygienic packaging. A huge variety of frozen raw meals specially formulated to match canine nutritional needs are available from companies such as Paleo Ridge and Naturaw.

Another consideration to bear in mind is you will need a big freezer to store your cocker's frozen raw food. This is an extra expense, and it is not always feasible as extra space is required to install it in the house.

Over the years, several variations of raw diets have been developed. The most significant ones are the Raw meaty bones, the BARF diet, and the Prey model raw, and they are discussed below.

Raw Meaty Bones

Renowned Australian veterinarian, Dr Tom Lonsdale advocates this diet, which consists mainly of the following:

- Raw meaty bones or carcasses when available. You should not feed cooked bones as thy can cause tearing of the oesophagus, stomach, or intestinal lining, which can cause internal bleeding or perforation.
- Both cooked and raw table scraps, such as vegetables.
- Fresh, clean water must always be available.
- Dr Tom Lonsdale also suggests you should feed your cocker the following foods:
- Poultry by-products, including heads, feet, necks, and wings.
- Turkey and chicken carcasses, after the meat has been removed for human consumption.
- Sheep, goat, calf, and deer carcasses sawn into large pieces of meat and bone.
- Whole fish and their heads.
- Other by-products include pig's heads, pig's trotters, tail bones, sheep heads, brisket, rib bones.
- Tripe, liver, lungs, trachea, hearts, omasums—stomach of ruminants.

Based on raw, meaty bones, an approximate food consumption guide for the average dog is 15-20 % of body weight in one week or 2-3 percent per day. That means, if your cocker has an average weight of 14 kg, they require up to 2.8 kg of carcasses or raw meaty bones every week. These figures are only a rough guide and relate to adult dogs in a domestic environment.

This diet claims, fish, birds, and low-fat game animals provide the best source of food for domesticated carnivores. If sourcing meat from farm animals—cattle, sheep, and pigs—avoid excessive fat, or any bones too large to be eaten.

Growing puppies and pregnant or lactating females might need much more food than adult animals of similar body weight.

Dr Tom Lonsdale also states:

'Providing scraps do not form too great a proportion of the diet, they appear to do no harm and may do some good. I advise an upper limit of one-third scraps for dogs. Liquidising scraps, both cooked and raw, in the kitchen mixer may help to increase their digestibility.

'Wild carnivores feed at irregular intervals. In a domestic setting regularity works best and accordingly I suggest that you feed adult dogs and cats once daily. If you live in a hot climate, I recommend that you feed pets in the evening to avoid attracting flies.

'I suggest that on one or two days each week your dog may be fasted—just like animals in the wild. On occasions you may run out of natural food. Do not be tempted to buy artificial food, fast your dog and stock up with natural food the next day. Puppies, sick or underweight dogs should not be fasted—unless on veterinary advice.'

Be aware:

- Older cats and dogs raised on a processed diet could experience initial difficulty when changed to a natural diet.
- Dogs with a dental disease or misshapen jaws might experience difficulties with a natural diet.
- Introduce variety as any nutrients fed to excess can be harmful.
- Whilst liver is an excellent food it should not be fed more than once a week.
- Although whole fish are a great source of food for carnivores, avoid constantly feeding one species of fish. Some species, such as carp, contain an enzyme that destroys thiamine—vitamin B1.

Foods to avoid:

- Excessive amounts of meat off the bone—not balanced.
- Too many vegetables—not balanced.
- Smaller pieces of bone—could be swallowed whole and become stuck.
- Cooked bones—they can splinter and/or get stuck.
- Vitamin and mineral additives—these create imbalance.
- Processed food—can lead to dental and other diseases.
- Large amounts of starchy food—associated with bloat.
- Garlic, onions, and chocolate—toxic for dogs.
- Currants, grapes, raisins, sultanas—toxic for dogs.
- Corn cobs and fruit stones (pits)—can get stuck.
- Milk—associated with diarrhoea. Animals will drink milk whether thirsty or not and subsequently get fat. Milk sludge sticks to gums and teeth.

You can find further information about this diet on Dr Tom Lonsdale's site: www.rawmeatybones.com.

If you are considering switching to a raw meaty bones diet, it is highly recommended that you consult your vet first.

BARF diet

The original raw diet is the Bones and Raw Food, or Biologically Appropriate Raw Food (BARF) diet, which was introduced by veterinarian Dr Ian Billinghurst in 1993. Like other raw diets, this diet is designed to mimic what dogs ate before they became domesticated. Although a dog's natural diet would be largely comprised of prey, they also scavenged for fruits and/or vegetables that were available to them. The BARF diet aims to replicate this and consists of roughly 70% meat, 10% bone, 10% offal—5% liver, 5% any other secreting organs—7% vegetables, and 3% fruit.

Prey Model Raw

A further version of the raw diet is the Prey Model Raw (PMR), which is like BARF but without the fruits and vegetables—there is a debate raging in the raw dog food arena about whether you should give your dog fruits and vegetables, and if so, how many. The guidelines for a PMR diet recommended 75-80% muscle meat, 10% raw edible bone, 5% liver, 5% other secreting organs, and 0-5% animal-based fibre, such as animal segments including fur or feathers.

The Dehydrated Diet

To preserve essential nutrients, vitamins, and minerals that occur naturally in the ingredients, dehydrated dog food (pictured) is made using a gentle, low-heat, drying method. The drying process mimics the natural process found in nature—the sun—preserving the ingredients. Drying food is a process that has been around for millennia, allowing you to keep food longer whilst it remains safe.

FACT ***Dehydrated recipes are made from minimally processed, fresh whole foods to create a healthy and nutritionally balanced meal to meet or exceed the daily dietary requirements of a healthy canine.***

Dehydrated dog food offers the benefits of raw diets without the hassle of defrosting. Therefore, it is convenient for travelling or camping since it is lighter and more nutrient dense than frozen, raw food, and does not require refrigeration.

Preparation is easy as you simply stir warm water into the food. The ratios/amounts are displayed on the feeding guide of the dog food bag, normally on the back. It is important to let it sit for 2-3 minutes, so the water fully rehydrates all the ingredients. The process guarantees all the nutrients, flavours, and aromas reach their optimum state ensuring your dog will love the taste and the benefits. If the food is not fully rehydrated it can swell in your cocker's stomach causing bloating and discomfort.

Once mixed with water, the dehydrated dog food looks like a stodgy form of gran's homemade stew. The chunks of ingredients in the food, such as chicken, barley, potatoes, flaxseed, organic oats, carrots, etc. are clearly visible.

The Freeze-Dried Diet

As with dehydration, freeze-drying is a way to remove water from perishable foods. The process of dehydration uses warm air to remove moisture, but freeze-drying involves three steps, freezing, primary drying, and secondary drying. By freezing before drying, freeze-dried foods (pictured) contain more nutrients than dehydrated ones because protein, vitamins, and minerals remain intact.

According to American holistic veterinarian Dr Marty Goldstein, your cocker will thrive when you feed them freeze-dried, raw food that contains three essential nutrients:

- Organ meat: a nutrient-rich source of energy for dogs.
- Omega-3 fatty acids: to help maintain brain health, make training easier, reverse aging, relieve joint pain, ease allergies, provide more energy for senior dogs.
- Natural prebiotics: flaxseed, pea flour, carrot, and ginger are prebiotics for good gut bacteria to promote digestion and serotonin production in dogs.

A freeze-dried, mostly raw meat diet with some healthy fats, vegetables, and fruits for good gut bacteria as well as powerful antioxidant support helps keep your dog healthy. Freeze-dried food is lightweight, easy to store, and simple to prepare, all you do is add a little water and wait three minutes for it to rehydrate. The freeze-drying process preserves all the nutrients that cooking destroys, so you can feed your cocker a healthy meal without losing any of its nutritional value.

The Dry Kibble Diet

There is no mistaking that, due to its convenience, dry dog food (pictured)—kibble—continues to be the most popular choice. There are several reasons why you might choose a dry kibble diet, such as:

- Dry kibble is usually more affordable.
- No refrigeration is required.
- Hard food exercises their jaws.
- It helps clean your spaniel's teeth.

Kibble brands have different ingredients, but all must be balanced and meet the nutritional needs of your cocker spaniel.

Kibble is prepared by processing raw ingredients together and cooking them. Typical ingredients include protein sources such as beef, poultry, fish, and eggs, as well as cereals, grains, vitamins, minerals, and antioxidants. Preservatives are necessary in all dry dog foods to prevent the fat from turning rancid. Some brands have high carbohydrate content or use low-quality ingredients and added sugar.

TIP ***Always check the label. Make sure the first ingredient in the kibble is a protein, not a grain. In quality kibble, protein dominates over starch, and many brands are even grain-free. The best kibbles have one protein source, such as lamb or chicken. Although there are grain-free kibbles,***

carbohydrates are necessary for energy. Also, the choice of grain is important since some dogs suffer from wheat, corn, or soybean allergies.

The Home-Cooked Diet

It is difficult to prove that taking the time to provide a home-cooked diet for your cocker spaniel is better than purchasing commercially produced dog food. However, one thing is certain, owners who prepare their own dog food know exactly what their dog is eating. There are several other considerations for choosing home-cooked food (pictured) for your dog, such as:

- To give variety to a picky eater.
- To provide fresh food with higher nutritional value.
- The ability to choose organic.
- Complete control over what they are eating.
- Alleviating fears over commercial food recalls.
- To avoid food allergy issues.

Although having complete control over what goes into your spaniel's dinner bowl can offer peace of mind, there are considerations to remember, including:

- The meal might not be balanced or address all the essential nutrients required by your dog.
- You need to make sure you do not choose ingredients that are unsafe for your cocker, such as onions, garlic, etc.
- It is challenging to find healthy and balanced recipes.
- Knowing how much home-cooked food to feed your dog can be difficult.
- You will probably need to add a multivitamin to ensure all vitamin and mineral requirements are met.

The bottom line is although a home-cooked diet certainly has its benefits, and when done correctly is a healthy alternative, there is much research and planning required to be certain the diet is nutritionally balanced.

The Canned (Wet) Food Diet

Some people would argue that a canned food diet is superior to dry kibble, as it:

- Contains fewer carbohydrates.
- Provides moisture.
- Is more appetising to most dogs.
- Contains no synthetic preservatives.
- Might contain fewer artificial flavours and colours.
- Usually contains more meat.
- Comes in air-tight packaging.
- Has a longer shelf life.

While the above list makes canned dog food look like a healthy option, there are a few things to consider about this dietary choice, such as:

- Canned food is usually more expensive.
- It cannot be left in a bowl for more than 1-2 hours.
- When exposed to the air, it can easily grow bacteria.
- Opened cans (pictured) must be kept refrigerated.
- It will only stay fresh for 2 to 3 days.

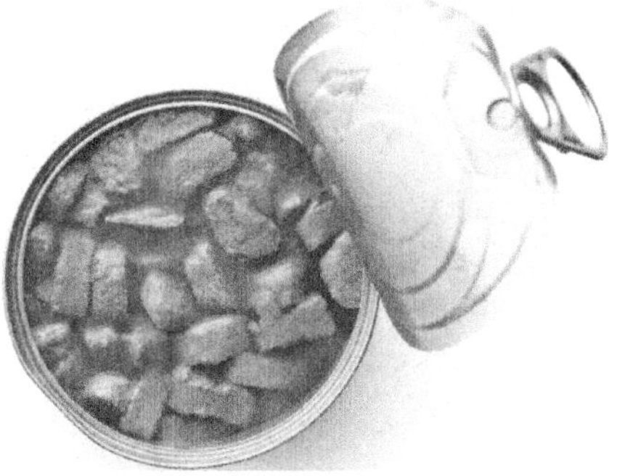

Many people choose to feed their spaniel a mixture of wet and dry food. This can cut the cost of your cocker's food while still giving them some of the health benefits and taste of wet food. If you decide to go down this road, make sure you still feed them the correct number of calories.

Several varieties of semi-moist dog food are available as well. These tend to be loaded with by-products and sugar, making them unhealthy as a primary diet for your dog. If your cocker is extremely picky, it is healthier to feed them wet food or mix some wet food into their dry food.

A Dog's Nutritional Requirements

Before deciding on the best food for your cocker spaniel and heading off to the pet food store, it is time well spent learning the basics about canine nutritional needs. Most of your dog's nutritional requirements should come from animal sources, including meat, fish, eggs, poultry, and seafood. Though dogs also need a balance of protein and fat in their diet, plus healthy carbohydrates to provide energy, fibre, and other essential nutrients.

Protein

The building blocks of protein consist of 23 amino acids, 10 of which must come from food. Protein is essential for survival and a strong immune system.

FACT ***Protein is the most important nutrient for your cocker spaniel and is required for healthy puppy growth and development. When your puppy is growing, protein helps them maintain lean muscle mass, so they do not become overweight or obese. Your puppy needs at least 22% protein in their diet, and when they reach adulthood, they need 18%.***

Fats

The second most important nutrient for your cocker is fat. While you might think of fat as a bad thing, it is an essential part of a balanced diet for your dog. Fat provides a concentrated source of energy and helps your dog absorb and utilise fat-soluble vitamins. Fat should come from healthy animal sources, such as chicken fat or salmon oil, and be at least 8% of your young cocker's diet. An adult dog requires a minimum of 5%.

Many kibble diets do not provide enough high-quality fats necessary to produce the much-needed energy in your dog's unique metabolism. Fat also helps keep your cocker spaniel's hair and skin healthy, reduces inflammation, and is necessary for the development and normal function of body tissues, muscles, and nerves.

High-fat diet concerns for people are not applicable to canines. You might not be aware that 90 to 95% of fat is easily metabolised by dogs and fats in their diet yield 2.5 times as much energy as proteins or carbohydrates.

Carbohydrates

Technically, even though your cocker does not have specific requirements for carbohydrates, they can provide energy as well as fibre and other nutrients. Your dog's body is not optimised for digesting and absorbing nutrition from plants as much as from animal products, which means carbohydrates in your dog's diet should be limited. They should come from sources such as whole grains, starchy vegetables, beans, or legumes.

TIP ***When your cocker eats a diet that contains a high amount of carbohydrates, instead of utilising the fat in the diet to fuel their metabolism, they use sugar. Burning sugar for fuel is known to place metabolic stress on your dog's body resulting in increased risk of serious health concerns, such as cancer, obesity, diabetes, and more.***

In many commercially prepared dog foods, cheaper, abundant carbohydrates that offer a long shelf-life are the dominant ingredient. The percentage of carbs found in the average off-the-shelf dog food is far higher than what would have been consumed in a dog's ancestral diet. Some statistics say the amount of carbohydrates has increased from 14% of the total ancestral diet to somewhere between 46 and 74% today.

It is important to choose healthy carbohydrate sources from plants and fruits called 'functional' carbohydrates. These contain minerals, vitamins, and phytonutrients that help promote your dog's optimum health and offer a wide range of additional health benefits, such as:

- Prevention and repair of DNA damage caused by daily exposure to environmental toxins.
- Reduced inflammation.
- Protection against heart disease.
- Regulation of hormone metabolism.
- Antioxidant protection of cell damage from free radicals.
- Enhancing their body's immune system and ability to fight disease.
- Blocking tumour activity.
- Killing cancerous cells.

Carbohydrates that are highly unsuitable for your cocker include anything processed with white sugar, salt, or flour. These are almost always empty calories that have had their nutritional value removed and quickly raise blood sugar levels. In moderate amounts, carbohydrates have their place in your dog's diet if they are 'functional' and healthy. The following are good sources of healthy, dog-friendly carbohydrates:

- Unprocessed whole vegetables and legumes—such as broccoli, Brussels sprouts, Bok Choy, carrots, cauliflower, cabbage, lettuce, parsley, spinach, black-eyed peas, garbanzo beans, kidney beans, lentils, lima beans, pinto beans, pumpkin, sweet potato, winter squash.
- Unprocessed whole fruits—such as apples, bananas, blackberries, blueberries, cantaloupe, pear, raspberries, watermelon.
- Whole grains—such as amaranth, buckwheat, millet, quinoa, sorghum, teff, gluten-free oats.

Minerals and Vitamins

If your cocker spaniel is not receiving all the minerals and vitamins essential for building strong bones and helping the many chemical reactions that take place inside their body, they need a supplement added to their diet. Even though vitamin and mineral requirements vary depending on your dog's age, all dogs have the following basic requirements:

- Minerals: calcium, chromium, copper, fluorine, iodine, magnesium, manganese, phosphorus, potassium chloride, selenium, sodium, sulphur, zinc.
- Vitamins: A, B family, C, D, E, K, Choline.

Water

Water accounts for half the weight of your adult cocker spaniel and is so important that a loss of just 10% can have fatal consequences. It is critical for your cocker's health for them to always have access to fresh, clean water. Water is the main component of healthy living cells in your dog's body and every vital function depends on it. An adequate amount of water:

- Helps digest food.
- Aids the absorption of nutrients.
- Cools the body and maintains normal body temperature.
- Helps release toxins and waste.
- Lubricates and cushions joints making movement easier.
- Keeps the cells hydrated.

Depending on their size, age, activity level, and the climate they live in, your cocker will usually need to drink approximately 30 millilitres (1 ounce) of water for every 0.5 kilograms (1.1 pounds) of body weight each day to maintain their health. As an example, a dog weighing 30 kilograms (66 pounds) will need to drink 1.8 litres (61 ounces).

FACT ***Humans can last about a week without water, but dogs may only last about three days. When your cocker is not drinking enough, it is highly likely they will become dehydrated, which can lead to kidney failure. Some signs of dehydration include a dry nose, dry eyes and dry, sticky, or light-coloured gums.***

When uncertain about whether your dog is suffering from dehydration, there is a simple test that helps identify it. Grab the skin at the top of the shoulder blades—where a mother dog might pick up a puppy—and lift it up. If it falls back into place quickly, there is likely no problem. However, if the skin slowly descends to its original form, this could be an indication of dehydration. Also, if your dog is suffering from an extended bout of diarrhoea, they can soon show signs of dehydration.

Reading Labels & Choosing Food

Learning how to correctly decipher those commercial dog food product labels can be more challenging than one might expect. Let us get used to the manufacturer's lingo, so we feel confident we are feeding a quality product to our spaniel.

The Law Versus the Lingo

Legally, pet food manufacturers must list what ingredients are in the food by weight.

However, what we mere owners may not be aware of is the weight is determined before the food is processed, including the moisture content.

Therefore, to avoid being tricked by clever wording, you need to be careful. Whilst 'deboned chicken' sounds good, it is full of weight-adding moisture. When the food is extruded and turned into kibble, all the moisture evaporates, and the chicken content is greatly reduced.

The meat content is extremely important and should be the first ingredient on the list, right? Yes, this makes sense, however, often the most misunderstood ingredient listed on pet food labels is 'meal'. Frequently, there are 'meat meals' used in the production of kibble and seen in the ingredients list, because when compared to fresh meat, the meal contains a higher protein content. This sounds good, but is it really?

FACT ***While the law states that a 'meal' must contain bone and meat, there can be other unnamed sources in the meal, including feathers, blood, dead animal carcasses, inedible meat scraps, hide, hooves, internal organs, fat, and bone. In other words, the meal could be almost exclusively comprised of the leftover animal parts that are unfit for human consumption.***

When a meal product is listed, the protein count is increased, and this can fool consumers into believing they are choosing a healthy product. The truth is the food they are choosing might not necessarily mean a high-quality product, as there may be very little beef, chicken, or other meat in the meal.

Of course, the next question on your mind probably is 'Should I buy dog food that lists 'meal' as an ingredient'. There is no simple answer to the question because making an informed decision requires discovering where the meal came from and exactly what is in it. This requires contacting the manufacturer and asking them to provide a written guarantee as to what is in the meal they list on their product, and by the time you get a definitive answer, they might have changed their ingredients.

The Rules

In the United States, the FDA enforces rules to regulate how a dog food label is written:

The 95% Rule – In food that has few ingredients, at least 95% of the product must be the named ingredients, excluding water added for processing and condiments. If the water content is included, the named ingredients must comprise 70% of the product. If a product is called 'Lamb Dog Food', for example, the product weight, not including water and condiments must be 95% lamb. Ingredients added for nutritional purposes, such as minerals, vitamins, and small amounts of other ingredients required to formulate the product make up the remaining 5%. As ingredients are listed in order of predominance by weight, 'lamb' should be the first ingredient listed on the label, followed usually by water, vitamins, and minerals. But bear in mind, the ingredients are listed by weight before being cooked, meaning beef is going to weigh a lot more pre-cooked. In the case of a mixed recipe like chicken and rice, 95% should be comprised of chicken and rice not counting water; when you factor in water, chicken and rice should make up at least 70%.

The 25% Rule – This applies to products often labelled as 'Dinner', 'Entrée', 'Platter' or 'Chow', such as 'Pedigree Chopped Ground Dinner with Beef'. To meet the 25% rule, the named ingredient must make up at least 10% of the total weight and at least 25% of the product weight not including water. With food that lists more than one ingredient in the name, like 'Beef with Vegetables & Potatoes', none of those named ingredients can be less than 3% of the total weight.

The with Rule – This rule applies to food labels like 'Honest Jack's Dog Food with Chicken'; the 3% or 'With' rule states that this food must contain at least 3% of chicken to the total weight. Any named ingredient must equal at least 3%. For example, 'Rover's Dog Food with Beef and Rice' must contain at least 3% beef and 3% rice.

The Flavour Rule – If the label says, 'Beef Flavour Dog Food,' then 'a specific percentage—of the beef—is not required, but a product must contain an amount sufficient to be able to be detected.' In this example, the word 'flavour' must appear on the label in the same size, style, and colour as the word 'beef.'

Unfortunately, without being involved in the manufacturing process or having access to someone who can vouch for the efficacy of the food, there is really no way to determine the true quality of a manufactured dog food simply by reading the ingredients list. Furthermore, there are many dog food labels that try to sell their products based on clever advertising ploys that portray healthy images of dogs playing or running with wild abandon over grassy fields and looking literally the 'picture' of health.

We can be part of a change for more transparent food labelling of pet food, when we take a more active role and get involved by calling the number on the food label and asking for product information that may not be as forthcoming as conscientious owners would like.

TIP ***When shopping for dog food, take the time to carefully read the information on the package, so you can determine the quality of the product. If you are going to make comparisons between different products, there are three specific things to look for on the label.***

Choosing a High-Quality Dog Food Brand

Analytical Constituents

In the United Kingdom, the next thing to look for is the Analytical Constituents—called Guaranteed Analysis in the U.S. This tells you the percentages of protein, fat, fibre, and moisture contained in the product. You can use the analytical constituents to make a direct comparison between products, bearing in mind the minimum values from the previous section. Because your cocker will have difficulty digesting too much fibre, look for products that keep the fibre content less than 5%.

Following are the ingredients you should look for in dog food products that constitute healthy food options, especially if they are organically sourced:

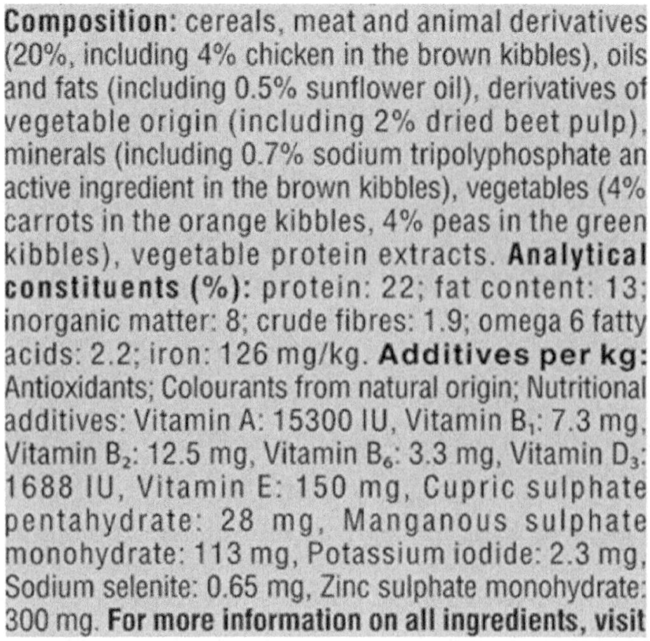

Composition: cereals, meat and animal derivatives (20%, including 4% chicken in the brown kibbles), oils and fats (including 0.5% sunflower oil), derivatives of vegetable origin (including 2% dried beet pulp), minerals (including 0.7% sodium tripolyphosphate an active ingredient in the brown kibbles), vegetables (4% carrots in the orange kibbles, 4% peas in the green kibbles), vegetable protein extracts. **Analytical constituents (%):** protein: 22; fat content: 13; inorganic matter: 8; crude fibres: 1.9; omega 6 fatty acids: 2.2; iron: 126 mg/kg. **Additives per kg:** Antioxidants; Colourants from natural origin; Nutritional additives: Vitamin A: 15300 IU, Vitamin B_1: 7.3 mg, Vitamin B_2: 12.5 mg, Vitamin B_6: 3.3 mg, Vitamin D_3: 1688 IU, Vitamin E: 150 mg, Cupric sulphate pentahydrate: 28 mg, Manganous sulphate monohydrate: 113 mg, Potassium iodide: 2.3 mg, Sodium selenite: 0.65 mg, Zinc sulphate monohydrate: 300 mg. **For more information on all ingredients, visit**

- Meat listed as the No. 1 and No. 2 ingredients.
- Carbohydrates—brown rice, whole oats, pearled barley, sweet potato, whole grains.
- Vegetables—sweet potatoes, peas, carrots.
- Fruits—apples, blueberries, blackberries.
- Healthy fats—omega-3, omega-6, olive oil.
- Vitamins—B, A, and E.
- Minerals and amino acids—zinc, potassium, calcium, manganese, L-Carnitine, DL-Methionine.
- No cheap fillers—corn meal, wheat gluten.
- No artificial preservatives—these are chemicals to make it last longer.

Composition List

GUARANTEED ANALYSIS	COMPOSITION:
Protein 36% Fat Content 16% Crude Fibre 4% Crude Ash 9% Omega-6 Fatty Acids 2,2% Omega-3 Fatty Acids 1,1% Glucosamine 900 mg/kg Chondroitin Sulphate 1200 mg/kg	Turkey 32% (Fresh Turkey 16%, Dehydrated Turkey 16%), Chicken 30% (Dehydrated Chicken 16%, Chicken Fat 8%, Chicken Gravy 6%), Peas 20%, Potato Protein, Beet Pulp 4%, Linseed 3%, Dried Potatoes, Salmon Oil 1%, Lignocellulose, Carrots, Apples, Yeast Extract (source of mannan — oligosaccharides) 0,5%, Dried Chicory Root (source of Fructo-oligo-saccharides and Inulin) 0,5%, Broccoli, Spinach, Tomatoes, Blueberries, Cranberries 0,01%, Dried Peppermint, D-Glucosamine Hydrochloride 100 mg/kg, Chondroitin Sulphate 100 mg/kg, Yucca Schidigera.

The final place to look is the Composition List—called Ingredients in the U.S.The composition list is in descending order by volume, which means the ingredients at the top of the list are used in the highest quantity, which is the same as the packages of food you eat.

You need to see healthy, high-quality ingredients at the beginning of the list, starting with a source of animal protein. Remember, your cocker's body is better at digesting and absorbing nutrition from animal sources.

AAFCO Statement of Nutritional Adequacy (if you are in the U.S.)

First, look for the Association of American Feed Control Officials (AAFCO) statement of nutritional adequacy. This is an organisation that sets and upholds standards for pet food and animal feed.

Before a product lands on the shelf, this organisation examines it to make sure it meets the minimum nutritional requirements for the intended animal, which in this case is your cocker spaniel. If the product is nutritionally balanced for your dog, you will see a statement like this somewhere on the label:

'[Product Name] is formulated to meet the nutritional levels established by the AAFCO Dog Food Nutrient Profiles'

If you see this on the package, you can rest assured it will meet your dog's minimum nutritional needs. However, the AAFCO statement does not guarantee quality—you still need to read the ingredients list noted on the package to determine whether it is a nutritious choice for your dog.

Choosing the Right Bowls

There are many different types and categories of food and water bowls for dogs, and it is important to choose one appropriately sized for your cocker.

The various water and food bowls in the market are:

Long Ear Bowl (pictured) – This bowl is designed with long-eared dogs, such as cocker spaniels in mind. It is narrower at the top, allowing your dog to put their head in it without getting their ears dirty or wet. Cockers are very prone to ear infections and this type of bowl will help to avoid them.

Elevated Bowls or Dining Tables (pictured) – These bowls provide easier access to food and water and a more comfortable drinking and eating experience as your dog is not bending down to floor level. For dogs who are messy eaters, elevated dog bowls are perfect, and according to some veterinarians, they are a healthier way for dogs to feed. Older dogs with stiff necks or backs can also find these feeders more comfortable.

Ceramic or Stoneware Bowls – The stylish, ceramic or stoneware bowl is another good choice for your spaniel. Though they can be broken if they are dropped onto a hard surface, they are easy to clean and available in many interesting shapes, colours, and styles. As they are heavier than other bowls, they do not slide across the floor as the dog eats. Often, they have cute pictures or wording that dog owners find very appealing. A chipped, cracked, or broken bowl should always be avoided, because when the surface is damaged it can harbour harmful bacteria.

Travel Bowls – As the name suggests, travel bowls are lightweight and often collapsible and can be a handy addition to your cocker's travel essentials. This bowl can be attached to the lead and be a lifesaver when out walking with your thirsty dog on a hot day.

Stainless Steel No Skid, No Tip Bowls (pictured) – This type of bowl is pretty much indestructible, easy to clean, and as the bottom is wider, it won't tip over. Also, the rubberised base prevents it from skidding across the floor. This kind of bowl can also be used as a slow feeder simply by turning it upside down.

Travel Water Containers – Your dog can be trained to drink water from a bottle, or you could carry a collapsible bowl and a regular water bottle. Additionally, there are many travel containers made especially for active dogs who need to quench their thirst. Whatever travelling water system is chosen, it is always a good idea to get your puppy used to drinking from it when they are still young. Otherwise, they may refuse to drink from anything other than their usual bowl.

Slow Feeder Bowls (pictured)– If your dog gulps their food too quickly, consider a slow feeder bowl to slow the speed at which they consume their food. To ensure your cocker takes time to digest their food correctly and not suffer from stomach pains or discomfort after eating, or life-threatening bloat, anti-gulp and slow dog feeders are an ideal way to control fast eating. Their specially designed rivets prevent dogs eating the complete bowl in just a few mouthfuls.

Gravity Water Container – Your cocker spaniel will drink a lot of water every day to stay healthy, and sometimes, you might be unaware their water bowl is empty. Choosing a larger water gravity container, or an automatic watering fountain, is a good way to ensure your cocker always has access to the water they need.

TIP ***When your cocker spaniel is a puppy, choose smaller bowls and as they grow, adjust the bowl so it is compatible with their size.***

How much food

This is a common question posed by owners. Unfortunately, there is no direct answer. Depending on the breed, age, weight, lifestyle, activity level, and metabolic rate, their needs vary. **Even two same-age cocker spaniels might have totally different caloric requirements, as one could be super energetic and the other a couch potato.**

A dog feeding adage says: 'Watch the dog, not the dish'. Portion sizes should be determined by body condition, not by how much is eaten or left in the bowl. The size of your cocker's appetite depends on their metabolism and body type, and nutritional needs vary from one dog to another. Do not worry if your puppy occasionally skips meals or picks at food. This could indicate they are ready to stop eating or you have given them too much and need to reduce the quantity served.

Following the advice of your vet and checking the feeding instructions on the dog food manufacturer's labels are important steps for managing your dog's weight. Therefore, you should remember the portion size recommended on the packaging is often more than is required. Label recommendations should only serve as a guide. Dogs' metabolisms vary the same as humans do, so the amount should be adjusted as they gain or lose weight.

TIP ***A practical way to check your dog's weight is to apply slight pressure to the sides of their chest. If you can feel their ribs without being able to see them, their weight is okay.***

In the hope of helping owners better understand their dog's daily food requirements, there are many online dog calorie calculators, such as the Pet Food Manufacturers Association (PFMA) calculator:

www.pfma.org.uk/dog-calorie-calculator-nrc-method

What you do is enter your cocker's weight and activity level and your chosen dog food % constituents, and the calculator tells you the recommended daily feeding amount. Again, bear in mind, these are just generic recommendations and each dog, and their energy requirements is different!

Feeding Puppies

Proper feeding is critical when it comes to puppies. Since cockers grow so quickly during their first few months, they need an especially nutritious diet to grow into healthy, strong adults. They require high calorie and nutritional levels of food, so they should be fed a high-quality puppy food brand. If puppies are fed regular, adult dog food, they are not likely to develop normally. Consult your veterinarian for specific recommendations, but the best puppy foods are high in protein, calcium, and calories.

How Often – Puppies need to be fed small amounts regularly throughout the day to avoid over-stretching their stomachs. This type of feeding also keeps their energy levels high all day long. Here is a typical cocker puppy feeding schedule:

- After weaning—around 8 weeks old—and up to 4 months old: 4 meals per day.
- Between 4 months and 6 months: 3 meals per day.
- Over the age of 6 months and for the rest of their life: 2 meals each day, morning, and evening.

Note, when feeding twice a day, one third is recommended in the morning and the rest at night, but not too late.

Your cocker spaniel puppy should have their meals evenly spaced. For example, if you feed them at 7:00 am—and they have 4 meals per day—their next meal should be at 11:00 am, 3:00 pm, and 7:00 pm. It is fine to change these times to fit your lifestyle but be sure to leave plenty of time between their last meal and bedtime to allow them to digest their food.

You should always ensure your puppy is eating and drinking enough throughout the day. The smaller the puppy, the more important this is.

TIP ***Before you bring your puppy home, the breeder might give you a small bag of puppy food together with instructions about their feeding schedule. It is recommended to continue feeding this to your cocker spaniel as the food is specifically formulated for your pup's growth and development during their early months, and their delicate stomach and digestive system is used to it.***

Transitioning to Adult Feeding – Once your cocker puppy reaches adulthood, they do not need as many calories. Unless they are highly active, continuing to feed rich puppy food to your adult spaniel can quickly lead to excessive weight gain, so their transition to adult food is important.

Typically, most puppies successfully transition to eating adult dog food by the time they are six to eight months old and certainly by the time they are a year old. When it is time to switch, select a dog food labelled '***Adult***'.

Here are a few puppy feeding tips that might come in handy:

- Leave your puppy to eat in peace. If you take their bowl away when they are eating it can make them anxious, which could lead to food aggression. To be certain your cocker feels comfortable if you approach them at mealtimes, add a small amount of food to the bowl while they are eating, so they see you as an ally, not a threat.

- You should never feed your puppy before travelling in the car, as this can cause carsickness.
- You should avoid feeding your puppy an hour before or after exercise as this could contribute to stomach dilation and torsion—also known as bloat. This is a life-threatening condition requiring immediate veterinary intervention.
- Growth-and-weight charts are available both in print and online. Weigh your puppy every week and record their progress, comparing them to breed-appropriate weight charts. Adjust their food intake to achieve an average rate of growth.
- Before implementing any major change in your cocker puppy's diet, consult your vet, and if possible, the breeder. Once you have a formula that works, stick with it. Any sudden changes in food can cause digestive problems.
- To ensure your spaniel puppy gets what they require, choose a food specially designed for them and buy the best dog food you can afford.

Feeding Senior Dogs

Just like people, as dogs become older, their metabolism slows down and they become less active than they once were. Continuing to feed them the same amount of food when the calories are no longer burned during vigorous daily exercise results in fat being stored, which could add excess weight. The last thing you want for your older cocker who could have weakened joints is extra kilograms to carry around.

TIP ***If your senior cocker spaniel is gaining weight, feeding a little less during mealtimes—20% fewer calories as a rule of thumb—will usually keep them trim.***

Conversely, some aging dogs begin to lose weight because their muscle mass diminishes. In which case, they need to have their caloric intake increased and more protein added to help maintain muscle mass.

Occasionally, an older dog suffering from kidney disease will urinate more often. In addition, some medications have a diuretic effect, making them more prone to becoming dehydrated. Therefore, always provide a fresh, cool source of clean water as drinking plenty is even more important in advanced age.

As dogs enter their senior years, their joints might not perform as well as they once did, and they could become stiff and feel pain from arthritis. In such an instance, your vet might recommend a dog food with added glucosamine, which many senior dog foods have. This can help reduce pain and allow your dog to get around easier. You can also buy glucosamine supplements and/or a natural pain reliever, such as CBD drops, to keep your dog more active and pain-free.

As your cocker ages, they might begin to lose fur or develop strange skin issues they never had in the past. Your vet might recommend dog food with higher fat content—specifically omega-3 and omega-6. These beneficial fats can be found in widely available fish oil supplements, which most dogs love the taste of.

If your cocker spaniel suffers from dental issues, you might want to move away from dry kibble altogether. You could try a softer dog food, such as wet canned dog food or fresh delivered dog food, both of which have a lot more moisture. This will let your dog eat comfortably, even with missing teeth or sensitive gums.

Many dog food companies manufacture dog foods with 'Senior' in the name or labelled for the 'Senior' dog. You might be surprised to learn there are no standards for what makes a 'Senior' dog food. In the U.S., the Association for American Feed Control Officials (AAFCO) has no 'Senior' life stage guidance for dog food nutrients. Therefore, every manufacturer can create any formula they want and market it as senior dog food.

While senior dog food might be marketed as a better diet for older dogs, there are no agreed upon standards for that being the case. Because this is the case, you should not feel the need to feed your dog a senior dog food. It is unnecessary to switch them from an adult dog food as they get older based on age alone. Most cockers do not need a special senior dog food to live a healthy life. If you have been feeding your dog a certain kind of dog food for years, there is no reason to switch them to anything else just because they are getting older. Of course, unless there are valid medical reasons that dictate a food change.

If you decide to switch to a senior dog food (pictured), it is important to gradually make the transition to their new food. Ideally, as with transitioning your puppy to adult food, this should be done over 7-10 days or more, with a complete transition to the new food within 14 days. If your cocker is prone to digestive problems, you might prefer to take longer to introduce the new food. If your cocker experiences digestive upset—vomiting, diarrhoea, or not eating—it would be best to stop the new diet and contact your vet.

If you are feeding your older cocker spaniel food that has been stored in the fridge, you will need to take it out up to two hours before mealtime to get it to the right temperature. If that is not possible, briefly microwave wet foods to warm them, but be careful to ensure it is not hot, or it could burn your cocker's sensitive mouth!

When it comes to mealtimes, consider feeding your older dog in a quiet place where they can eat in peace without being interrupted. If you have more than one dog, so one doesn't bully or snatch food from the other, feed them separately, but at the same time.

Treats

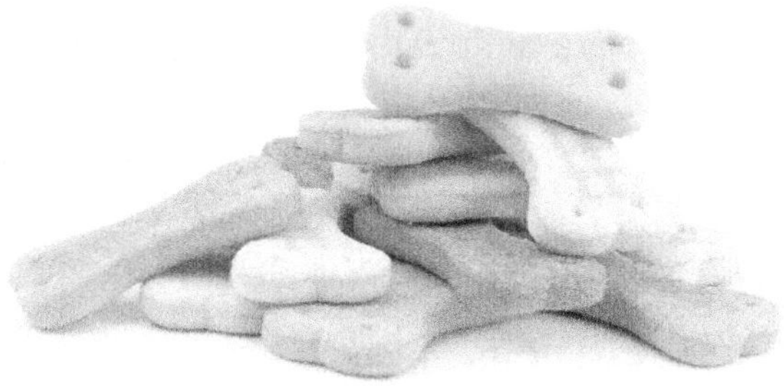

Most pet shop and grocery stores have their shelves lined with endless choices of dog treats (pictured), which can make it an overwhelming task to choose wisely, unless one simple rule is kept in mind: **Choose treats that contain either one ingredient or very few ingredients.**

Nevertheless, if you treat your cocker too often during the day, they can become overweight. Treats are usually very flavourful and appealing to your dog's palette. But too many tasty treats throughout the day can create a picky eater. The clever dog knows if they wait long enough, treats will soon be coming their way, therefore, they might be less excited about consuming their dinner.

Your puppy will probably consume more treats or snacks as incentives during training. However, it is suggested to feed no more than 10% of your dog's recommended daily caloric intake when giving treats or snacks. This is called the 90/10 rule.

FACT ***Researchers in Sweden have discovered that dogs were happier when they had to earn their treats as a reward for completing a task, rather than just being given one for looking cute. Just like humans who experience that happy 'eureka' moment when finally solving a problem, the same is true for dogs.***

Dangerous Treats

It is important to carefully read labels and take note of where treats are manufactured, because not all countries maintain the most stringent manufacturing protocols. As well, there are some treats that you absolutely should NOT be feeding to your dog, which are the following:

Rawhide (pictured) – Rawhide is made from the inner layer of horse or cow hides. During manufacturing, rawhide is soaked in an ash/lye solution to remove every particle of meat, fat, and hair, then soaked again in bleach to remove any remaining traces of the ash/lye solution. Now the product is technically no longer food, it does not have to comply with food regulations.

The wet rawhide is shaped into chews, and when dry it shrinks to approximately 25% of its original size. Then, arsenic-based products are used as preservatives, and antibiotics and insecticides are added to kill bacteria. Some rawhide treats include beef, chicken, or liver flavourings to make them more appealing to dogs.

Although rawhide chews are tough and long-lasting, when your cocker gnaws one, they will ingest many harsh chemicals. Also, when your dog swallows a piece of rawhide, it can swell to four times its size inside their stomach, which can cause anything from mild to severe gastric blockages This could become life threatening and require emergency surgery.

As convenient as it might be to give your cocker a treat that will occupy them for a considerable time, if it is rawhide, just say ‘***No***’.

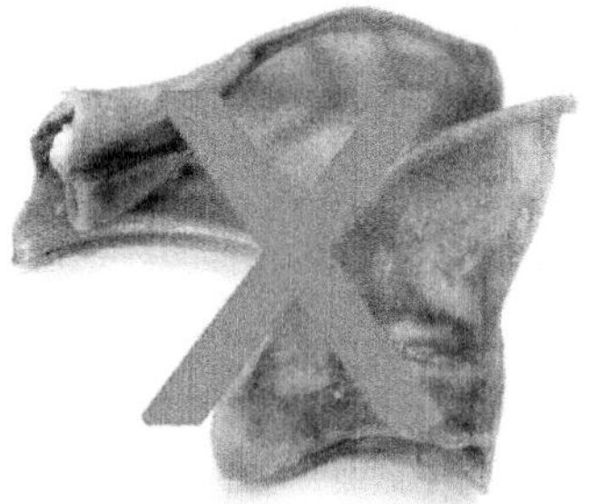

Pig’s Ears (pictured) – Pig’s ears are exactly what you might think they are—the dehydrated ear of a pig, specifically the flap of the ear called the pinna. This part of the ear is made up of skin and cartilage, and has barely any muscle, making them more flexible for dogs to munch.

These are very attractive to dogs and most eagerly devour them, and they are ‘natural’ as they are ears, so what could be wrong? They are thin, crispy, and very high in fat, which can cause stomach upsets, vomiting, and diarrhoea. Also, sharp pieces can break off and become stuck in your dog’s throat or cause perforations in the mouth, throat, or digestive tract.

Pig’s ears are often processed and preserved with unhealthy chemicals. As a discerning dog owner, you will NOT want to feed them to your dog. Just say, ‘***No***’.

Hoof Treats (pictured) – These are cow, bison, horse, and pig hooves that are cleaned, shaved, and dried for pet resale. They are marketed as healthy and ‘natural’ treat choices for dogs. The truth is after processing with harsh chemicals and preservatives, hooves retain little, if any, of their ‘natural’ qualities.

Furthermore, hooves are very hard and can cause the chipping or breaking of your cocker spaniel’s teeth as well as perforating their mouth, throat, or intestinal tract, or create blockages in their intestines. Another downside of giving hooves to your dog is the smell, which gets worse as they are chewed, and the stench can linger on carpet for days or even weeks.

Again, just say, '***No***'.

Healthy Treats

As there are so many healthy treat choices available, there is no excuse for feeding your cocker unhealthy, toxic, nutrient-deficient, or dangerous treats that could harm them.

Examples of healthy treats include:

Hard (Crunchy) Treats – Known as dog biscuits, these come in a range of shapes, sizes, and flavours and are designed to help keep your cocker's teeth cleaner. As an everyday reward for your dog, these are a great choice.

Soft Treats – Soft, chewy treats are also available in endless varieties and flavours. Due to their pleasing taste and soft texture, for immediate gratification small pieces are especially useful during training. As your dog can swiftly devour the treat, it is clear to them this a reward.

Dental Treats or Chews (pictured) – Dental treats are designed with the specific purpose of helping your spaniel maintain healthy teeth and gums by exercising their jaws and massaging their gums, while removing plaque build-up near the gum line.

TIP ***Even though the best way to take care of your cocker's oral hygiene is to brush their teeth every day, dog dental chews can be an excellent top-up between brushing or for dogs who will not let you get anywhere near their teeth without a struggle.***

Dental chews come in edible and non-edible varieties. Many cockers love these and think of them as a tasty treat. Non-edible chews are a bit like toys for many dogs and satisfy their natural urge to chew, while helping to clean their teeth at the same time.

Freeze-Dried and Jerky Treats (pictured) – These treats offer a tasty morsel most dogs find irresistible as they are usually made of simple, meaty ingredients, such as liver, poultry, and seafood. Be careful when choosing jerky treats, as they are often processed with too much salt.

As they are so flavoursome, many dog owners find these treats extremely useful when training. It is important to find a reputable manufacturer of jerky treats. Alternatively, if you have a food dehydrator, you can make your own meat jerky treats for your dog.

TIP ***Always check labels for high quality, making sure the treats chosen are the right size for your cocker spaniel and try to find treats with just one ingredient—or just a few ingredients.***

Supplements

Most commercial pet foods are formulated with a view to meeting all the requirements your dog needs to thrive. Nonetheless, all foods are not created equal, and neither are all dogs. The better pet food companies create their foods based on monitored feeding trials. However, there are many companies that do not go to such lengths and simply develop, package, and sell a formula that might have never been fed to a dog.

Just as they can for humans, supplemental vitamins and minerals can improve your cocker's health, as they help to protect the immune system and ensure your cocker's nutritional needs are met. It could be helpful to discuss this with your vet who is well versed in optimal diet requirements for cocker spaniels.

The following are the most popular supplements recommended for dogs:

- Glucosamine.
- Fish Oil.
- Antioxidants.
- Probiotics.
- CBD oil.
- Chondroitin sulphate.
- Multi-vitamins.

Glucosamine – This is the most popular supplement for dogs. Glucosamine is an amino sugar found naturally in the fluid around the joints and helps to build cartilage. It comes from the shells of shellfish and can also be made in the laboratory. Many dog owners and veterinarians believe glucosamine for dogs is effective in treating arthritis. In older dogs, it can relieve joint pain and improve mobility. It comes in several forms, including pills, powders, and as treats. Glucosamine supplements are usually formulated with chondroitin sulphate, which occurs naturally in the connective tissues of bone and cartilage.

Fish Oil (pictured) – The second most common supplement given to dogs is fish oil. It contains omega-3 fatty acids that are thought to ease skin allergies and improve coat quality and shine. A study in the American Journal of Veterinary Research suggests that fish oils also reduce inflammation, and many dog owners use it for this purpose.

Even if there is not a single symptom that points to an omega-3 deficiency in your spaniel, there are a few signs you should keep an eye out for. These are dull or dry coat, hair loss, obesity, eye problems, poor wound healing, or muscle weakness. Before giving your cocker a fish oil supplement, it is recommended to discuss it with your vet first. They will be pleased to put your dog's need for omega-3 in context by customising their diet and daily intake of supplements.

FACT ***Omega-3 might also influence your cocker puppy's mental development. Studies have shown that an omega-3-rich diet in your dog's infancy can improve cognitive functions, memory, and learning ability as they grow.***

Antioxidants – Antioxidant supplements (pictured) help slow and/or counteract the effects of the aging process by fighting 'free radicals', which are part of the normal metabolic process in both dogs and humans. They are cells that are missing a molecule, and when this happens, the cell tries to repair itself by stealing molecules from other healthy cells. This process then damages your cocker spaniel's DNA, which in turn makes them more prone to disease.

When your dog's body's natural defences against free radical damage are hindered, the result is chronic disease and increased aging that often includes cancer, heart/kidney/liver disease, damage to the joints, and brain dysfunction. Antioxidants' function is to strengthen the body's natural defences against free radical damage. Although antioxidants are naturally found in foods containing vitamins C and E, such as apples, blueberries, pumpkins, strawberries, the introduction of Coenzyme Q10 (CoQ10), which is a powerful and natural antioxidant, can easily be added to your cocker's diet.

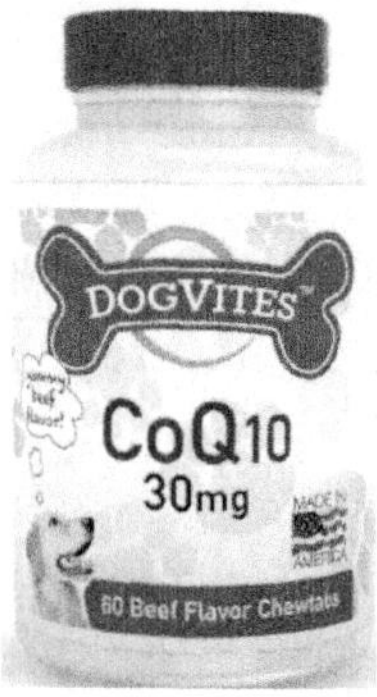

CBD Oil – Cannabidiol (CBD) oil (pictured) is extracted from the flowers, leaves, and stems of cannabis plants. Note that it does NOT contain the chemical 'tetrahydrocannabinol' (THC) that gives the well-known 'high' people get from smoking cannabis. Research is still in its infancy with respect to any long-term effects when giving your cocker CBD oil. What is known is many human studies have shown it can relieve chronic pain, anxiety, seizures, aggression, muscle spasms, and even neurological disorders. Since both people and dogs have an 'endocannabinoid' or complex cell-signalling system, it stands to reason that both species can benefit from the use of CBD oil in their diet.

There is a great deal of anecdotal evidence from doting dog owners who strongly believe adding CBD oil or treats to their spaniel's diet provides many benefits and relief from chronic conditions.

N.B. When considering an additive for your cocker's diet, the chosen product should be as pure and organic as possible and discuss it with a professional, as there can often be a trial-and-error period before determining correct dosage amounts.

Probiotics (pictured) – With the increase in the use of probiotics in humans, it is hardly surprising that probiotics for dogs have also become popular supplements. Probiotics live naturally in the body in the form of yeasts and live bacteria that aid digestion and intestinal health. As supplements, they are used to treat diarrhoea and other digestive problems. Probiotics come in several forms, including yogurts, capsules, chews, powders, and dog food formulations.

Chondroitin Sulphate – This joint supplement is often used in combination with glucosamine as it is a healthy building block of cartilage. The School of Medicine and Health Sciences at the University of North Dakota carried out a study of the benefits of combining chondroitin with glucosamine and found that this combination can help repair and even reverse cartilage damage.

Chondroitin sulphate is a chemical that is part of a protein molecule found in both human and animal cartilage. This protein promotes the retention of water to provide elasticity in the cartilage. This is important for proper nourishment of the tissues to ensure shock absorption during movement.

Supplements containing chondroitin and glucosamine are regularly used for dogs with joint stiffness and reduced mobility. The right supplement could help to aid your dog's mobility and support their joint structure. Discuss with your veterinarian before adding to your cocker's diet.

Multi-Vitamins – This simple supplement can help ensure your cocker spaniel is receiving all the vitamins and minerals they need in their daily diet. Usually, in a tasty chew to appeal to the canine taste buds, they contain minerals and vitamins that support many different areas of your dog's body, including the coat, digestion, heart, joints, skin, and immune system. There are specially formulated products for spaniels of all ages and sizes.

The Canine Fitness Centre in the United Kingdom stated: 'The International Centre for Nutritional Excellence, an independent laboratory specialising in nutraceutical analysis, surveyed label claims of human joint supplements and found 6 out of 10 failed to meet label claims.' Their advice is, 'consumers need to be very careful when purchasing such supplements be it for themselves or for their pets'.

The healthiest choice here would be to look for one free of artificial flavourings, preservatives, corn, and soy. However, it is advisable to discuss your cocker's current diet with a specialist to ensure that adding a supplement will not result in an excess of vitamins that could be harmful.

Anxiety

Loud, booming noises can unsettle some dogs and make them nervous. Choosing an anti-anxiety or calming supplement might help your cocker spaniel relax.

Many dogs suffer from anxiety-related stress. Whether it is the fear of being left at home alone, the stress of a loud home environment, or anxious pacing during celebrations when fireworks are exploding, there are natural supplements—called 'canine chill pills'—that help as they contain ingredients promoting relaxation. The following are the most common active ingredients found in anti-anxiety supplements, which are often given as a tasty treat or chew:

- CBD Oil – See above in dedicated section.
- L-theanine – Increases dopamine in the brain to ease anxiety.
- L-tryptophan – Raises serotonin levels in the brain, which can reduce aggression and hyperactivity.
- Melatonin – This is a hormone that promotes relaxation especially for dogs suffering from hyperactivity.
- Valerian Root (pictured) – Not for all dogs, especially those on medication. There have not been any conclusive studies done on the effects of valerian root for dogs. Although it is thought that it can have multiple benefits. If your dog is particularly fearful of specific scenarios, such as visits to the vets, when you have visitors, or during thunderstorms, it could prove helpful.

FACT ***Synthetic supplements are not as good for your dog as natural sources for the same nutrients—such as fresh fruits and vegetables. When it comes to mineral supplements, chelated minerals are ideal—these are minerals that have been bound to protein molecules, making them easier for your cocker's body to utilise. If you see 'dried fermentation products' on the list, do not be alarmed – these are probiotics that can support your dog's digestion.***

Top Feeding Tips

Apart from purchasing the healthiest food for your cocker spaniel, here are some tips to ensure a pleasant and comfortable feeding experience for your dog:

1. Observe the speed at which your cocker eats their food. Eating too quickly can cause health issues that can be prevented by choosing a slow feeder bowl.
2. Get your puppy used to activity around them during feeding time, so they do not become food possessive and get into the habit of growling when anyone comes near. Put a small amount of food in their bowl, wait until they have eaten it, then give them more so they associate people approaching their bowl with receiving something they like.
3. It is important for your cocker puppy to know you oversee the food source and they must be respectful and patiently wait for their dinner. Tell them to '***Sit/Stay***' and wait for their food bowl to be offered before they are permitted to eat.
4. By using a scoop or measuring device to place food into your dog's bowl could be a missed opportunity for 'telling' them you are in control of their food supply. Instead, when you mix the food with your hands, your scent is on their food, which lets them know you are their leader. This mimics what happens when a pack of wild dogs is out hunting as the leader always eats first, leaving their scent on the food, while the rest patiently wait their turn before eating what is left over.
5. Some adult cocker spaniels prefer to eat a single meal each day. If your cocker seems to have little interest in a morning meal, perhaps once a day is their preferred eating plan.
6. When your dog is a picky eater, it is easy to make sure they understand there is only a 'window of opportunity' for eating their dinner. Give them 20 minutes, and if they do not eat, simply confiscate their food, and make them wait until the next feeding time.
7. If your dog is a fussy eater, they might be enthusiastic about eating more flavourful food, such as a canned or home-cooked meal, rather than dried kibble.
8. It is never a good idea to let your dog eat cat food, as it usually has more protein than a dog requires and can cause diarrhoea, vomiting, or hair loss.
9. Regularly weigh your dog, especially if they have a lot of hair that camouflages the extra kilos. Occasionally, it can be difficult to notice them gaining weight until it is too late.
10. Cleaning their dog bowls daily is a good habit to get into. While they may look clean, they will have a film of saliva and food residue all over them, where unhealthy bacteria will quickly grow.

11. Not feeding them immediately after an energetic play session or a large drink of water will help prevent stomach upsets or possible bloat. Wait until they are relaxed and calm enough to eat slowly.
12. Monitoring your cocker's poo habits can help you discover potential health problems. For instance, if they are suffering from diarrhoea that lasts longer than a couple of days, they may have a gastrointestinal problem requiring a visit to the vet for diagnosis.

13. Waiting at least an hour after they have eaten before taking them for a car ride will ensure their stomach contents have settled. Some dogs are more prone to motion sickness and if they throw up in the car, they could begin to associate vehicle outings with something unpleasant.
14. Avoid taking away your puppy's food bowl while they are still eating. Doing so can create anxiety or food aggression, especially in a dog with a healthy appetite as they will think someone is stealing their food.
15. When feeding more than one dog, give each of them their own space. Allow them to be at least two metres (six feet) apart, so they do not feel threatened or worried that the other dog might try to take their food.
16. Always avoid feeding your cocker any foods that are high in salt and sugar as doing so can lead to obesity, diabetes, and dental problems.
17. If your dog is a fussy eater, simply adding a little chicken or beef broth—unsalted—grated parmesan, or a highly-flavoured topping often encourages them to eat.
18. Instead of just giving your cocker their meal, use mealtime as an opportunity to help with training and patience. Practise the '***Sit/Stay***' command, and work on the '***Okay***' release command, so they learn to sit and wait patiently until they hear the '***Okay***' command that permits them to eat their food.
19. If your dog's activity levels change during certain seasons, to avoid adding extra unhealthy weight, feed less when they are less active and more when they are highly active.
20. Dogs such as the cocker spaniel who are highly intelligent are easily bored and appreciate being fed via a food puzzle. This type of toy dispenses food, while simultaneously exercising memory and manipulation skills.

Weight Control

Cockers are renowned for being slightly more rotund than they should be through overeating. No matter what time of day it is, they are always ready to eat and therefore prone to obesity. Conscientious dog owners who want the best for their furry friends need to control their dog's weight, as this will avoid future health problems that could be serious enough to dangerously affect their dog's life. Packing on the kilos will soon create a pudgy pup who could suffer from many health problems, such as:

- Diabetes.
- Heart disease.
- Respiratory ailments.
- Stress to the joints and skeleton

An underweight dog can also suffer from health problems, such as:

- Reduced bone density.
- Muscle loss.
- Weakened immune system.
- Increased number of infections.
- Lethargy and decreased physical stamina.
- Skin and coat problems, including hair loss.

While being overweight is far more widespread than being underweight, both conditions warrant immediate attention that might also include professional intervention to get your cocker spaniel's weight back in proper balance.

FACT ***Sometimes, a medical condition, such as Cushing's disease or hypothyroidism makes a dog gain weight, as can advancing age when their metabolism naturally slows, and your dog is***

not as active. Also, some breeds, like the cocker, are naturally prone to easily gaining weight, which means their food intake must be carefully monitored.

Helping Lose Weight – The first step towards helping an overweight cocker spaniel lose weight is to have their weight assessed at the vet's. They will then tell you how many kilograms your dog needs to shed to regain their trim figure. Next, based on their age, activity level, and how overweight they are, no doubt your vet will ask what they are being fed and how much.

TIP ***Depending on the size of your dog, simply changing from feeding a heaped cup to a level one could have a significant effect on their weight. In cases where your dog needs to lose more than 2.2 kilograms (5 pounds), once they have been checked for possible hormonal conditions and there are no health issues, the vet might suggest an increase in exercise in combination with reduced daily calorie intake.***

Sometimes, all that is required is to cut back on the amount that you are feeding your dog, keep track of how many extra treats are given, and increase their daily exercise.

Helping Gain Weight – Being underweight is seen less often in well-cared for canine companions. If your cocker cannot maintain their ideal weight, this is still a cause for concern and should be discussed with the veterinarian. If there is no underlying medical condition requiring treatment, there are several steps that will help an underweight dog put on some needed kilograms, including:

- Feed a higher calorie diet—higher protein and fat.
- Feed a larger meal at night to encourage fat storage.
- Supplement main meals with snacks throughout the day.
- Make a dry diet more enticing by adding fresh or wet foods.
- Boost fat and fibre by adding canned pumpkin or sweet potato.
- If your dog does not like their current diet, find one they do like.
- Feed organic peanut butter treats before bed.
- Try more exercise to build muscle.

Dogs and Human Food

Many cocker spaniel owners have questions about what human foods are suitable for feeding to their furry friends. There are many human foods that are a definite no-no (see Toxic Food, Plants, and Products, Chapter 15). However, there are also many other foods you can safely feed them. Below are some of the most frequent questions asked about dogs and human food.

What Fruits Can My Dog Eat?

Fruits are higher in natural sugars than vegetables and should be given in small quantities, especially for overweight cockers. The following fruits are safe to feed them, and add helpful vitamins and antioxidants:

- Apples.

- Bananas.
- Blackberries.
- Blueberries.
- Cantaloupe.
- Cranberries.
- Kiwi.
- Oranges.
- Pears.
- Pineapple.
- Pumpkin.
- Raspberries.
- Strawberries.
- Watermelon (pictured).

When feeding organic fruit treats, try to keep this to no more than 10% of your cocker's daily diet and do not forget to add the extra calories to their daily calorie count.

What Vegetables Can My Dog Eat?

Spaniels can understandably get fed up eating the same meat-based food every day and appreciate a little variety. Plus, there are many benefits to be gained from feeding vegetables, as they are rich in enzymes, minerals, phytonutrients, and vitamins.

Pureeing provides optimum digestibility from the following dog-friendly vegetables:

- Asparagus.
- Beets.
- Broccoli.
- Butternut squash.
- Carrots.
- Celery.
- Cucumber.
- Green beans.
- Kale.
- Mushrooms.
- Parsley.
- Peas.
- Spinach.
- Sweet Potatoes.
- Courgette

Although feeding your cocker just vegetables is not a replacement for a well-balanced meal, supplementing it with healthy vegetables enhances health and will prolong your dog's life.

What Meats Are Safe for my Spaniel?

The following list contains meats that are safe to feed your dog:

- Beef.
- Bison.
- Chicken.
- Duck.
- Goat.
- Lamb.
- Ostrich.
- Pheasant.
- Pork.
- Quail.
- Rabbit.
- Salmon.
- Tilapia.
- Turkey.
- Venison.

The safest meat sources are grass fed, organic, free range, or wild caught. Depending on the meat source you choose, the protein and fat content will vary.

Can My Dog Eat Chocolate?

Many people are confused about the feeding chocolate as many remember the 'doggy' chocolate drops.

Although many cockers have snatched a piece of chocolate and seemed to suffer no ill consequences, chocolate contains a chemical called 'theobromine', which is poisonous to dogs. To keep your dog safe, do not feed chocolate in any amount.

Can My Dog Eat Ice Cream?

It might be tempting to want to share this tasty treat with your furry friend, and most cockers will certainly devour it with much gusto if they get the opportunity. However, there are several good reasons to avoid giving a dog ice cream, including:

- They are not designed to digest milk after weaning.
- They could be lactose intolerant.
- They might be allergic to milk and dairy products.
- It may make them throw up or give them diarrhoea.
- They might develop itchy, red skin.
- Sugar can contribute to obesity and other health issues.
- 'Sugarless' ice cream often contains xylitol, which is toxic to dogs.
- Some flavours are toxic to dogs.

TIP ***Before considering sharing an ice cream with your dog, choose an alternative wholesome dog snack that is good for their health instead.***

Can I Feed My Dog Porridge?

There are some health benefits associated with eating porridge, including a host of nutrients, antioxidants, and minerals that help keep your cocker looking and feeling their best. Although, there are some considerations to bear in mind:

- Feed porridge that is simply bland and plain.
- Make it with water, not milk.
- Do not use fancy, flavoured packets high in sugar.
- Do not use instant porridge as it can contain artificial sweeteners.
- Read the label and make sure it is 100% whole, rolled oats.
- If possible, buy only organic.
- Be aware than 200 grams of cooked porridge has 150 calories.
- Do not feed more than 1 tablespoon for every 9 kilograms of your cocker's weight.

Feeding porridge should be considered a treat or an addition to a well-balanced main meal and not a replacement. As healthy as porridge might be, it still lacks many of the minerals and vitamins necessary for the maintenance of a healthy cocker.

What Grains Are Safe for My Cocker Spaniel?

FACT ***Grains (pictured) contain valuable nutrients and provide carbohydrates, fat, and antioxidants. Grains can be part of a healthy, canine diet. However, not all dogs can easily digest some grains, especially wheat and corn, particularly those who already have digestive problems.***

This can give your dog unpleasant and painful symptoms such as stomach-ache and constipation. Cocker spaniels with digestive issues benefit from a grain-free diet that provides carbohydrates via fruits and vegetables.

In addition, some dogs exhibit allergies to certain grains. If your regular dog food triggers allergic symptoms, switching to grain-free foods might be a better option.

Here are some common and ancient grains you can try adding to your dog's diet:

- Amaranth.
- Brown rice.
- Chia.
- Corn (only non-GMO).
- Einkorn.
- Emmer.
- Kamut.
- Millet.
- Porridge—Oatmeal.
- Quinoa.
- Sorghum.
- Spelt.
- Teff.
- Wild rice.

Other Human Foods Cockers Can Eat

There are some other human foods that can be given in small amounts as a treat and will not usually be harmful to your dog:

- Eggs—free range.
- Cashews—no added salt.
- Cheese—but only in small quantities.
- Honey—pollen helps with allergies.
- Yogurt—plain.
- Peanut butter.
- Pineapple.
- Popcorn—nothing added.

When deciding whether to feed treats that are high in fat, such as peanut butter, consider your cocker's weight.

Dogs can eat peanut butter but never feed them one that contains xylitol, as this is toxic to dogs. You should never feed dairy products as a treat if your spaniel is intolerant to lactose.

Common Eating Issues

While there can certainly be as many 'common' eating issues as there are dogs, some of the more usual ones are noted below.

Eating Too Quickly

Eating food too quickly is also called 'wolfing', 'scoffing', 'bolting', 'gulping', 'inhaling' or 'hoovering'. This habit can lead to an upset stomach, burping, passing wind, throwing up immediately after eating, or suffering from the serious, life-threatening condition called 'bloat'—gastric dilatation volvulus. No matter what the reason is for your dog wolfing their food down in record time, it is important to slow them down to a healthier pace. Here are some techniques to do this:

- Hand feeding.
- Give their food in a slow feeder bowl.
- Present their food in a puzzle feeder.
- Turn a stainless-steel bowl upside down to reduce its size.
- Place a fist-sized rock in the centre of their stainless-steel bowl.
- Feed smaller meals more frequently.
- Make sure their food is providing the nutrients they need.
- Feed on a regular timetable.

Picky Eaters

Although many dogs become fussy eaters, it is often the smaller and less-active breeds that tend to be being picky eaters. There are some dogs who live to eat, and others who eat to live. Some of your dog's eating habits may simply be the result of the breed's genetics.

FACT ***Cocker spaniels are known to have quite robust appetites and can be quite picky. However, it also depends on the individual dog.***

Occasionally, your dog will 'tell' you they simply do not like the food being offered, and a sure-fire method to get this message across, is refusing to eat. In the case of a kibble diet, it might be wise to check the ingredients to make sure it contains all the nutrients your cocker needs. If the kibble is well-balanced, perhaps they just need a stronger flavour to entice them, such as adding a wet topping.

When your dog has sore gums—from teething or dental disease—or loose or broken teeth, they could refuse to eat hard kibble food as it hurts to chew it. Adding warm water to soften the food or changing to a softer canned or home-cooked meal could be the answer. If their kibble diet has very large pieces of kibble and their jaws are smaller, they can have difficulty chewing the large pieces and simply refuse to eat them. If size is the problem, a simple solution is to break the large kibbles into smaller, more easily chewed pieces, and next time buy one that has smaller kibbles.

Your cocker could refuse to eat their main meals because they have already received plenty of treats or snacks and are not that hungry. Not being so generous with treats and snacks between meals helps a fussy eater to feel hungrier at mealtimes.

All dogs thrive on adequate daily exercise. A dog who is not exercised enough will not expend sufficient energy to feel hungry. It might make a huge difference to how they approach mealtimes if they are first taken out for a walk and some fun exercise. Then, once back home, after they have had 10 or 15 minutes to settle down, give them their meal.

Stress is caused by any number of underlying sources—such as disharmony between family members, a new carpet, a new baby or pet, moving to a different location, painting a wall, unidentified noises—and can make your dog go off their food. If there has been significant change in your cocker spaniel's usual environment, this could be the problem. Usually, once a little time has gone by and they have become used to the changes, their normal eating habits will resume. Nevertheless, if they are very sensitive and prefer a harmonious environment, and squabbling family members are upsetting them so they do not eat their meals, eliminating their stress will re-establish peace and tranquillity.

Finally, your cocker spaniel can become a fussy eater if they suffer from an underlying medical condition. If all other possible causes have been eliminated, and they are refusing to eat their dinner for more than 24 hours, it could be time to consult your vet.

Pica

Pica in dogs refers to a health condition characterised by the compulsive eating of non-food items.

These are such things as cardboard, wood, paper, cloth, or plastic. Periodically, your cocker puppy might eat such things simply because no one has told them they should not, or they are exploring their new world and increasing their sensory bank by tasting everything.

Most cocker spaniel puppies will grow out of putting everything in their mouth by the time they are six months to a year old. However, some might have learnt to like the taste of fermented grass clumps or worms that have surfaced after rain, and it can take a considerable time to discourage them from this activity.

The root cause of pica is either behavioural or medical. If this habit is behavioural, it could be from issues not addressed during puppyhood. These include anxiety, boredom, or stress that has made your dog act in a destructive manner by ripping up bedding, items of clothing, or chewing the wooden legs of your coffee table.

There are several symptoms that will show if your puppy has pica through swallowing non-food items, such as:

- Lack of appetite.
- Tiredness or inactivity.
- Diarrhoea.
- Vomiting.

FACT ***While chewing up the occasional tissue might not be worrisome, pica may become a problem when an older cocker continues to chew and swallow non-food items such as***

plastic, which can cause perforations of the intestines or stomach or blockages that require surgery.

Behavioural pica can be eliminated by providing your dog with a more interesting and engaging lifestyle—more fun, vigorous exercise, mental stimulation, trick training, socialising, off lead playtime—and appropriate items to chew. It also helps if you keep non-food items they like to eat safely out of their reach. When trying to work out what triggers could be making your spaniel ingest these things, look at their environment to identify any obvious stressors that might be creating this unwanted behaviour, such as:

- Other pets in the home.
- Teasing children.
- Too much time alone.
- Inadequate exercise.
- No interesting toys to play with.
- Not enough mental stimulation.
- High-pitched noises.
- Loud neighbours with aggressive dogs.

If pica is the result of a medical condition or a nutritional deficiency, once your vet has identified the problem and devised a treatment plan, the condition should resolve itself. For instance, if there is a nutritional deficiency, a different kind or amount of food, adding a supplement or experimenting with a different feeding schedule could be all that is necessary.

9. Care and Grooming

'When you adopt a dog, you have a lot of
very good days and one very bad day.'
~ W Bruce Cameron ~

Cocker spaniel grooming is more than just brushing and bathing your dog. The process also involves checking their ears, eyes, claws, and teeth, which is vital for their health. The best time to establish simple, healthy routines that are part of the rest of their life is when you bring your puppy home. This chapter explains how to take care of your cocker spaniel's coat, teeth, nails, ears, and paws.

Coat Care

The cocker spaniel has a double coat, which means they have two layers of hair, an outer coat, and an undercoat. The outer coat around the head is short and fine, and longer on the body, especially the chest, underside, and ears. Their coats are silky and either flat or wavy, and the colours vary widely.

FACT ***Undercoats are short and dense, acting as insulation that prevents cockers from becoming too hot or too cold. This is ideal for sporting dogs such as the cocker spaniel but can increase shedding and grooming time.***

Their double coats are high maintenance, requiring regular brushing and combing to keep them clean and presentable. This is due to the length, particularly the feathered parts, which are prone to matting, knots, and tangles. These should be removed as they can cause pain and discomfort for your dog. They also have large, delicate ears that need to be handled carefully when brushing and their coat must be trimmed regularly in certain places to maintain the right length.

As mentioned earlier, cocker spaniels shed moderately throughout the year and are not considered hypoallergenic dogs.

Putting this into perspective, English springer spaniels and cavalier King Charles spaniels shed about the same amount of hair. As a result, you will find some hair around the house, especially if you do not keep up with brushing your cocker. You might notice an increase in moulting during periods of seasonal change, but nothing too extreme. When compared with heavy shedders, such as the Saint Bernard or Labrador retriever, their shedding is not nearly as conspicuous. However, they do moult more often than low-shedding breeds, such as the Irish water spaniel.

There are several traditional hairstyles for the cocker spaniel designed to show the breed's silky coat to its best advantage.

Best-In-Show Cut – The most visible feature of this showstopping cut is the smooth back and flowing skirt of longer hair that begins just below the top of the ribcage and almost kisses the floor. The legs are swathed in long, flowing hair, and the ears are kept long. When the dog prances elegantly around the show ring, it looks as if they are riding a wave of shining, silky fur.

Traditional Cut – More practical and without the clearly defined lines, this cut leaves the fringe of hair longer around the cocker's torso, with the face trimmed short, and the ears left long. This flowing, wavy coat requires regular bathing and grooming to keep it looking its best.

Puppy Cut – This short cut is preferred by those who like a coat without the high-maintenance upkeep, as there is less chance of it becoming tangled or matted. Usually, the coat is shaved so the hair is approximately 2.5 cm (1 in) over the entire body, legs, and ears.

Hair Brushing

Typically, cocker spaniels require brushing every three days to keep their luscious look, but if you walk your dog in the countryside, you may need to brush them more frequently to remove grasses and burrs. You can begin by brushing your cocker's coat once every three days if you are unsure how often you need to do it. If the brush collects lots of loose hair, increase the grooming frequency to once a day or every other day.

Taking a few minutes to brush the coat will make your dog feel good while giving you an opportunity to check for lumps, scrapes, hot spots, bugs, and dry skin or hair. Here are a couple or brushing tips:

- Use a soft bristle brush (pictured) for removing dirt, debris, and dead hair while distributing natural oils to keep the coat looking healthy and shiny.

- Start at the base of the neck and work your way down the back and sides, always brushing in the direction of hair growth.
- Next, brush down each leg, then have your dog roll over so you can brush the underside, and finish with the tail.

An effective home brushing regimen includes not just surface brushing, but also getting to all those sensitive areas easily missed around the ears and collar, the armpit and stomach, and the back end and tail.

TIP ***Many cockers develop a heightened sensitivity, especially about having their legs and feet held, ears inspected, teeth brushed, or nails clipped, and will do anything they can to avoid these necessary, lifelong procedures.***

Therefore, try getting your cocker used to a grooming routine early on, rewarding them for calm behaviour with a tasty treat, and maintaining a habit of carrying out regular sessions so grooming can be a pleasant experience both you and your dog look forward to.

Removing Tangled Hair – While tangles can be removed with a brush, a comb is frequently more effective. When buying a stainless-steel comb, look for one with rotating teeth (pictured) as this will tug far less on tangled fur, reducing any discomfort from having their hair pulled. Comb slowly and carefully when removing tangles, and take the following steps:

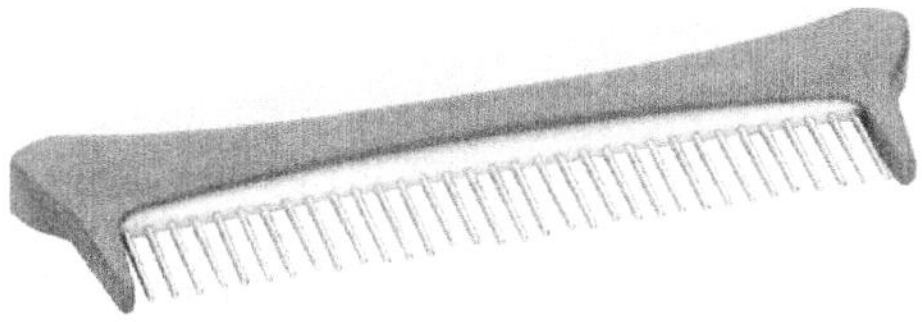

- Hold their hair close to the skin.
- Gently brush the tangles with a bristle or slicker brush.
- Separate persistent tangles with a stainless-steel comb before brushing.

Tangles are not usually a problem if you are vigilant about daily and weekly coat maintenance. It is important to note the cocker spaniel tends to suffer from painfully matted fur far more frequently than other breeds. Sometimes, it may not be obvious that the fur behind their ears, the long hair in their tail, or the fine hair on the stomach has become tangled.

Removing Matted Hair – When hair becomes tightly matted together, it will pull on your cocker's skin—especially if it is wet—which can be both irritating and painful. In this case, a special, sharp mat splitting tool is needed (pictured). Here is how to remove mats from your cocker spaniel's coat:

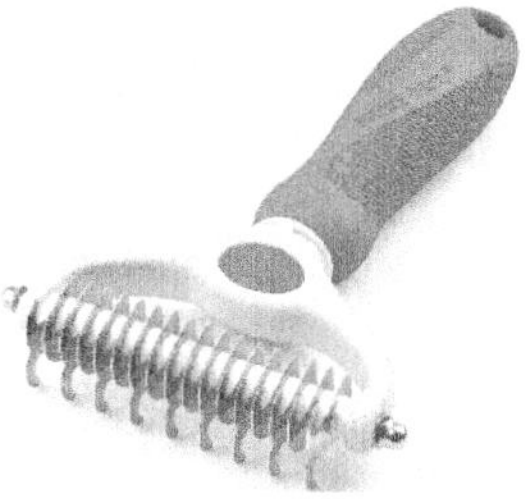

- Hold their hair close to the skin—not so easy if the mat is already tight against the skin.
- Slowly and carefully comb through the matted hair with the splitter.
- Once the mat is broken up, it is possible to comb it out.
- If the mat is very tight and behind their ears or between their foot pads, it is probably best to carefully snip it out with scissors.

The procedure for removing matted hair can vary significantly depending on where the mat is, how severely, and how much hair is matted. In an extreme situation where your dog has not been regularly brushed or properly groomed for many months, their entire coat should be closely clipped by a professional groomer, rather than having your cocker spaniel suffer the pain of a lengthy session to remove endless mats.

Clipping the Coat

Every six weeks or so, your cocker spaniel's coat will need to be clipped. What you need to ask yourself is whether you wish to learn how to groom your own dog, buy all the necessary equipment, and have the time to do the work, or should you simply have them groomed at a doggy spa.

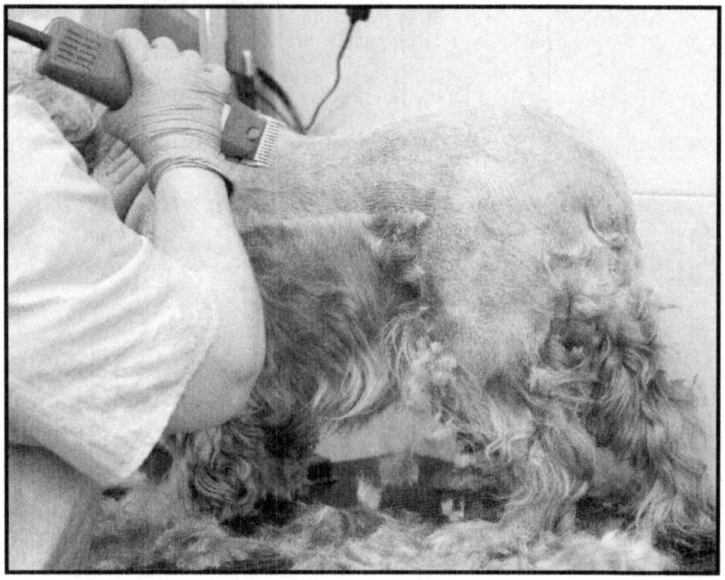

To make life easier, most owners prefer to have their dog professionally clipped. By doing so, you can avoid mats and knots and save some time brushing. This is often followed by a thorough bath and nail trimming. Do not forget that paying someone to groom your cocker spaniel is not cheap and will cost you a great deal per year. A rough cost estimate per grooming session is £29 to £54 ($40 to $75) or more.

It is highly recommended to expose your puppy to a professional grooming environment early on. Even if they do not need a bath or a clip, the experience while young is invaluable for your cocker as they need to accept the grooming process as it is part of their life.

For those who decide to groom their cocker themselves, there are many helpful online videos for when you are starting out. Another option is to hire a professional groomer who is willing to let you watch and/or video how to groom your cocker spaniel in the style you prefer.

Equipment Required – Exactly what equipment is required for clipping your cocker depends on the condition of their coat, and the preferred style of clip. The following is a generic list of the essential items you need:

- Clippers (pictured)—professional brands: Andis, Wahl, Oster.
- Detachable metal blades—minimum a No. 10 and a No. 4F or 5.
- Professional set of sharp, stainless-steel scissors.
- Stainless-steel comb with rotating teeth.
- Slicker brush.
- Spray to cool, disinfect and lubricate blades.
- Grooming table.

When buying grooming equipment, especially scissors and clippers, it is recommended to purchase the best quality you can afford. Choose professional brands that will stand up to frequent use and make grooming easier.

TIP ***While many clippers come with a set of plastic combs for clipping the hair shorter or longer, these combs tend to easily become caught in their hair, making them frustrating to work with. It is far easier to buy the right size metal blade compatible with the chosen clippers.***

The cost of buying dog grooming equipment varies considerably. Professional-grade equipment will ensure a professional outcome that takes less time to accomplish with less stress for both owner and dog.

The Puppy Clip or Cut – For those who have decided to learn how to clip their own cocker's coat rather than making appointments at the pet grooming salon, it is helpful to consider what is involved. Beyond learning how to do it yourself, remember the initial cost of professional grooming equipment could be considerably more than you imagine.

A puppy clip is the most popular style for those who wish to have their cocker spaniel with a low-maintenance coat. There are several ways to define exactly what a 'puppy cut' looks like. Typically, the coat is cut short to a length of 2.5 to 5 centimetres (1 to 2 inches) over the entire body, while the beard, ears, and tail area are left a little longer. Keeping the coat shorter has many benefits, such as:

- Helps prevent mats and tangles.
- Easier to keep clean.
- Less shedding.
- Less frequent brushing.
- Keeps your dog cooler.
- Easier to see if there is an injury.
- Easier to identify hitchhikers—fleas, ticks.
- Makes your dog look like a sweet puppy forever.

TIP ***Before beginning the grooming session, your cocker needs to have their coat bathed, conditioned, and completely dried. Otherwise, clipping a dirty coat can damage the clippers and scissors and make them dull and difficult to use.***

Hopefully, your dog has been desensitised to the sensation of the clippers before their first grooming session. This process requires showing them the clippers, letting them hear the noise they make and feeling the vibration long before they need to be clipped.

Here are the step-by-step instructions for the puppy clip, which should take approximately 30 to 45 minutes to complete:

1. Set up the grooming table.
2. Have the clippers—plugged in or fully charged—scissors, comb, and slicker brush close at hand.
3. Place your dog on the table.
4. Remove their collar.
5. Attach the No. 4F or 5 blade to the clippers and turn them on.
6. Begin at the neck by holding the clippers parallel to the body.
7. Using long strokes, clip through the coat in the direction of the hair growth.
8. Continue clipping until their entire body, neck, and chest areas are the same length.
9. If their ears are quite thick, you can use the same blade on them.

10. Clip their head—not the beard—in the direction of the hair growth.
11. Carefully clip down each leg and the base of their tail.
12. Lift their tail and shave against the hair growth to make it half the length of the body hair in the anal area.
13. Check that the clippers are not too hot and if they are, use spray coolant or take a rest until the blade cools down.
14. Turn the clippers off and switch to the short No.10 blade.
15. If hair is growing over their eyes, comb it forwards and trim with the scissors and/or clip the corner of their eyes with the No.10 blade.
16. Pick up each foot and trim the hair between their pads.
17. Turn the clippers off and use the scissors to trim around their feet.
18. Use the scissors to trim their tail, beard, and ears to the desired length. If their beard is very thick use the thinning shears.
19. Check their entire body for any hairs sticking out.
20. Use the No. 10 blade to trim their armpits and tummy short.

When learning how to groom, it can take several sessions before you get your cocker looking exactly the way you want. Do not expect the first clipping session to be perfect.

Bathing

Introducing your Puppy to Bathing – Everyone has stories about how their cocker spaniel hates having a bath, how they run away, hide underneath the bed, or do anything to avoid it. When your puppy is introduced to the bathtub in a fun and rewarding way, the trauma can be avoided, and your dog will be delighted to get into the tub on their own.

TIP ***When introducing your puppy to bathing, it is far better to do it when they are young. The procedure should be initiated slowly, in small steps that include tasty treats over several weeks, so the puppy learns to trust and accepts the routine.***

The following steps will help your cocker learn to love bath time:

1. Put your cocker in the tub without water and give them a treat. Do this several times during the session.
2. The next day, put your dog in the tub, give them a treat and wet their feet. Praise them for getting their feet wet, give another treat, dry their feet with a towel and end the session. Repeat this step for a couple of days.
3. Put your dog in the tub, give them a treat and wet their entire legs. Praise them for getting their legs wet, give them another treat, dry them off with a towel and end the session.

4. Continue gradually getting your puppy a little wetter every day until they are entirely wet. Dry them with a towel and give them a treat.
5. Once you can get your dog completely wet, you should also get them used to shampooing. Add some shampoo, work it through their fur and shower it off before drying them and giving them a treat.
6. The final step is to have your puppy wait a little longer after shampooing, so you can condition their coat before drying them and giving them treat.

Hopefully, by now your puppy is a calm and patient participant at bath time and instead of running to hide, they will happily jump into the bath whenever you ask.

Equipment and Products – Before getting your dog ready for their bath, you need to make sure you have all the necessary bath products and they are close at hand, such as:

- Canine Shampoo.
- Canine Conditioner.
- Sponge.
- Non-slip mat for the sink or bathtub.
- Plenty of towels.
- Hairdryer.

Regular care of your cocker's coat should typically include bathing them every 4-6 weeks. You can increase the frequency to bi-weekly if they regularly get dirty running in muddy fields. However, overbathing your dog can dry out their skin and cause itching and flaking, as it depletes the skin's natural oils.

Canine Shampoo (pictured) – It is important to know that shampoo for people can harm your cocker's coat and skin, as it usually contains strong detergents that strip the natural oils from your dog's coat, leaving them with dry, itchy skin. The following is a list of the many kinds of canine shampoos, some designed for a specific purpose:

- Anti-bacterial, anti-fungal—to eliminate bacteria or fungus.
- Anti-itch—with anti-itch, anti-inflammation properties.
- Brightening and whitening—often used on white coats.
- Deodorising—for a dog who just rolled in something unsavoury.
- Flea and Tick—to eliminate unwanted parasites.
- Hypoallergenic—for allergies or fragrance sensitivity.
- Natural—containing gentle, natural ingredients.
- No more tears—gentle shampoo for puppies.
- Organic—100% natural and non-toxic ingredients.
- Waterless—for spot cleaning between baths.

Whatever type of canine shampoo you choose, it must always have a pH of between 7.0 and 7.52. When picking a shampoo, unless you need one for a specific purpose, it is always best to go for an organic, 100% natural shampoo free of any ingredients that might be toxic.

Canine Conditioner (pictured) – After their bath, it is a good idea to take the extra time to condition your cocker's coat. Doing so will not only make them look and feel better, but has many additional benefits, such as:

- Prevents the loss of natural oils and moisture.
- Keeps their coat cleaner for a longer time.
- Repairs a dull, damaged, or dry coat.
- Restores a soft, silky feel to their coat.
- Helps their coat dry quicker.
- Protects from the heat of the dryer and hair breakage.

The benefits of spending the extra two minutes to condition your spaniel's coat will be welcomed by both owner and dog alike. Plus, your cocker will have healthy, moisturised skin and a coat with a smooth feel and natural shine.

Bathing Step-By-Step – Before you start your cocker spaniel's bath, be sure to brush out any debris, dead hair, mats, or tangles from their coat. Removing any debris or mats beforehand makes the entire procedure easier and faster and avoids clogging up the drains with dead hair.

1. First, lay down a rubber bathmat to provide a more secure footing for your dog and prevent the tub from being scratched.

2. Have everything you need for their bath next to you, so you do not have to search for them when your cocker is already wet. Place cotton balls in your dog's ears to prevent accidental splashes from entering the ear canal as it could cause an infection.
3. Fill the tub with 10-15 cm (4-6 in) of lukewarm water—not too hot as dogs are more sensitive to hot water than people—and place your dog in the water. Completely wet your cocker's coat down to the skin by using a detachable showerhead. If a spray attachment is not available, a cup or jug will work just as well.
4. Apply a line of shampoo along your dog's back and work down the sides, under the body, and down the legs and tail. Wet the sponge, add shampoo, and scrub it around the head area. Be careful not to get shampoo in their eyes, nose, mouth, or ears (pictured). Once your entire dog is lathered up, comb the shampoo lather through their coat with your fingers, making sure you do not miss the areas under their legs and tail. No dog enjoys having water poured over their head and into their eyes, so use a wet sponge or flannel to wet, lather, and rinse their head.
5. After allowing the shampoo to remain in your spaniel's coat for a couple of minutes, thoroughly rinse it out with clean, lukewarm water using the spray attachment. Comb through their coat with your fingers to ensure all the shampoo residue has been completely rinsed away. Shampoo that is not thoroughly rinsed out of your dog's coat can lead to irritation and itching. While rinsing, be especially thorough in their armpits and underneath the tail area. Finish by using your hands to gently squeeze their body and down the legs to help remove excess water from their coat.

6. Apply a line of conditioner starting at the top of the head and along their back to the tail and work it through the coat. Leave the conditioner in your cocker's coat for two minutes, then rinse again with plenty of lukewarm water, unless the conditioner is a leave-in, no-rinse formula. Now, your dog is ready to be dried (see below).

TIP ***Dogs who live in warmer climates may benefit from a brand of conditioner that contains sunscreen to protect them from ultraviolet radiation when they spend time outside on sunny days.***

Drying Step-By-Step – Place dry towels close at hand and on the floor of the bathroom or where your cocker is being bathed.

1. Close the shower/bath curtain and let your dog shake off excess water.
2. Place them on a towel on the floor, wrap them in another clean, dry towel and gently squeeze out the excess water.
3. Wrap them in another clean, dry towel, so they won't get cold and begin to shiver (pictured).
4. Remove the cotton balls from their ears.
5. Unless it is a warm day out, you need to dry them straight away with a hairdryer.
6. Place them on a dry towel and begin to blow-dry their coat on a warm setting. Place your hand between the dryer and the coat so the hot air will not get too close to their skin.
7. Use your hand or a soft brush/comb to lift and fluff longer hair to help it dry faster. Never blast hot air directly into your cocker's face or ears.
8. Give your dog a tasty treat as a reward for good behaviour.

Top Tips for a Healthy Coat

There are many things you can do to ensure your dog has a beautiful, soft, shiny, healthy coat, looking as if they are just stepping onto the show ring:

1. Include quality protein in the diet. As your cocker's coat is 95% protein, it is essential to provide food that contains high-quality animal protein, such as chicken, lamb, and fish. They contain special amino acids that ensure the skin and coat are properly nourished, maintaining healthy structure and function. Just keeping their coat and skin in good condition requires up to 35% of your spaniel's daily protein intake.
2. When feeding dry meals, add a teaspoon of organic coconut or pumpkin seed oil, as they contain zinc. Often, a rough or dry coat, or red/dry skin is the result of insufficient zinc in their diet, so adding this mineral helps to improve the condition of the skin and coat.

3. Feed single ingredient, organic treats. These have no unnecessary added ingredients, sugars, salts, or preservatives that can cause an itchy skin and dull coat.

4. Include eggs in your cocker spaniel's diet. They are rich in protein and a good source of linoleic acid and fat-soluble vitamins, such as vitamin A, which are perfect for your dog's skin and coat.
5. Feed herbal horsetail and spirulina to enhance their coat quality. Horsetail contains silica, which is an important ingredient in maintaining healthy skin, bones, and coat. Spirulina contains vitamin B and carotenoids that nourish the skin and coat.

6. Provide a clean, water source to keep your dog well-hydrated. Proper hydration promotes a healthier skin and coat, while also removing any toxins such as chlorine that may cause tear staining and damage to your dog's skin.
7. Add omega-3 to your cocker's diet. Small, freeze-dried oily fish treats, such as herring, mackerel, and sardines or the oil made from them is rich in fatty acids, which are essential for a heathy skin and coat.
8. Adding a vitamin B supplement (pictured) can improve the quality of your dog's coat. The deficiency of this vitamin can make the skin dry and crusty, which leads to a brittle and dull-coloured coat.
9. Use a leave-in conditioner during sunny weather. This helps hydrate your spaniel's skin and coat, improves hair elasticity to prevent breakage and protects from the harsh rays of the sun during warm, dry weather.
10. Have a regular grooming schedule of brushing and combing your cocker and taking them to the groomers. This will keep their coat at a manageable length and prevent uncomfortable mats.

11. Brush their coat thoroughly every few days to distribute natural oils. It removes dead hair and lubricates growing hairs, so they flow together in the same direction to improve skin protection and retain heat.
12. Apply sunscreen (pictured) or protective clothing during hot, sunny weather. Sunscreen reduces the risk of certain skin cancers. Just like shampoo and conditioner, it is essential to only use canine sunscreen on your cocker spaniel and make sure they do not lick it off. Otherwise, protective clothing such as a light-coloured T-shirt will provide an even higher UPF protection.
13. Rinse off any salt or chlorine from sea or pool swimming. The salt that dries on your dog's skin after a swim in the sea can cause itching and scratching. Dogs who swim in pools will also get dry skin and a brittle, dull coat from the chlorine in the water. Chlorine can even bleach their coat or turn it green.
14. Prevent fleas and ticks. Keeping your cocker's coat clean helps to prevent infestation, as parasites take up residence easier in a coat that is in poor condition.
15. Make a DIY coat treatment with aloe vera and coconut oil. This mixture helps soothe irritated skin while restoring moisture and elasticity to your spaniel's coat. Before rubbing into their coat and skin, first test on a small area to ensure there is no allergic reaction.

Rub their coat with a dry, leather chamois to make it shine. This buffs and polishes the hairs and helps them to lay in the same direction.

Choosing a groomer

Under the Animal Welfare Act 2006, in the United Kingdom, a dog groomer is responsible for meeting your cocker's needs whilst in their care. Although recently there have been cases that have highlighted the need for owners to think carefully when choosing a groomer. When equipment has been faulty or where animals have been left unsupervised whilst being dried, dogs have suffered severe burns or even fatalities in grooming establishments.

Therefore, if you decide to have your cocker groomed by a professional, it is extremely important to leave them in the care of a responsible and reputable adult who will meet all your spaniel's needs. When choosing a groomer, be certain to:

- Consult your vet—they might be able to recommend a reputable groomer. Ask friends and family for recommendations about establishments they have used.
- Before employing them, meet the groomer. You need to be assured they will care for your dog properly, and they will get on well with your cocker. The grooming visit should be an enjoyable experience for your dog. Therefore, it is important that you are confident the groomer will meet your dog's physical and behavioural needs when left with them.
- Check that the facilities are clean and secure? It is important the establishment is suitable for your spaniel, and they will not be at risk while they are there. It should be somewhere you are comfortable to leave your dog.
- It is important that there are enough staff to look after the needs of the animals in their care. A groomer who runs on an appointment-only basis might be certain to each give your dog the correct amount of time, so the job is done properly. Working in this way also means fewer dogs are groomed at any one time.
- If your dog has any special requirements, such as sensitive skin, then make sure you are satisfied that the groomer will discuss these needs with you and cater for them. Your cocker might also be of a nervous disposition or does not like particular parts of their body being touched. If you decide it is still necessary to visit the groomer, will they recognise signs of anxiety in your dog and know how to respond?
- A good groomer might also be willing to show you how to groom properly at home using the correct techniques and the right tools. This will enable you to carry on their good work between visits.
- Be realistic about the price. Though £10 might sound like a bargain for a grooming session, it could also reflect the quality of the service being provided.

Teeth Care

As your cocker's teeth do a lot of work, they need to be properly cared for, otherwise, your dog can suffer from dental problems. This is extremely important as they use their teeth and mouths for more than just eating, including playing, exploring, and tasting much of their surroundings. You know how miserable a toothache can be—imagine your poor dog who cannot tell you how miserable they feel.

How Often and When?

Teeth brushing is important for every healthy dog. Establishing a strict, teeth brushing routine for your dog can totally prevent dental problems. It is a good idea to get into the habit of brushing your cocker's teeth at least two to three times a week. If the task can be managed once a day that would be preferable. Before bedtime, after all their meals and snacks are finished, would be preferable.

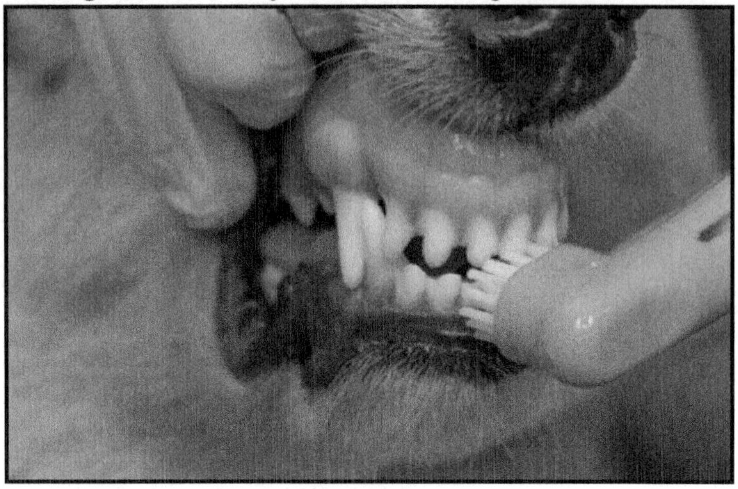

When brushing their teeth, it is important to be able to see what you are doing. To achieve that, get your cocker up on a table or worktop that is padded with a non-slip surface. Alternatively, one person could pick up your dog and hold them at chest level, while the other person brushes their teeth. Wherever teeth brushing takes place, make sure your dog is comfortable and has a secure footing.

Keeping your cocker's teeth healthy is a much easier task if the routine is introduced to them soon after your new puppy is brought home. Getting your pup used to having their mouth handled and fingers rubbing their teeth and gums is beneficial as they grow older.

TIP ***Reward them with a treat before brushing begins—not after—so there are no food particles to cause plaque build-up in the mouth overnight.***

When adopting an older cocker spaniel who has never had their teeth brushed before, introducing them to it is the same as with a young puppy. Go slowly and gently, give treats to reward calm behaviour but do not rush the process.

Step-By-Step Teeth Brushing

Here are the steps to follow to brush your cocker puppy's teeth and get them used to the idea:

1. Check your puppy's teeth and gums often to see what is normal so you can spot any issues or problems.
2. When your cocker pup is stress-free and a little sleepy, lift their lip and rub their gums with your finger several times every day for a week.
3. When they are comfortable and relaxed, gently stroke the outside of their cheeks with your finger for 1 or 2 minutes.
4. Next, buy some canine toothpaste specially formulated for dogs (pictured) and apply this to your puppy's teeth with a finger several times a day for a week.
5. Get a finger cap toothbrush (see Top Teeth Care Tips below for definition) and continue rubbing your cocker's gums and teeth several times every day for another week.

6. Next, move to a soft bristled toothbrush. Add a little doggy toothpaste and slowly brush their teeth for a few seconds, several times a day for a week—but do not press too hard as their gums may bleed.
7. If you wish to, you can change to an electric brush once your puppy has their adult teeth. It is best to get your puppy used to it while they still have their milk teeth. Show it to them, turn it on, and let them feel the buzzing while you are manually brushing—do not rush brushing with the electric toothbrush, yet.
8. Once your puppy has their adult teeth, let them feel the buzzing sensation on their body, while moving the electric toothbrush slowly towards the head and muzzle.
9. When your cocker puppy allows you to touch their muzzle while the brush is turned on, lift their lip and quickly brush a couple of teeth at a time, until they get used to having them all brushed at the same time.
10. While brushing, angle the bristles so they extend underneath the gums to help prevent plaque build-up.
11. When going slowly, your spaniel pup will become familiar with the buzzing and vibrating of the electric brush. The latter cleans their teeth and removes plaque faster than a manual toothbrush, and all you need to do is hold the brush against their teeth.
12. Always praise your cocker puppy for letting you brush their teeth, especially when they are first introduced to the routine.

Teeth Scaling – Scaling is cleaning the areas of their teeth just below the gum line with an ultrasonic or handheld instrument. Using this tool helps to remove stubborn tartar build-up that might be hidden beneath the gums. Most accumulation is found on the outside of the teeth and on the back molars, near the gum line.

This is usually done by a professional while your cocker is anaesthetised, as they have all the necessary tools and can polish the teeth afterwards to remove any scratches and prevent further accumulation.

Top Teeth Care Tips

1. Hydrogen peroxide is effective for killing germs, whitening, and cleaning your dog's teeth and is far less expensive than canine toothpastes. As there is so little on the brush, you do not need to worry about your cocker swallowing it. Just dip the toothbrush in a capful of hydrogen peroxide, shake off the excess, and brush their teeth. You can use it full strength or combine hydrogen peroxide—3% food grade— aloe vera juice (1:1) and a pinch of baking soda.
2. Feeding bones at least once a month helps to prevent tooth plaque, bad breath, and tartar build-up. Bone munching will also polish and whiten your cocker's teeth.
3. Choose only large bones so there is no danger of swallowing. Do NOT boil the bones first, as this makes the bone soft, which defeats the purpose of removing plaque and makes the bones splinter into smaller pieces that could create a choking or puncturing hazard for your spaniel.
4. Feeding a daily dental chew or hard biscuit can help to remove tartar while exercising their jaws and massaging their gums. Some dental chews contain natural, breath freshening cinnamon, cloves, or chlorophyll.

5. Coconut oil can eliminate bad breath while giving your cocker's digestive, immune, and metabolic functions a boost at the same time. Most dogs love the taste and all you need to do is add ¼ teaspoon to their dinner.
6. Remember, frequent teeth brushing is a prerequisite for keeping your cocker healthy. Once a day after dinner is good, after every meal is perfect.
7. The many canine toothpastes on the market are usually flavoured with beef or chicken to appeal to your dog's taste buds. Some others are infused with mint or other breath freshening ingredients.
8. Some doggy toothpastes are formulated with active enzymes designed to work chemically by breaking down tartar or plaque to keep build-up at bay. These do not need to be washed off your cocker's teeth and are safe for them to swallow. However, whether they remain on their teeth long enough to do any good might be debatable.
9. Another usual ingredient in toothpastes is baking soda. This is the same mild abrasive found in many human toothpastes and is designed to gently scrub their teeth. Again, the issue is how much time you have before they have had enough, as it might not be sufficient to produce any results.

10. Water dental additives, such as Arm & Hammer Fresh Coconut Water Additive (pictured) are simply chemicals added to the water in your spaniel's drinking bowl. They may use natural or non-natural chemicals, some of which could be anti-bacterial or antiseptic in nature. These products are designed to break down minerals and plaque in your dog's mouth when they drink. They also help to rid the drinking bowl of bacteria and keep your cocker's mouth cleaner.
11. Feed your dog Himalayan Yak Cheese treats. These high protein, natural, hard cheese treats make excellent chews that last a long time for even the most aggressive chewer, while helping to scrape and clean their teeth at the same time.
12. Antimicrobial dental wipes are usually formulated with chlorhexidine gluconate—disinfectant and antiseptic. This chemical works with your dog's saliva to remove plaque and bacteria while also freshening their breath. Simply wipe over your cocker's teeth and gums.
13. Hard rubber or nylon toys with bumps help to exercise their jaws and clean their teeth.
14. There are many dental sprays and gels on the market that promise to remove plaque and tartar from your dog's teeth. These products are helpful and keep plaque at bay between regular brushing sessions.
15. Performing a weekly check of their gums will alert you to possible problems. If your cocker has a healthy mouth, their gums should be pink. Any other colour could be an indication of dental disease.

16. A finger cap toothbrush is the easiest way to get your cocker puppy used to having their teeth brushed. As the name suggests, this is a soft, silicone cap that fits over your finger and has small, raised bristles on the end. While they are too soft to effectively clean an adult dog's teeth, they are a great way to begin desensitising your puppy to the idea of regular dental care. Furthermore, there is a finger cap brush, 'Waggletooth' designed by a dentist to be stronger for adult dog teeth with bristles all around.
17. Most manual toothbrushes designed for dogs have a long handle. Some have a larger brush on one end and a smaller brush on the other, such as 'Enzadent Dual-Ended Toothbrush' (pictured) for getting to your cocker's difficult to reach back teeth. When

choosing a manual toothbrush, make sure the bristles are soft and it is the right size for your spaniel's mouth.

18. The three-sided manual toothbrush—Espree Oral Care—is designed to reach all their teeth and stimulate your cocker's gums at the same time. This toothbrush cleans their teeth in fewer strokes, which is convenient for both you and your dog.
19. The easiest and most effective way to keep your dog's teeth clean and their gums in healthy condition is with an electric toothbrush, such as the rotary 'Oral-B'. A child's size is perfect for your dog. This brush does all the work for you and there is less worry about possibly brushing too hard and making your cocker spaniel's gums bleed.
20. It is helpful while brushing their teeth to give your dog a piece of hard material—rubber or leather—to bite down on, so they can relax without fully closing their mouth.

Nail Care

FACT ***Allowing your dog to have long, untrimmed nails can result in various health hazards, including infections or an irregular and uncomfortable gait that can damage their skeleton.***

Although most cockers do not particularly enjoy having their nails trimmed, regular trimming is an important grooming practise that should never be overlooked. When your dog comes to terms with having their nails trimmed while young, they will learn to quietly tolerate the process for the rest of their life.

How often your cocker needs their nails trimmed varies considerably. There are several factors that dictate the frequency, including:

- The consistency of the nails—soft, medium, or hard.
- How quickly their nails grow.
- Your cocker's age and activity level.
- The different surfaces they walk on.

TIP ***As a rule, you need to have your cocker's nails trimmed every two to four weeks. Yes, trimming your dog's nails is a lot of work. However, you will save your dog a lifetime of trauma by deciding straight away this is necessary work that cannot be avoided.***

Dewclaws – These are the claws located on the side of the foot that never touch the ground, but they continue to grow. Some puppies have their dewclaws removed when very young by a veterinarian, and growing dewclaws will never be a problem.

Dewclaws on adult dogs can be more difficult to clip, but it is very important to do so regularly. If they are not trimmed, they can grow so long they curl into a circle, which can even grow back into your cocker spaniel's leg causing immense pain.

Clippers, Scissors – Toenail scissors are a good choice for trimming the curved tip of your puppy's softer nails.

There are also 'guillotine' nail clippers (pictured) that have a hole where your spaniel's nail is inserted. This type of trimmer is recommended as: (1) it is difficult to get the nail into the hole at the right depth; (2) it is hard to see how much of the nail is really going to be sliced off; and (3) the likelihood of cutting into the quick and causing your dog pain and blood loss is much higher.

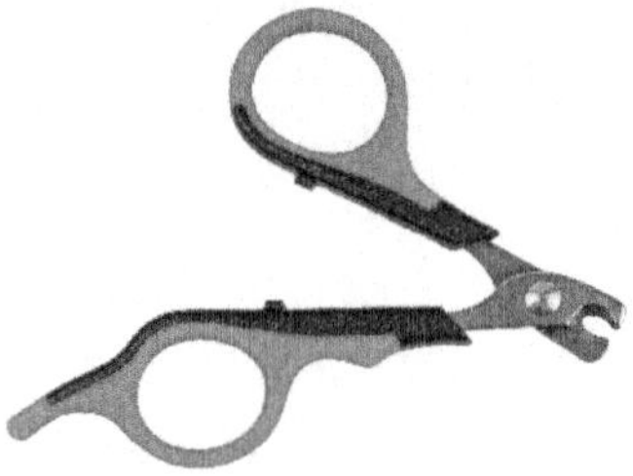

Introducing a Puppy to Nail Clipping

Foot holding – Many dogs develop an aversion to having their feet held, which then transmits to having their nails trimmed. The only way to avoid this problem is to get your cocker puppy accustomed to having their feet touched and toes inspected as soon as they come home from the breeder.

When your cocker puppy is relaxed and tired after a walk, have them sit beside you while you hold their paws—one after the other—and separate their toes while inspecting their nails. If your pup does not try to pull their foot away, give them a treat and move on to the next foot. If they object, simply hold the foot again and before they can pull it away, give a treat. If you perform this foot holding and inspection exercise every day and reward them with treats, your spaniel puppy will soon learn to accept this as an enjoyable part of their day.

Nail Scissors – Once this is accomplished, it is time to introduce the nail scissors. Let your puppy see and sniff them and give them a treat. Hold one paw, separate the toenail and snip off just the curved tip. Give them a treat for not making a fuss. It is okay if you just get one paw snipped each day instead of doing too much and possibly upsetting your cocker pup. Make the procedure as pleasant as possible and stop before they play up.

Once your puppy is approximately six months old, their nails will have grown stronger, thicker, and much tougher. This is when you should switch from the nail scissors to a rotary trimmer/grinder or plier clippers (pictured).

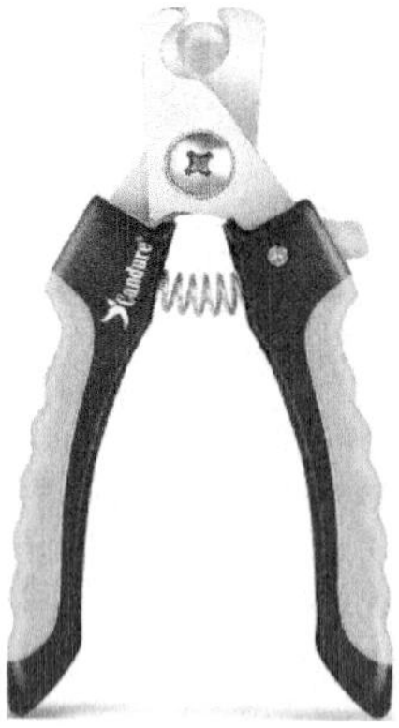

Plier-type Nail Clipping

You probably already know leaving your dog's nails too long can lead to many problems later in life, such as sore feet, painful joints, back pain, and difficulty walking. Therefore, to take good care of your cocker, you need to learn how and when to perform this necessary task.

Rotary trimmer/grinder – If you plan to use a rotary trimmer, it is important to introduce this to your cocker when they are young, so they learn to calmly accept the noise and vibration. Here is how to do this:

- Show the grinder to your puppy.
- Lt them sniff it and turn it on so they get used to the sound and vibration.
- Hold it against their feet one at a time, so they learn not to fear the vibration.
- When they do not object, give them a treat.

FACT ***Depending on the variety of surfaces your dog is walking on and how tough their nails are, plan to clip or grind them every two weeks.***

Step-by-Step Instructions

When trimming their nails, be sure to snip only the tip. You do not want to accidentally cut into the vein, as this is painful and will make your cocker's nail bleed. Here is how to trim your dog's nails using the plier-type clippers.

- Hold your dog's paw firmly but gently.
- Trim the nail below the quick—where the dead nail begins—at a 45o angle, removing small slices at a time.
- Continue until you reach the white inside the nail—this is dead nail—with a small, black dot at the centre. If you cannot see the dot yet, and the nail is completely white, you can trim off a little more.

Rotary Nail Trimming

TIP ***Trimming your cocker's nails with a rotary device MUST be done with a tool designed especially for dogs (pictured). Otherwise, the tool's speed might be too high and burn your dog's nails.***

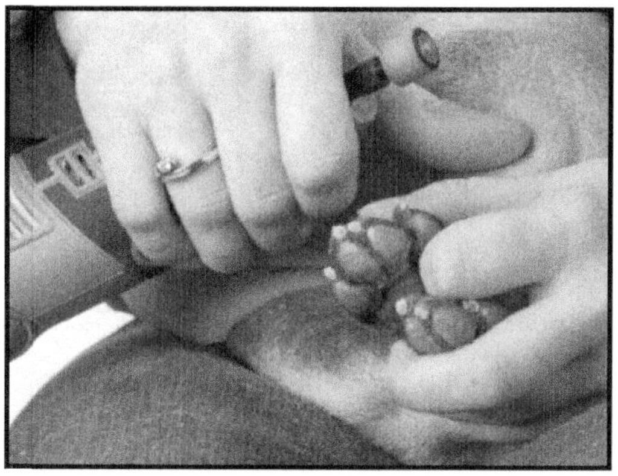

Some spaniels prefer having their nails trimmed with a rotary device that grinds away the excess nail. Once your dog is familiar with a rotary trimmer, this type of tool might be all you ever need. Plus, your dog's nails will always be smooth and rounded with no sharp edges that are left when a plier-type clipper is used.

There are several benefits inherent in using a rotary tool to keep your dog's nails trimmed:

- There is less chance of cutting into the vein.
- It is easier to keep their nails short.
- Many dogs prefer it as there is no squeezing sensation or clicking sound.
- A rotary trimmer is usually quicker than plier-type clippers.
- When you use this tool every week or two, you will never have to clip their nails.

Step-by-Step Instructions

The following is a step-by-step process for trimming your cocker's nails with a rotary trimmer:

1. Trim their nails when your dog is relaxed—after a walk or play session.
2. Have your spaniel lay beside you on the sofa or sit on the floor with them.
3. Have some favourite treats nearby.
4. Turn on the trimmer and pick up one paw.
5. While holding their paw in one hand, separate a toe and firmly hold the nail you are going to trim between your thumb and forefinger.
6. Hold the sanding disc lightly against the end of the nail until you see how your cocker reacts and how much pressure you need to apply.
7. Move the sanding disc around the end of the nail until the dead part has been ground off and it is smooth with a rounded shape. Stop before the disc cuts into the vein.

8. You may also need to sand underneath the nail to remove sharp edges.
9. Repeat the process on all four feet (16 nails). If they also have dew claws, do not forget to trim those, too.
10. Check online videos that show how to use a rotary trimmer.
11. The first few times you use the rotary trimmer, go very slowly, and give a treat after just one nail. Once your cocker realises the procedure will not hurt them and they are rewarded with a treat, you can trim the rest of their nails.

TIP ***Make sure you have good lighting when trimming your dog's nails, or sit in the sunlight, so you can clearly see what you are doing.***

Accidents – Of course, you always want to avoid causing any pain when trimming your cocker spaniel's toenails, and you do not want to destroy their trust in you when performing this necessary task. However, sometimes accidents do happen. If you clip it too short and inadvertently cut into the vein in their toenail, your dog will be in pain, and it will bleed.

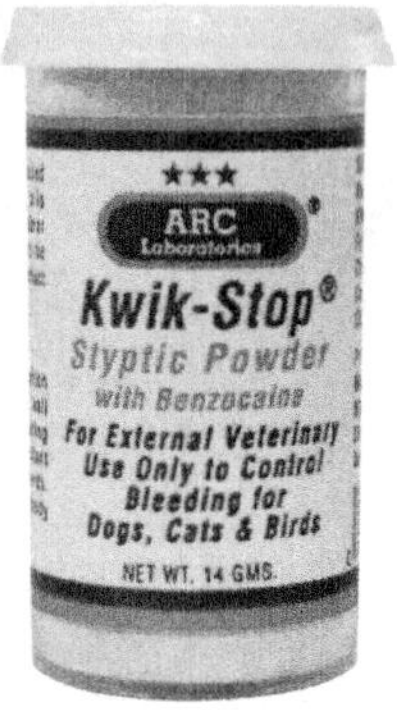

For such incidents, keep some styptic powder (pictured) —often called 'Kwik Stop'—in your grooming kit. This yellow powder is quick and easy to use. Hopefully, you will never need it, but it will give you peace of mind knowing you have it to hand. Dip your moistened finger into the powder and apply it with a little pressure to the end of the bleeding nail. This will stop the bleeding in just a few seconds.

Ear Care

Cocker spaniels often suffer from painful ear infections. Being familiar with your dog's usual habits and noting if they change and keeping their ears clean and dry can help prevent this health issue. If your dog is scratching at their ears, moaning, crying, or constantly shaking their head, it is time for a trip to the vet as they could have an infection.

Aim to clean your cocker's ears regularly, at least monthly. It is a good idea to keep ear powders and cleaning solutions in your dog's grooming kit. Proper preventative care will minimise the chances of irritating and painful ear issues.

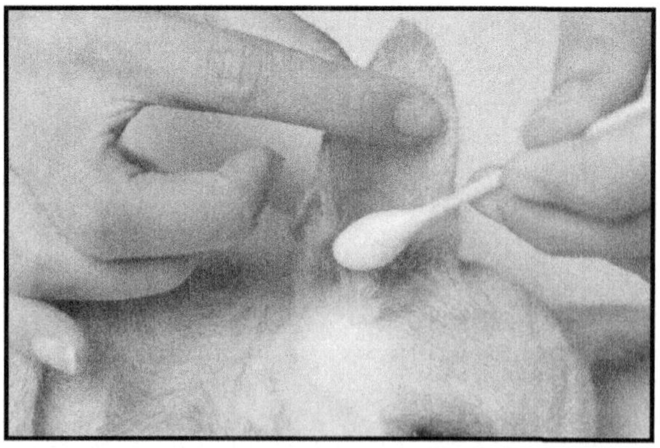

Ear Powders – These can be purchased at any pet store and are designed to keep your cocker's ears dry, while inhibiting the growth of bacteria that can lead to infections. Ear powders are also used when removing excess hair growth from inside your dog's ear canal, making it easier to grip the hair.

Ear Cleaning Solutions – All pet stores offer a wide variety of ear cleaning creams, drops, oils, rinses, or wipes specially formulated for cleaning doggy ears.

TIP ***Your cocker's ears are very sensitive. It is always important to read the labels before purchasing products and avoid any solutions that list alcohol as the main ingredient.***

Ear Cleaning Step-By-Step

1. Lift your cocker's ear, holding it between your thumb and forefinger to get a good look inside.
2. Gently wipe around the entrance of the ear canal with damp cotton wool, removing dirt or excess wax.
3. Insert the tip of the bottle containing the ear cleaning solution into the ear canal, making sure not to push it in too far, then squeeze to release the cleaner.
4. Massage the base of the ear to help the cleaner pass inside the ear canal and wipe away any excess with damp cotton wool.
5. Repeat the process for the other ear.
6. If there is an infection and your vet has prescribed drops, it is best to apply them straight after your spaniel's ears have been cleaned. This will ensure the medicine enters the ear and is absorbed without being blocked by excess wax.

Ear Care Tips

- Establish a regular, healthy ear care programme early on that includes cleaning and inspection for foreign objects and foul smells.
- Check inside your cocker's ears for redness. When the inside appears red and irritated, this could be the first sign of a problem.

- Look for excess hair growth in their ears. Some dogs grow hair inside their ears, and if it is not removed, it can cause itching and hearing loss.
- Regularly check inside your dog's ears for any discharge or odour. If they smell bad, they might have a highly itchy yeast infection, which smells like beer or bread baking. Time for a vet visit.
- A gentle ear cleaner formulated for dogs such as 'Ear Pro', (pictured) will remove debris, eliminate excess wax, and relieve inflammation.
- Frequently inspect for bacterial infections. Depending on the type of bacteria, your cocker might be scratching or whining, and their ears could smell like bad breath or rotten chicken, or smell sweeter, like caramel or grapes. If you notice any of these signs, it is time for a visit to the vet.
- Regularly check for parasites. If your cocker is shaking and tilting their head, it might indicate tiny mites in the ear canal. These are extremely itchy, very irritating, and usually smell like rotten rubbish. Mites are often difficult to spot until they build up and start to resemble coffee grounds. Veterinary attention in this case is required.

- Scratching or rubbing their ears and tilting or shaking their head often indicates an infection that needs immediate attention by the vet.
- Ear wipes, such as 'Vet's Best', (pictured) could help between ear cleaning sessions, as they freshen the outer areas of the ear and help decrease odours.
- Many home remedies can clean your cocker's ears just as efficiently without the high price tag. Witch hazel is recommended, or a 50:50 solution of organic cider vinegar and purified water, another option is a 50:50 solution of hydrogen peroxide and purified water.
- After swimming, always check to make sure your cocker spaniel's ear canals are dry. If salt water has got inside their ears, rinse them thoroughly with fresh water and completely dry to prevent infection.

Paw Care

It is important to regularly check your cocker's paws to ensure they are in good condition and be aware of potential problems before they become serious.

TIP ***Anyone living in a wet climate where your cocker could come home with muddy feet after each walk, should consider purchasing a 'MudBuster' portable dog paw cleaner. These are simple to use and will keep the mud out of your home. Just add warm water, insert your dog's foot, give a twist, and like magic the soft, silicone blades will remove the mud.***

Since dogs do not usually wear shoes, their feet get into everything and sometimes pick up burrs, spear grass, or even chewing gum. After a walk, take a minute to check between the pads to make certain there are no foreign objects that could cause discomfort.

15 Paw Care Tips

1. When out walking, your dog's nails shouldn't touch the ground. Their nails need to be trimmed if you hear them clicking or scratching as they walk.
2. After running or jogging with your dog, always check their paws for injury.
3. When visiting the beach, always check your cocker's paws after arriving back home. There may have been sharp barnacles at the beach that can cut or injure their paws.
4. Hot pavements, sand, or road surfaces can burn your dog's paws. Bear that in mind on hot days and walk your cocker in shady areas or on grass that are cooler than concrete pavements, roads, or sand covered areas.
5. Check for spear grass when visiting a park or wooded area. There are many varieties of dangerous spear grass that flourish during the summer months. These invasive grasses easily cause great discomfort and can lead to emergency surgery. Some of these grasses have a Velcro-like surface and a needle-like point that can easily pierce any area of your cocker's skin. Always have a look between their toes and all over your dog's body after visiting an area where spear grass is growing.
6. Inspect for mats between the pads. Cocker spaniels often grow excessive amounts of hair between their paw pads. If this hair is not regularly clipped away, it can form mats between the pads that feel like tiny rocks and make walking painful.
7. Dogs walk on all sorts of debris, from chewing gum to sticky plant leaves and sap from trees that can stick to their feet. Checking for any foreign objects and removing them after a walk helps to ensure your dog has healthy feet.
8. Consider dog booties for walking your cocker in cold weather. If you start using them from when they are a pup, your dog will readily accept wearing booties when walking on snow and ice-covered ground that could have been sprayed with salt.

9. Try 'Musher's Secret Paw Protection Wax' (pictured) during cold winter months. This product creates an invisible boot around your dog's paws to protect the pads from salt, snow, and ice.
10. If your cocker doesn't venture out very often, rough ground could cause them injury as their paws are unused to it. Take them outside for short periods, gradually

increasing play or walk time so their paws become accustomed to the environment, making them more hard-wearing.

11. Use a long-lasting moisturiser, such as 'Bag Balm' (pictured). It will treat cracked and damaged noses and paw pads. Your dog will not only love you for providing a special spa day for their paws, but they will also feel better as their moisturised paws are softer and less prone to injury or cracking. To improve circulation to your spaniel's paws, massage them by gently rubbing between their paw pads, and in a circular motion on the back of their paw.

12. Eliminate toxic floor cleaning products your dog might walk on, as toxins can enter their body through the pads of the feet.
13. Do not use pesticides or herbicides in the back garden. When your dog walks on the grass, these products enter through their paw pads.
14. When out walking with your dog, take note of oil or petrol spills on the road and avoid them so the toxins will not get stuck onto their paws.
15. Be careful not to walk your cocker through building sites or areas with falling and abandoned buildings where they might step on a nail or other sharp object.

If your dog continually licks or chews their paws, it could be a sign of injury or irritant. Check their paws and remove any debris before wiping them with antimicrobial hydrogel. This will soothe any irritation and promote the healing process. If your cocker continues to lick or chew, contact your vet for advice about further treatment.

If their paws are cut or cracked, rinse the affected area with a wound care solution to clean away any irritants. Then, apply an antimicrobial hydrogel to soothe and heal the injury. To prevent any further damage to the paw, wrap it in a bandage.

Paw care needs to be part of your regular, dog care routine, in the same way as exercise and grooming are.

Removing Parasites

Removing Fleas – Fleas are the bane of every dog who walks through grassy fields or explores the local park or nature trails. For more information about fleas, please refer to Allergies and Canine Skin, Chapter 14.

TIP ***You will need a flea comb specifically designed to remove tiny mites or fleas from your dog's coat. Usually, small for manoeuvring in tight spots, these combs often have a plastic handle with metal teeth spaced closely together to trap and remove tiny, hiding pests.***

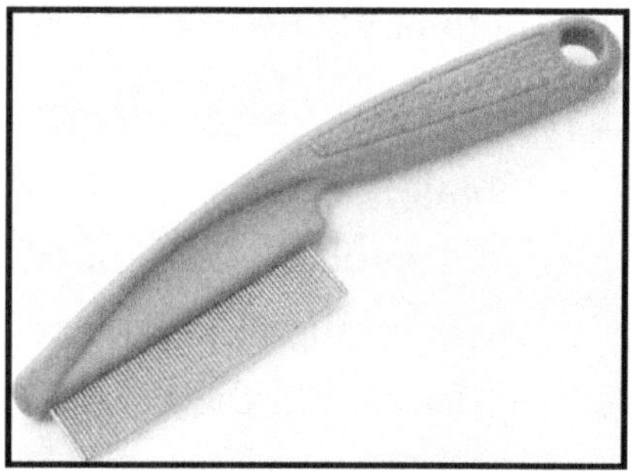

Mostly, an infestation of fleas is found when brushing your cocker spaniel. Unless the infestation is too large to handle at home and requires the intervention of a veterinarian, you should immediately get busy eliminating these annoying pests.

Most vets recommend a monthly spot-on or pill flea treatment. If you prefer a more natural approach without the harsh chemicals, there are many alternative products and shampoos available designed to eliminate fleas, such as:

- Shampoos containing pyrethrum—botanical extract found in small, white daisies—or citrus, cedar, or tea tree oil.
- 'Cedarcide' shampoo and spray—100% safe for everyone, non-toxic, and highly effective in killing biting and crawling creatures on contact. You can bathe your dog with the shampoo and spray carpets, beds, or even yourself.

Depending on the length and density of your cocker's coat, removing fleas with a flea comb (pictured) can be an arduous task.

Although you can never be 100% certain they have all been removed, the following steps will help:

1. First, bathe your dog with a shampoo designed to kill fleas and then condition—it is easier to comb through a clean, conditioned, and dry coat.
2. Prepare a container with hot water and washing up liquid.
3. Begin at the head, and work towards the back, slowly combing through small sections.
4. As the comb fills with dead hair, flea eggs, dirt, and fleas, push down on the teeth of the comb and deposit the contents trapped in the teeth into the soapy mixture.
5. Work down the chest and sides and then the stomach.
6. Finish by combing your cocker's legs and tail.
7. As fleas scurry around and a second pass may get the ones that were missed the first time, repeat the process.
8. Focus under the chin, tummy, and tail areas where fleas tend to congregate.
9. Let the soapy water stand for at least 10 minutes before discarding it to make sure all trapped fleas have drowned.

Although using a flea comb is a time-consuming task, it is a safe, effective, and inexpensive way to remove these pests. Remember to wash all bedding, or spray with a treatment designed to kill them, so any fleas, eggs, or larvae are removed from your spaniel's environment.

Removing Ticks – Before learning how to remove them, read about ticks in Allergies and Canine Skin, Chapter 14 to find out what ticks are.

As ticks are larger than fleas, ranging in size from tiny larvae to the size of a human fingertip, they are usually easier to find. The following tips will help you find ticks on your cocker spaniel:

1. Start at the head and run your hands over their body to feel for lumps or bumps that were not there before.
2. When checking around the neck, do not forget to feel underneath the collar and inside their ears.
3. Then search the rest of your cocker's body, inside the groin area, underneath the tail, and between the toes.

There are several tools that can be used to remove ticks. While you can certainly remove one with the tweezers you have in your medicine cabinet, having a tool purpose-built for easy and complete removal of an embedded tick is always better:

- A fine-tipped pair of tweezers, such as 'Tick Ease' has a V-shaped slot that will remove the entire tick, including the mouth pieces.
- Tick Twister (pictured) is a simple device for painlessly, easily, and quickly removing ticks that have embedded themselves in your cocker's skin.

There are many natural and chemical-based tick repellents designed to prevent or kill ticks—and other crawly creatures—including oral tablets, shampoos, tick collars, sprays, and spot-on treatments.

FACT ***There are hundreds of kinds of ticks, and many diseases they transmit can be harmful to both animals and humans. The deer tick is more worrisome than some others, as it infects both dogs and humans with Lyme disease. It takes several hours for an attached tick to transmit disease, which is why looking for ticks after each walk and immediately removing them is very important.***

The best type of tick prevention for your spaniel depends on where you live, where your dog spends most of their recreation time, and how prevalent ticks are in the area. Choosing effective tools and repellents, plus taking precautions by not walking your cocker in areas known to be infested with ticks will help to avoid these bloodsucking parasites. If your dog does get ticks, here is how to remove or kill them:

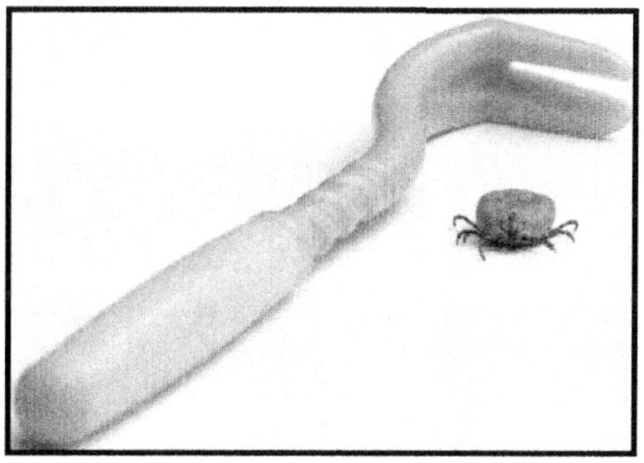

- Tick Twister – Hold close to the skin and engage the tick from the side so it is securely in the narrowest part of the V-shaped hook, lift very lightly and twist the hook two or three times until the tick is detached from your cocker's skin. Disinfect with alcohol.
- Tweezers – Spread the fur, grasp the tick as close to your cocker's skin as possible and pull it out in a steady, slow, straight upward motion to prevent the mouth from breaking off and remaining embedded in your dog's skin. Disinfect the area afterwards with rubbing alcohol.
- Cedarcide spray – Lightly mist your spaniel's coat or apply with your hands. Massage into their coat and cover their legs, under belly, and around the ears and tail. Apply to your dog's face with your hands, avoiding their mouth and eyes.

Seasonal Care

Unless you live in a part of the world where the day-to-day climate remains constant, the chances are you will need to consider care items to keep your dog comfortable in every season.

Summer Care – While summertime usually entails enjoying more outdoor adventures, it can also mean biting ticks and flea season, burnt paw pads, or heatstroke that can seriously injure your cocker.

The ideal temperature for fleas and ticks is between 21-29º C (70-85º F), which is why these pests are more common during summertime. Make sure you are vigilant about your tick and flea prevention/treatment routine (as described in the section above) during those hot, summer months.

Your cocker should never be left alone in a parked vehicle, even on mild days, as they can suffer from heatstroke within a few minutes. Even though the car might be parked in the shade and have the windows cracked, this will have little effect on how hot the vehicle gets. In a matter of minutes, it can become considerably hotter inside the car compared to the outside temperature. **The best rule is to never leave your cocker alone in a vehicle.**

When walking your dog outside during the heat of summer, bear in mind that hot tarmac, carparks, and pavements can cause burns and blistering to your spaniel's foot pads very quickly. For example, when the air temperature is 30o C (86o F), the road surface can reach 57o C (135o F), which is far too hot for your cocker's feet to endure. Also, your dog's body will be heated from below—radiating up from the surface—and from the sun's rays beating down from the top, which increases the possibility of heatstroke. Always test the surface temperature with your hand before setting out with your dog. If it is too hot, choose to walk in shady or grassy areas, or walk during cooler times of the day.

Anyone who has ever been to the beach on a hot, summer day will have experienced the sand becoming so hot it is almost impossible to walk on it without burning your feet. If the sand is hot enough to scorch your feet, it will be just as hot on your cocker spaniel's feet.

Just like people, dogs are at risk of burning in the sun if they are not protected—especially lightly coloured or thinly coated dogs. But the good news is most pet shops stock specially formulated suncream for your cocker spaniel. Ask your vet if you are unsure whether your dog needs suncream.

Regular clipping and/or grooming will keep your cocker's coat clean and free from knots. This is particularly important in the summertime as matting traps heat and makes your spaniel feel extremely hot.

It is important to help your dog keep as fit and healthy as possible all year round. It is especially important to help them maintain a healthy weight during warm weather. Your dog will probably be less active when it is hot, and any walks or playtime should be moved to cooler parts of the day with plenty of breaks. Giving them time in the shade can be a good idea. Adjust the amount of food you give them to reflect how much energy they are using.

FACT ***Dogs do not sweat the way people do and can only regulate their temperature by panting. They need access to drinking water during hot weather. Never forget to take water with you when you go out walking in warmer temperatures.***

You can buy evaporative cooling vests that will keep your dog cool when the weather is hot. These work by soaking them in water before putting them on your cocker. Another simple way to help your dog stay cooler when the sun is shining is to have them wear a T-shirt or vest that is a lighter colour than their own coat.

When your dog is panting excessively and feeling uncomfortably hot, this is how to make them feel better:

- Have them rest in the shade.
- Get them to stand in cool water.
- Use a wet towel.
- Give them a cooling bath and let them air dry.
- Spray your cocker with the garden hose.
- Provide them with a paddling pool full of water.
- Place your spaniel in front of a fan.
- Add some ice cubes to their water bowl.

Winter Care – Because your cocker has a fur coat, there is a misconception that they can tolerate the cold better than we do. Unfortunately, this is not necessarily the case. Like us, our fur-coated friends are used to the warmth of an indoor shelter and cold weather is as hard on them as it is on we humans. Whatever your view of winter, one thing remains certain, it is a time when our beloved dogs need a little extra care. Here are some tips to think about as you explore the winter landscape with your cocker spaniel:

If it is too cold for you to stand at the door without your coat, it will probably be too cold for your dog. Pay attention to their behaviour when they are outdoors. If your cocker spaniel is whining, shivering, acting anxious, or they stop playing and appear to be looking for places to burrow, it is time to bring them in.

Coat – Your dog might need to wear a coat or jumper when out for winter walks. A cosy coat should reach from your cocker's neck to the base of their tail and protect their stomach. Remember, coats do not prevent frostbite on their ears or feet, so do not keep your spaniel out too long in freezing temperatures.

Walk timing – If your cocker feels the cold, try walking them in the late morning or early afternoon hours when temperatures are a little higher, avoiding early morning or late evening walks. While it is sunny, spend time playing outdoors. The added benefit of sunshine is that it provides both you and your dog with vitamin D.

Limit outdoor time – Take your spaniel out for frequent walks, exercise, and play. However, when the temperature drops, do not leave them outdoors for long. A good rule is to go out with them, and when you are ready to come in, they will be too.

Warm bedding – To ensure your dog stays warm, it is vital to choose the right bedding. Warm blankets create a snug environment. Heated dog beds can help keep the stiffness out of aging joints. Place your cocker's bed in a favourite spot where they sleep every day, so the area does not feel unfamiliar.

Heating sources – Cockers often seek heat during cold winter weather by snuggling too close to heating sources. So, it is important to avoid space heaters to prevent your pet from being burnt. Fireplaces can also pose a major threat, so make sure you have a dog-proof system to keep your heat-seeking spaniel out of harm's way.

Grooming – Your cocker spaniel needs a clean, well-groomed coat to keep them fully insulated. This is especially important if they spend a lot of time outdoors. If they need a bath, thoroughly dry them afterwards, especially if you are going to allow them outside.

Moisturise their skin – Cold and dry weather can adversely affect your cocker's skin. To prevent dry, flaky skin, add a skin and coat supplement to their food. Coconut oil is an excellent, natural moisturiser that will help keep your dog's skin and coat healthy.

No overfeeding – Although your cocker might need an extra layer in winter, make sure it is provided by a coat and not a layer of fat. Cold temperatures often bring on lazy behaviour and the need for fewer calories. Be attuned to your dog's activity level and adjust their calorie intake accordingly.

Antifreeze – With winter comes antifreeze, which tastes sweet, and your cocker will readily lick or drink it. It is extremely toxic, and a small amount can prove fatal. It is best to keep your dog out of the garage and off the driveway where they could encounter antifreeze or other harmful chemicals.

Do not leave your spaniel in the car – In the same way as cars can get dangerously hot in summer, freezing cold winter temperatures are equally dangerous for your dog. Leaving your car running involves additional risks that include carbon monoxide poisoning if your car is parked in the garage. When you go out to run errands, leave your cocker at home.

Special care for seniors – Cold weather often aggravates existing medical conditions in dogs, particularly arthritis. It is essential to maintain an exercise regimen for your arthritic cocker but be careful of slippery surfaces and make sure your dog has a warm, soft rest place to recuperate in after their activity. If you do not give your senior dog a natural joint supplement to lubricate the joints and ease the discomfort of arthritis, you might want to consider adding one in the winter months. Just like people, your cocker spaniel is more susceptible to other illnesses during winter weather.

Snow in their paws – Inspect your dog's paws and dry them thoroughly after they have been out in the back garden. With long-haired dogs, this is especially important as they are prone to snow compacting between their toes and turning into ice balls, which can prove very painful. If they will let you, trim the long hair between your cocker spaniel's toes to help prevent this.

Recall command – In foggy or snowy conditions, the cold weather frequently brings reduced visibility. Therefore, if you are letting your cocker off their lead, be certain they have good recall to avoid them becoming lost. As always, you need to make sure their microchip details are up-to-date, and it has your correct contact information.

Conspicuousness – As the nights are drawing in and the sun begins to rise later, attach a small light to your spaniel's collar so they can be seen when out walking in reduced visibility.

Watch where they play – Although your cocker is probably having a great time outdoors, give them frequent indoor breaks for water and to allow them to get warm. And remember not to stay out too long. If you are walking or playing in an are unfamiliar to your dog, keep them close. It would be easy for them to venture onto unsafe surfaces such as frozen ponds or lakes. These could be covered in snow and not easily visible.

During holiday times – such as Easter, Halloween, and Christmas there are often more foods easily within reach that are toxic for dogs, such as chocolate or other sweet treats. Also, holidays often mean firework displays—Halloween, New Year's Eve—that can be exceedingly unsettling for our furry friends. Remember to leave them indoors where they are in familiar surroundings and disguise the disturbing sounds with soft, soothing music.

10. Socialisation

'A dog is the only thing on earth that
loves you more than they loves himself.'
~ Josh Billings ~

What is meant by socialising? It is the learning process your cocker puppy must go through to learn key life skills to ensure they are secure and content in their environment and can communicate effectively within their social group.

This is achieved by introducing your puppy to everyday sights, sounds, and situations to get them used to their surroundings. This should be done in a positive and non-threatening way. Socialising your cocker spaniel puppy is one of the most important steps towards guaranteeing they will live a happy and stress-free life with their new family. Not taking the time to properly socialise your puppy can lead to unwanted behavioural issues later. A dog acting aggressively towards a person or other animal can be so severe that they find themselves in danger of being put down or having to wear a muzzle every time they go out in public. The good news is any sort of aggressive tendencies your cocker might display are usually avoidable if thorough socialisation steps are taken. Although early socialisation of your puppy is very important, it is also vital that you continue socialising them throughout their lifetime.

Every dog needs a leader to guide them. The cocker spaniel is an independent-minded breed with a history as a gun dog for hunting birds. If your cocker is not properly socialised, trained and taught to respect your word as their owner, they could feel forced to take over the family 'pack' and make their own decisions. This can lead to all sorts of unwanted trouble, especially if your dog decides to act in an aggressive manner towards other dogs or people. Aggression is a huge stress on both dog and owner, and as most people are aware, stress can shorten your life and prevent you from experiencing happiness.

Socialising Puppies

Socialising your new cocker puppy can be a fun and entertaining time for both of you and is one of the most important aspects of raising a well-behaved companion who is a joy to be around.

TIP ***It is far easier to socialise a puppy than an adult dog. When bringing your new spaniel puppy into your home, you should take advantage of the critical socialisation period between 3 to 16 weeks of age.***

Though this is the age when your puppy is more accepting of new things they are introduced to, it is never too late to get started. When this important period in your puppy's life is over, it does not mean socialisation is at an end.

Before embarking on the socialisation journey, it can be useful to think about what your plans might be over the next 10 to 15 years, and then imagine how you would like your cocker to react in those circumstances. For instance, if you plan to fly frequently to visit relatives, you will want your dog to enjoy staying in a travel crate and not be freaked out by the noise of the plane.

Or perhaps you might wish to spend your leisure time enjoying open-air concerts. In this case, getting your puppy used to large crowds and loud music is essential. However, it is never a good idea to take your dog to any event that involves fireworks.

Maybe you like to go kayaking, paddle boarding, or surfing. It is easy to each a young puppy not to fear these fun water sports when they are young. In other words, when you think of your daily life, what you enjoy, and places you want to visit, it makes sense to begin socialising your cocker puppy in those areas.

Additionally, taking your puppy to places they do not normally visit or doing things they wouldn't ordinarily be exposed to also helps them feel more confident and comfortable as they move forwards in life. When socialising your cocker puppy, the following check list for their exposure will help you start:

People

- Babies, toddlers, and children of all ages.
- Men and women of all ages and ethnicities.
- Men with beards.
- People wearing masks, hats, and backpacks.

- People carrying boxes or using a walking stick.
- People lying down or limping.
- People jogging, riding bicycles, skateboards.
- People on crutches, in wheelchairs, or on scooters.

Dogs

- Small dogs.
- Large dogs.
- Young dogs.
- Old dogs.
- Energetic dogs.
- Calm dogs.
- Aggressive dogs.
- Dogs with short muzzles.
- Dogs with no tails.
- Dogs with cropped ears.

Vehicles

- Motorcycles.
- Cars.
- Trucks.
- Buses.
- Ambulances.
- Fire engines.
- Planes.
- Trains.

Sounds

- Babies crying.
- Beeping noises.
- Children screaming.
- Doorbells.
- Door knocking.
- Sirens.
- Smoke Alarms.
- Noisy traffic.
- Planes landing and taking off.
- Children playing in a schoolyard.
- Animal and bird noises.
- Loud music.
- Hoovers.
- Cars backfiring.

Surfaces

- Smooth floors.
- Tiled floors.
- Gravel.
- Stairs.
- Bridges.
- Grates.
- Metal surfaces.
- Mirrors.

Situations

- Busy pavements.
- Quiet lakeside walks.
- City parks.
- The vet's office.
- Riding in a lift.
- Long car rides in a crate.
- Inside a Sherpa bag on a plane—while still small.
- Inside dog-friendly stores.
- Visiting a friend's house.

You should always let your cocker puppy know when they are doing well during socialisation sessions. Reward them with praise and a tasty treat when they react calmly in any of the above situations and look to you for direction. Never force your puppy into a new situation. If they seem nervous or frightened in any way, move away from whatever is causing stress and try again at another time. Successful socialisation involves ensuring that every new experience is a pleasant one.

Socialising Adult Dogs

The same puppy checklist above also applies when socialising an adult dog, which will often be a far more time-consuming task. Nevertheless, if you are patient and do not force issues too quickly, anything is possible. The process typically takes longer as an older dog is more apt to act with fear aggression when exposed to sounds, people, animals, and situations they have not experienced before.

TIP ***All dogs are curious about their environment and love to check it out. The best way to start socialising an older dog is to take them for frequent walks. This will expose them to many new social situations and plenty of opportunities to practise proper behaviour.***

If your cocker spaniel growls, barks, or appears to be fearful when seeing a person or dog approaching, the best course of action is to remain calm and confident. Remember, this is all new for them. Simply move away from the stressful situation by turning in another direction to increase space so they can calm down.

By implementing the socialisation of your older dog slowly and remaining composed, they will feel your energy and soon become more confident and less concerned about the new situation. Every time they stay calm and look to you for direction, reward them with a treat and loving praise. Soon, your dog will realise going out to socialise is a rewarding experience they look forward to repeating.

If your adult cocker has never had the opportunity to socialise with other dogs at the park, it is important not to force this but let them observe from a distance. When they are relaxed, slowly move a little closer and carefully watch their reaction. Should they respond with fear or aggression, move farther away until they calm down. Gradually introduce your spaniel to the park and reward their good behaviour. By doing this, your dog will soon want to move closer for a sniff with the other dogs. Before you know it, they will be eager to visit their new friends every day.

Socialising with Unknown Dogs

Despite their personality, any cocker who is not regularly socialised can become shy, nervous, afraid, suspicious, or overly bossy around unfamiliar dogs. Daily on lead walks are the perfect opportunity for your cocker to see and possibly meet other dogs, as well as practise proper behaviour when out and about.

Always take it slowly and never put your spaniel in the uncomfortable situation where they feel forced into being around other canines who might unsettle them. Whether a puppy or an adult dog, your cocker should always be given the option to walk away to create space.

Below are some tips to help your spaniel quickly make friends:

1. When walking on a loose lead, encourage your cocker to keep their attention on you. When they do, reward them, and keep practising until they calmly walk on lead.

2. Walk at a distance from other dogs. Make sure your cocker's focus stays on you and remain far enough away for them not to become excited or agitated. Be sure to have some treats with you so you can reward their calm behaviour.
3. Gradually reduce the distance between your cocker and other dogs.
4. Once they are accustomed to seeing other dogs, arrange a walk with a friend and their dog. That way, your spaniel will learn to walk alongside them. At first, keep both dogs on lead.
5. If both dogs are relaxed, let them greet each other on lead. Once they have said hello and had a sniff, you can move on.
6. When they have got to know each other and are relaxed, you can let them off their leads to play together. Just be sure you have trained your cocker to come back when you call them.

Always remember to go at your spaniel's pace. If they seem overwhelmed or unsure at any point, go back to the stage where they were calm. Then continue at a slower pace.

When you start to socialise your cocker puppy or adult dog, it is best to introduce them first to the calmer and friendlier dogs, as opposed to overly boisterous or less friendly dogs. Any sort of negative experience can result in teaching your dog to be afraid or feel they must take an aggressive stance.

Be vigilant when visiting the park where there could be dogs with different personalities and play styles. Matching dog sizes is a good idea as your spaniel puppy needs to be protected from playing with a dog who is ten times their size. The moment any dog is playing too roughly or causing your dog to yelp or feel afraid, you need to step in and immediately stop the play.

Socialisation with Senior Dogs

When your puppy has had all their vaccinations and can visit the park to meet and greet fellow canines of all shapes, sizes, and ages, one of the important ages is the senior dog. While it is important to carefully supervise any interaction between any dog and your excited, bouncing cocker puppy—who has not yet learnt to control their enthusiasm—it is even more important around a senior dog.

Some senior dogs are extremely tolerant and will put up with crazy puppy energy and others will not. Close supervision is key around an older dog who might not appreciate being pounced on, having their ears pulled or tail bitten by razor-sharp puppy teeth. Here are a few steps to keep your puppy under control while teaching them respectful greeting skills:

- Take your cocker puppy for a walk to tire them out before visiting the park.
- Lift your puppy up and let the senior dog sniff their bottom.
- If the senior dog is agreeable, let your puppy sniff their bottom.
- If all seems fine, let your puppy play under close supervision.
- The second your spaniel seems to be aggravating the senior dog, step in and stop the play session.

Depending on the age of your puppy, the play session with a willing, elderly dog may not last long before they both have had enough, and it is time to head home. A senior dog could have aches and pains and not be all that interested in playing. If the elderly dog has had enough, they might decide to give your puppy a nip. While a good-natured senior dog will probably not really harm your cocker, it is always best to avoid any situation that has the potential to frighten your puppy enough to make them afraid of other dogs.

Socialising with Unknown People

Proper socialisation also means taking your cocker spaniel everywhere and introducing them to different people of all ages, sizes, and ethnicities (see the People checklist at the beginning of the chapter), so they will learn what is normal and acceptable behaviour in their daily life.

First Meeting Introductions – When a new person or child is approaching for a first meeting with your cocker, ask them to practise the following:

- Approach calmly and slowly.
- Hold out the back of their hand rather than trying to pat your cocker's head.
- Let your dog sniff their hand and approach at their own speed.
- Never force your dog to get closer if they do not want to.

Introducing your dog to your children

Introduction – You should introduce your new cocker spaniel to your children sooner rather than later. This will help them to become accustomed to one another. Start slowly, but do not to rush them into it as they might not hit it off immediately. Brief, frequent encounters are the best way to gradually let them interact together.

When children wish to play with your dog, always supervise so no one becomes nervous or overwhelmed.

An older dog will usually have much more stamina for long play sessions. They will also be stronger, and when playing too vigorously with very young children they could unintentionally be bowled over or scratched.

Your cocker puppy will tire easily, so keep their play sessions short. Be especially careful when allowing young children to play with your small puppy who might accidentally be hurt. You do not want your puppy to become fearful of children, as this could lead to fear or aggression issues later in life.

When introducing your child and cocker spaniel, the 'sniff test' is normally the best place to start. Hold your child's hand out to allow your dog to learn their smell. This is important before your child tries to stroke them. If your cocker appears uncertain after sniffing, they might not wish to be touched. Instead, encourage your child to speak softly to your dog to soothe their nerves and wait for your dog to approach them.

If you are adopting a new cocker, involving your child in the selection and adoption process is a good way to teach them about the responsibility that comes with it. It will also initiate the bonding process between them. Your child needs to learn that there are certain times when they should not approach the dog. This includes when they are eating, when they are playing with a toy, when they are going to the toilet or while they are asleep. Special care should be taken if your dog is blind or deaf as they can easily become frightened.

Playing together – One of the mutual benefits of dogs and children playing together is the exercise and stimulation they gain from their interaction. Young children are often overly enthusiastic and loud when playing. This could frighten or over-excite your cocker, so it is essential for you to teach them to play calmly and quietly with the dog. Rough, aggressive games could encourage aggressive behaviour in your dog.

To help them form a strong bond, have them play together with your cocker's favourite toys, such as a pull rope, or let them run together. Teach your child how to recognise when their pet is scared or anxious—tail tucked in, ears flattened, or hiding—and get them to back off straight away.

Never leave your cocker and child to play unattended, particularly if they are young, as your dog could easily misinterpret the situation and become overly excited. Discourage jumping up, as your dog could knock over an infant, and teach your child to keep dog toys away from their face.

If your spaniel appears unhappy or too boisterous, be ready to intervene to prevent them biting or scratching. When your dog shows signs of tiredness or over-stimulation, it is time for a nap in a quiet and safe place away where they will not be bothered.

It is vital to remind your child to handle their pet gently and respectfully as children can perceive pets as cuddly toys. Also, some dogs don not like being picked up, and smaller breeds are often quite delicate. So, teach your child to be patient with their cocker and let them come to them in their own time. Discourage your child from getting too close, as some dogs dislike face-to-face contact. Teach your child to treat their spaniel as they would another child. They should not climb on them, pull their ears or tail, and there should be no rough play.

Other tips – Often, puppies steal, chew, and swallow children's toys and clothes, so teach your child to keep them safe by tidying up after themselves and storing their toys out of paw's reach.

Most children love nothing better than sharing their food under the table, without realising it could be unhealthy for their cocker. Keep a watchful eye on your dog if they are sniffing around for titbits, or better still, leave them in a different room at mealtimes.

Sometimes, nervous dogs cope better around children when they have somewhere to escape to if things get too much for them. Crate training your dog offers a safe place filled with their favourite blanket or toy away from loud or excitable children. Be certain your child understands that the dog crate is off limits to them.

Depending on your child's age, it is a good idea to get them involved in your pet care routine. They can learn the valuable lesson about the constant care and attention pets need to live happy, healthy lives through filling their water or food bowls, walking your cocker, or cleaning their toys and bedding.

TIP ***When it comes to protecting themselves from small children who might not understand how to respect a dog's space, the cocker spaniel is usually gentle and patient. Still, bear in mind, any***

dog who is pushed too far may feel the need to protect themselves from a child who is invading their space, getting too close to their toys and food bowl, or treating them roughly.

Fear of Loud Noises

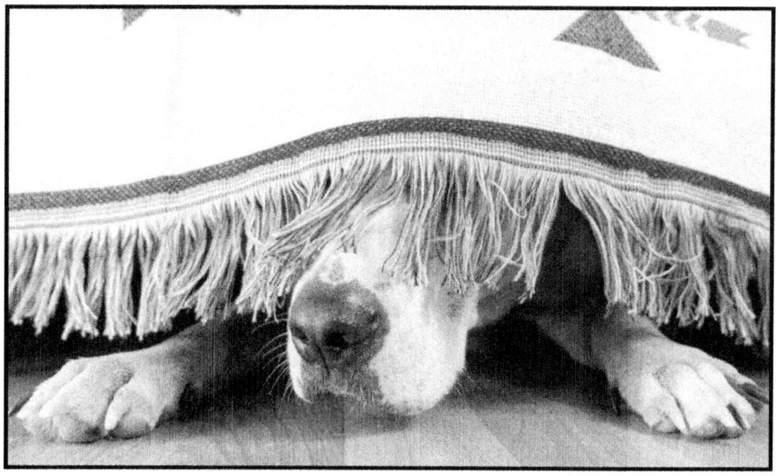

Many cockers show extreme fear of loud noises and piercing noises can be very painful for your dog's sensitive ears. The best way to prevent or eliminate this fear is to take the time to desensitise your dog to these noises when they are very young. However, it is still entirely possible to achieve that with an older dog. Once your dog learns that these sounds are not to be feared, it is far less stressful for them when they hear them.

Desensitisation Devices – There are several devices you can use to desensitise your cocker, so they are not traumatised by high-pitched alarms, and loud, popping or banging noises, such as the following:

- CDs – Purchase CDs that are a collection of unusual sounds, such as vacuum cleaners, aeroplanes, sirens, smoke alarms, fireworks, guns firing, people clapping, children playing, and more. Play them while working in the kitchen or relaxing in the living room or lounge. If you show that everything is normal while listening to the CDs, the next time your puppy hears these sounds elsewhere, they will not become upset or agitated, as they will have already learnt to ignore them.
- Bubble Wrap – There is a simple way to desensitise your spaniel if they are fearful of unexpected popping sounds. Show them the bubble wrap, pop a few of the cells and if they do not run away, give them a treat. Begin with the bubble wrap that has small, quieter cells, and then graduate your puppy to the louder, larger celled bubble wrap.
- You can also take things even further by blowing up some small paper bags or balloons and loudly popping them in front of your cocker puppy, or even taking them to a rifle range. When you reward them with a tasty treat for not showing fear or running away, they will soon associate these sounds with receiving something pleasant.
- Relaxation Collars – There are basically two kinds of collars designed to help relax or calm your upset puppy. One uses scent or calming pheromones, while the other plays music at the appropriate decibel level to calm a fearful or stressed dog.
- TV or Radio – Sometimes, all that is required to calm your cocker puppy who is stressed by loud noises is to turn on a TV or radio station that is playing relaxing music. Play it louder than you might normally to help disguise the exterior noises.
- Thundershirts – Some dogs respond well to wearing a 'Thundershirt'. This is a vest designed to reduce anxiety or trauma from loud, rumbling, popping, or banging noises. The idea behind the design is that the gentle pressure it creates is like a hug, which has a calming effect.

FACT ***Some dogs literally lose their minds and do things that make no logical sense when they hear the loud popping or screeching noises of fireworks and various alarms. They start trembling, running, or trying to hide and will not listen to you at all.***

Make certain your cocker cannot harm themselves trying to escape from these noises. If possible, calmly hold them until they start to relax. Always act appropriately when your dog is under this kind of stress by not panicking or having 'feeling sorry' or 'angry and frustrated' energy around them. This tends to make matters worse.

When you are the person who is supposed to be your dog's support system and you are also feeling weak or acting unstable, your cocker will have nowhere to turn. A better idea is to pretend nothing is wrong and talk to your spaniel in a soothing, yet assertive and reassuring tone.

11. Training

'Heaven goes by favor. If it went by merit,

you would stay out and your dog would go in.'

~ Mark Twain ~

As soon as your adorable cocker puppy arrives at their new home, they will learn who is really in charge and where they fit in the family hierarchy. While we tend to believe all people are created equal, this is not the case in the dog world. With respect to our beloved canine companions, there is a pecking order whether you are an animal or person. As an owner if you are not quick to demonstrate to their puppy that they are higher up the totem pole than the pup is, and do not maintain some sort of consistency with rules, your spaniel puppy will soon begin to test the boundaries. You can demonstrate that by being a strong leader during training sessions and your daily encounters with your dog.

This does not mean being harsh, loud, or mean. It simply requires that you find the right energy (see Energy and Body Language Chapter 7) within yourself that your dog responds to best. For example, when teaching your dog to '***Sit***' on command, if your voice sounds too weak or questioning—rather than giving a command—your puppy will probably ignore you. Dogs need to have a dominant leader who they trust and respect, so they can learn to obediently follow commands and understand the rules and boundaries

Basic Rules and Boundaries

TIP ***You can prevent many future behavioural problems when you take the time to teach your cocker spaniel basic rules and boundaries. All that is necessary for effectively teaching your puppy these basics is a composed, consistent, and firm approach, combined with endless patience.***

Basic rules and boundaries include things such as:

- No barking at every little noise.

- No dogs allowed in the kitchen when preparing food.
- No begging at the dinner table.
- People through the door first.
- No sleeping in the owner's bed.
- No raiding the rubbish bin.
- No jumping up on tables or worktops.
- No jumping on people.
- No chasing the neighbour's cat.
- No digging in the flowerbed.

When teaching a 'rule' or 'boundary', you need to 'tell' your puppy when they have done something you do not agree with. The way to do this is through tone of voice to get your puppy to remove themselves from the unwanted activity.

For example, if your cocker is engaging in out of control barking every time someone knocks on the front door or rings the doorbell, you must take control and 'tell' your dog to stop barking and move away from the front door. The following simple steps can help:

- Walk to the front door.
- Stand between the door and your cocker.
- Make eye contact with your dog while pointing away from the door and firmly saying, '***Go!***'
- If your spaniel does not move away, walk towards them so they must back up.
- Keep pointing and forcing them to back away.
- Firmly say, '***Go!***' again.
- Once your dog has backed away at least three metres, keep an eye on them while returning to the door to let your guest in.
- If your cocker immediately rushes to the door when it opens, again step between them and your guest while firmly saying, '***Go!***' and pointing away.
- Walk to the front door.

Every situation is unique, and every dog is different, which means it might take only one or two of these scenes to teach your cocker to desist from this unwanted behaviour or it may take considerably longer. Persistence and consistency are key, and the same steps outlined above can be very effective when teaching many different rules and boundaries.

TIP ***To establish boundaries, it is useful to have a 'Discipline Sound'. You can use it to redirect your puppy when they engage in unwanted behaviour. They will quickly learn what they can or cannot do.***

The best sounds are short and sharp ones that immediately get the attention of your puppy, so they can easily be interrupted or redirected before they make a mistake. It doesn't really matter what the sound is, if it gets your dog's attention and everyone in the family is consistent. In most cases, a simple 'Uh!' said sharply and with emphasis is very effective. Most dogs respond immediately to this, and if caught in the middle of something they are not supposed to be doing will quickly stop and give their attention to you.

Enrol your cocker in a training class

If you are a new owner, it is highly recommended that you book your puppy in a puppy training course. It is a good way to socialise your cocker with other dogs whilst learning basic obedience and commands. Your puppy can then implement what they have learnt when meeting other dogs at the park or on walks as they grow older.

With an expert on hand to guide you and your cocker, taking your dog to a professional training class is an excellent way to build your relationship in a safe and structured environment. If possible, it is recommended that you attend a class rather than just training at home. A professional trainer can give you tips to help you teach your dog in an effective way and will probably offer advice on subjects you may not have thought of.

Before booking, it is advisable to go along and watch a class without your dog to get a feel for what is involved. Good classes have:

- An approachable trainer who helps dogs and their owners in a positive way.
- A calm atmosphere that has no overly excited dogs or a cacophony of barking, which can be a sign of stress. Both dogs and owners should be relaxed.
- The dogs should not be playing uncontrollably.
- The ratio of trainers to dogs should be sufficient that they are able to handle the number of dogs in the class.
- There should be positive and reward-based training methods. If the dogs are punished, or equipment such as choke or electric collars are used, do not enrol.

It is worth noting that there are no regulations for dog training classes, so how good they are differs greatly. Blue Cross only recommends training classes where the trainer uses modern, science-backed training methods. These focus on rewarding your dog with praise, food, and play for doing well rather than punishing them when they get it wrong. If you make it clear your cocker has performed well, they are far more likely to repeat their clever work, and positive training is an effective way to build their confidence in themselves and trust in you.

Avoid trainers who use aversive training equipment, such as choke or pinch collars, or punitive methods such as physically forcing a dog into a sit or yanking them into another position. These training techniques can be stressful for your dog, and some can cause them pain.

You should search the Association of Pet Dog Trainers or Puppy School websites to find a trainer local to you. Also, the Kennel Club in the United Kingdom—and the AKC in the U.S.A.—offer many training classes offered as do other dog trusts and funds, which can either be online or in person. Additionally, many veterinary clinics offer dog training classes.

The largest dog training programme in the U.K. is The Kennel Club Good Citizen Dog Scheme. It is open to all dogs, young or old, whether pedigree or crossbreed. Your dog does not need to be registered with The Kennel Club to take part. The purpose of the scheme is to promote responsible dog ownership by teaching owners to train their dog for everyday life situations. It has four award levels: Puppy Foundation, Bronze, Silver, and Gold.

20 Top Training Tips

1. Begin training straight away as soon as your cocker puppy arrives home. Puppies are much more susceptible to learning new things when they are very young.
2. Always train with an upbeat attitude and positive energy. Dogs learn quicker when they do not feel any stress from their owner. If you are not in a friendly and positive mood when training, your dog might become confused. When all training sessions are fun-filled with plenty of food rewards, your cocker will be a content, attentive student who trusts and respects you and looks forward to learning new commands, tricks, and routines.
3. Use positive reinforcement for good behaviour—toys, treats, play, games, love, walks, happy praise. Give the treats or other rewards to your puppy immediately after they complete the desired behaviour. The faster you confirm the behaviour you want, the easier it is for your puppy to understand what you are trying to teach them.
4. Train your puppy often and for short periods—5 to 10 minutes. Puppies have short attention spans, so if training sessions are too long, they will zone out and this will not be a very productive time.
5. Do not train your puppy when they are hot, tired, or in the middle of vigorous playtime. You want them focused and eager for a training session.
6. Eliminate distractions while training. Choose a quiet place away from noises, children, or other pets. When puppies are young, they are easily distracted by movement and noises and will have a more difficult time concentrating on training.
7. Be consistent when teaching and always follow the same routine. Changing the way you are teaching a certain command/trick or using a different method will only confuse your cocker and make it more difficult for them to learn.
8. Resist using too many confusing words—one-word commands work best. For instance, when teaching your dog to lie down on command, rather than saying, 'Clover, lay down', simply say, 'Down'.
9. When teaching commands, use the hand signal and the command word at the same time. Once your dog has learnt the hand signals for the commands, it is no longer necessary to say the words.
10. Never become short-tempered, frustrated, or impatient during a training session, as your dog will feel this negative energy and get confused. If you feel you are about to lose your cool, quietly end the session and try again later in the day. Yelling at your spaniel could make them nervous and they will stop paying attention to you. If they fear training they might decide following directions is not for them.
11. Say a command word, such as 'Sit' or 'Down' only once. Dogs are smart, so they hear your command and can follow it the first time. Repeating the cue word multiple times will not help your pup sharpen their listening skills, and like a teenager, they will tune you out.

12. Schedule your training session before your cocker's regular meal. This way they might pay closer attention to the instructions so they can earn a tasty treat.
13. When several family members are involved in the training process, everyone needs to use the same command words and hand signals. Otherwise, your dog might get confused.
14. Use what your dog loves best as a reward for learning commands or routines, such as a toy, treat, playtime, or a walk. Some dogs are keener to receive a food treat for learning, while others prefer a toy or a game of fetch as a reward after a training session.
15. Have realistic expectations that take into consideration your puppy's mental and physical limitations. Do not expect too much too soon with a very young puppy. Exercise patience and do not give up on your cocker puppy if they take a little longer to learn what you are teaching them.

16. Dogs learn quicker when they receive a reward for good behaviour (pictured). For instance, if your dog is barking at the postman, calmly correct them and give them a treat when they stop barking.
17. Dogs live in the moment, two minutes after they have done something, they have already forgotten about it. So when your cocker pup is doing something bad, use your chosen 'Discipline Sound' straight away so they can make the association between the behaviour and the correction. Consistent repetition will reinforce what they have learnt.
18. Avoid using punishment such as lead corrections or yelling. Punishment can make your cocker confused and unsure about what is being asked of them.
19. Always end a training session on a cheerful note, with plenty of loving praise, scratches, tummy rubs, a toy, a treat, a walk, or a game. If your puppy has trouble learning a new behaviour, end the session by getting them to do something they have already learnt. Then give them plenty of praise and a reward for their success. We always want our dogs to look forward to their next training session and the best way to ensure that is through positive reinforcement.
20. Begin training straight away as soon as your cocker puppy arrives home. Puppies are much more susceptible to learning new things when they are very young.

Basic Obedience Commands Training

A puppy needs to learn the basic obedience commands, which will ensure that they remain safe in almost every circumstance. For example, when your puppy correctly learns the '***Come***' command, you can always quickly call them back if there should be any danger approaching. Also, when teaching these commands, you are further establishing your leadership role, and if your cocker understands that you are the boss, they will be a safe and obedient follower. If it is fun, your puppy will look forward to their next session.

It is important to use the hand signals that go with the verbal commands during training your cocker spaniel. These hand signals can be a very helpful aid during the senior years of your dog's life when their hearing might be compromised.

When you take the time to teach your cocker hand signals for all basic commands, you are communicating with them at a level they instinctively understand. Furthermore, you are helping them to become a focused follower, as they must watch you to understand what is required of them.

The Three Ds

Sometimes, you can be certain that you have trained your dog to do something, only for them to act as if they do not remember. Perhaps your cocker stayed beautifully when you stood beside them in your quiet kitchen. But when you ask them to '***Stay***' from 7 metres away in the park, they ignore you. Although you might have trained them well in the kitchen, but you need to consider the three Ds of dog training.

The three Ds are duration, distance, and distraction, and they affect almost every command. Dogs are not good at generalising, meaning if they learn to stay in front of you, they do not automatically understand that '***Stay***' has the same meaning if you are on the other side of the room. As each D increases, it is harder for your cocker to know how to successfully perform your command. And if all three come into play without you individually training your dog for each D, the chance of them doing what you tell them is slim.

Duration is the length of time your dog can maintain a command. Some commands, such as spinning in a circle or jumping over a bar have no duration factor, but other commands that require your dog to hold a position, such as '***Sit***' or '***Down***', the longer they must hold it, the more difficult the task becomes.

Whenever you teach a new command, start with a very short duration, such as a second. Then increase the time one second at a time. If your cocker gets it wrong, reduce the duration to something you know they can handle and start building one second at a time from there.

Distance is how far away you can get from your dog before they break the command. The farther away you are, the less reliable your dog will become. As with duration, when you are training distance, start small and build slowly. Ensure your cocker can handle a relatively long distance with you in front of them before you move to their side or behind them. Keep leaving the room for last. Your dog knows when you cannot see them, so turning your back or walking out of sight is particularly challenging for them.

Distraction involves everything that is going on around your cocker when they perform a command, from a squirrel running across the garden to the sound of the doorbell. Anything your dog finds exciting, or disrupting is a distraction. Some dogs even find extra special treats distracting. Make sure your dog has mastered duration and distance before you add distractions. Start by training new commands in a familiar, quiet environment where you are the most interesting thing in the room.

When training your cocker spaniel, only work on one D at a time. You should only combine the Ds once your dog has learnt each D on its own. So, when working on distance, reduce the duration to one second and keep any distractions to a minimum. Set your cocker up for success by not rushing them.

If you see your dog struggling to perform a command you thought they already knew, consider the three Ds. The chances are something is too difficult for them to handle. By incorporating duration, distance, and distraction into your training, it will ensure your cocker understands what you are asking of them no matter what.

Come

The first and most important command to teach your cocker is the '***Come***', or '***Recall***' command.

- Start inside your home and go into a larger room, such as the living room or hallway.
- Place your puppy in front of you and attach their lead or a longer line to their collar, while you back away from them a couple of metres.
- Say the command '***Come***' in an excited, upbeat voice and hold your arms outstretched wide.
- If your cocker does not immediately come towards you, gently tug on the lead, so they understand what they are supposed to do.
- When they come to you, enthusiastically praise them, and offer a treat your puppy likes.

Once your puppy can accomplish the '***Come***' command almost every time inside the home, they can be taken to a nearby park or quiet outside space to repeat the process where there are many more distractions. The goal with the '***Come***' command is to keep you and your dog safe. Successful implementation of this cue is when your cocker spaniel always comes to you when asked, despite nearby distractions.

A helpful tool when practising the '***Come***' command is an extra-long, lightweight line 6-12 metres (25-50 feet). You can use this to attach the puppy to you and encourage them in the right direction should they become distracted by noises, scents, and other dogs.

When first teaching the '***Come***' command outside, choose a time of day when there are fewer distractions. For example, if there are swiftly moving balls and many dogs at the local park at certain times, these are a difficult distraction when first teaching this command. Instead, choose times when the park is quiet, such as early in the morning.

TIP

The most important thing to remember is that 'Come' MUST always be a pleasant experience for your cocker. If you ask your dog to 'Come' when you are upset about something your dog has done, and they come when called only to be disciplined, your dog will soon learn to ignore this important command. You should always give positive praise and/or a treat when your cocker returns to your side when called.

Once your dog always comes happily running to you when asked, it is no longer necessary to say the '***Come***' verbal cue, but you can simply show them the signal. The best thing about the arms wide open hand signal is that it can be seen from a great distance. A well-trained puppy will come running even if they are on the other side of the park.

Also, bear in mind that, even after successfully teaching your dog the '***Come***' command, sometimes they can still be distracted when outdoors if an interesting scent or fast-moving object or creature distracts them. It is a good idea to keep your young cocker on lead in an area where they can easily run off in pursuit of any distraction.

Sit

The '***Sit***' command is important and easy to teach. It will help to keep your puppy safe and can be a valuable behaviour for them to learn. For example, if you teach your dog to sit at kerbs it will make crossing roads safer and asking your dog to sit when they greet people means they are less likely to jump up.

- Ask your dog to '***Sit***'. If they do not understand the command yet, show them what you mean by gently squeezing the area across the back that joins with their back legs with your thumb and middle finger.
- Do NOT just push them down into a sit, as this can cause damage to their back or joints.
- When they sit, give them a treat, and praise them.
- When saying the word '***Sit***', at the same time show the hand signal for this command.
- The universal hand signal for '***Sit***' is right arm—palm open facing upward—parallel to the floor, and then raise your arm while bending at the elbow towards the right shoulder.
- Once your dog is reliably sitting on command, remove the verbal '***Sit***' and replace it with just the hand signal.

Every time you take your cocker out for a walk—which is often a cause of excitement—get into the habit of asking them to sit quietly and patiently at every stage of the walk, including:

- When putting on your puppy's lead.
- While you are putting on your shoes or jacket.
- Before you open the door.
- When you are on the other side of the door.
- While you lock the door.
- Every time you arrive at a road junction.
- Every time you stop during your walk to speak to a neighbour, greet a friend, or admire the view, etc.

When persisting and taking advantage of the many opportunities during a walk to ask your cocker puppy to 'Sit', it will be automatic for them to calmly sit every time you stop walking. Congratulations! That is called an 'automatic' sit.

When asking your cocker spaniel to '***Sit***', they are learning several things at once. You are telling them they must remain still while paying attention to you and you are their boss. Also, they must look to you for direction and respect you as their leader.

Remember, a sitting puppy is easier to control than one standing alert, ready to bolt out the door or jump on someone. Also, because the action of sitting helps to calm the mind of an excited puppy, teaching this command can enhance their daily interaction with family members, friends, and even strangers.

Stay

Once your cocker can '***Sit***' reliably, it is time to add the 'Stay' command. This command instructs your spaniel to remain stationary where you tell them until they are released. Use this command in correlation with a movement command such as '***Sit***' to help your cocker understand what is expected of them.

The biggest mistake people make when teaching '***Stay***' is instructing their dog to break the position rather than hold it. For example, if you ask your dog to '***Stay***' then walk away and call them to you, you are teaching them to break the position you just asked them to hold. Smart dogs will anticipate your release and the '***Stay***' will become less reliable.

- Place your dog in a '***Sit***' and say the word '***Stay***' with authority in your voice. Hold your arm outstretched, your palm open towards your cocker's head while backing away a few steps.
- If they try to follow, calmly say, '***No***' and put them back into '***Sit***'.
- Give them a treat and then repeat, '***Stay***' with the hand signal and back away a few steps.

Down

One more basic command every dog should know is the '***Down***' command, which tells them to lie down. This is a useful thing to get your dog to do when you want them to settle on the floor, either at home or when you are out and about—in shops, restaurants, etc.

- Start with your dog in the '***Sit***' position, then hold a treat about 15 centimetres in front of their nose.
- Slowly lower the treat to the floor in front of them, moving your hand farther away as you lower it.
- Simultaneously say, '***Down***' in a firm but encouraging voice.
- You want your dog to stretch forwards and slide down, following the treat.
- Once their tummy hits the floor, give them the treat and plenty of praise.

- With patience, consistency, repetition, and tasty treats, this is a command that most dogs learn very quickly. Practise often and in different places. Once your cocker is happily lying down on command in your home, continue training in more distracting environments, such as the garden or your local park.

Leave It

As owners, sometimes it is necessary to take things away from your cocker spaniel. For example, if they have picked up something dangerous or are playing with your favourite shoe instead of a toy. Getting your dog to '***Leave it***' is about teaching them it is all right to have something taken away from them as it means they will be rewarded. Follow these basic steps:

- Offer your dog a tasty treat and encourage them to take it in a cheerful, friendly voice.
- Hold another treat in your hand with your fist closed around it. Your cocker is likely to nudge and lick your hand to get the treat out. Do not respond to any of their attempts.
- Wait patiently and say nothing. Wait for your dog to back off from your hand, even just momentarily. As soon as they do and there is a small gap between your hand and your spaniel's nose, open your hand, release the treat, and shower them with praise.
- Repeat these three steps until they consistently make the choice to move away from the treat.
- Once your dog always moves away from the treat you can add the cue word '***Leave it***'. Say this as they back off in a gentle tone and then open your hand to give them the treat and praise them.
- Once your cocker has made the association between the words '***Leave it***' and backing off from the treat, you can start making it harder. Place a treat on your open palm, so your dog can see and smell it. Ask your dog to leave it by saying '***Leave it***'.
- If your dog does not touch the treat, reward them with lots of praise and a treat from your other hand. If your cocker goes to take the treat from your open palm, simply close your hand and wait for them to back away.

Practise the above basic commands everywhere at every opportunity and use them as frequently as possible to ensure their success. As your puppy matures and their attention span increases, you can train them for longer periods and introduce more complicated routines.

Teaching Tricks

Many people only associate the basic dog training commands above when thinking about dog training. Although those are important, you should not underestimate the benefits of training your dog to do tricks. They are a great way to give your cocker spaniel some much needed mental stimulation. Several tricks are built around the basic commands. Also, it can be a lot of fun training your dog some cool tricks to show off to friends!

Shake a Paw

Who doesn't love a well-trained dog who knows how to shake a paw—give a handshake? This is one of the easiest tricks to teach any dog.

- Stand or sit in front of your cocker.
- Place them in the sitting position.

- Say the command '***Shake***' while putting your right hand behind their left or right paw. At the same time, pull the paw gently towards you until you are holding their paw in your right hand.
- Immediately praise them and give them their favourite treat.
- Most dogs learn this trick quite quickly. Soon, once you put out your hand, your cocker will immediately lift their paw and put it in your hand without your assistance or any verbal cue.

Practise every day until they are 100% reliable with this trick, and then it is time to add another one to their repertoire. Most dogs are naturally either right or left pawed. If you know which paw your dog favours, ask them to shake that one.

Roll Over

You will find that just as your cocker is either right or left pawed, they will also want to roll either onto their right or left side. Take advantage of this by asking your dog to roll to the side they naturally prefer.

- Sit with your dog on the floor and put them in a lie down position.
- Hold a treat in your hand and place it close to their nose without allowing them to grab it.
- While they are in the lying position, move the treat to the right or left side of their head—their nose will follow the treat—so they must roll over to get to it.
- You will very quickly see which side they want to naturally roll to. Once you see this, move the treat to that side.
- When they roll over to that side, immediately give them the treat and praise them.
- Say the verbal cue 'Over' while you demonstrate the hand signal—turning your right hand in a circular motion—or move the treat from one side of their head to the other with a half circle motion.
- With enough practise, your cocker will roll over when they see just the hand signal.

Sit Pretty

'***Sit pretty***', or '***Beg***' is a cute trick. Your cocker spaniel starts in the sit position then raises their front legs until they are sitting on their back legs with their front legs curled and held in front of them. While this trick is a little more complicated, remember, every dog is different so always exercise patience.

- Sit or stand in front of your dog and ask them to, '***Sit***'.
- Have a treat nearby—on a worktop or table. When they sit, use both hands to lift their front paws into the sitting pretty position, while saying the command, '***Sit pretty***'.
- Help them balance in this position, while you praise them and give them a treat.
- Repeat the above until your cocker can perform the balancing part of the trick without your help.
- Sit or stand in front of them while holding the treat above their head level with their nose and tell them to, '***Sit pretty***'.
- If they attempt to stand on their back legs to get the treat, you could be holding it too high, which will encourage them to stand on their back legs to reach it. Go back to the first step and put them back into the '***Sit***' position and again lift their paws with their backside on the floor.
- After they learn the trick on verbal command, try saying the verbal cue while demonstrating the hand signal. Holding your arm straight, fully extend it over your cocker's head with your fist closed.

- Make this a fun and entertaining time for both of you and practise a few times every day until they can '***Sit pretty***' with just the hand signal command every time you ask.

Collar, Harness, and Lead Training

Adjusting the collar/harness

Whether you decide to have your puppy in a collar or a harness, you will first want to ensure these fit properly before teaching them to walk beside you on their lead.

TIP ***When fitting your cocker's collar, you do not want it so tight that it almost chokes them, and you do not want it too loose as your puppy could pull their head out of it. When adjusting a flat collar, it should be approximately five centimetres larger than your puppy's neck.***

When adjusting a Martingale collar, the two outside rings should never come together when the lead is attached and there is tension on the lead.

To adjust a harness to fit correctly, you should make it snug around the broadest part of your cocker's chest, so they cannot slip out of it, but not so tight that they cannot move freely.

Putting on the collar/harness

It is always a clever idea to introduce your cocker puppy to their collar or harness shortly after you bring them home from the breeder, so they get used to the sensation even before the lead is attached. Below are the required steps for putting on their collar, but are identical for a harness as well:

- Ask your puppy to come to you and calmly sit.
- Let them see and sniff the collar and then start putting it on. Have tasty treats at the ready to distract them if the sensation of the collar causes them to act as if they are being tortured.
- If your puppy fights about having their collar put on, offer a treat, or play a game to distract them. Only remove their collar when they stop fretting, at which time you can give them another treat.
- Soon, they will learn that when the collar goes on, they receive something they want—a tasty treat.

Attaching the lead

Once your cocker puppy is used to the feel of the collar—or harness—it is time to introduce their lead.

Some new dog owners experience a frustrating situation when first introducing the lead to their puppy who immediately runs away. Instead of sitting quietly while their lead is attached, now there is a game of catch me if you can. This type of game is very entertaining for your puppy and now every time they see you pick up their lead, the chase is on. You can avoid this type of situation by following the steps below every time you attach their lead:

- First, stand or sit in front of your puppy and show them the lead.
- The second your cocker shows any interest in sniffing it, immediately give them a treat.
- Put the lead behind your back for a few seconds and then show it to them again, and immediately give them a treat. Now your puppy is learning to associate seeing their lead with receiving a treat.
- Next, attach the lead to your puppy's collar and again follow with a treat to help form a positive association with their lead.
- Take their lead off and put it away. Then, repeat this process several times during the day until your cocker is consistent with calmly sitting while their lead is attached.

Of course, all this is practised before going out for your first on lead walk. Once your puppy learns to also associate their lead with a fun, outdoor adventure, they will not need a treat for sitting quietly while you attach it.

Walking on a lead

Before your cocker's first outside lead walk, attach the lead to their collar—or harness—and practise a few short, inside walks. This will help them get used to the feeling of being confined or restrained by the lead. If they flatly refuse to follow and there is tension on the lead because your puppy just lay down, keep some forward tension on the lead and encourage them to walk towards you. When they do, give them a treat. Continue short, indoor lead walks until your puppy no longer refuses to follow.

Now, it is time to set out for the great outdoors with your puppy on lead. A young puppy who has not yet roamed around their new neighbourhood will be distracted by many sights, sounds, and smells. Depending on your cocker spaniel puppy, their first lead outing could be the source of much excitement and darting everywhere, while a timid puppy might hesitate and be slower to explore.

Whichever type of puppy is on the end of your lead, you should be patient and take the time to show them lead walking is not an exercise in who is pulling who but is about walking together with no tension or lead pulling.

FACT ***There are two important habits that you want your cocker to grasp early on in their lead training: (1) looking to you for direction; and (2) never moving forwards when there is tension on the lead.***

Habit 1: When your puppy looks to you for direction, they understand that they are not simply out walking alone but are walking with you. Forming this habit begins with the very first on lead walk:

- As you walk, cheerfully say your puppy's name, and the second they look at you, reward them with a treat or happy praise.
- Repeat, repeat, repeat, and soon your cocker puppy will regularly look to you for direction when out on a walk.

Habit 2: At the same time, you want your cocker puppy to form the habit of never moving forwards when there is any tension felt on the lead. Some people call this exercise 'Red Light/Green Light' or 'Stop/Go'. Whether you call it a game or an exercise, all it means is your puppy can only move forwards when they are

NOT pulling on the lead. Of course, there could be many outdoor walks that end up going nowhere fast. That is okay, because if you practise the following steps, after a while, on lead walks will be a breeze:

- Start walking slowly with your spaniel by your side.
- The second your puppy begins to pull on their lead, simply stop moving—Red light.
- Wait for them to look towards you.
- Encourage them to come closer—with praise or a treat—which will release the tension on the lead.
- Start walking again and keep going as long as there is no tension on the lead—Green light.

Practicing these two habits every time you take your puppy outside for an on-lead outing will soon result in a comfortable walk with no pulling and an attentive dog who is always checking in with you.

Leads

Leads (pictured) come in many types, materials, and lengths. When choosing a lead for your dog there are several considerations to bear in mind, including:

- The size of your dog—larger dogs need a stronger lead.
- The width of the lead—a wide lead might be uncomfortable to hold.
- The size of the clip at the collar end—a large and heavy clip will not be suitable for a small dog.
- The length of the lead—1.5-2 metres will work for any size of dog*.
- The strength of the lead—a lighter lead for a smaller dog.

FACT› ***N.B. In the U.K., dog owners must keep their dogs on short, fixed-length leads—two metres or less—in some circumstances under the Countryside and Rights of Way Act 2000. However, many councils have made the decision to reduce this to 1.5 metres and in Devon one council has reduced this further to 1 metre.***

As there are so many styles and designs of dog leads to choose from, it can be difficult to decide which one you really need. Your best option is to choose one that is functional and fits your personal lifestyle. Here are the main lead types:

Standard Lead – These leads are for basic training and everyday use. They have a loop handle at one end and a metal clip at the other end to attach to your cocker's collar. Typically, they are available in lengths from 1.2-2.4 metres (4-8 feet), the 1.8-metre (6-foot) length is ideal for most dogs. The leads are made from leather, nylon, cotton web, or rope and can be flat or round. Flat leads come in a variety of widths, usually the thicker and wider ones are for larger and stronger dogs. Leather leads are more durable, and some owners feel they are more stylish. Normally, rope leads are round instead of flat and extremely tough.

Hands-Free Lead – These leads keep your hands free as they attach around your waist or over your shoulder—like a sash. This is a good option for someone who has things to carry, or perhaps, when jogging with your spaniel.

Double Lead – The double lead is convenient for walking two dogs at the same time as it has two leads together with one handle. This type of lead works best with two similarly sized dogs, as it requires the dogs to move in tandem.

City Lead – A city lead—also called a 'traffic lead'—is a short lead—less than 1.2 metres (4-feet)—used to keep better control of your dog. It is useful when walking on busy pavements or heavily crowded areas where you want to keep your cocker's head close by your side.

Flexi-Lead – The flexi, retractable or extendable lead (pictured) is usually spring-loaded and very long—normally 8 metres (26 feet). A thin cord winds up inside a plastic compartment with a handle and a button to control how much lead is extended. These leads are often high on lists of pet peeves for several reasons, including:

- They can be dangerous for human and dog alike. Do not let your dog out of your sight when on the lead, especially at longer lengths. The lead could become tangled, or your dog might get into a hazardous situation. These leads are also serious tripping hazards that can be the cause of broken bones and rope burn injuries.
- Your dog can get in the wrong walking position. These leads should only be used after your dog has been trained to walk by your side on a regular lead. Otherwise, you will teach your dog that it is permissible to pull on the lead, which is an extremely bad habit.
- The large plastic handles are heavy, clumsy, and difficult to grip securely. If your dog suddenly lunges or changes direction, the chances of losing grip are quite high.
- They are prone to accidentally breaking. Be sure to periodically check along the entire length of your retractable lead for frayed, worn, or otherwise damaged areas, as this is quite a common occurrence.

Some dog owners choose to use several kinds of dog leads for different purposes. One lead could be for daily walks and another for hiking with your cocker in the mountains or for bike rides. You might choose a certain type of lead specifically for dog training.

TIP ***If you want to choose a single lead for your cocker spaniel, it is recommended that you buy a standard 1.2 metre (4-foot) lead. This provides better control, improved training, safety, and will make your life easier in most circumstances.***

Collars

It is especially important to choose the 'right' kind of collar for your cocker. However, there is an ever-increasing array of tempting colours, materials, and styles to choose from. This makes it v easy to become distracted and forget about choosing what is most appropriate for your dog. Here are the most common collar types:

Flat Collars (pictured) – What is most important in a collar is its ability to keep your cocker safe and secure. Flat collars , unless they are so tight, they almost cut off your dog's air supply, can prove relatively easy for most dogs to get out of. Even though you have a firm grip on the lead, your cocker could back away, wiggle, twist and contort themselves in an instant, flip their head and the collar is off—bye, bye doggy!

Martingale Collars – While the Martingale collar is considered a 'training' collar, there is no reason why it cannot be your spaniel's everyday collar as it is very comfortable for them to wear. There are several reasons why this type of dog collar (pictured) is considered superior to a flat collar:

- It is comfortable for your dog to wear all day.
- They are strong and safe, and your dog cannot wriggle out of it.
- They are the best training collar.

The Martingale collar looks much the same as a flat collar, with one very important difference—there is a triangular piece of chain in the middle of it. This chain is attached to the collar—the red loop in the picture—with two rings, and a third ring in the middle of the chain, which is where you attach the lead.

When there is no tension from the dog pulling on the lead, the collar hangs loose and comfortable. However, when there is tension on the collar, the little piece of chain tightens so your cocker cannot get out of their collar. The chain also makes a slight noise when you sharply tug or jiggle it, which sends a message to your dog that you want their attention on you. This is considered one of the best collars for teaching your dog to walk calmly by your side and to remind them that you are in charge.

Some Martingale collars have a plastic clip attachment. However, these are not as strong as the ones that fit over the head.

When buying one of these collars, take your cocker with you as it needs to be the correct size to fit over the widest part of their head. Then, once you have the right size for your spaniel, you need to learn the correct way to adjust the collar for maximum effect and safety. Adjust the length so when the lead is attached to the outside ring and pulled tight, and the two inside rings come together, there is still a gap between the two rings of approximately two finger widths. The two inside rings should never touch.

Bark Collars – There are three different sorts of bark collars. Some vibrate like a mobile phone, others release a strong-smelling citronella spray, while others emit a high-pitched sound only audible to your cocker. All these methods are designed to interrupt your dog's barking and may or may not be effective.

FACT ***This negative type of training tool has the potential to create fearful, anxious, or even aggressive behaviour in your dog, especially in the hands of someone who does not understand how to properly use them.***

Choke Chain Collars – Also known as a '*slip chain*', this type of collar can cause pain and discomfort. This is a negative method of training your cocker spaniel not to pull when out lead walking.

There is a great deal of controversy about these collars among the dog owning population because, as the name suggests, when your dog pulls against the lead, they feel a choking sensation. While this type of collar can be helpful for training larger dogs when used correctly, there are better ways to teach a dog to walk without pulling that do not involve a negative experience.

Halti (Head) Collars – This type of collar is known by several different names, including '*gentle leader*', '*Halti*', '*head collar*' or '*head halter*'. It is designed like a halter on a horse to provide better control of your dog's head and prevent them from pulling when out lead walking.

Depending on your dog, and how early you introduce them to this type of collar, it might be an appropriate training tool. However, some people think the Halti is a muzzle and will avoid you because they believe your cocker could be dangerous. Furthermore, some dogs will fight this type of collar and do everything to remove it, while others can become overly subdued.

Prong or Pinch Collars – This type of aggressive looking collar tightens when your cocker pulls on their lead and the inward-facing prongs twist and pinch the skin of your dog's neck and scruff causing pain. The idea behind the collar is to prevent a large and powerful dog from pulling when lead walking. It is never a good idea to use pain as a deterrent, as this can backfire and create other problems, especially as there are so many other positive methods for teaching proper lead walking.

Relaxation Collars – There are two types of collars designed to help relax or calm your upset spaniel. One uses scent or calming pheromones, while the other uses species-specific music at appropriate volume levels to calm your fearful or stressed dog.

Harnesses

There are many different types, styles, and colours of harness arrangements, some of which have D-rings in multiple locations, reflective stripes for safety in low lighting, pockets for carrying gear, or convenient handles for lifting your dog.

Although your dog might not be a puller, harnesses are comfortable and offer excellent control of your dog. Here are the main types:

Vest – The vest harness is a good choice for dogs who do not pull. If your dog is a puller, this is not for you. The real advantage of this type of harness is that they fit comfortably like a piece of clothing and are less likely to chafe under your spaniel's armpits.

You need to consider all your options when choosing the harness that works best for you and your dog. Take into consideration your cocker's weight and character when determining what size and type of dog harness is best. The various styles of harnesses fit differently. Measure around your spaniel's rib cage to ensure you are buying the right size. If the harness is too tight it will be painful for your dog, but if it is too loose, your dog might easily slip out of it.

It should not be possible to pull the harness over your cocker's head, but you should be able to fit two fingers under all the straps that attach it to your dog. To test the dog harness, have your dog walk around your home with it on so you can be certain the harness does not move around loosely on their body, or rub uncomfortably against their skin.

Consider how much or how hard your dog pulls when choosing your cocker's harness. Buying the wrong harness can result in it being easier for your dog to pull you around. You should buy an 'anti-pull' harness if your spaniel is a puller.

FACT ***Harnesses work by distributing the weight and pressure of the lead away from your cocker's collar and neck and onto their shoulders, chest, and back. This will significantly reduce the risk of neck strain or choking.***

Back Clip – One of the most basic harnesses and versatile types on the market is the back clip. The harness has a metal D-loop sewn into the fabric where the lead attaches at about the middle of your dog's back. This type of harness might encourage a puller to pull even more.

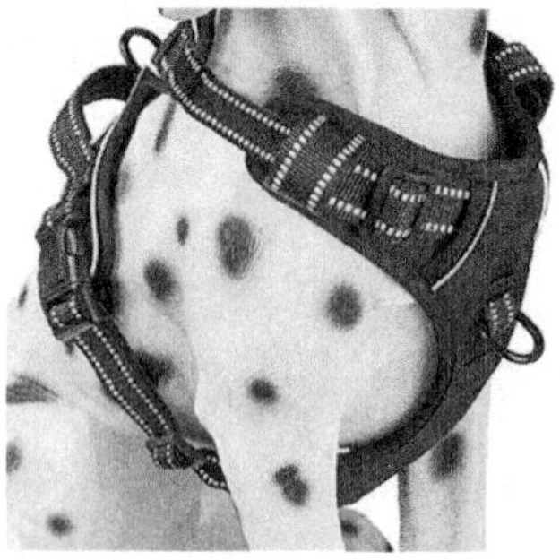

Front Clip – This is also known as an 'anti-pull' harness and is like the back-clip, but the clip is in front of your dog's chest. These can help teach your cocker spaniel not to pull and tug on their lead.

Side Clip – This type of harness is also considered an 'anti-pull' type, as it has the D-ring at the side, so when your dog begins to pull on their lead, they are directed back towards you.

Training Methods

There are many different types and combinations of dog training methods. For most dogs, the most effective training method is positive reinforcement. There is another form of this method called clicker training that utilises a clicker.

Positive Reinforcement (Training with Rewards)

As the name implies, this training method involves teaching your cocker commands, routines, tricks, or sports by rewarding them for desired behaviour. The reward could be anything your dog likes, such as treats, toys, praise, being groomed, going off lead during walks, playing in water, or travelling in the car. Every dog is different, so they naturally find different things rewarding. Nevertheless, nearly every dog enjoys food, toys, and attention.

TIP ***Reward training is all about teaching your cocker spaniel that good things happen when they make a right choice. If your dog receives a reward, they will associate it with whatever they just did, which will make it more likely for them to do the same thing next time.***

The best way to encourage your dog to behave the way you want them to daily—such as learning to settle themselves down when you are busy—is to train them with rewards for the following reasons:

- Science tells us that reward-based training is the best way for dogs to learn.
- Training with rewards is fun and helps build a positive bond between dog and owner.
- Owners who train using rewards report fewer behavioural problems with their dogs.
- Reward-based training can help build confidence and encourage dogs to think for themselves.

Note that since positive reinforcement is the training method of choice, all the training instructions of the various commands, tricks, and routines presented in this chapter are reward-based.

Reward your puppy whenever you catch them doing something good, instead of only telling them off for doing something wrong. Make sure it is a reward your cocker really wants. Rewards can be such things as a gentle fuss, stroking them, or just speaking softly to your dog when they are behaving calmly so the reward does not suddenly make them too excited. By contrast, if they are doing something active, such as running over to you as soon as you call them, rewarding this behaviour with an active and energetic game is the perfect prize.

When you start teaching your spaniel a new skill, it is important to reward them every time they succeed. You can change the type of reward once they have learnt the new behaviour and can do it well in several different environments. By doing this, it is unnecessary to give them a treat for obeying the '***Sit***' command for the rest of their life. Instead, you can say, '***good dog***' and occasionally give them a treat as a bonus.

For example, if you use food to teach your cocker a new behaviour, to begin with, it is useful to reward them every time until they really understand what you want them to do. As soon as they reliably and consistently do it, reward them every other time, then every third time. Then alternate when you give a food reward and when you just give them verbal praise or make a fuss of them. This will keep your spaniel interested as they will not know when to expect their favourite type of reward.

It is a good idea to have a marker that is a signal to let your cocker know when they are doing something you are happy about. The marker tells your dog, '*Yes, you got it right and I am about to give you a reward.*' It is essential to always reward your dog immediately after the marker, so your dog becomes confident they did things correctly.

Some owners use a short, punchy word, such as '***Yes***' or '***Nice***', but you might prefer to use a mechanical clicker device, or simply give them a thumbs up. Whatever marker you choose, make sure everyone uses it, so your cocker never becomes confused no matter who is training them. When teaching them a new behaviour, use the signal at the precise moment your dog is doing what you want. That will tell your spaniel their reward is on its way, and they will have learnt exactly what to do again to get their next reward.

At different time and places, you might need to offer different rewards. There could be times when your dog requires an extra or different reward. Sometimes, what was easy for your dog in the comfort and calmness of their own home can become far more difficult for them when the environment is busier and more distracting. What was rewarding at home might no longer be as exciting for them outside. If there are distractions that make it hard for your cocker to respond, you might need to use something particularly tempting in that location. It could be a treat your dog especially loves, a game, or a toy.

One of the favourite rewards your cocker spaniel craves is your attention. Often, we underestimate how important our attention is, and most dogs feel good any time we look at, touch, or talk to them. We constantly influence their behaviour with our attention, and not only by offering treats and toys. Make sure your dog receives your valuable attention for the good choices they make, not just when they do something you do not want them to.

The Effect of Punitive Training on Emotion

Dogs who are trained using duress and force, i.e., trained to respond through fear or pain, suffer much higher stress and anxiety levels than those trained using positive reward methods. Studies show that if your dog is punished by being pinned down on their back or side in an 'alpha roll' for example, cortisol releases into the body during their restraint. Cortisol is a stress hormone produced by an activated amygdala—the part of the brain primarily involved in the processing of emotions and memories associated with fear—and readies the body for danger. If high levels of cortisol are released, the brain becomes overwhelmed, and the resulting state overrides rational thought. An owner might think their cocker is being submissive or becoming calm while they are being held down, however, the opposite is happening.

Stress from threat will make your spaniel 'shut down,' effectively freezing them until the threat disappears. In this state of anxiety, your dog will stop learning and become more insecure, frightened, and/or angry. If your dog cannot practice avoidance, the only option left is to bite, which is why so many trainers and owners who use this method of punishment are bitten. Most dogs get up and shake themselves after they experience an 'alpha roll'. This is called the 'shake off' and is an effective way for them to relieve stress after a negative experience.

Clicker Training

FACT ***Clicker training and positive reinforcement training are the same thing, with the added benefit of a clicker. A clicker is simply a small, mechanical device that makes a clicking sound when you press a button.***

The value of the clicker (pictured) is that it tells your dog exactly which behaviour you are rewarding. By clicking at the appropriate time, you can 'mark' the moment your cocker does what you want. Rather than having to guess what you approved of, the click tells your dog exactly what they did right.

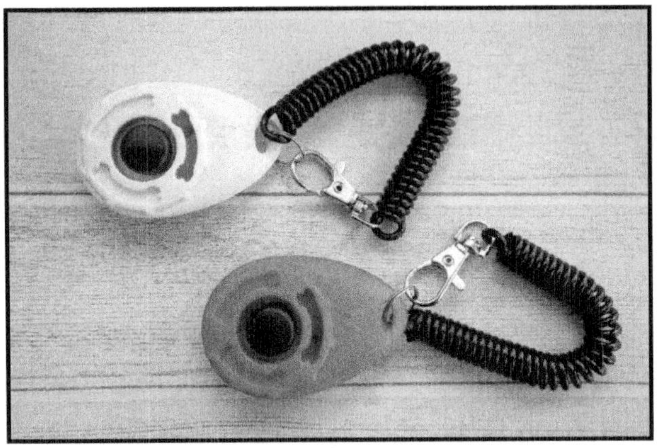

The clear and loud sound of the click also removes the different tones that come from your mood when voice training your cocker spaniel. The precise sound of the clicker helps your dog focus by removing some of the confusion that occurs with voice commands.

When clicker training, the most important aspect is timing. It is critical to click at the exact moment your dog exhibits the requested behaviour, and then immediately offer the treat. This will encourage your puppy to work out exactly what they did to receive the treat reward. Very quickly, most puppies learn to associate the click sound with the requested action and they will be eager to do what you ask to get the tasty treat.

Firstly, if you decide to use a clicker, you need to teach your spaniel what the click sound means. Sometimes referred to as 'loading the clicker,' you must pair your chosen marker—the clicker—with a reward. Hold the clicker in your hand with treats at the ready. Have your dog in front of you, click the clicker and immediately give them a treat. Repeat this several times until your cocker realises that the sound of the click means they get a treat. Now, you can move on to using the clicker to teach some basic commands:

'***Come***' command with a clicker – Use the hand signal to ask your cocker to '***Come***' (see Commands Training section above) and the second your dog comes to you, CLICK the clicker, and give them a treat.

'***Sit***' command with a clicker – Have your dog in the same room and then use the hand signal for '***Sit***'. The second your dog's bottom touches the floor, CLICK the clicker, and give them a treat.

'***Stay***' command with a clicker. – Have your dog sitting in front of you and give the hand signal for '***Stay***' while you back away a metre or two. When your cocker remains sitting, immediately CLICK the clicker, and return to give your dog a treat.

You can use this training method for acknowledging good behaviour. If your cocker is lying quietly on the mat instead of begging at the dining table, click then reward their behaviour. Or if the doorbell rings and your dog keeps all four paws on the floor, instead of jumping on your guests, click that moment.

TIP ***A clicker is a tool that can be used to increase the efficiency of positive reinforcement training. After the clicker has been repeatedly associated with a treat or reward, it will become a conditioned reinforcer. Note that this type of training method might not be very effective for a dog who is not particularly food motivated.***

Whilst you can use your marker with lure-and-reward training—using a reward to lure your dog into the behaviour you are looking for—it is also useful when shaping their behaviour. Shaping entails building a complex behaviour by taking baby steps. Fox example, training can be used to teach your cocker to put all their toys back in the toy box.

With patience and repetition your spaniel will soon learn to identify their toys, pick them up, take them to their toy box and drop them in it with just one word, '***Toys***'. For full details on how to train your cocker spaniel to perform this task see Top Mental Stimulation Tips, Chapter 12.

12. Exercise

'Money can buy a fine dog, but

only love can make him wag his tail.'

~ Kinky Friedman ~

Cocker spaniels are usually energetic dogs with plenty of stamina. They have a lively and playful temperament, love to chase and romp, and are happiest and content when given a job to do. Depending on what you might be into, this spaniel can be a great hunting companion or a blue-ribbon performer in many different canine sports.

Supervision during play exercise with other dogs is always important with a young spaniel puppy who has not yet learnt the rules and boundaries and is excited to see other dogs. To prevent possible squabbles, you need to be fully in control and capable of intervening quickly to shut down any unwanted situation, such as dogs exhibiting dominance.

Bear in mind how active you are will have a definite effect on the energy level and exercise tolerance of your dog. Maintaining your cocker's fitness through regular exercise goes beyond keeping them in shape. Here are some of the benefits of dog exercise:

- It burns excess calories to prevent obesity.
- Keeps them well behaved, as they do not have to find other ways to entertain themselves, such as chewing on furniture or barking.
- It keeps their brain active, especially if you include mental stimulation games and puzzles in their exercise routine.

- Exercising with your dog is a good stress reliever, letting both of you unwind.
- It reduces the risk of health problems such as arthritis, hip dysplasia, and obesity related diseases such as diabetes and heart disease.
- It strengthens your relationship when you are out and about and exercising in a variety of ways.

Puppies

When cocker puppies are very young, it is far more important to focus on short walks as part of their toilet training procedure, completing their vaccination schedule, and simply letting them get other exercise through indoor play sessions.

As a rule, they should not be exercised beyond 2-4 short walks as part of training them to use the outdoors for their toilet routine. Puppies need a lot of time for napping and growing, which means during the day these walks should just be interspersed with play sessions, napping, and feeding.

Another consideration will be your puppy's vaccination schedule. Your puppy should not venture out into the real world until approximately two weeks after their final vaccinations are complete.

TIP ***To give your cocker puppy plenty of rest and time to grow without harming young bones and muscles, vigorous exercising or long walks should only be considered once they are at least six to eight months old.***

Young puppies will do fine with entertaining games involving retrieving toys or balls, but they also need mental stimulation to grow their minds. Often teaching simple tricks and basic commands can begin when they are young. Also, introducing your puppy to food puzzles, how to walk on lead or an exciting game of hide-and-seek will tire them out faster than a physical walk. Taking the time for regular play sessions with your new puppy will certainly make them happy. Try to set aside times during the day when you stop your chores and engage your cocker spaniel puppy in fun games for 5 or 10 minutes.

By the time they are 6 months old, their bone structure has developed, so they can go for longer walks. Do not let them become exhausted, but gradually increase their exercise routine.

Adults

Adult cocker spaniels need a fair amount of exercise every day to keep them active, healthy, and to stop them getting bored. They are more than happy to go out walking a few times a day and love any opportunity to play with their owner. You could find that if your dog comes from parents bred to work, they will probably need more time to run around than your average cocker spaniel.

Your cocker spaniel will need a minimum of an hour exercise every day. Most adult cockers will be very happy having a brisk walk for about 30 minutes morning and evening with plenty of opportunity to have a good sniff around. They will also need off lead exercise in a secure area—such as your back garden—so they can run off their excess energy. In addition, they need lots of playtime with you and enjoy training sessions and games to challenge them (see Mental Stimulation section for games).

FACT ***The cocker spaniel is a quick and agile dog, so they tend to do well at agility—look online to find a local place to train your dog. They also like to play with a ball or Frisbee. This is a great way to burn off energy and have fun. In most cases, they will be glad to walk with you for considerable distances, so you can easily go out together for long, country walks at the weekends.***

Seniors

When your dog reaches their senior years, even those who have led a high activity lifestyle will eventually begin to slow down and be satisfied with shorter walks, more sedate play sessions with other dogs, and less vigorous daily exercise schedules. You need to pay attention to how quickly your cocker seems to get tired or to be less interested in energetic pursuits or wild play sessions with friends and adjust their lifestyle accordingly.

Dogs thrive on routine, which means exercise still needs to be a regularly consistent occurrence in the life of a senior dog. Exercise is beneficial for the senior dog too, because it keeps the joints and muscles moving and the mind active, both of which can extend their life.

While your senior dog may sleep more, the walks and ball retrieval games might be shorter, and they could be less interested in participating in play sessions with the younger crowd. Although they will still enjoy walks and activities that do not wear them out too much.

When your dog reaches middle age, they are more likely to develop joint problems, physical conditions, and other medical issues. For cockers 7-9 years old, replace high impact sports with shorter sessions of moderate exercise. Swimming, walking, or other joint friendly routines are ideal for them to stay in shape without any risk.

Top Exercise Tips

Here are some useful tips you should remember when training your cocker spaniel:

1. If your dog is unaccustomed to regular exercise, but you want to introduce a routine, start out gently. You will have an easier time, and your dog can build up stamina. You should begin your dog's exercise routine with short periods of activity at slow speeds, gradually increasing the time, speed, and distance until your cocker is getting the appropriate amount of exercise.
2. Avoid exercising your dog right after or before they eat, as a full stomach combined with walking or running can upset their system. Also make sure your dog has enough water at mealtimes, so they stay hydrated and ready for exercise.

3. Remember, your puppy's physical abilities are limited, and their bones are still growing and more susceptible to injuries. As a rule, puppies should have no more than 5 minutes of exercise for each month of age, twice a day.
4. Dog exercises should not just be long, boring treks, they should be fun and varied. Dogs become bored just as much as their owners if they do the same thing every day. Add variety to your routine to keep it fresh, and you will both be happier to exercise. Plan several dog walks you can switch regularly, and make sure to incorporate playtime with fun games.
5. Give your cocker the chance to release all their pent-up energy, but do not push them too hard. Think about how long they can run around before becoming tired, and make sure they have the energy to get back home.
6. If your dog has a history of medical problems, you could consider consulting your vet to plan a suitable exercise programme that is beneficial for their specific needs.
7. Remember your dog loves to spend time with you, so make it really special rather than just plodding around the same old park every day. Meeting new dogs is all part of the fun.

8. Do not throw sticks (pictured) for your dog to chase—they can splinter and injure your cocker's mouth and throat. If you throw a ball, make sure it is not too small as your dog could swallow it.
9. Always allow your dog to have a good sniff around—this is important for their mental health.
10. 'Varied walking' can be good for you and your dog—this is where you speed walk for about 30 seconds, walk at normal pace for about a minute, then speed up again and repeat. It is a good exercise for both of you and something you can do randomly throughout your walk.
11. Just like people, not all dogs enjoy exercise, and they have different exercise needs. You can often find dogs of the same breed who are completely different with one being high energy and the other much more laidback.
12. Exercise as much as necessary. If your dog is not getting tired or is still full of energy when you get home, they might need more exercise. If your cocker is struggling, or refuses to go at all, you could need to cut back. Just follow the signs.

13. Most cockers love the water (pictured), and swimming is great for dogs with joint problems, as it provides low impact exercise. It also helps improve their circulation and boost the metabolism. A life jacket can help your dog stay in the water longer for an optimum cardio workout.
14. Fetch does not have to be boring. Shake up your dog's fetch routine by making them run uphill to retrieve a ball, or by tossing it into the water. Alternate between balls, Frisbees, or other prized toys to keep your dog on their toes.

15. If you are looking for a great dog exercise for your cocker, you could consider a treadmill. With careful training, your dog might grow to love their treadmill workouts. While they are not a replacement for a walk or a run outside, treadmills build endurance and do not rely on decent weather.
16. Climbing stairs is the perfect way to build your leg muscles. Place your dog on their lead and walk up and down your stairs. Be sure to vary it by adding some high steps and side steps to work various muscle groups.

Visiting the Park

Visiting the local park with your dog can be the highlight of their day if you are aware of proper etiquette, how to keep them safe, what to bring and when to avoid.

For many dog owners, the first time they visit their local park is after their puppy has finished their vaccination schedule and they want to get busy socialising. While this is a great idea, you will have a much easier transition into this new world when keeping a little basic etiquette in mind.

For instance, being new to the park, your cocker puppy might become overly excited about meeting and greeting other canines. However, an extremely excited, rambunctious puppy will sometimes be too much for older dogs to tolerate, and they might react with growling or snapping.

TIP ***Before going to the park, take your puppy for a disciplined, on lead walk to burn off some of their high energy so they will be more sedate when first meeting the new canine crowd.***

Once at the park, keep your puppy on lead until you are certain they will meet politely and not simply pounce on every other dog with wild abandon. Carefully observe your cocker spaniel's reaction to their exciting new world and that of the other dogs they meet to make sure none of them are becoming overwhelmed or obnoxious.

Keeping your puppy safe when visiting the park requires you being vigilant about several things, including:

- The size of other dogs.
- The behaviour of your puppy and the other dogs.
- The intensity and length of play.
- Your cocker's hydration level.

While it is entertaining watching dogs having fun in the park, sometimes they play too vigorously or do not know when to call it quits. You should always be watchful and make sure your dog is not playing too hard for too long and getting overtired, overheated, or dehydrated.

Also, allowing your small spaniel to play enthusiastically with a dog who outweighs them many times over can lead to accidental injury. While the larger dog might have no ill intentions, your puppy can easily be injured during boisterous play. Do not let your cocker interact with large breeds.

In general, dogs prefer to play with members of their own breed or dogs of a comparable size. However, sometimes your feisty little puppy will be excited and have no idea of their size and no fear when placing themselves against a much larger dog during a play session. This is when you need to step in to prevent any accidents.

Observing the behaviour of the other dogs in the park will also help to keep your puppy safe. If the other dogs are playing and seem to be quite intense with lots of shoulder checking, body slamming, nipping, and pouncing on one another, this is the time to keep your cocker on lead and simply observe from a safe distance.

Other instances when it would be wiser to **simply avoid the park** with your dog, include when:

- There are many dogs in a small space.
- Your dog seems nervous.
- The dogs are being overly dominant with one another.
- Play is becoming too aggressive or out of control.
- The owners do not seem to be paying attention.
- It is a hot day and there is no shade.
- There are unknown dogs.
- There are unpredictable strong breeds in the mix.
- Someone arrives with a dog they cannot control.

Things to Bring – While depending on the games you and your dog like to play at the park, you might want to bring along more items, there are at least three things you will never want to be without:

- Lead (always).
- At least 3 poo bags (always).
- Water (always).
- Treats (optional).
- Ball (optional).
- A vest for your dog to reflect the sun (optional).
- Frisbee (optional).

Responsible dog walking

Going for a walk is an important part of your cocker spaniel's day, and the countryside can be the perfect place to do this. Follow our simple tips for a safe countryside dog walk to keep you, your dog, and other animals safe.

Crops – Follow the designated footpaths, always close the gates behind you, and never stray into fields. Dogs and people walking on them can easily damage crops that are in early and later stages of growth.

Litter and dog poo – Wildlife and farm animals can suffer serious harm if they try to eat discarded litter and poo bags, thinking it is food. Always dispose of all your rubbish and dog poo in a bin or take it home with you.

As a dog walker, you can play a key role in keeping the countryside safe and clean for everyone by picking up any litter you see, even if it is not yours.

Wildlife – No matter where you go in the countryside wildlife will be nearby, even though you might not be able to see it. They could hide in bushes or hedgerows, but your cocker spaniel can still sniff them out thanks to their fantastic sense of smell. There could be young wild animals waiting for their parents to return, or adults keeping their young safe, such as ground nesting birds sitting on their eggs. Be aware of places where wildlife might hide and make sure your dog does not disturb them, as it could make the parents abandon their young or your dog might chase them and cause significant injury.

You need to keep your cocker safe too, as wild animals often become aggressive when they think they are going to be attacked and feel the need to defend themselves or their young. This is important to remember all year round, but especially in the spring and summer as that is when most wild animals breed and have vulnerable offspring. Between early May and late June, if you walk your spaniel in an area where deer reside, keep an eye out for new-born deer as they are particularly vulnerable at this time, and many are killed or injured by dogs.

Should you decide to walk along beaches or near areas where seals come out of the water to rest, be certain your cocker is on their lead and remain at least 50 metres away and as far from the seals as possible to avoid disturbing them.

Livestock – Most dogs show an interest in livestock, and even if you believe your cocker will not harm another animal, accidents do happen. Dogs easily frighten animals, especially ewes and lambs. Encountering dogs can create fear, which makes ewes abort their unborn lambs, become separated from the herd, or seriously injure themselves. Give livestock adequate space, and never try to feed them as this might cause them harm.

Mental Stimulation

All dogs need mental stimulation in their day and without it they can decide to create their own entertainment by acting in ways you may not appreciate.

First, let us discuss what 'mental stimulation' is as the term can be confusing or have a different meaning for different people. We have known for a long-time physical activity that exercises the body is vital to keep your dog healthy, but what about your cocker's brain? Mental stimulation simply means finding ways to make your dog think. This exercises their brain, makes them smarter and far less likely to spend their time being mischievous because they are bored.

FACT ***Mentally challenging games, tasks, or sports are more tiring than any type of physical effort that may take three times longer to complete.***

One of the reasons most dogs get into trouble with their owners is because their day involves no regular thinking tasks. In other words, they are not being mentally challenged or stimulated.

A suitable time to begin games or tasks that are mentally challenging for your cocker spaniel is as soon as your new puppy arrives home. The sooner your puppy's brain is engaged in solving tasks or being involved in learning something new, the better for their mental health.

How much mental stimulation a dog requires depends on their breed and age. A smart, working breed such as the cocker needs far more daily mental stimulation to keep them happy and out of mischief than a breed bred solely as a lapdog.

When your spaniel is less than six months old, shorter mind games of 5-15 minutes are sufficient. As your dog matures, add longer and more challenging tasks that keep their mind occupied, such as an invigorating canine sport to their routine.

Top Mental Stimulation Tips

Although every dog is different with respect to what sort of mental tasks they find interesting, the following tips will help you keep your cocker spaniel mentally challenged:

1. Teach your puppy rules and boundaries so they learn what they can and cannot do. For instance, when your puppy is taught that they are not permitted into the kitchen when you are preparing food, they have learnt a 'rule'. Teach them this by firmly saying, '***Go***' while pointing away from the kitchen. If they do not go, simply walk towards them, forcing them to back away. Giving a treat once they leave when told to will help reinforce this rule.
2. Teach basic tricks that require positive reinforcement. Most dogs love to learn tricks, and this gets their brain working. You can start by teaching the 'Shake-a-paw' trick (see Training chapter).
3. Take them for walks in locations where there are dissimilar smells and dogs. When you walk your cocker in the same place each day, it is not as stimulating or mentally exciting for them as the new smells and sights they can encounter when they are taken to a new place.
4. Take your dog to off lead parks, so they can interact with other dogs. Dogs like to meet, greet, and play with different dogs, and the park is good place to have this type of interaction. Do not forget the park 'safety and when to avoid' rules.
5. Hide treats inside a puzzle toy (pictured) so your dog must use their mind to figure out how to get the toy to release them. Your cocker's sense of smell will identify a treat they want, and then they must engage their brain to figure out what they need to do to get the puzzle to release the treat.

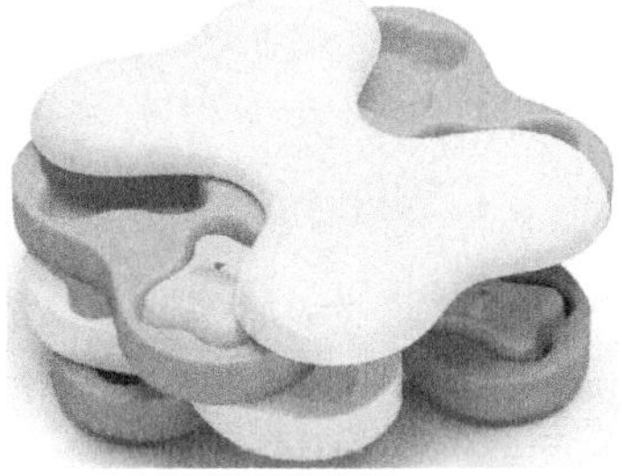

6. Set up an agility course in the back garden. You can buy agility obstacles online, or simply create your own. Set up a course that involves jumping up onto a box, leaping over a hurdle, weaving through poles, and crawling through a tunnel. This only restriction being your imagination.
7. Teach your cocker to swim and retrieve an object that floats. Start with something simple like a ball that floats when tossed near the shoreline, and when your dog brings the ball back, give them a treat to reinforce this behaviour. Slowly introduce greater distances until your cocker must swim to grab the floating object and return it to you.

8. Enrolling your dog in an obedience class can be beneficial if you are a first-time owner and you need a little help teaching the basics. A beginner class usually includes the basic commands (see Training, Chapter 11), whereas an advanced obedience class may focus on off lead skills, such as recall when the dog is out of sight, and hand signals.
9. Teach your smart dog to help with daily chores. Cockers love to work and have interesting tasks that are part of their daily routine to keep their mind active. There are many tasks your dog can help with around the house. Begin with something simple, such as collecting the post from the doormat. Once your dog has accomplished this daily chore, think of other tasks they could learn.
10. Play the 'cupcake tin' game. Get a cake tin, place treats in some of the cups and cover them with dog approved tennis balls. Then, your spaniel must sniff for treats and figure out which balls to remove to get to them.
11. Teach your cocker the names of all their toys and then get them to fetch each one by name. This takes patience and repetition, and when the toys have short names, it is easier for your dog to remember them. For instance, if they have a stuffed cat toy, call it '***Cat***', or if they have a ball toy, call this '***Ball***' and so on. Begin with just two toys—Cat and Ball—and place them in front of your dog. Say the word, '***Cat***' and point to the cat toy. When your dog picks up the cat, give them a treat. Repeat this exercise with the ball until your dog picks up the correct toy every time they are asked. Now you can add more toys for more mental stimulation.
12. Get a toy box and teach your dog how to put their toys away. Ask your cocker to pick up a toy—or give them one—and say, '***Box***' then lead your dog immediately to their toy box and say, '***Drop***'. When your dog drops the toy in the box, give them a treat to reinforce this behaviour. This can take some patience and repetitions before they understand when you say '***Box***', it means put the toys in their toy box.
13. When out lead walking, ask your dog to follow you around trees, poles, jump up on benches, walk along retaining walls, do figure of eights or circles, stop, and start suddenly, varying walking speeds and directions. Changing speed and direction when walking helps your cocker learn their correct walking position—beside your leg—without pulling. It also makes them think, as they will be unable to anticipate which direction you might take next.
14. Researchers in Sweden have discovered that dogs are visibly happier when they must earn their treats as a reward for completing a task (pictured), rather than just being given a treat for looking cute. Apparently, just like people who get that happy 'eureka' moment when they finally solve a problem, so do our canine counterparts. Before giving them a treat, ask your spaniel to perform a trick or command.

15. Teach your dog a freestyle dance routine. Freestyle dance is a canine sport that can take much dedication, patience, and many hours of practise to perform. Choreographing and designing a trick training routine to a piece of music is a creative challenge for the owner and a huge mental exercise for any dog. There are many organisations that can be a good starting point for learning how to dance with your dog, such as the Canine Freestyle GB, the Musical Dog Sport Association, and the World Canine Freestyle Organisation.
16. Join 'Dognition', an online game assessment that helps you better understand and connect with your dog. All you do is provide information about your dog in the canine personality questionnaire and then play science-based games with your cocker and a friend. Games take around ten minutes and test five dimensions of your dog's cognition: communication, memory, reasoning skills, and how cunning or empathetic they are. The results are analysed in your spaniel's profile report.

Indoor Food Games

Kong wobblers, food puzzles and the shell game are interactive games that involve solving puzzles to get the reward of food, while the game of search involves finding a treat hidden somewhere inside the home.

FACT ***Most cockers are highly food motivated, which is why playing indoor games that involve finding food treats are almost always a winner.***

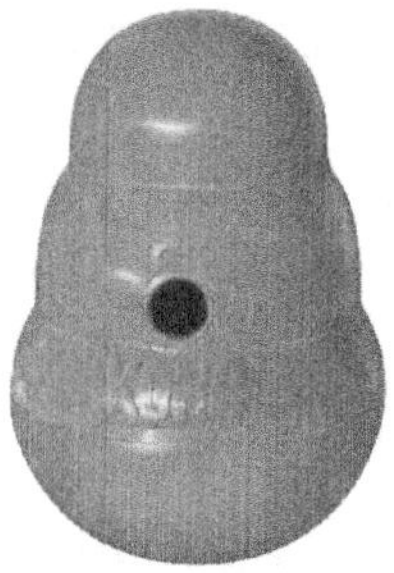

Kong Wobblers/Feeder Balls – These fun toys (pictured) will make your dog work to get their treats, as they dispense the treats while your cocker is playing and pushing the toy around.

Food Puzzles – There are many different types, sizes, and difficulty levels of interactive food puzzles that involve moving levers, pulling out drawers, toppling cones, flipping cups, sliding compartments, and rotating discs.

The Shell Game – This is a simple, beginner-level game you can play indoors with your cocker that involves nothing more than three cups and one treat. Have your dog sit and stay while they watch you place three cups upside down on the floor. Place a treat under one cup, change the position of the cups, then release your dog to find the cup that hides the treat. This is a game any dog will quickly figure out because their nose tells them which cup the treat is hidden under. Once they have found the right cup, they must figure out how to overturn it to get the prize.

Search – This game is also easy to teach to any dog who has already mastered the sit/stay commands. To begin, first ask your spaniel to sit/stay while you slowly back away and place a treat where your dog can still see it. Return to where your dog remains in a sit/stay and say, 'Okay! Search' while pointing to where the treat was placed. Each time this game is played, you can make it increasingly more difficult by placing the treat farther and farther away and then finally completely out of your dog's sight before they are released to search.

Scatter Feeding – Scatter feeding is one of the easiest games you can start with. It encourages your cocker spaniel to search for their food and helps build their natural hunting and foraging behaviour.

Essentially, scatter feeding is what it sounds like. Instead of placing your cocker's food in their bowl, scatter it on the floor, around the house, or in the garden. It is preferable to do this on a hard, easy to clean surface if you play this game indoors. As your dog's ability to use their nose to find the food improves, scatter it over a larger area or an uneven surface, such as grass.

You can start hiding small pieces of food for them to find after your dog has mastered this skill. Choose places you do not mind them rummaging around in, and where there is no danger of things getting damaged. As their confidence grows, make the hiding places more difficult to find, or even conceal the food beneath something such as a flowerpot.

If your cocker finds it too hard to find the food and becomes frustrated, you can help them by moving them closer to the food.

Other Indoor Games

Hide and Seek – This is a simple game that exercises both mind and body, and is fun for dogs of all ages, children, and adults alike, especially on those cold or rainy days when nobody is particularly interested in an outdoor adventure.

When first teaching your young puppy to play hide and seek, have a family member or friend hold your spaniel while someone takes a treat and hides where your dog can see where they hid. Then the person hiding calls out 'Find me' and the assistant releases the dog. As soon as your dog runs to the hiding place, they receive the reward of a treat or a toy.

Once your puppy grasps the concept of this fun game, family members can make it increasingly difficult by hiding farther away in more complex locations, so your cocker must search and use their nose to find the person hiding. Make the first few times easy on your puppy and give them a treat when they find you.

iDig – This interactive game provides a safe and rewarding way for dogs to exercise their natural desire to dig. It comes with three different digging flap challenges that you fill with toys or treats to provide mental stimulation while your dog hunts for treasure.

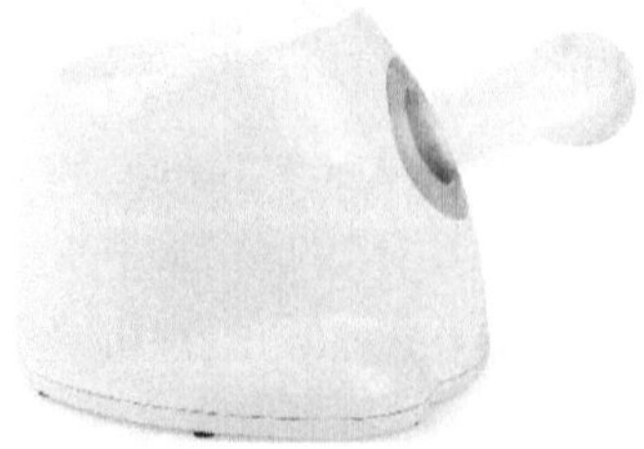

iFetch – This automatic ball launcher (pictured) has three increasing distance settings. Your cocker will be mentally challenged as they must figure out where to drop the ball so it can be launched from the machine. They are rewarded with chasing and bringing it back again.

Obstacle Course – It is easy to set up an indoor obstacle course for your dog and then teach them the routine—sort of like your own indoor agility course. It is fun to get the whole family involved in creating obstacles by using whatever is close at hand.

For example, make a tunnel out of a couple of chairs and a blanket or a large box, or use a step stool as an obstacle to jump onto or over, a coffee table to crawl under, or arrange boxes so your dog must weave their way through. There is no end of fun for all when creating a homemade obstacle course for your cocker.

Tug-of-War – In this game, you and your dog are pulling at opposite sides of a rope tug toy (pictured) until one of you gets the toy. This is both an indoor and outdoor game that also teaches basic impulse control. Dogs who enjoy this game become quite excited and can get their teeth too close to your fingers. If this happens, it is time to stop the game.

The impulse control comes into play when teaching your dog to '***Leave it***' when it is time to end the game. This is easy to do with a tasty treat as a reward. Simply stop pulling, and while still holding the end of the tug, firmly say '***Leave it***' and offer a treat.

Outdoor Games

Though it is certainly possible to move all the same games that everyone enjoys playing indoors to an outdoor location, there are some games that are much more conducive to an outdoor arena, such as fetching balls or Frisbees.

Search – Playing this game inside, where the dog receives the reward of eating the treat once they find it, can also be played in a grassy back garden. Simply take some favourite treats and place them in random locations in the grass so your dog must use their nose to find them.

TIP ***While it is fun to create an indoor obstacle course, if you have a convenient back garden, you can easily set up your cocker's very own agility course. Creating a digging pit for your dog is also a fun activity for back garden play, because you can bury their favourite toys and your cocker can dig for them.***

In addition, there are many organised activities and canine sports that are mentally challenging for our canine friends:

Agility – This is an organised obstacle course (pictured) involving jumps, tunnels, balancing boards, and navigating various walkways in a specific order, with direction from their owner.

Barn Hunt – A relatively new canine sport, barn hunt is based on the traditional roles that many breeds were bred for, which was eliminating destructive vermin from barns, storage areas, and homes. This sport is open to any breed or crossbreed that can fit through a 45-centimetre (18-inch) tunnel in a straw maze. The rats used in this sport are carefully protected inside aerated tubes so no harm will come to them.

Canicross – This sport is cross-country running with dogs. Your dog is placed in a harness connected to a bungee that is attached to the runner—you—with a belt around your waist. Originally designed to exercise sled dogs during off season, many dogs run in front, although beside is also perfectly acceptable.

Conformation – Also known as 'a dog show', this is simply the best of the best strutting their stuff around a ring in front of judges who decide which dog best conforms to the ideal characteristics of their breed.

Disc Dog – Dog and owner, or handler teams are judged in disc-throwing routines involving distance/accuracy and the chasing speed and catching ability of the dog.

Lure Coursing – This is a very fast-paced, timed sporting event that appeals to those breeds with a strong chasing instinct. The dogs compete for the best time as they chase an artificial lure across an open field without putting any small animals in harm's way.

]**Dock Diving or Jumping** – As the name implies, this organised sport involves water-loving dogs jumping off a dock into a body of water (pictured) to retrieve a toy or ball thrown by the owner. The object of this sport is to get the dog to jump the longest distance possible.

Field Trials – In this competitive event, the dogs are judged on how well they retrieve out in the field over a long distance.

Flyball – This is a time-recorded relay race involving teams of four dogs. The first dog runs down a course that involves jumping hurdles and then presses a panel to release a ball, which they grab and run back to their owner before the next dog sets off.

Herding Trials – Even some non-herding breeds enjoy learning how to herd, whereas those who come by this instinct naturally but do not live on a farm enjoy being able to satisfy their natural born talents.

Mushing – This competitive category includes bikejoring, carting skijoring, scootering, and sledding and simply refers to one or more dogs pulling a person on a bike, cart, skis, scooter, or sledge, either on dry land or snow.

Nose Work – This sport is designed to mimic what detection dogs are trained to do, which is to locate a specific odour and alert their owner or handler that they have found it. They are rewarded with a treat or a toy when they have found their target.

Rally Obedience – This is a type of obedience course open to all breeds to compete for championships and titles. The course is made up of specific obedience tasks that must be completed as dog and handler navigate their way through the course.

Schutzhund – This is a protection dog sport that includes obedience and tracking. These dogs are highly intelligent and display a strong desire to work. They are tested for traits that are found in a wide variety of working or service tasks, such as police work or search and rescue.

Tracking – This is a type of test that uses your dog's strongest sense—smell. Following a scent trail imitates what search and rescue dogs are trained to do, so if they become good at it, perhaps they will have a part-time job!

Weight Pulling – While some criticise this sport, there are many breeds that were traditionally used to pull carts to market or sledges across miles of snow. In a weight pulling contest, the dog is attached to a cart or sledge loaded with concrete weights by a special harness to minimise injury and asked to pull the weight across carpet, dirt, grass, or snow.

13. Health

'Everyone thinks they have the best dog
in the world. None of them are wrong.'
~ Unknown ~

The last thing you want to worry about as a cocker owner is what kind of health issues your dog might encounter in their lifetime. Nonetheless, part of being a responsible dog owner is learning about the conditions that commonly affect cocker spaniels and making sure you have access to a veterinarian. There are some conditions that can be hard to detect, and you should never wait until it is too late. Look at some of the most common health issues affecting spaniels, and what clinical signs to watch for to ensure the best health and quality of life for your dog.

Please do not panic reading these pages. Remember, the cocker spaniel is typically a healthy breed and most likely will not suffer from any of these issues, especially if you follow the health tips outlined below. But the key to protecting your dog's health is looking for these health problems, doing all that is possible to prevent them, learning what to do if an accident occurs, and having regular check-ups at the vet's.

Diet – The cornerstone of Health

Note that there are three ingredients found in almost all dog food manufactured today—including 'organic' food—that are literally compromising our dogs' health and shortening their lives:

- Preservatives, such as BHA and propylene glycol that can create poor digestion, skin and coat issues, weight gain, and more.

- Fillers that are contributing to increasing canine cancers at an alarming rate. These can be anything the food company puts into the food that does nothing for your dog's health, such as heavy grains—barley, flour, oatmeal, soy, wheat, white rice.

Meat by-products, often called 'meat meal' or 'bone meal', is slaughterhouse waste that may contain beaks, brains, feathers, feet, intestines, and other waste.

FACT ***Many health problems can be attributed to poor breeding practises and indeed some breeds are more prone to certain health concerns. However, the number one health destroyer for dogs that most dog lovers are not aware of is their dog's diet.***

A wholesome, balanced diet is the cornerstone of keeping your cocker healthy. Firstly, research companies that use high-quality ingredients and create foods that are nutrient-rich and balanced. Next, choose a quality diet that your dog enjoys.

Many companies offer samples you can try before you buy a case or bag. Some other brands offer money-back guarantees if your dog does not like the food. Discuss your options with your vet first if you choose to provide a homemade diet. Numerous studies have shown that most recipes available in books or on the internet are not nutritionally balanced or complete. Next, make small batches until you are sure your cocker likes it, and schedule regular vet visits to ensure your dog is receiving all the nutrition they need.

During the first few weeks after you find an appetising diet, watch how your dog responds. Symptoms such as low energy, gastrointestinal problems, and a dull coat might warrant a change of diet. If you do change your spaniel's food, be sure to do it gradually by mixing some of the old food with the new to avoid gastrointestinal upsets or food aversions. Your vet can also provide nutritional advice, especially if you have noticed changes in your dog's health. Water is also essential to keep your dog healthy, so make sure they have access to fresh, clean water always.

FACT ***Apart from diet, there are many other factors that can influence your cocker's lifespan, both positively and negatively. Our dogs are like small children whose health can be put at risk when exposed to only small amounts of toxic products, fumes, and foods.***

There are many little things we can do that may seem insignificant, yet together, over the years they can have a substantially positive health effect and increase your dog's lifespan. These are covered in detail in other sections of the book but include:

- Not overfeeding.
- Providing sufficient daily exercise.
- Teaching games and routines that exercise the mind.
- Giving them a calm, safe, and stress-free environment.
- Early socialisation with other dogs and people.

- Removing toxic products and cleaners from the home.
- Removing pesticides and fertilisers from the garden.
- Removing toxic plants.
- Keeping harmful foods and liquids away from your dog.
- Regular check-ups at the vet's.
- Regular bathing and grooming sessions.
- Purchasing pet insurance.
- Providing a securely fenced back garden.
- Training basic commands to prevent possible accidents.
- Becoming familiar with canine body language.
- Keep your dog on lead when in high-traffic areas.
- Not exposing them to toxic fumes or smoke—car exhaust, cigarettes.

Signs of a Healthy Cocker

We all want our cockers to look, feel, and be healthy, both inside and out with a sound body and mind. The following are the most important signs that indicate your dog is healthy:

Skin

Healthy skin is soft, smooth, and free of scabs, growths, white flakes, or red areas. Whether your cocker has a spotted coat or a solid coat, spotted skin is normal. Check your dog for fleas, ticks, lice, and other external parasites. You can do this by blowing gently on your spaniel's stomach or brushing the hair back in a few places to see if any tiny specks, fleas, or ticks are attached to the skin. Black 'powder' on your dog's skin or bedding could signify a flea infestation.

Coat

Whether short or long, a healthy coat is glossy and pliable, free from dandruff, bald spots, and excessive oiliness. It should smell fresh and feel smooth. Their coat should not shed excessively. The appearance and texture of your cocker's coat can be affected by illness or stress, which can cause excessive shedding. A dull, lacklustre coat can be a sign of hormonal imbalances, parasites, digestive disorders, and cancer.

Ears

Ensure that the skin inside your cocker's ears is clean and light pink. There should be some yellow or brownish wax, but excessive amounts are abnormal. Your dog should not scratch their ears or shake their head excessively. There should not be any redness or swelling inside the ear. A dog with long ears that hang down, such as the cocker, requires extra attention to keep their ears dry and clean.

Mouth, Teeth, and Gums

FACT ***Gums that are healthy are pink, black, or spotted, just like the skin of your dog. Young dogs have white teeth that tend to darken in time as your dog ages. Adult dogs typically have 42***

permanent teeth, while puppies have 23 baby teeth. Baby teeth begin to fall out as the permanent teeth grow in.

Try talking to your dog gently, then put your hand over their muzzle and lift the sides of their mouth. Ensure that adult teeth are coming in properly and are not being crowded by baby teeth. Verify that the gums are healthy, and their breath does not smell foul. Check for soft, white matter and hard, white, yellow, or brown matter. This is plaque or tartar and needs to be brushed away by a professional. An infection in your cocker's mouth can lead to serious problems in the gums and other parts of the body, including the heart, so it is important to take care of your dog's teeth and mouth.

Eyes

A healthy pair of eyes is shiny and bright. The presence of mucus and watery tears is normal but should be minimal and clear. Their eyelids should have a pink lining that is not inflamed, swollen, or discoloured. At the inside corner of your spaniel's eye, you can sometimes see their third eyelid, a thin, transparent membrane. During sleep, this may slowly engulf and cover the eye. It is important that the whites of your dog's eyes are not yellowish. Their eyelashes should not rub against the eye.

Nose

The nose of your dog should be cool and moist. Depending on the breed, it may be black, pink, or self-coloured—the same colour as the coat. There should be no yellowish, thick, bubbly, or foul-smelling nasal discharge. Dogs with cool, wet noses are not always healthy, and those with dry, warm noses are not necessarily ill. Taking their temperature is a more reliable health indicator.

Breath

The breath of a dog does not smell bad, unlike what many people think. Obviously, it does not smell minty fresh, but there should not be any offensive smell either. If your dog has bad breath, it could be the result of bacteria build-up that can cause gingivitis and periodontal disease. Certain odours may indicate illness. For instance, if your spaniel's breath smells like ammonia or urine, it could be the result of kidney disease.

Elimination

The colour of the urine is an indicator of your dog's health and should be clear yellow. On average, adult dogs have one or two bowel movements each day. They should have brown and firm stools. Symptoms such as bloody, runny, or watery stools, excess urination, and straining require veterinary attention.

Heartbeat and Pulse

The heartbeats of dogs vary depending on their size. In a resting dog, a normal heart beats between 50 and 130 times per minute. Puppies and small dogs have faster heartbeats, while large dogs in good condition have slower ones. You can check your cocker's heart rate by placing your fingers over the left side of their chest and feeling the strongest beat. When testing the pulse, which is the same rate as the heartbeat, press gently on the inside of the top of the hind leg. An artery runs through that area and the skin is thin, so it is easy to feel their pulse.

Weight

The weight of a healthy dog is determined by the balance between diet and exercise. If they are eating right and exercising regularly, but still seem overweight or underweight, they might have a health problem. Avoid giving your dog too many between meal treats; obese dogs typically develop serious health problems. You can tell if your dog is overweight by feeling their rib cage. Ribs should be easy to feel under the surface of the skin without much padding.

Alertness and attitude

When your cocker spaniel is happy, you can tell by their body language. Your dog should be eager to engage with you, aware of their surroundings, and lively. Rather than showing signs of nervousness or anxiety, they should appear happy and content. They should be enthusiastic about life and full of energy. Their posture should be relaxed and confident.

Top Illness Indicators

Your dog cannot tell you how they feel. However, they use their body language in a very expressive way (pictured). Instinctively, in the early stages of an illness, your dog will not show you that something is wrong. Knowing your cocker spaniel, you might be able to recognise some subtle changes in their behaviour and personality. Typically, these changes indicate a health issue. You can help your dog recover quickly by seeing there is a problem as soon as possible. A few warning signs that your dog might be ill and need veterinary treatment include:

Vomiting or Diarrhoea

The most common reason to seek veterinary care is vomiting or diarrhoea. Such problems can be transient and mild, or they can be life-threatening. It may be due to a change in diet, an ingestion of nondigestible objects, viral or bacterial infections, or getting into the rubbish.

Temperature

The normal temperature for a dog is between 38.3 to 39.2o C (101 to 102.5o F). As your dog's body temperature is naturally higher than a human's, feeling warmer than you is not always cause for concern.

FACT ***A dog with a temperature of 39.5o C (103o F) or higher is considered to have a fever, and in this case, you should call your veterinarian.***

Loss of Appetite

It is common for dogs to have their own eating habits and to eat varying amounts of food depending on the day. However, an on-going loss of appetite is often indicative of underlying problems. These can range from mild to serious. Anorexia can indicate dental disease if it is accompanied by bad breath. It might help to offer your dog their favourite treats. A vet should be consulted if the problem lasts more than a day or is associated with other symptoms such as lethargy, vomiting, and weakness.

Changes in Personality

In pain or feeling unwell, dogs display changes in behaviour, such as decreased energy levels and lethargy. Dogs who are normally social might start to withdraw when they are sick. A loving and energetic dog may show signs of snippiness or aggression. Observe if your dog growls whenever you approach a specific place on their body. Not all sick dogs display negative behaviour. Some dogs might become clingy or show signs of increased neediness.

Coughing, Wheezing, or Trouble Breathing

Coughing, wheezing, nasal discharge, and trouble breathing are signs of respiratory problems. The symptoms can indicate something as simple as a cold, to more severe conditions such as canine influenza, kennel cough, or heart failure. Honking noises can be an indication of a condition known as tracheal collapse, which is common in small breeds. Consider your cocker's condition as an emergency if they have difficulty breathing or their tongue or gums appear blue. Coughs should be closely monitored, and if they do not go away or develop in conjunction with other symptoms, they should be evaluated.

Joint and Spine Issues

Cocker spaniels are known to suffer from several musculoskeletal problems. Even though it may seem overwhelming, every condition can be diagnosed and treated to prevent unnecessarily painful outcomes. If you observe your dog carefully at home and know about any conditions that could affect their bones, joints, or muscles, you can provide them the necessary care throughout their life.

Hip and Elbow Dysplasia

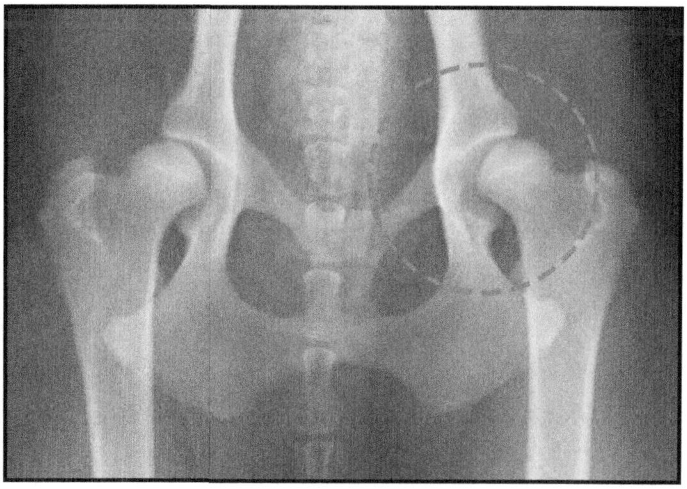

Hip dysplasia (pictured) is a deformity of the hip that occurs during growth. The hip joint is a ball and socket joint. During growth, both the ball—the head of the femur, or thighbone—and the socket in the pelvis—acetabulum—must grow at equal rates. In hip dysplasia, this uniform growth during puppyhood does not occur. The result is looseness of the joint, followed by degenerative joint disease (DJD) or osteoarthritis (OA), which is the body's attempt to stabilise the loose hip joint. In other words, the head of the dog's femur does not fit properly into the hip or elbow joint socket.

Clinical signs include weakness and pain in the hind legs. The dog appears wobbly and avoids rising from a sitting or lying position. Many dogs limp or seem to be reluctant to climb stairs. The signs can be seen in puppies as young as a few months old, but they are most common in dogs between one and two years of age. Dogs with mild hip dysplasia can develop minimal arthritis without showing clinical signs until they are more elderly. Even though hip dysplasia typically starts in puppies, most dogs do not show any clinical signs until they are older. It often takes years of progressive bone degeneration for a dog to exhibit symptoms.

FACT ***Hip dysplasia is a genetic condition that is influenced by factors such as diet, environment, exercise, growth rate, muscle mass, and hormones. The disease is most often seen in breeds of large dogs, but it can be seen in smaller breeds as well, such as the cocker spaniel. According to a study from the Orthopaedic Foundation of Animals (OFA) in the U.S., on average, 6.5% of cocker spaniels suffer from the condition.***

Diagnosis – Your vet can diagnose hip dysplasia by taking an x-ray of the hip.

Treatment – Clinical signs and your dog's level of discomfort determine the appropriate treatment. Non-steroidal anti-inflammatory drugs (NSAIDs), such as Meloxicam, provide excellent pain relief. There is no one-size-fits-all approach to selecting medications, and various drugs might be tried before finding the most effective one.

In most cases, dogs with hip dysplasia should be given glucosamine, chondroitin sulphate, and omega-3 fatty acid nutritional supplements. Many dogs suffering from painful hip dysplasia benefit from regular injections of polysulfated glycosaminoglycan. A moderate amount of exercise, avoiding high impact exercises such as jumping, might help the patient dog to stay mobile.

In addition to other treatments, physical therapy has been shown to significantly improve the quality of life for affected dogs. Weight loss is strongly recommended for overweight dogs as excess weight causes undue stress on the hip joints.

Surgery is an alternative to NSAIDs and medical therapy. A variety of surgical procedures are available to treat hip dysplasia. Total hip replacement and femoral head ostectomy are the two most common surgical treatments. Your dog's age, health condition, and lifestyle determine the type of surgery required. The best recommendation for your cocker will be provided by your vet.

Hip Dysplasia Screening Scheme – In the United Kingdom, the British Veterinary Association BVA—the OFA in the U.S.—reviews x-rays for abnormalities in dogs' hip joints. Each x-ray is graded by a panel of experts. Your vet can arrange for your cocker's x-rays to be scored and relay the results to you.

Scrutineers of the BVA evaluate each hip joint based on nine different aspects. A score for each hip indicates how severely your spaniel has been affected by hip dysplasia. Scores range from 0 to 106—0 to 53 for every hip—with a score of 0 representing the least and a score of 53 representing the most severe degree of hip dysplasia. Over the last 15 years, the average hip scope for cocker spaniels has been 11, so you could use that as your benchmark.

Patellar Luxation

Patellar luxation is when your cocker's kneecap—patella—slips out of place, which occasionally happens.

During a run, you might notice that your dog picks up a back leg or skips and hops for a few steps. Then, they may kick their leg out sideways to pop their kneecap back into place. Both are common symptoms of patellar luxation. Cocker spaniels are particularly susceptible to this problem.

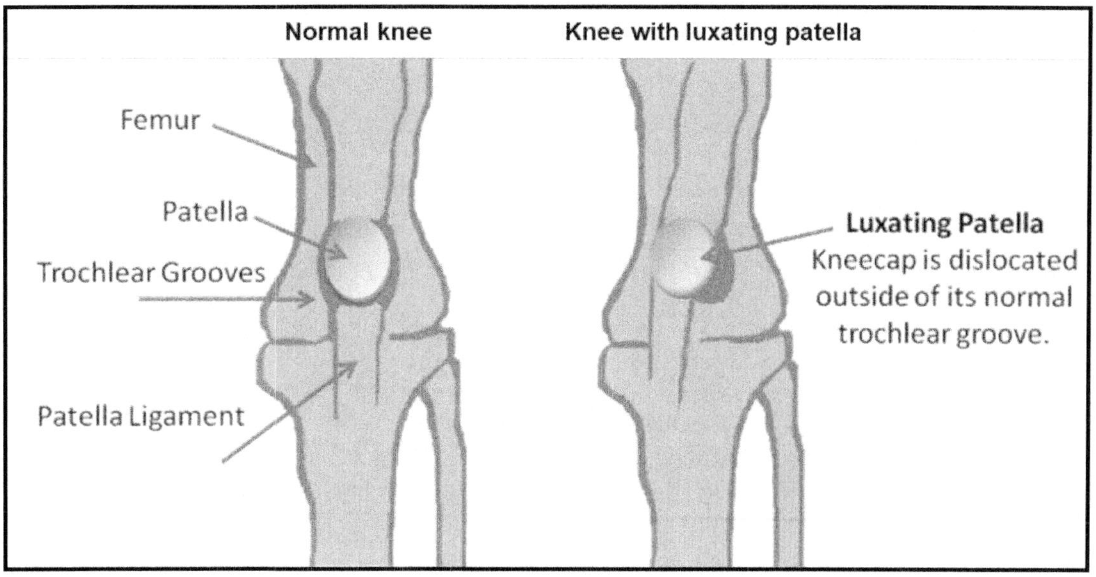

The kneecap slides up and down a groove in the thighbone when a healthy knee bends. Kneecaps should not slip out of the groove, and if they do, it is referred to as a luxating patella—dislocating kneecap. When the kneecap dislocates, it prevents the knee from bending, causes a limp, and rubs past the bone as it slips, which over time can result in pain and arthritis.

One or both knees can be affected by patellar luxation, which ranges from Grade 1 to Grade 4:

Grade 1 – Kneecap is loose but stays in place when your dog moves. If forced by your vet, it will dislocate, but returns instantly after release. Often, grade 1 patellar luxation is not much of a problem.

Grade 2 – The kneecap dislocates occasionally when your dog moves, but usually returns on its own. The severity of grade 2 symptoms depends on how frequently the kneecap dislocates.

Grade 3 – The kneecap is permanently dislocated, and it can be pushed back into place by the vet, but it slips straight out again if the vet lets go.

Grade 4 – The kneecap is permanently dislocated and cannot be put back in its original position.

Diagnosis – To check the stability of your cocker's kneecap, your vet will feel it carefully and perform a few different tests. They will also look at your dog's cruciate ligaments, because cruciate disease is common in dogs with patellar luxation. For a full diagnosis, some dogs require a general anaesthetic and x-rays, especially if their knee is very painful.

TIP ***If your dog limps only occasionally—every few weeks—physiotherapy and controlled exercise might be able to manage their patellar luxation. However, if your dog is in pain or regularly limps, surgery might be the solution.***

Treatment – The type of treatment your dog needs is dependent on the grade of their patellar luxation and their symptoms.

The mildest cases of patellar luxation—grades 1 & 2—can be treated without surgery. Physiotherapy and controlled exercise can be used to strengthen the leg muscles and stop kneecaps from slipping. Dogs with severe cases—grades 3 & 4—could require surgery. You can choose from a few different surgical options, and your vet will help you pick the best one for your cocker. You should be aware that all surgeries come with pros and cons, and some of the more complex ones can only be performed by a specialist veterinarian at a referral centre.

Most dogs with patellar luxation—except some grade 1s—experience pain at some time during their lives. As needed, your vet can prescribe NSAIDs to relieve pain. The higher the grade of luxation, the more complicated and expensive the treatment will be. Specialist knee surgery tends to be the most expensive procedure. Discuss your finances with your vet as well as what you believe is best for your dog.

Intervertebral Disc Disease

Intervertebral Disc Disease (IVDD) is a very serious and common disease affecting thousands of dogs every year. Dogs with short legs and long backs, such as dachshunds and basset hounds, are most affected. However, it can also occur in other breeds such as the cocker spaniel.

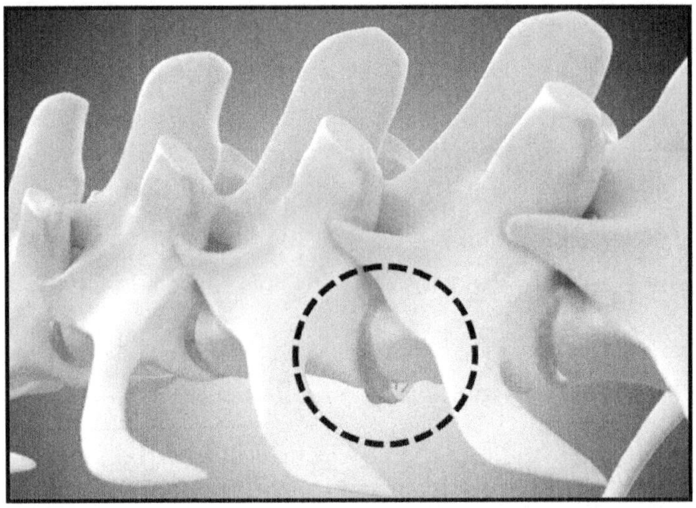

Your dog's intervertebral discs are little cushions between each vertebra—backbone. These pads absorb shocks and provide support to your spaniel as they move. This condition causes the intervertebral discs to gradually lose their elasticity, become hard and fragile, and often slip out of place (pictured). A slipped disc presses on the spinal cord, causing pain, weakness in the legs, and sometimes paralysis and incontinence.

IVDD symptoms can occur gradually or rapidly, and include back pain, wobbliness, weak legs, falling, tripping, and difficulty getting up.

Diagnosis – When your vet examines your dog, they might suspect IVDD, but further tests are typically needed to confirm the diagnosis. These tests might include:

- An MRI scan is the best way to diagnose IVDD since it provides a detailed view of the spine, nerves, bones, and discs. An MRI scanner is a very large, expensive piece of equipment, so they are often only available at specialised veterinary hospitals.
- An x-ray will show some of the changes caused by IVDD and a slipped disc, but not all of them as nerves and the spinal cord are not visible on an x-ray.
- Other tests might be required for your dog, depending on your vet's findings, such as blood tests, spinal taps, or CT scans.

Treatment – If your cocker only exhibits mild symptoms of a slipped disc, you might want to treat them conservatively. In conservative treatment, your dog is given pain medication, rest, and physical therapy. They will also need assistance going to the toilet if they cannot urinate or poo. In most cases of IVDD, strict rest is essential for several weeks. The dog needs to be kept in a crate or a small space and only come out on their lead to relieve themselves. You should make sure your dog does not jump, run, or climb stairs while they are recovering from a slipped disc. Another essential component of conservative management is pain relief. A tablet or liquid can usually be given at home, but if that is not enough, your dog could require stronger injections, or even be hospitalised for pain control.

In severe cases, such as pain that is severe or an inability to walk, surgery is likely to be needed. In many cases, surgery is very successful if it is carried out within a few days of the onset of the symptoms. However, spinal surgery is a major procedure, so talk to your vet about the possible risks, recovery time, and costs before proceeding. Unfortunately, some dogs are so severely affected that putting them to sleep is the best option.

IVDD treatment costs vary widely depending on the treatment needed. If your dog needs specialist treatment or spinal surgery, the costs could amount to several thousand pounds.

Dental Issues

Unfortunately, it is a fact that most dogs suffer dental issues at some point in their life. Studies have revealed that 80% of dogs suffer from dental disease by the time they are five years old. This is a sad statistic as dental issues are all entirely preventable. The only reason so many dogs suffer with teeth problems is that we sometimes neglect to establish a dental routine that includes daily brushing.

It is important to commit to a healthy teeth routine early on with your cocker puppy and never put off making sure they have their teeth brushed at least once every day. After every meal would be even better.

Cocker spaniels tend to have more dental problems than other breeds. As the cocker spaniel's jaws are so small their teeth can become overcrowded, making them hard to keep clean, which causes a build-up of tartar and plaque.

Read on to learn about the most common canine dental issues.

Dental Disease

When bacteria in the mouth combines with fluids, food, and saliva, they create a sticky, clear or pale-yellow biofilm called plaque, which settles between the teeth and along the gum line. Within just 4 to 12 hours after their teeth have been brushed, plaque starts forming in their mouth and sticking to every tooth surface. This constantly forming film is the root cause of many dental problems and the major reason why brushing your cocker's teeth is so important.

When plaque is not removed with brushing, it mineralises into hard, cement-like tartar—within 24 to 36 hours of eating—that builds up along the gum line, pushing the gums away from the teeth, causing dental disease. Effectively removing plaque once it builds up requires scrubbing.

The bacteria in the plaque attack the tooth enamel. The enamel loss causes cavities, infection, pain, inflamed, swollen gums that bleed easily, and gingivitis—gum disease. The latter then causes bad breath, loose teeth, and eventual tooth loss. The only scientifically proven way to decrease plaque and tartar is the same for dogs as it is for humans—daily brushing combined with routine removal of any accumulated hard tartar deposits by a health professional.

FACT ***Vigilant care of your cocker spaniel's teeth throughout their lifetime will add at least 2 to 5 years to their life.***

Gingival Hyperplasia (Gum Disease)

This refers to a medical condition in which your cocker's gums or gingival tissue becomes inflamed, swollen and enlarged because of irritation from dental plaque or other bacterial growth along the gum line. Over time, more of the tooth is revealed as the gums recede and connection to the socket is loosened. In almost all cases, this painful condition can be prevented with good, oral hygiene habits. When a dog is suffering from gum disease, they have an increased chance of being affected by other serious health issues, including cancer, diabetes, and heart disease.

Loose Teeth

The only time your dog should have loose or wobbly teeth is when they are very young, and their milk teeth are being replaced by their adult set of teeth. When an adult dog has a loose tooth, it is usually because of an underlying gum problem resulting from poor dental hygiene.

Malocclusions

Abnormal tooth alignment is known as malocclusion. There are two types, skeletal and dental. A skeletal malocclusion is when the jaw length is abnormal, creating a malalignment of the teeth. A dental malocclusion, or malposition, happens if the upper and lower jaw lengths are normal but one or more teeth are out of normal alignment.

If a dental or skeletal malocclusion causes trauma to the oral soft tissues or other teeth, the condition is called non-functional or traumatic and treatment is needed, including:

- Extraction.
- Moving the offending or offended tooth/teeth.
- Surgically creating additional space for the mispositioned tooth to occupy.

Retained Milk Teeth

Mostly, puppies lose their 28 puppy—or milk—teeth without intervention by a vet. However, sometimes they do not all naturally fall out (pictured). If your puppy has not lost all their baby teeth on their own, any remaining ones need to be pulled by the vet to allow room for their adult teeth to properly grow in.

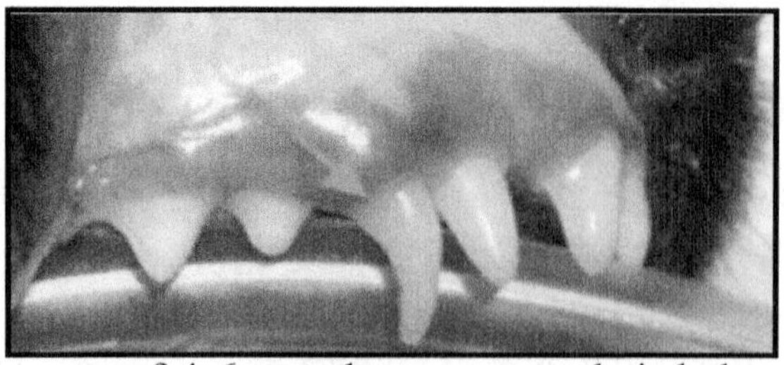

Remember to keep a close watch on your puppy's teeth around the age of 4-6 months to ensure their baby teeth have fallen out and their adult teeth have space to grow.

Periodontal Disease

This disease begins with inflammation caused by infection of the tissue that surrounds the tooth—the periodontium—called gingivitis. As the disease progresses, the covering of the root surface—the cementum—

is affected, followed by the ligaments that attach the tooth root to the bone—the periodontal ligament. When left untreated, the infection spreads into the tooth socket, destroying the bone. At this stage, the tooth becomes loose and over time will fall out.

Anyone who has ever had a toothache can easily imagine how painful this disease must be. Unfortunately, your cocker spaniel cannot tell you that their teeth are painful, and the only indication will most likely be a disgruntled dog who refuses to eat or have anyone touch their face. You can prevent this from ever occurring simply by practicing good dental hygiene.

Worn Down Teeth

It is natural for your cocker's teeth to show some signs of wear as they age, especially since they are always chewing on something. However, severe tooth wear, known as attrition—which is the loss of the protective layer of dentin—can be the result of chewing inappropriate items, such as tennis balls, rocks, antlers, or other hard objects.

Some dogs literally fetch anything, including stones and hard rocks. You should never get in the habit of tossing rocks for your dog, because these can crack, chip, and eventually wear down their teeth. Once your dog has learnt to pick up rocks, this can be a difficult habit to break.

TIP ***Never allow your dog to play with tennis balls. These are very corrosive and can wear down their teeth, as they contain fibreglass.***

Bad Breath

A healthy dog should not have bad breath, unless they have just raided the cat's litter box. When your dog has bad breath, this could be the first sign of an unhealthy mouth and gum disease caused by plaque build-up on their teeth. Beyond poor oral hygiene, which is the most common cause of bad breath, there may be other contributing factors, such as:

- Diabetes.
- Too much bad bacteria in the gut microbiome.
- Gastrointestinal issues.
- Airway infections in the lungs, sinuses, or windpipe.
- Bowel obstruction.
- Kidney Disease.
- Liver Disease.

In addition, if your dog is drooling excessively, this could also be a symptom of dental disease. Drooling can mean the salivary glands are reacting to inflammation from excessive bacteria in the mouth. When noticing your dog drooling—and it is not because they are anticipating the steak grilling on the BBQ...—you should have them professionally examined by your vet.

How to Check the Teeth

Knowing how to check your spaniel's teeth can help to minimise teeth issues by alerting you to potential situations before they become serious.

While checking your dog's teeth is best done while carrying out their daily teeth brushing, if this routine has not been established, begin with your dog sitting quietly beside you or up on a worktop where there is a good light source. Lift their lip so you can clearly see your dog's teeth and look for the following:

- Brown colour—teeth should be white.
- Tartar and plaque build-up—the precursor to serious disease.
- Red and swollen gums—the beginning of periodontal disease.
- Bleeding gums—usually the result of plaque beneath the gum line.
- Lumps or growths on the gums.
- Teeth that are chipped, cracked, broken, or worn.
- Loose or wobbly teeth—might need to be removed.
- Smelly breath—can indicate gum disease.

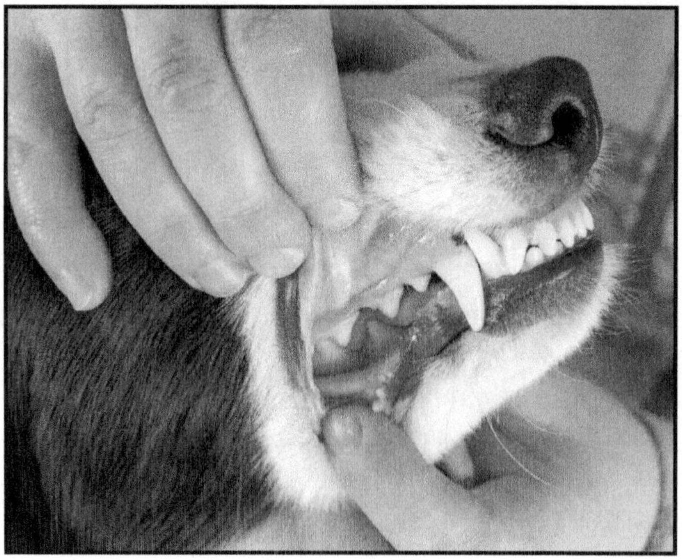

All the above conditions require intervention and closer observation by the vet. A routine course of action typically performed by the vet is a professional cleaning of your cocker's teeth to remove all the plaque, reduce the gum swelling and get the teeth and gums back in good health.

What Should the Gums Look Like?

Pale Pink or White Gums are usually an indication of anaemia or low blood count. This can be a warning of a serious problem that requires immediate attention by your vet.

Bright Red Gums can indicate that the dog is overheated, suffering from heat stroke or from infected inflamed gums—gingivitis—that bleed easily.

Blue Gums are usually an indication that not enough oxygen is being circulated through your dog's blood supply. Difficulty breathing, heart disease, or pneumonia can be the cause and requires immediate intervention by your vet.

TIP ***The colour of your dog's gums can alert you to the health of your cocker spaniel. Healthy gums should be wet or smooth and slippery and a powdery pink colour. This colour should fade to pale pink or white when pressed with your finger and return to the deeper pink within two seconds of removing your finger.***

Growths or Tumours found on the gums may be benign and disappear on their own, they could be a contagious viral problem, or they might be cancerous. Appearance of growths on the gums need to be assessed by your vet.

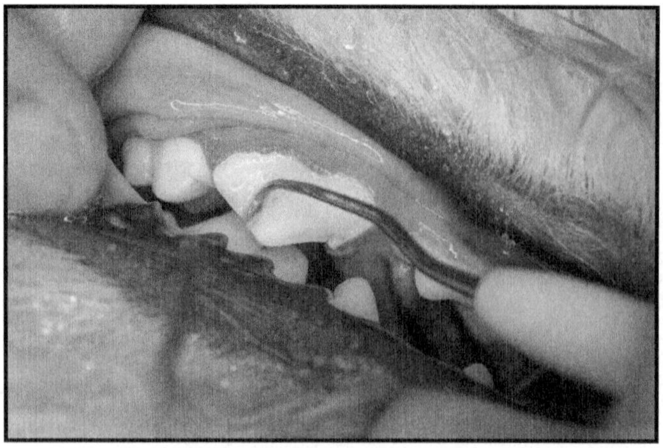

Healthy Chewing Toys

There are many popular chew toys and objects in the market that can be dangerous for canine teeth and their health overall. It is important to always keep the following in mind when choosing toys:

- They are vet approved.

- They are softer than their teeth—otherwise they might damage your cocker's teeth.
- They are size appropriate so your dog cannot swallow them.
- They are designed for the level of chewing force of your dog.
- They do not contain toxins.
- They engage your spaniel's mind and keep them occupied.
- No soft or plush toys if your dog likes to rip things apart.
- Only balls that are designed especially for dog's teeth.

Eye Issues

Many dogs are born with eye issues or develop them over time as part of the aging process. The following are the most common eye issues that could affect your cocker spaniel throughout their life.

Cataracts

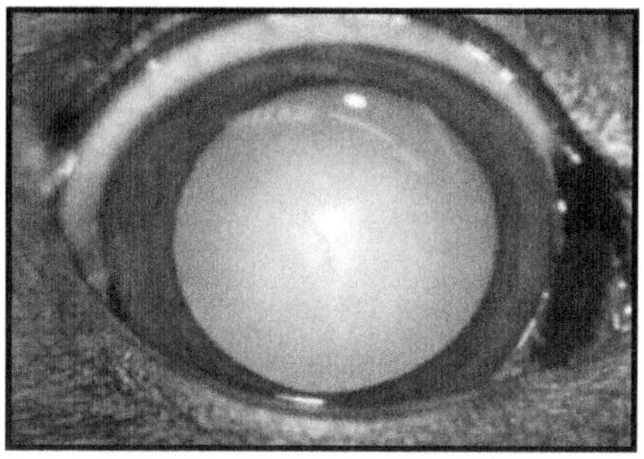

Cockers are prone to cataracts (pictured), a major cause of blindness. Cataracts are cloudy spots that form on the clear lens of the eye that focuses light on the retina at the back of the eye. Eventually, these spots completely block the light from reaching the retina. As the lens becomes cloudier, it dims the light reaching the retina to the point where your dog could become blind. Even though cataracts are not painful, they increase the risk of injury, especially if your dog is unfamiliar with their environment.

Since cataracts are often hereditary, their progression differs from breed to breed and individual to individual. In some breeds, cataracts develop relatively early, whilst in others, the first signs are detected at an older age and progress is so slow that the dog can maintain reasonable vision well into old age.

At least 70 breeds are affected by hereditary cataracts. Despite this fact, little is known about their genetic cause. There are breed-specific characteristics associated with cataracts, such as their appearance, age at onset, rate of progression, and whether they occur bilaterally in both eyes.

Cataracts in cocker spaniels were first recognised in the 1970s. Their development can begin as early as 3 to 4 years of age and affect the entire lens or a selected part of it. Their progression can be rapid over weeks or gradual over years, and they might occur in one eye before the other.

FACT ***Statistics show that 7.3% of American cocker spaniels examined had some form of cataract. Even though this number includes cataracts from non-hereditary causes, it is significantly higher than the 1.6 percent found in mixed breeds.***

It is rare for cataracts to give rise to diminished vision if they obscure less than 30% of the eye's lens or if only one lens is affected. Visual impairment is usually evident when opacity covers about 60% of the lens. Your dog will become blind in the affected eye if the opacity advances to 100%. Cataract progression or stability depends on the type, breed, and other risk factors.

Today, no topical medications—e.g., drops—have been shown to slow the progress of genetic cataracts. However, topical aldose reductase inhibitors have been shown to be effective in treating cataracts generated by diabetes. A veterinary ophthalmologist can surgically remove cataracts and restore your cocker's vision.

Most dogs recover quickly from surgery and are back to their normal activities, running and playing within a few days.

Glaucoma

FACT ***The cocker spaniel is one of the breeds that is susceptible to this eye problem. Glaucoma (pictured) is a condition in which aqueous fluid builds up inside the eye and results in pressure build-up.***

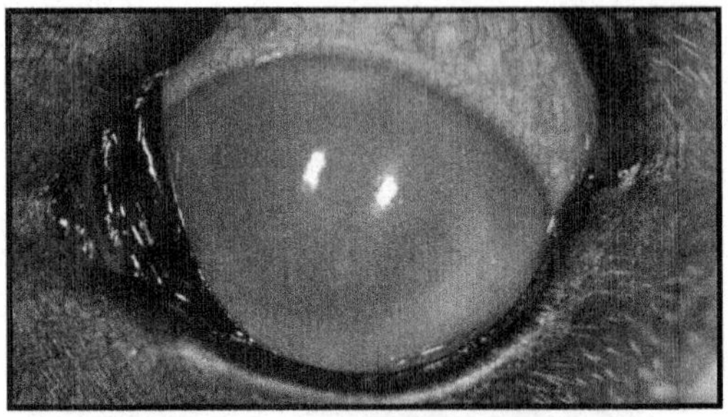

The pressure of the eye, called intraocular pressure (IOP), increases when too much fluid is made or not enough is drained, damaging the retina and optic nerve. This is a problem as the retina converts images into nerve signals and the optic nerve sends these signals to the brain to produce vision. Due to this, an increase in intraocular pressure almost always leads to blindness in the affected eye due to damage to the retina or optic nerve.

Glaucoma can be classified as either primary or secondary. In primary glaucoma, the flow rate of fluid into or out of the eye is abnormal, resulting in increased pressure. The condition is often inherited due to a genetic predisposition within certain breeds. Unlike secondary glaucoma, it is not the result of an underlying disease. Primary glaucoma can occur at any age, but most dogs are diagnosed in their middle or late years, between the ages of 3 to 7.

Secondary glaucoma occurs owing to another concurrent eye condition. There can be bleeding, swelling, inflammation, scar tissue may form, and fluid drainage can be hindered if not blocked entirely. Compared to primary glaucoma, secondary glaucoma is more common in dogs. The triggers include infection, advanced cataracts, inflammation, and other conditions.

As your dog ages, the clinical signs could first manifest in one eye and then the other. The signs are rarely experienced simultaneously or equally in both eyes. It can also take years for the second eye to be affected. Check your cocker for glaucoma immediately if you see any signs and symptoms. Time is critical when this condition occurs. It is not only painful, but it can also lead to irreversible blindness if left untreated.

Dogs with glaucoma suffer more severe pain than humans. Some of the symptoms to look out for are:

- Eye pain—Rubbing their eye against the floor or other object or with their paw.
- Eye redness.
- Squinting.
- Watery eyes.
- Avoiding light.
- Having a weakened blink response.
- Eyelids fluttering.
- Pupils appear to be different sizes.
- Vessels in the white of the eye.
- Swollen, bulging eye.
- Vision problems—bumping into objects, struggling to find items, cautious when walking.

Your vet will measure intraocular pressure of your cocker spaniel's eye with a tonometer, a device that measures the amount of pressure the eye's fluid exerts.

Glaucoma treatment depends on the severity of the disorder, as well as any underlying conditions that may have contributed to it in the first place. Those issues must be addressed to prevent a recurrence. The treatment options are medications, cyclocryotherapy—cold temperatures are used to kill the cells producing intraocular fluid—and surgery.

Sadly, in most long-term cases, the eye must be removed. If glaucoma goes undetected for a long time, the optical nerve can be damaged beyond repair, which means surgery and possible removal of the eye.

Cherry Eye

A cherry eye (pictured) is a common condition in cocker spaniels.

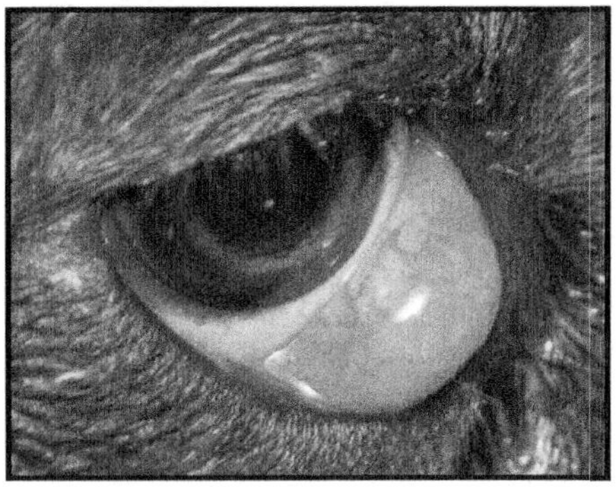

This is a genetic eye problem where the gland of the third eyelid prolapses or slips in the corner of the eye, because of weakness of the connective tissue surrounding the gland. This causes a pink, fleshy protrusion to extend or bulge over the edge of your dog's eyelid. In other words, the prolapse of the third eyelid gland produces a red, swollen mass that forms on the lower eyelid near the nose or muzzle. Its name comes from the resemblance to a cherry. It can be large and cover a considerable portion of the cornea, or it might be small and appear only occasionally. Veterinary attention should be sought as soon as possible in the event of cherry eye.

Treatment involves surgically replacing the third eyelid gland. To minimise permanent damage to the eye or third eyelid gland, it is crucial to treat the condition as soon as possible. This is vital as the three eyelid glands produce about 50% of the watery—aqueous—part of the tear film. In the absence of sufficient tear production, your cocker is far more likely to develop dry eye, which can severely impede their vision. Your vet will assess your dog's condition and decide which surgical technique is best for them.

After surgery, the gland usually returns to normal function in a few weeks. There is a possibility of re-prolapse of the third eyelid gland in about 5 to 20 percent of cases. Many dogs with a prolapsed eye will eventually experience the same prolapse in the other eye.

Retinal Dysplasia

Retinal dysplasia in dogs is the formation of clumps known as 'rosettes' or 'folds' in the eye retinal tissue e. There are many causes of retinal dysplasia, but the condition is usually genetic in nature, with several different dog breeds particularly prone to the condition. The cocker spaniel is one of the breeds most at risk of inheriting retinal dysplasia. This condition can affect your dog's vision, but it is not painful or progressive.

Normally, a retina is comprised of two layers that form and develop together. In retinal dysplasia, folds, or creases form between the two layers when they do not develop properly. In addition to genetic factors, retinal dysplasia can also be caused by a variety of other reasons, such as vitamin deficiencies, damage to the eye itself, and viral infections.

The condition cannot be observed with the naked eye, and therefore the first sign of something amiss is more often the concern that your cocker's vision might not be 100%. For example, if they seem particularly clumsy or always bump into things.

A veterinary ophthalmologist would need to examine your dog with an otoscope or even perform a more complex examination to positively identify the condition.

Currently, it is not possible to reverse or treat retinal dysplasia. A dog who develops the condition will have it for the rest of their life. This eye issue is hereditary, so dogs with any form of retinal dysplasia should not be bred.

The associated vision loss may be entirely manageable, depending on the severity of the condition. Dogs with retinal dysplasia can live healthy and happy lives with very little difficulty. After retinal dysplasia is diagnosed, it will not worsen over time, as it is not progressive. However, as your dog ages, they might develop additional eye problems or have failing sight.

Progressive Retinal Atrophy (PRA)

FACT ***An inherited disease in dogs, progressive retinal atrophy engenders blindness slowly over several months or years. It is also called generalised progressive retinal atrophy or GPRA. The condition can occur in nearly any breed. However, it is most common in miniature and toy poodles, cocker spaniels, and Labrador retrievers.***

This is an inherited autosomal recessive disorder that causes the retinal cells in your cocker's eye to degenerate and die. As light enters the eyes, retinal—rod and cone—cells transmit information to the brain, where it is translated into vision. The rod cells, which function in low light, are the first to degenerate causing night blindness. Next, the cone cells, which function in bright light or daytime, begin to deteriorate, leading to complete blindness over time.

Symptoms usually appear when the dog is around 3-5 years old, and blindness can occur in older dogs. When PRA is diagnosed, an ophthalmoscope is used to examine the back of the eye for characteristic signs of retinal degeneration. This is performed by a veterinarian who specialises in ophthalmology. In cases where the retina cannot be examined, such as when cataracts are present, a brief anaesthetic may be required. This test is called an ERG—electroretinogram—and measures the electrical activity and function of the retina.

There are DNA tests available for cocker spaniels. A DNA test can detect whether your dog has the potential to develop progressive retinal atrophy or to pass it on to any offspring.

Unfortunately, there is no effective treatment for PRA at present, and affected dogs will likely become totally blind. There have been suggestions that antioxidant therapy could delay vision loss in affected dogs, but there is still no solid evidence that this is effective. Although gene therapy research might provide some hope for the future, treatment is still a long way off.

Since PRA is an inherited issue, dogs with the disease should not be bred. In general, many dogs adapt well to vision loss, especially if the condition develops gradually, as in PRA.

Ear Issues

Ear Infections

Knowing the anatomy of your cocker spaniel's ear will help you understand why they are susceptible to ear infections. Cocker spaniels have long, pendulous ears, which make them more likely to develop ear infections than other dogs with pointy ears. The reasons why cockers tend to have more ear problems than other breeds are:

- They have floppy ears. An ear canal that has reduced air flow has a moist, warm, and humid environment. Yeast and bacteria thrive in such an environment.
- They have sensitivities and allergies to food and the environment. Infections and inflammation of the ear can occur even without symptoms on other parts of their body.
- Compared with other breeds, cocker spaniels produce more sebaceous oil from their ears and skin.
- When there is more oil, more earwax is produced, which means increased ear problems.
- Cockers can exhibit thyroid problems. Hypothyroidism, or low thyroid (T4) function, can predispose your dog to chronic ear infections.

FACT ***Cocker spaniels with their floppy, hanging ears are prone to ear infections. Infections in the ear are caused by a build-up of bacteria or yeast in the ear canal. These infections tend to be caused by underlying conditions such as ear mites, a skin issue, or excessive earwax and are the most common ear condition in cockers.***

When your cocker's ears are damp after swimming, bathing, or walking in the rain, the trapped moisture serves as the ideal breeding ground for ear infections. By keeping your dog's ears dry, you can prevent this problem.

Symptoms of ear infections in dogs include head shaking, itchiness that causes scratching, rubbing their ear on the floor, red and swollen ear canals, whining due to pain, a dark coloured discharge, odour, and crusts in the ears. More serious ear infections can make dogs lose their balance, walk in circles, have unusual eye movements, or appear to have hearing loss. When your cocker's head tilts or they lose balance, the infection has spread deeper into the ear. Consult your vet if you suspect your dog has an ear infection. The faster your dog is treated, the quicker their recovery will be.

Typically, your vet will examine your dog's ears using an otoscope to determine the pain level, and then swab the ears to collect a sample. They usually use a medicated cleanser first, then recommend some of the following:

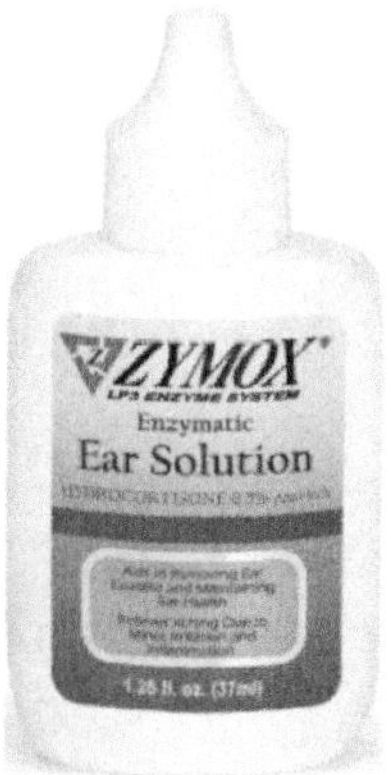

Eardrops – The use of medical ear drops (pictured) containing antibiotics, antifungals—to kill yeasts—and anti-inflammatories can alleviate swelling and pain. Ensure your dog gets the whole course of drops—even if it appears that their ears are improving.

Ear cleaning – As your spaniel heals, you need to keep the inside of their ears clean. Ask your vet how to do this and what product you should use. Do not use cotton buds.

Anti-inflammatory pain relief – When your dog is in a lot of pain, your vet might prescribe anti-inflammatory pain medication.

Antibiotic tablets – A very severe infection could require your dog to receive both antibiotic pills and eardrops. In most cases, eardrops are enough.

Treating the underlying problem – Most ear infections are the result of an underlying condition, such as an allergic reaction to the skin. Treatment of the underlying cause is just as important as treating the actual infection since untreated infections will recur.

When your cocker's ear infection is caught and treated early, it is likely to clear up quickly. Your dog will need a follow-up check-up to ensure the issue has been resolved. If your dog's ear does not improve, your vet might decide to examine or treat it under anaesthetic. Some ear infections take several weeks to resolve. Some cases of severe infection require surgery because the infection continues for so long that the ear becomes misshapen.

Dogs who suffer from ear infections, or are prone to them such as the cocker, need ongoing ear care:

Ear checks – Regularly check your dog's ears for problems. The smell is usually the most obvious sign. As you become familiar with how your dog's ears normally smell, you will notice when an infected sour/pungent smell develops.

Cleaning – Your cocker might need help keeping their ears clean if they are susceptible to infection. Your vet will be happy to show you how to check and clean your dog's ears at home, so ask for advice on cleaning them regularly. An effective ear cleanser for cockers is Zymox. It is a non-irritating cleanser for long-term use on non-infected dry ears. Zymox products contain LP3 enzymes, which can be safely used by dogs of all ages.

Hairy ears – Often, hairy ears are very warm and moist, making them a perfect breeding ground for bacteria and yeasts. By plucking or trimming the hair, air can be introduced into the ear.

Foreign Objects in the Ear

TIP ***Rarely, a foreign object can become lodged in your cocker spaniel's ear canal. If your dog scratches at their ears without apparent reason, it could be spear grass or another foreign object irritating their ear.***

Grass seeds (pictured) are a common foreign object that causes ear problems in dogs. The problem usually occurs during the summer months when they have been playing in long grass. The sharp tip of the seed creates irritation by piercing the skin and becoming lodged. It is possible for the grass seeds to burrow into and through the skin, and they may even travel elsewhere on the body. When this happens, they can be difficult to locate. Symptoms of this problem include:

- Frequent ear scratching.
- Head shaking.
- An accumulation of seeds in or around the ear.
- Inflammation of the ear or its surrounding area.
- You may also notice some blood in your cocker spaniel's ear if the seed has become inflamed.

Your vet will first remove the grass seed—or any other foreign object. This can require anaesthesia or sedation depending on where it is and the temperament of your dog. A long pair of tweezers called crocodile forceps will often be used. Locating the seed is frequently the hardest part. X-rays are ineffective for this as grass seeds are invisible to them. Sometimes, they can be seen by ultrasound. After the seed has been removed, the infection will likely result in an abscess requiring medication to treat it. It could be necessary for your cocker to wear a buster collar and/or bandage.

Mites

Another common ear problem seen in cocker spaniels is ear mites, also known as otodectes cynotis. These tiny parasites generate intense itchiness in the ears and are picked up from another dog. This is a mild parasitic infection that is highly contagious and commonly irritates the outer ear canal. You might notice some or all the following symptoms if your cocker spaniel has ear mites:

- Head shaking.
- Scratching excessively around the ears and head.
- Brown particles that resemble coffee grains inside their ears.
- Waxy black or brown secretion.
- Further complications might result in blood pooling, as blood vessels in the ear can rupture when scratched and shaken.

Mites are microscopic and infectious organisms that resemble tiny, white dots, which can barely be seen with the naked eye. To confirm their presence usually requires a microscope to detect them.

- Ear mites feed off ear wax and skin oils and live on the skin of the ear canal. Normally, an adult mite lives for approximately two months. They multiply quickly and their eggs take four days to hatch and a further three weeks to develop into adult mites ready to breed.
- Irritation in your dog's ear is often due to allergies, leading to infections other than ear mites, so it is crucial to get your dog to the vet for a proper diagnosis. Without visiting their vet, many owners incorrectly assume their dog has ear mites when, in fact, they are suffering from a bacterial or yeast ear infection. Misdiagnosis can lead to weeks of inappropriate treatment and allow the condition to worsen.
- Ear mites are contagious and other dogs and cats in the household can easily catch them. Even if your other pets are showing no symptoms of ear mites, it is imperative that you also treat them at the same time. Due to their lifestyle habits, cats are the most prone to catching ear mites. In

extremely rare cases, dog owners have developed skin rashes when their pet has ear mites. The ear mites that infect dogs are not the same as the parasite that affects humans.

- Several spot-on flea treatments also treat and prevent ear mites. This is far and away the easiest way to protect your pet from these parasites. Normally, this most popular form of treatment requires only one or two applications and is less stressful for you and your pet than ear drops.
- Some ear drops require at least three weeks of treatment as the medication does not kill the parasite's eggs. If using ear drops, it is crucial that you administer them as prescribed for the recommended period. Other stronger topical treatments only need to be used for 10 to 14 days. These kill the eggs as well as adult mites and include medication to tackle the parasitic infection
- Always consult your vet about the best and most appropriate treatment to use.

Heart Disease

As with humans, our four-legged friends can suffer from heart disease, which sounds scary to any dog owner. However, keeping the health of your cocker's heart in check will enable you to recognise any symptoms of heart disease—or worse, congestive heart failure—as well as get them the appropriate treatment if needed.

Here is what you need to know about heart disease in dogs, how to spot the signs, and the best ways to prevent the condition for your dog to live the best and longest life.

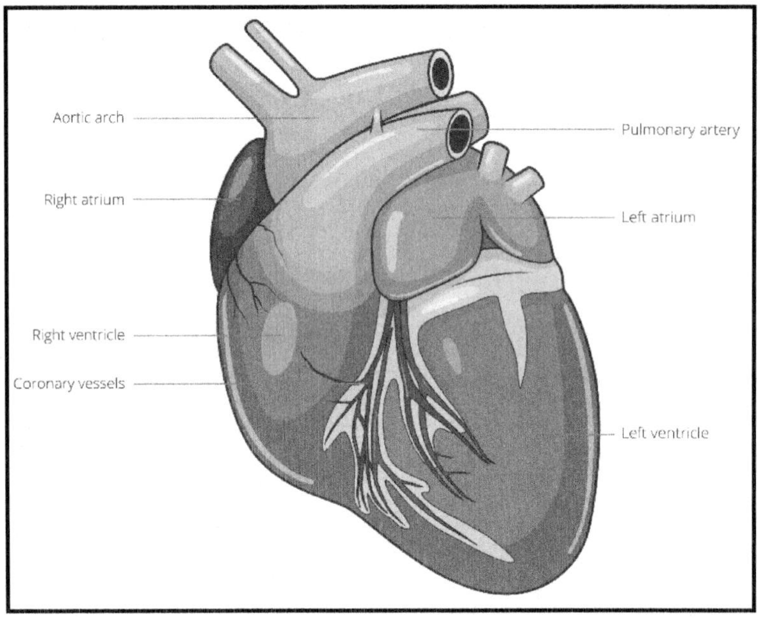

Facts – The heart (pictured) is split into different parts to pump blood through the body. The right side of the heart, which comprises the right atrium and ventricle, pumps blood to the lungs so the blood cells can collect oxygen, which is then delivered back to the heart. In the left side, the left atrium and ventricle pump newly oxygenated blood throughout the body via the circulatory system.

If your cocker spaniel develops heart disease, their heart will have to adapt or change so it can continue to function efficiently and deliver oxygen to the rest of their body. In most cases, these changes occur slowly over time—often over years—and cause the heart to enlarge. This stage is known as preclinical heart disease, since dogs show no obvious signs that they suffer from the condition.

However, heart disease can develop into heart failure over time. This stage of the disease is called the clinical stage because signs of heart failure begin to show—including weakness or fainting after exercise, coughing or difficulty breathing, or fluid build-up. In essence, heart failure—including congestive heart failure—involves a back-up of blood in the lungs or other organs, which compromises the heart's function.

Although dogs can be born with heart disease, it frequently occurs as they age. The most common form of the condition in dogs, accounting for 75% of all cases, results from degeneration of the mitral valve—the valve between the left atrium and the left ventricle. This creates a leaky valve, making your cocker's heart chambers enlarge. The condition is called mitral valve disease (MVD). This problem can eventually lead to heart failure. It can also lead toa hcart murmur that your vet can detect. The second most common form of heart disease is called dilated cardiomyopathy (DCM), which when the heart becomes so large, thin, and weak that it can no longer pump blood efficiently. Cocker spaniels are particularly susceptible to this life-threatening condition.

FACT ***Heart disease is rare in dogs younger than 5 years old but becomes more common with aging dogs. In some cases, it can occur even earlier or later in life.***

Symptoms – The symptoms of heart disease in dogs can go unrecognised for years. The most prevalent cause of heart disease, mitral valve disease, has a long, preclinical stage during which your dog is asymptomatic. Therefore, the early signs of heart disease are likely to go unnoticed by owners but may be detected by your veterinarian.

Even though not all dogs suffering from heart disease will develop heart failure, there are several clinical signs of heart failure to be on the lookout for, including:

- Breathing too fast—more than 30 breaths per minute—when your dog is resting or sleeping.
- Increased effort required for breathing.
- Having trouble sleeping; moving around a lot and changing positions.
- Gagging or coughing.
- Depressed attitude, quiet, and not interactive.
- Weakness.
- Fainting or collapsing.
- Decrease in appetite.
- Losing weight.
- Distended stomach.

Contact your vet if your cocker spaniel exhibits any of these signs. Diagnosis usually involves x-rays, an electrocardiogram, and an echocardiogram.

Treatment – For dogs diagnosed with dilated cardiomyopathy, several drugs are available for treating the symptoms. However, there are no guarantees in medicine. DCM is a serious disease that requires accurate diagnosis and aggressive treatment. While some dogs with DCM can benefit from treatment for some time, others will never be able to live a normal life again. Dogs who respond well to treatment live between 6-24 months.

A vet cannot predict how long your cocker will live if the condition is mitral valve disease. All cases are different and life expectancy depends heavily on the severity of the symptoms, the progression of their MVD, and their response to medication.

While some dogs with MVD live without symptoms for many years—sometimes their whole lives—some require medication and respond well, and others suffer from more severe MVD that does not respond to medication. Unfortunately, in severe cases of MVD that do not respond to medication, life expectancy may even be days or weeks.

Heart Murmurs

Dogs often have heart murmurs. It is an abnormal heart sound, usually heard when listening to the heart with a stethoscope. Heart murmurs are the result of turbulent blood flow in the heart. Murmurs may be deemed 'innocent' or 'physiologic', but they can also be pathologic or caused by disease. Pathologic heart murmurs can be due to structural heart issues—cardiac disease—or problems outside the heart—extracardiac problems.

The loudness of a murmur is related to the amount of blood flow turbulence within the heart and does not always indicate the severity of the illness. The intensity of murmurs is usually measured on a scale of 1-6. Grade 1 murmurs are very soft or quiet, intermittent, and often only heard on one side of the chest. Grade 6 murmurs are very loud, detectable everywhere you can hear the heart, and can be felt if you place your hand on your spaniel's chest in the heart area.

Your vet can detect a heart murmur by listening to your dog's heart with a stethoscope.

Depending on the cause of the murmur, the prognosis can range from excellent to grave. If the murmur is physiologic, no treatment is necessary, and the prognosis is usually good to excellent.

In cases where the murmur is caused by an extracardiac disease—i.e., not related to heart disease—or a functional issue that can be treated, it might resolve itself over time.

If your cocker has a murmur caused by heart disease, the long-term prognosis varies greatly depending on the specific type of defect. Usually, dogs with mitral valve disease can be managed with long-term medications. The prognosis for a dog suffering from dilated cardiomyopathy varies, but if there are signs of heart failure, the outlook is grim.

Depending on the results of the diagnostic tests, your vet will determine the prognosis and treatment options for your spaniel. It is necessary to monitor the condition on an ongoing basis and conduct periodic diagnostic tests throughout your dog's life.

FACT ***A physiologic or innocent heart murmur is one that does not affect your dog's health. Puppies, especially large breed puppies, are prone to developing an innocent heart murmur as they grow rapidly. Innocent heart murmurs typically become evident at 6-8 weeks of age, and puppies will outgrow them by about 4-5 months of age. These murmurs are benign.***

Other Common Health Conditions

There are some other common health conditions that can affect a cocker's quality of life. While a well-cared for and healthy dog will probably never suffer from any of these, it is always a good idea to be aware of them.

Diabetes

Diabetes is a chronic disease that affects humans, dogs, cats, and other animals—including pigs, horses, and apes. Dogs can develop diabetes as young as 18 months old, but mostly the condition is diagnosed between the ages of 7 to 10 years old. Fortunately, the cocker spaniel is not prone to this disease, as it is not in their genes. Although, they often develop diabetes in later life, this is normally because of obesity or a poor long-term diet.

FACT ***An interesting statistic is that about 70% of dogs with diabetes are females. The disease can affect any breed, but cocker spaniels, dachshunds, poodles, miniature schnauzers, Cairn terriers, and springer spaniels are at a higher risk.***

Mechanism – During digestion, the canine body breaks down some nutrients into glucose, which is a type of sugar that provides energy to the cells and organs. Glucose is absorbed into the bloodstream through the intestines, which then transports the glucose to every cell in the body. In addition, the pancreas secretes insulin into the body. The insulin acts as a 'gatekeeper', telling cells to pull glucose and other nutrients out of the bloodstream and use them as fuel. The glucose-insulin connection does not function properly in diabetes. There are two forms of diabetes in dogs:

Insulin-Deficient Diabetes – This happens when your dog's body does not produce enough insulin because the pancreas is damaged or otherwise malfunctioning. For dogs with this type of diabetes, daily shots are necessary to replace the missing insulin. Diabetes of this type is the most common in dogs.

Insulin-Resistant Diabetes – This happens when your cocker's pancreas is producing some insulin, but their body is not using it as it should. The cells do not respond to the insulin's 'message' and cannot absorb glucose from the blood. Diabetes of this type is often seen in old, obese dogs. During pregnancy or while in heat, female dogs can also develop insulin resistance.

Regardless of the type of diabetes, the effects on the body are the same. It means there is an excess of sugar in your dog's bloodstream, and yet cells in the body cannot access it. As a result, diabetes causes two adverse effects in your dog's body:

- The cells are starved of vital 'fuel'. Cells in muscles and certain organs are deprived of glucose, a fuel they need for energy. As a response, the body begins to break down fats and proteins to use as fuel.
- Many organs are damaged by high blood sugar levels. In the absence of insulin—or in insulin-resistant cases—high levels of glucose build up in the bloodstream. As a result, this abnormal blood chemistry acts as a poison and eventually damages many organs. Often, damage occurs to the kidneys, eyes, heart, blood vessels, or nerves.

Symptoms – Usually, the first signs of this disease will be a normal appetite, with an increased consumption of water, followed by weight loss. Even though your dog might be eating normal amounts of food and seem to be hungry all the time, they begin to lose weight. This is because the cells in the body are not receiving the glucose they need to function properly.

As the disease progresses, your cocker might begin to show signs of depression, loss of interest in their food, lack of energy, and episodes of vomiting. When the signs are not detected, and a treatment protocol is not put in place, there can be other serious health effects, including cloudy eyes leading to cataracts, enlarged liver, kidney failure, ketoacidosis, seizures, and urinary tract infections.

Risk factors – Even though diabetes can occur in any dog, there are some factors that increase the possibility of the condition developing:

Age – Most commonly, middle-aged to senior dogs develop diabetes. Noticing any changes with eating or drinking habits in a dog older than 5 can help to detect the early signs of the disease.

Chronic Pancreatitis – When the inflammation of the pancreas is a repeated or chronic occurrence, this can cause damage to the pancreas, which can then result in diabetes.

Cushing's Disease – This condition makes your dog's body over-produce internal cortisol steroids, which can then develop into diabetes.

Genetics – While diabetes can affect any breed of dog, whether purebred or hybrid, it is believed that genetics could predispose certain breeds to having a higher incidence of this condition.

Gender – A female dog who has not been spayed is 50% more likely to suffer from diabetes than a male dog. Simply having the female spayed will help to prevent diabetes.

Obesity – Too many of our canine counterparts are overweight, which contributes to a higher incidence of insulin resistance, pancreatitis, and diabetes. Making sure your cocker receives enough daily exercise and is not being overfed can go a long way towards preventing diabetes and other weight-related health issues.

Steroid Medications – The long-term use of steroid medications can cause diabetes. This possibility should be discussed with your spaniel's vet.

Treatment – Once diagnosed by a veterinary professional, diabetes is a treatable condition. Most diabetic dogs require daily insulin injections (pictured) to return their blood sugar to an acceptable level. You will need to learn how to give insulin injections, which is not as hard as it sounds.

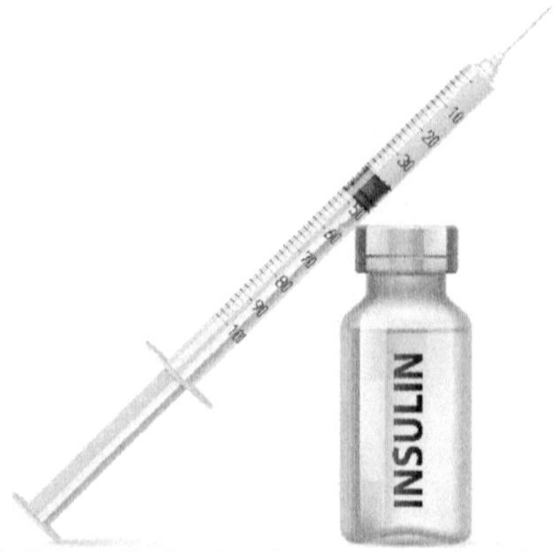

Regular blood and urine testing is needed to ensure normal blood sugar levels. It might also be necessary for you to carry out in-home urine glucose level checks.

Your dog's vet will emphasise the importance of maintaining proper insulin and feeding schedules. A dog receiving insulin therapy needs to maintain a normal consumption of food. Your cocker needs to eat regular meals to balance the effect of the insulin injection that removes the excess sugars from the bloodstream. To prevent sudden spikes or drops in glucose levels, it is crucial for diabetic dogs to maintain a moderate but consistent exercise routine.

There are signs that indicate whether your dog is receiving too much or too little insulin including loss of appetite, excessive urination, weakness, tremors, or seizures. If these signs are observed, your spaniel will need to immediately to visit the vet or an emergency clinic for examination and possible changes in dosage or frequency of their insulin injections.

With early detection and proper management that includes ongoing veterinary care, a diabetic dog can live a long and healthy life.

Cancer

FACT ***Our canine friends suffer similar varieties of cancer issues at roughly the same rate as their human counterparts. According to studies, dogs have the highest rate of cancer of any mammal on Earth, with the most affected areas being the skin, the digestive system, and the mammary glands of females.***

Common in cocker spaniels, cancer is a leading cause of death in the breed. The most common cancers include basal cell tumours, melanoma, fibrosarcoma, and anal sac adenocarcinoma.

This disease used to be associated with the old but has now started affecting the much younger too in both people and dogs. While some breeds are more susceptible to certain kinds of cancer, it is estimated that overall, 1 in 3 dogs will develop and eventually succumb to cancer, making it the leading cause of canine death over the age of 10.

Cancer is the unrestrained division and growth of cells. Usually, cell division is tightly regulated. If a single cell undergoes a series of genetic mutations, it can result in cancer, making cell division unregulated, which results in a tumour.

The following are the most common cancer types in dogs:

Mast Cell Tumours – Mast cell tumours are a type of skin cancer. Mast cells reside in the connective tissues, especially the nerves and vessels near the external surface of your dog—skin, lungs, nose, and mouth. The grading of mast cell tumours is based on their location on the skin, presence of inflammation, and how well they are differentiated.

Melanoma – Melanoma, a common type of cancer in dogs, is the most common malignant tumour in a dog's mouth. Among the most common tumours found in dogs are skin tumours, many of which are benign.

Lymphoma – Lymphoma is a cancer of the lymphocyte blood cells and lymphoid tissues. Normally, lymphoid tissue is present in many parts of the body, including the lymph nodes, spleen, gastrointestinal tract, liver, and bone marrow.

Bone Cancer (Osteosarcoma) – Osteosarcoma is the most common bone tumour found in dogs. Whilst it is more commonly found in the larger breeds, bone cancer can affect any breed of dog.

Hemangiosarcoma – This cancer is highly malignant and can spread rapidly, causing tumours almost anywhere in the body. It is often found in a dog's heart and spleen. Frequently, it is in an advanced stage before it is diagnosed.

Diagnosis – As cancer can occur in any part of your cocker's body, its symptoms are extremely varied. Many of the symptoms are common to an extensive range of diseases—therefore, a diagnosis cannot be made on symptoms alone.

If you have discovered a bump or lump on the surface of their skin, you should certainly take your dog to the vet, but not all surface lumps are cancerous. Any sore that will not heal should be investigated. Other signs of tumours affecting internal organs—benign or cancerous—include:

- Changes in eating habits.
- Discoloured areas of skin.
- Laboured breathing.
- Swelling of the abdomen.
- Sudden weight loss.
- Diarrhoea or vomiting that lasts longer than 1 or 2 days.
- Bleeding from the mouth, nose, or other orifices.
- Heat, pain, or lameness that cannot be explained.

Typically, your vet will take blood samples and x-rays. They might also suggest an ultrasound or MRI scan. These tests can help discover whether the cancer has spread to other areas of your dog's body—a process vets call 'staging'. They can give your vet an indication of the soundness of your cocker's health. This affects their ability to withstand treatment.

FACT ***A biopsy—examining a small sample under a microscope—can help identify the tumour and see whether it is cancerous. Making a definite diagnosis can sometimes be difficult. For example, even when examined under a microscope, biopsies do not always contain enough good quality material.***

Treatment – There are various types of tumours and treatment is available for both non-cancerous and some cancerous ones. Surgery might provide a cure for an isolated lump that has not spread within the body. Though it depends on where the tumour is growing. In an area such as your cocker's brain, even a benign tumour cannot be easily removed. Where cancer is spreading inwards, the opportunities for treatment depend on the type of cancer and how far it has spread. Clearly, quality of life is important and if your dog is in severe pain that cannot be relieved, your vet will probably encourage you to choose euthanasia.

There are three fundamental types of treatment—surgery, radiotherapy, and chemotherapy. Several other new therapies may also be available, such as photodynamic therapy or immunotherapy. Certain treatments require frequent visits to your vet, or to specialists, and it can be important for treatment to be given at specific intervals.

Often, surgery is chosen for tumours of the skin or internal growths that are apparently distinct. To find out whether it is likely to have spread, the lump removed at surgery normally needs to be analysed. With internal growths where the size of the tumour is giving rise to illness, surgery can sometimes relieve the symptoms, although the risk of recurrence remains.

Several types of cancer respond well to chemotherapy. Because the doses used are smaller than those used for humans, veterinary chemotherapy mostly has few side effects, or none. Unfortunately, it does not normally cure the cancer—the aim being to reduce the symptoms and slow the cancer down.

If removing the entire cancer has not been possible, sometimes, chemotherapy is performed following surgery to try to slow down recurrence. Also, it is used in widespread cancers such as those involving the white blood cells—leukaemia—that cannot be surgically removed. Your vet maybe able to provide some types of chemotherapy, but others require specialists.

Usually, it is necessary to make regular visits to your vet for treatment and sedation could be required during treatment. You may need to give your cocker tablets as well. There are several possible side effects from chemotherapy, which include a short period of reduced appetite, vomiting, or diarrhoea. Occasionally, the drugs cause the white blood cell count to drop. This can increase the likelihood of infections, so blood tests are commonly taken to check for this during treatment.

Only a few specialist centres provide radiotherapy treatment. Again, this does not normally cure the cancer, and regular visits are frequently required for some time. Because your spaniel needs to be perfectly still for the treatment, a short, general anaesthetic is given during each treatment.

It is not possible to predict life expectancy with any certainty. The kind of cancer and how far it has advanced when diagnosed gives some indication. For certain cancers there are more specialised tests that help with the prognosis. Nevertheless, as with all illnesses, cancers do not necessarily follow a set course. Regrettably, sudden deteriorations can sometimes ensue.

Your vet will be aware of the importance of keeping your cocker spaniel pain-free, and current painkillers are extremely effective. Unfortunately, any dog with an incurable cancer will eventually come a point when they are suffering and have lost their quality of life. You should collaborate with your vet to recognise when this happens and then opt for euthanasia. However, all vets agree that a healthy, happy animal does not need to be euthanised, even if your cocker's disease is incurable.

Familial Nephropathy (FN)

Familial nephropathy is a hereditary disease of the kidneys in cocker spaniels and one where young dogs can suffer from early-onset kidney failure. Dogs who have the condition are born with an abnormal structure in the walls of the kidney tubules. This affects your dog's ability to remove waste products from their blood and to produce urine. As the disease makes the walls of their kidney tubules excessively leaky, it results in abnormally elevated levels of protein passing from the blood into their urine. These further damages the kidney tubule walls.

As the damage to the kidneys is irreparable and eventually the kidneys cease to function, familial nephropathy is progressive and fatal. The onset of the condition is rapid and affects young dogs, normally between 6 months and 2 years of age.

Although there is no cure for familial nephropathy, diets formulated for dogs with renal failure, or the administration of an angiotensin converting enzyme inhibitor can reduce the clinical signs.

Most dogs with familial nephropathy have abnormally high levels of proteins in the urine—proteinuria—before they are one year old. They will develop kidney failure between 6 months and 2 years of age. However, the progression rate of the disease varies between individuals. Some dogs become seriously ill at a faster rate than others.

Currently, there are no published data available for the number of dogs affected by the condition. For English cocker spaniels in Europe, 11% are reportedly affected by familial nephropathy.

Diagnosis – The clinical signs are usually the same for familial nephropathy as those seen in any kind of chronic kidney failure, and include loss of appetite, excessive thirst and urination, lethargy, vomiting, anorexia, halitosis—bad breath—poor coat quality and pale mucous membranes. An early diagnosis can be difficult to make as the signs are non-specific.

In young cockers, a persistently high level of protein in their urine is frequently due to familial nephropathy. The best diagnostic tool to start with is urine sampling. Nevertheless, a biopsy is necessary to confirm diagnosis.

Genetics – Familial nephropathy is an inherited trait that is autosomal—i.e., it is not carried on the sex chromosomes and therefore affects both males and females—and is recessive. This means your cocker must inherit two copies of the mutated gene for the disease to affect them. If your dog has only one copy of the mutation, they will not be affected but will be a carrier and could pass the mutated gene on to their offspring if the other parent is affected or also a carrier.

Available in Europe and North America, DNA testing can reliably be used to identify the mutation for familial nephropathy in cocker spaniels. DNA analysis can be done from either blood samples or mouth swabs. This test can identify dogs who are affected, carriers, and those without the condition. In the United Kingdom, The Kennel Club website has a list of animal laboratories that provide DNA testing for familial nephropathy:

https://www.thekennelclub.org.uk/health-and-dog-care/health/getting-started-with-health-testing-and-screening/dna-testing/dna-test-fn/

Gene and DNA tests for familial nephropathy are also available through the French company, Antagene, and the American company, Optigen.

There are ongoing efforts to eliminate the disease from the cocker spaniel breed using DNA testing and cautious breeding practises. To produce unaffected offspring, it is advisable to mate only two clear dogs, or one clear and one carrier dog. It is not recommended to mate affected dogs, or two carriers as this will produce some offspring who are affected by the condition.

Hypothyroidism

Your cocker spaniel could have hypothyroidism if they have been extremely tired of late or having issues with their skin or hair. Fortunately, thyroid problems in cockers are easy to diagnose and manage.

In both dogs and humans, the thyroid is a butterfly-shaped gland in the neck, located next to the windpipe. Being part of the endocrine system, the thyroid gland produces the hormones needed for cells to function normally. The thyroid affects your dog's metabolism.

They can develop signs of hyperthyroidism, including diarrhoea, increased heart rate, anxiety, and hyperactivity if your dog produces too much thyroid hormone. When the thyroid gland does not secrete enough thyroid hormone, the exact opposite occurs. Hypothyroidism is the most common thyroid problem for dogs.

It is most frequently diagnosed in dogs between 4 and 10 years old. Mostly, the autoimmune disorder shrinks or inflames the thyroid tissue causing hypothyroidism. There genetic causes are unknown. However, medium to large breeds are at greater risk than toy and miniature breeds, according to the American Kennel Club. The cocker spaniel, miniature schnauzer, dachshund, Doberman pinscher, golden retriever, Airedale terrier, and Irish setter are among those more likely to contract the disease.

Although uncommon, cancer of the thyroid gland can also develop into hypothyroidism in dogs. There is an apparent increase in the risk for spayed and neutered dogs. However, the suspected risk may be outweighed by the many benefits of spaying and neutering.

Signs – In dogs, hypothyroidism affects every system in their body, including the nervous system, the gastrointestinal system, and the circulatory system. If your dog has not been spayed or neutered, hypothyroidism could also affect their reproductive system.

The most prevalent signs of low thyroid problems in dogs include:

- Excessive tiredness.
- Mental depression or dullness.
- Gaining weight.
- Infections of the skin.
- Intolerance to cold.
- Skin and coat changes, such as excessive shedding, hair loss, excessive dandruff, a dry or dull coat, and hyperpigmented skin.
- Excessively long heat cycles for female dogs who have not been spayed.
- Generalised weakness and other neuromuscular problems.

- Walking stiffly or breathing loudly due to laryngeal paralysis—the loss of normal function of the larynx.

Diagnosis – Unlike human thyroid problems, the good news is thyroid problems in cockers are usually easy to diagnose and manage. If you think your dog might be suffering from a thyroid problem, make an appointment with your vet. Your vet will ask questions, conduct an examination, and most likely want to run some lab tests—normally blood work and urine testing.

A common indicator of hypothyroidism in dogs is high blood cholesterol. Most clinics can test for thyroid hormone levels in dogs with a simple blood test.

Treatment – Should your cocker spaniel be diagnosed with hypothyroidism, do not worry. Although hypothyroidism in dogs is uncurable, with an oral thyroid supplement, it is usually easy and relatively inexpensive to manage. The effect of thyroid hormone on the body is mimicked by the supplement. If successful, your cocker will regain their energy, lose weight, stop shedding hair, and have a brighter attitude.

When treating thyroid problems in dogs, the most important thing to remember is the importance of balance. If your cocker takes too much thyroid supplement, they can develop signs of an overactive thyroid, which is the opposite of what you want. If your vet prescribes a thyroid supplement for your dog, it is important to follow the instructions regarding the dose—talk to your vet before changing the dosage.

Once your spaniel has started on a thyroid supplement, your vet will probably ask you to come back in a couple of weeks for a follow-up blood test to ensure your dog's thyroid hormone levels are correct. Once they have been stabilised, your vet will most likely wish to check them every six or twelve months.

Epilepsy

FACT ***Epilepsy is one of the most reported canine neurological problems. It is estimated to affect 0.6-0.7% of all dog breeds in the U.K.—around 1 in 130 dogs. In most cases epilepsy is a lifelong disease. While it is not painful to the dog, it is nonetheless a dramatic experience for the owner.***

Epileptic seizures are the result of excessive—abnormal—neuron activity occurring in the cerebral cortex area of the dog's brain. The neurons in the brain communicate with each other through neurotransmitters that either inhibit or excite other neurons. When there is a healthy balance of neurotransmitter activity, all is well. However, when there is an imbalance that increases the firing of excitation neurons, this can cause a seizure. Epileptic seizures are the result of abnormal electrical activity occurring in your cocker's brain.

Cocker spaniels are among the breeds most likely to suffer from seizures with an estimated 2-4% of the breed affected according to studies from the University of Missouri College of Veterinary Medicine.

There are several types of seizures and how they will display depends on what percentage of the dog's cerebral cortex is abnormally firing. The different types include:

Partial (Focal seizure)

This can be more difficult to recognise because only one part of the cerebral cortex will be involved with little spreading to other areas of the brain. There are two types of partial seizures that can be simple or complex and will last a couple of minutes.

Grand Mal (Generalised tonic-clonic seizure)

This type of seizure occurs when both hemispheres of the cerebral cortex are activated at the same time. It is the most easily recognised and commonest, typically lasting from a few seconds to a few minutes.

Your dog may lose consciousness and fall to the side with rhythmic muscle contraction displayed as chewing jaw movements, paddling motions, or jerking of the limbs. During a grand mal seizure, your cocker spaniel may also drool and lose control of the bladder and bowels.

Simple Seizure (Focal motor)

When neurons are firing only in the motor area, a dog may remain conscious, while there are involuntary muscle movements of the face or jerking of the limbs.

Complex Partial Seizure (Psychomotor)

This is the most difficult to recognise, because while consciousness may be impaired, this type of seizure may just seem like passing abnormal behaviour. For instance, a dog may appear to be biting at unforeseen flies, staring in the distance or suddenly act out with aggression.

Causes – There are many different causes that may trigger a seizure, including exposure to toxins, kidney and liver disease, anaemia, cancer, inflammation or infection of the brain, head injury or genetics that are passed down to puppies from parents that are predisposed to seizures.

'Symptomatic' epilepsy means that there is a cause or reason for the seizure occurring that can be identified.

'Idiopathic' epilepsy means a seizure that has no known cause (perhaps the dog ate a toxic food), and these types of seizure more often occur between the ages of 6 months and 6 years.

How to Help – If you suspect that your dog may be suffering from seizures, it will be very important to have them immediately diagnosed at the vet's office.

Since isolated seizures are usually self-limiting and not usually life threatening, make sure the dog cannot injure themselves (fall off a chair or down a flight of stairs). Stay calm and keep track of how long the episode lasts, so you can report to your veterinarian. Also, keep your hands out of the dog's mouth, because they will not know what is happening and you may accidentally be bitten.

Some dogs are born with this neurological condition and sadly there is currently no known cure. Studies have demonstrated promising results for controlling epilepsy by feeding a special diet that is rich in MCT (Medium Chain Triglycerides). These fatty acids are derived from various plant-based oils such as coconut oil, are known to improve brain function.

The addition of supplements or herbs (vitamin E, melatonin, taurine) to improve liver function may also help to reduce the severity and/or frequency of seizure events. As well, some believe that acupuncture treatments can help to reduce the frequency of seizures.

When a seizure is not stopping on its own (within 5 minutes), or two or more are occurring within 24 hours, this should be considered a life-threatening emergency that requires prompt medical intervention.

Treatment with anti-epileptic—anti-convulsive—drugs to reduce frequency, length and severity of seizure activity is an available option.

- It can take time to find the right dose of medication that will offer therapeutic relief from seizures, and regular blood testing will be required. Phenobarbital is usually the first drug of choice prescribed for a dog experiencing seizures. Careful blood monitoring will be required; if the levels of Phenobarbital in the blood are too high, this can lead to the development of liver disease.
- Potassium bromide is another drug that can help to control seizures. This will also require regular blood testing to ensure stable levels in the blood stream, because this drug is linked to the development of canine pancreatitis.
- Other, newer seizure medications may be prescribed, including levetiracetam (keppra) and zonisamide—the latter can be used alone or in combination with other medications. When your cocker spaniel is having a seizure, short acting drugs—diazepam or midazolam—could also be prescribed.

While a diagnosis of epilepsy is not something any dog owner wants to hear, this is usually a manageable condition. With a solid treatment plan in place, your dog will usually live a happy, long, and normal life.

von Willebrand Disease

Von Willebrand's disease (vWD) is one of the most common inherited bleeding disorders in both humans and dogs. A deficiency of a specific protein causes the condition. This protein helps platelets—blood cells necessary for clotting—to clump together, and seal broken vessels, and it is called von Willebrand factor (vWF).

FACT ***There are usually three types of this disease, type I, type II, and type III. A dog with Type III bleeding disorder runs an elevated risk of spontaneous bleeding and serious bleeding caused by trauma and surgery. Type I is a milder form.***

A dog with vWD might suffer nose bleeds, excessive bleeding from the gums, and prolonged bleeding during or after whelping. In some instances, there is prolonged bleeding from the umbilical cord at birth or when the pup sheds its baby teeth. The first sign of this condition in a dog is often excessive bleeding following surgery or trauma. It is also possible to see blood in the dog's urine or stools. Symptoms reported can differ significantly. Some dogs bleed profusely, while others do not show any bleeding at all.

This is an autosomal-recessive condition. Meaning an abnormal gene must be inherited twice—from the mother and the father—for your cocker's health to be affected. Dogs who inherit only one copy of the abnormal gene—from either their mother or father—show no signs of the disease but will be carriers who can pass it on to their offspring. More than thirty breeds are affected, though the Doberman pinscher has the highest prevalence of vWD. **Cocker spaniels are also susceptible to this disease.**

This condition can be diagnosed by your veterinarian using a buccal mucosal screening test. The presence of prolonged bleeding in the test can raise suspicion of this disease, especially in breeds that are at risk. A laboratory test precisely determines the amount of von Willebrand factor present in the blood to confirm the diagnosis.

It is common for dogs to go their entire lives with no signs of this bleeding problem until they undergo surgery or are injured, at which point the disease is discovered. If your dog has von Willebrand disease and is actively bleeding, then their bleeding needs to be stopped and their blood replaced. The procedure involves using clotting sponges or styptic powder, giving a blood transfusion, and sometimes administering Desmopressin, a medication that temporarily increases the amount of von Willebrand factor in the blood. Von Willebrand disease has no known cure.

PFK Deficiency (PFKD)

The phosphofructokinase (PFK) deficiency is an autosomal recessive genetic disorder in which there is an absence of the enzyme phosphofructokinase. This enzyme is necessary for your cocker to convert glucose into energy. As a result, a PFK-deficient dog is frequently exhausted and weak.

Due to PFK deficiency's recessive nature, dogs can carry the disorder without displaying any symptoms. A recent study estimates that at least 10% of the cocker spaniel population is a carrier, which underscores the significance of genetic testing. **It should be noted that only American cockers are affected, not English cockers.** An offspring from two carriers of PFKD has a 25% chance of inheriting both mutated alleles from their parents and developing the disease.

The symptoms associated with this disorder vary depending on the degree of PFK deficiency. Among the common ones are fever, depression, lethargy or general weakness, muscle wasting and cramps, and exercise intolerance. Anaemia and other abnormalities of red blood cells are typically found in blood tests. A biochemistry profile usually shows abnormally elevated levels of potassium, calcium, magnesium, urea, and total protein.

A veterinarian must first stabilise and rehydrate your dog. They might require fluid therapy or blood transfusions, especially if they have severe anaemia. A bone marrow transplant is the only known treatment for phosphofructokinase deficiency, which is expensive and requires a healthy donor.

Many dogs can live healthy lives if they are properly cared for, but some might develop fatal complications due to severe anaemia or kidney failure. A calm, stress-free environment away from other pets is crucial for your spaniel, who should not be allowed to exercise strenuously or be kept in overly hot environments.

Canine Obesity

Canine obesity is one of the most common and preventable health hazards. The Association for Pet Obesity Prevention has estimated that 56% of dogs in the United States are overweight or obese. That's more than 50 million dogs, which means that obesity in the canine population can easily be considered an epidemic. There are serious weight related health conditions associated with obesity that can shorten and make a dog's life miserable, including arthritis, cancer, diabetes, heart disease, high blood pressure, kidney disease and more. Statistics tell us that being just 10% overweight may decrease a dog's life by as much as one-third.

But just like with human obesity, it's not always a clear-cut case of too much food and not enough exercise. There are some congenital causes of canine obesity. Certain breeds, such as the beagle, cocker spaniel, collie, Labrador, golden retriever, and basset hound are more prone to obesity than others. Also, if your dog has been spayed or neutered, they can experience a drop in metabolism. This might cause problems if you do not change your feeding and exercise routine as they grow older. Hormonal disorders can also result in weight gain. Underactive thyroid glands are linked with cases of canine obesity, which is a condition called Cushing's disease. When your dog's adrenal glands produce too much cortisol, fat is disproportionately distributed to the abdomen, resulting in a pot-bellied appearance.

FACT ***Today, people live a more sedentary lifestyle, and when our dogs are part of that, they can suffer from being overweight, too. Cockers are active athletes who need to run and explore their world every day. They also love to eat, but when you combine their love of eating with little or no exercise, they easily become obese.***

Obesity is a serious condition that plagues many breeds of dogs. Scientists at the University of Cambridge have identified a genetic variation known as 'POMC', which may explain why some breeds—such as the 'food obsessed' Labrador retriever—are more prone to being obese than others. However, further research is required as some breeds that also carry this variation are not known to be prone to obesity.

Most cockers are always hungry and will eat anything that comes their way. When the size of your cocker spaniel is getting out of control, the following steps will help you get your dog trimmed down:

- Document when and what treats they are given.
- Feed only the recommended amount for the size of your dog.
- Desist from feeding human table scraps.
- Only give treats sparingly.

- Weigh your cocker each week.
- Understand the risks obesity poses to your dog.

If you are uncertain about the ideal weight for your cocker, you should make an appointment to discuss this with your vet. The following chart will give you an estimate of what your dog's ideal weight should be, so you can keep your cocker in the ideal range.

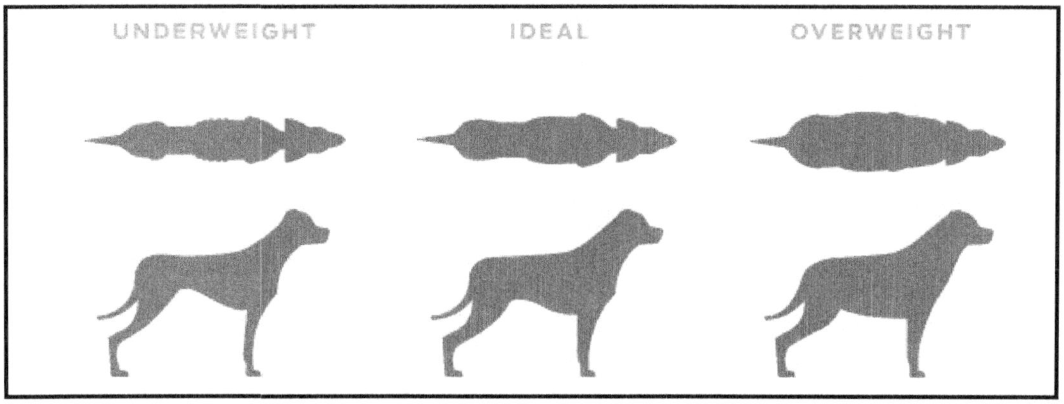

Canine Bloat

While any dog can suffer from bloat, it is seen more often in larger, deep-chested breeds.

Bloat, also known as 'Emergency Gastrointestinal Syndrome' or 'Gastric Dilatation Volvulus', is a common, life-threatening incident. This condition can happen quickly, especially if your dog is fed right after vigorous exercise, or if they are a very fast eater and gulp in large quantities of air with their food. Their stomach then distends with food, wind, and fluid, which can make the stomach twist 180 degrees or more and close. When the stomach is closed off, the food is then trapped inside where it ferments and makes the stomach bulge. Their bulging stomach can in turn create dangerous problems, including:

- Decreased blood flow to the heart.
- Obstruction of blood flow to the veins in the abdomen.
- A tear in the wall of the stomach.
- Low blood pressure.
- Shock and damage to internal organs.

Symptoms can occur very quickly and include:

- Restlessness.
- Drooling.
- Swollen stomach.
- Looking anxious.
- Pacing.
- Attempting to vomit.
- Stretching with the front end down and the back end up.
- Weakness.
- Shortness of breath.
- Rapid heartbeat.
- Pale gums.

FACT ***The reason that bloat is referred to as 'Emergency' Gastrointestinal Syndrome is because it is a serious condition that requires immediate, emergency veterinary intervention. Based on statistics, 50% of dogs that develop bloat do not survive.***

While treatment is dependent on the severity of the condition, it includes:

- Placing a tube down the throat to the stomach to release pressure.

- If the stomach is twisted, inserting a large hollow needle through the belly to relieve pressure.
- Provision of IV fluids and antibiotics.
- If the x-ray confirms a twisted stomach, emergency surgery is performed to untwist the stomach and return it to the proper position.

While bloat can be a very frightening occurrence requiring immediate intervention, there are steps that can be taken to prevent it from ever occurring in the first place, including:

- Not feeding right after vigorous play or running.
- Rather than feeding one or two larger meals, feed several smaller ones.
- Using a slow feeder bowl to slow down the eating pace.

Useful health tips

Visiting the vet – Rather than worrying about causing your dog trauma and stress every time they must visit the vet's, there are several things you can do to prevent 'vet trauma', including:

- Social visits before your dog needs to attend for any treatment, when they can visit the staff, become familiar with the smells, and have a treat.
- Practise exams at home on a table, so your cocker will not be fearful of the vet's examination table—look at their eyes, ears, open their mouth, feel their spine, and hold their feet.
- Exercise before visiting, so your dog is more relaxed. A tired dog will feel less anxious.
- Check your energy, as having a negative 'feeling sorry' energy can make things worse. Your dog needs your confidence when being subjected to new smells and procedures they might feel nervous about.

TIP ***The frequency of visits to the vet will depend on your spaniel's stage of life. Your young puppy will require more frequent visits for their vaccination schedule and spaying procedure. A healthy adult dog with no problems should only need to visit the vet once a year for a wellness check-up. For a senior dog, increase vet visits to twice yearly to make sure everything is functioning well, and they are maintaining a healthy weight.***

Although a well-cared for and healthy adult cocker will not spend much time in the vet's, there are occasions when no time should be wasted in getting them assessed. For example, this can be when your dog is bleeding, unconscious, shaking with pain, vomiting blood, etc.

Taking your Dog's Temperature – If you suspect your dog might be ill or have a fever, you should check their temperature. You can accomplish this in one of two ways, depending on the type of thermometer you have in your canine first aid kit.

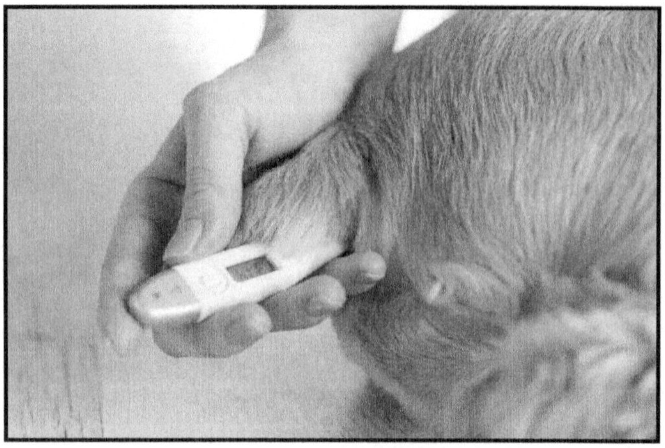

Rectal Thermometer (pictured) – A rectal thermometer is easier to use when you have a friend to help hold your spaniel still, by following these steps:

- Have your dog lie down on their side.
- Shake the mercury down in the thermometer.

- Lubricate the thermometer with petroleum jelly.
- Lift your cocker's tail and locate their anus.
- With a rotating motion insert 2.5 to 7.5 centimetres (1 to 3 inches).
- Talk soothingly to your dog while holding the thermometer in place for two minutes.
- Remove the thermometer and wipe it clean.
- Read the height of the mercury on the gauge.
- A normal rectal temperature is 38 to 38.8 o C (100.5 to 102 o F).

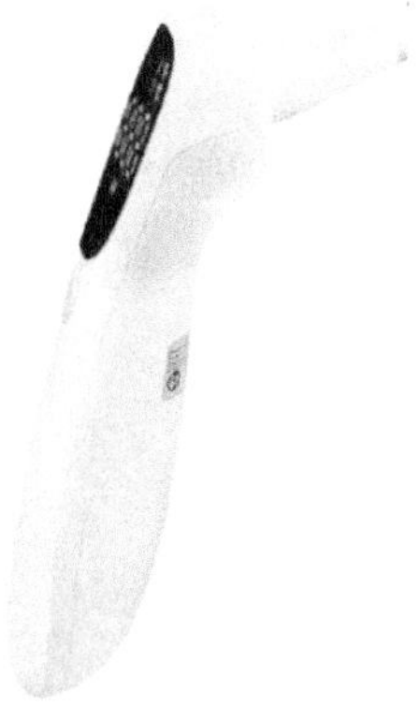

Ear Thermometer (pictured) – When used correctly, an ear thermometer is a less invasive and often more easily tolerated way to take your cocker's temperature, as follows:

- Have your dog sit or lie down.
- Lift their ear flap.
- Insert the thermometer deeply into the horizontal ear canal.
- It should only take a few seconds to register their temperature.
- Normal ear temperature is 37.7 to 39.4o C (100 to 103o F).

If your cocker spaniel's temperature is out of the normal range—either above or below—it is time to take them to the vet for examination to hopefully determine the reason.

My dog is Limping – There are many reasons why your cocker might be limping. They could have a foreign body stuck between their toes, or a sore muscle from rough play with a heavier dog. They could have a cut on their foot or a broken claw, or if they are of advanced years, they might have arthritis in their joints.

When your dog is limping, first determine whether the problem is minor, as they may recover shortly on their own, or if your dog has been seriously injured and needs to be taken to the vet. For instance, most dogs will not attempt to walk on a broken leg. However, if the injury is minor, they could lightly touch their foot on the ground and limp along. If they allow you to examine their leg and foot without biting you—because it is too painful— usually the injury is not severe.

TIP ***If there is swelling from a bruise or pulled muscle, rinse it with cool water and apply an ice pack to reduce the swelling. If the limping continues for more than 24 hours, you should make an appointment with your vet.***

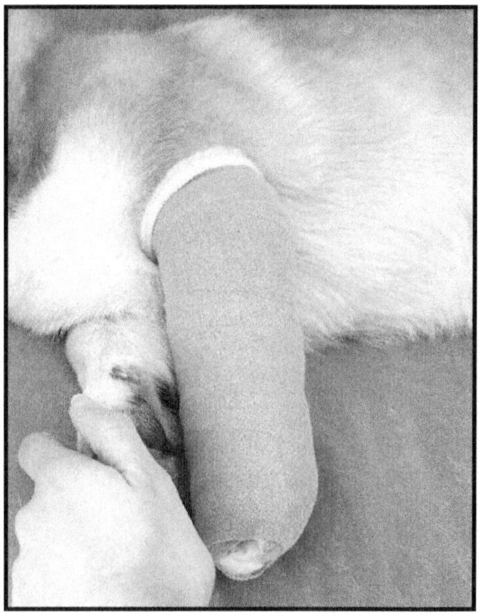

My Dog Broke a Leg – Whatever the reason for your cocker breaking their leg, they will be in severe pain and need to be carefully transported to the vet clinic for immediate assessment and treatment. Ask a friend or family member to drive, while you try to keep your spaniel as calm as possible to minimise pain and further injury to the leg. Once at the vet's, first your dog will be stabilised by providing intravenous fluids, pain medication and possibly antibiotics.

If their broken leg (pictured) is a simple, closed fracture, all that is required is to splint or cast the leg. However, if their leg has been broken in multiple places and is severely damaged, with the knowledge that dogs can adapt very quickly to getting around on three legs, you might be asked to consider amputation.

The length of recovery, which could be between 4 and 12 weeks, depends on the diagnosis, treatment, and age of your cocker. The veterinary team will provide guidance, and might recommend underwater treadmill therapy, or at-home physical therapy that includes massage, joint flexion exercises, and ice treatments to aid recovery time.

Disclaimer: The author of the book is not a veterinarian. This chapter has been compiled to give a thorough overview of the medical conditions that might affect your cocker spaniel, but it is not intended to give medical advice. For a firm diagnosis of any health condition, and for a treatment plan suitable for your dog, you should consult your vet or health care consultant.

14. Allergies and Canine Skin

'Dogs got personality.

Personality goes a long way.'

~ Quentin Tarantino ~

As with humans, the skin is the largest organ of your dog's body and comprises 12 to 25% of their entire body weight. Their skin regulates temperature while providing a protective barrier against environmental influences. Without healthy skin, your cocker spaniel will not have a shiny and lustrous coat.

FACT ***Skin consists of the epidermis (outer layer), the dermis (middle layer), and the subcutis—inner layer—and there are other important appendages, including claws, hair, subcutaneous fat, and muscles.***

Your cocker's skin should be regularly checked for lumps, bumps, redness, insect bites, sores, dandruff, dull coat, and hair loss by brushing and parting their hair to inspect the skin. If their skin and coat does not look healthy, your dog should be inspected by your vet before any problems become more serious. There are many skin issues that can affect your dog's health and the condition of their coat. Allergies are on the rise and a growing concern for most dog breeds.

Allergies

You might have heard from your vet or a friend that perhaps the symptoms your cocker is experiencing are the result of allergies, but what does that mean? An allergy is simply a reaction by your dog's immune system to a substance in the environment, on the coat or skin, or in the food. While different allergies usually require various treatment protocols, their symptoms are often similar, and include:

- Red, inflamed skin.
- Hives.

- Swelling of their ears, eyelids, earflaps, and face.
- Itching skin.
- Runny eyes.
- Sneezing.
- Chronic ear infections.
- Itchy ears.
- Constant licking.
- Constant scratching.
- Rubbing their face.
- Unhealthy skin and coat.
- Diarrhoea.
- Vomiting.

Inhalant Allergies (Atopy)

Atopy is one of the most common allergies in dogs. When your cocker has an inhalant allergy, their immune system overreacts to an airborne or inhaled allergen. There is a wide variety of allergens that might cause atopy, which are like the causes of hay fever in people. When the affected dog inhales pollens, dust, or moulds an allergic response occurs. **Cocker spaniels are one of the dog breeds most affected by atopy.**

A dog with an inhalant allergy is usually itchy during certain seasons of the year. However, some atopic dogs can exhibit non-seasonal signs. An affected dog typically chews, licks, and scratches all over, especially the feet and face. Your dog's saliva might stain their light-coloured hairs, resulting in reddish-brown or orange hair. When affected your cocker might also rub and scratch around their eyes and ears, armpits, groin, or the inside of their thighs. Moreover, dogs occasionally show respiratory signs in addition to itching. Seasonal allergy and atopy are similar terms used to describe the same type of allergic skin condition.

Diagnosis – Diagnosis is not easy and is based on the presence of clinical signs and ruling out other causes, such as flea or food allergies. Bear in mind that the clinical signs and itching caused by grass pollen are the same as those caused by dust mites and many moulds. This means your cocker spaniel might be allergic to several different things with the result being the same—excessive scratching and itching. A thorough medical history of your dog will help narrow down the causes. For instance, if itching occurs during spring, when certain pollen is present in the air, this narrows the extent of investigation.

Treatment – Once the diagnosis is complete, it might be possible to desensitise your cocker to the offending allergens. To achieve this, a specific allergy serum is prepared based on the results of the allergy tests and is given in a series of shots. The principle behind desensitisation with allergy shots is to control the injections by increasing doses of the offending allergens, which will re-adjust your spaniel's immune system and reduce their hypersensitivity. On average, these allergy injections result in significantly reduced itching for about 50% of dogs.

Anti-inflammatory drugs, including corticosteroids and antihistamines, as well as other targeted therapies will often give your dog relief from itching. In addition, omega fatty acids—omega-3—can provide some relief for many dogs with allergic skin disease. Antibiotics might be needed if there is a secondary bacterial skin infection such as pyoderma.

If infected, your cocker could benefit from frequent bathing with specially formulated hypoallergenic shampoos. Research has shown that certain allergens are absorbed through the skin. Therefore, regular bathing can help reduce the number of allergens your dog absorbs. Some of these special shampoos also contain omega fatty acids, which can be absorbed by the skin and help reduce itching.

treatment.

Food Allergies

Food allergy or hypersensitivity is known to affect many breeds, but cocker spaniels are at greater risk of developing this kind of allergy. Most likely, your cocker will experience itchiness in their ears and feet and scratch them fervently. Any affected areas will be red, irritated, and swollen. When touching your dog's ears or feet, you might also feel bumps and warmth. The food allergies in some spaniels can involve the gastrointestinal tract, triggering vomiting, diarrhoea, or blood and mucus in the faeces and vomit.

In a dog with a food allergy, the immune system overreacts and produces antibodies to substances that it would normally tolerate. During an allergic food reaction, antibodies are produced against some part of the food, usually a complex carbohydrate or protein. This type of allergy usually occurs after prolonged exposure to one brand or type of food. Food allergies affect dogs in a different way than humans. While a person typically feels nauseous or sick after eating something they are allergic to, your cocker is more likely to develop skin problems or throw up what they just ate. Some of the more usual signs that your dog is suffering from a food allergy include:

- Shaking their head.
- Scratching their ears.
- Ear inflammation.
- Chronic diarrhoea.
- Wind.
- Stomach upsets—vomiting.
- Itchy, red, and swollen skin.
- Licking or chewing their feet.

FACT ***Proteins are the number one food allergen in dogs, particularly those that originate from dairy products, beef, lamb, chicken, chicken eggs, soy, and wheat gluten. An allergic dog consuming these substances develops symptoms when the antibodies react with the antigens. In addition to the ones listed above, there are also other more subtle symptoms that can develop, such as hyperactivity, loss of energy, and aggression.***

Food allergies are not always easy to diagnose. Discovering what is causing the allergic reaction can take time—up to 12 weeks—as it involves what is known as an 'elimination diet'. This diet means completely stopping feeding your cocker their usual diet and then slowly reintroducing their previous foods until an allergic reaction occurs. Furthermore, specialised blood tests can reveal what foods your dog is allergic to. These are called serum IgE tests, and your vet will decide if these could be helpful in diagnosing your dog's condition.

As soon as the offending food is identified, a diet free of that ingredient can be followed. The good news is that there are several tasty, hypoallergenic diets available today that can be fed for the rest of your cocker's life. Based on the test results, your vet will recommend the best treatment options for your dog.

Flea Allergy Dermatitis

FACT ***Flea allergy dermatitis (FAD) is a major cause of allergic reactions in dogs. In this type of allergy, their body's immune system overreacts or is hypersensitive to a substance called an antigen that is normally harmless.***

FAD is a frequent cause of itching in dogs. Adult fleas need to bite a dog and obtain a blood meal to reproduce. Normally, fleas will not stay on your cocker except for the minutes to hours when they are being fed. Therefore, you usually will not see live fleas on your dog's skin, unless there is a severe flea infestation in their immediate environment. While fleas feed, they are injecting a small amount of saliva into the skin. It is the proteins or antigens in the saliva that cause the itchy response to sensitive dogs.

Diagnosis – Clinical signs often give the first clue that your dog may suffer from flea allergy. Typical symptoms include itching and hair loss in the area from the middle of the back to the base of the tail and down the rear legs—known as the flea triangle. A specialised blood test (IgE test) or an intradermal allergy test—a skin test like those performed on humans—can confirm a flea allergy in your dog.

Treatment – Since what causes the allergic response is the injection of flea saliva, it is critical to prevent fleas from biting your dog. In other words, strict flea control is essential. It is important to continue rigorous flea treatment and maintain environmental control even if you have not seen fleas on your cocker for a while. Typically, flea infestations happen during warmer seasons, but can also occur year-round. Monthly oral and topical flea preventive products are an important part of good pet care for your spaniel. Do not forget that flea prevention is always the best form of

Contact Dermatitis

There are two types of contact dermatitis: allergic contact dermatitis and irritant contact dermatitis. It is hard to tell one from the other as the symptoms typically appear to be same. Irritation, soreness, inflamed patches of skin, thickening of the skin, fluid discharge from the skin are all possible symptoms. Both dogs and cats can suffer from contact dermatitis. It can occur at any age and is a direct result of the irritating nature of the offending substance.

During allergic contact dermatitis, the skin becomes sensitive to a particular element, which is normally harmless. As soon as the body encounters it, the immune system responds by thinking it needs to protect itself, leading to the symptoms given above. For example, if your cocker spaniel is allergic to a certain soap, they will develop symptoms of dermatitis whenever you bathe them with it.

Irritant contact dermatitis occurs when your dog touches something that irritates their skin, such as salt on the road. If your cocker has this condition they will probably suffer from rashes and/or bumps that appear on the skin where it met the ground—i.e., the chin, neck, chest, abdomen, groin, anal area, scrotum, tail, and between the toes. These rashes often stop abruptly at the hairline. Other symptoms include swelling, and itching, which is normally severe.

Breeds that are more likely to develop contact dermatitis include: cocker spaniels, golden retrievers, poodles (and hybrids), shih tzus, and bulldogs. However, any breed of dog can develop this type of allergy.

Diagnosis – Your vet will want to run a few diagnostics to find out what the offending irritant is:

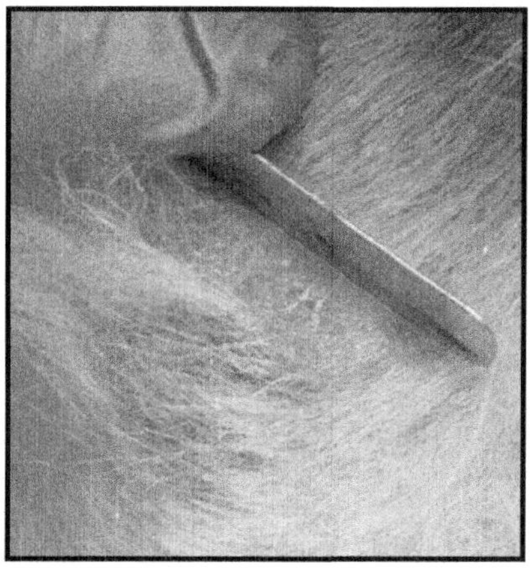

- A skin scraping (pictured) might be collected to check for a bacterial infection or parasitic infestation. The vet will scrape off a thin layer of your cocker's cutaneous skin in a small area. They will take the sample and look at it under the microscope to rule out any type of skin mite that could cause the same symptoms.
- A patch test can be performed. The suspected substance is placed on a patch and taped to the skin for 48 hours. Any reaction is then assessed.
- Your dog is removed from the offending environment for a period and then returned to the location, monitoring what happens and whether it has had any impact one way or the other.
- Bacterial cultures might also be performed. A clip of hair will be taken from a patch in an area that is not affected, applied to a sample of the suspected antigen, and observed for possible reactions.
- Skin biopsies are also sometimes required.

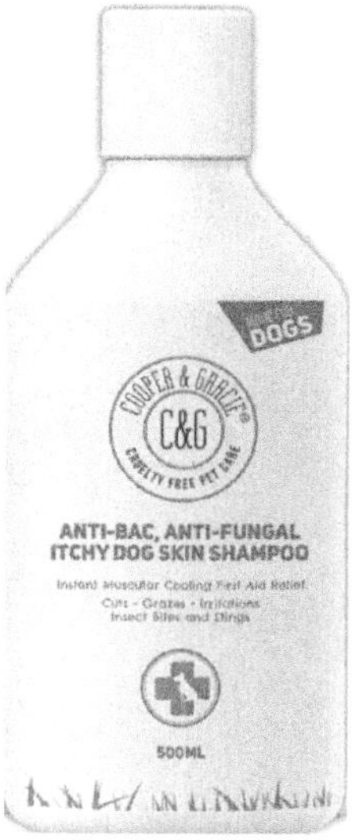

Treatment – Medications, such as antihistamines or steroids, will be prescribed to offer your dog relief from itching. A cream or ointment might also be prescribed by the vet to apply to the affected areas. If a secondary infection develops, your cocker will need antibiotics.

TIP ***You will also need to bathe your spaniel multiple times a week with a specially formulated shampoo (pictured). These shampoos have hypoallergenic, antiseptic, antifungal, and antibacterial properties that will help your dog's skin to heal.***

Firstly, the most essential, yet difficult thing to achieve is removing your cocker from the environment where the condition began. If the dermatitis is the result of an irritant and not an allergy, once the irritant is identified your dog's recovery will be quick. However, if the dermatitis is due to an allergy, it could have developed over months or years. Should your spaniel be exposed again, the symptoms will be apparent three to five days after exposure and could persist for weeks. Once the antigen is identified and removed, your dog's health will most likely be back to normal within a few weeks. If it is not possible to identify the allergen, there is a chance you will have to treat the symptoms with medications for the rest of your cocker's life.

Allergy Medications

You might wish to discuss possible allergy medication options with your vet, as there are many that are designed to relieve symptoms, such as the following:

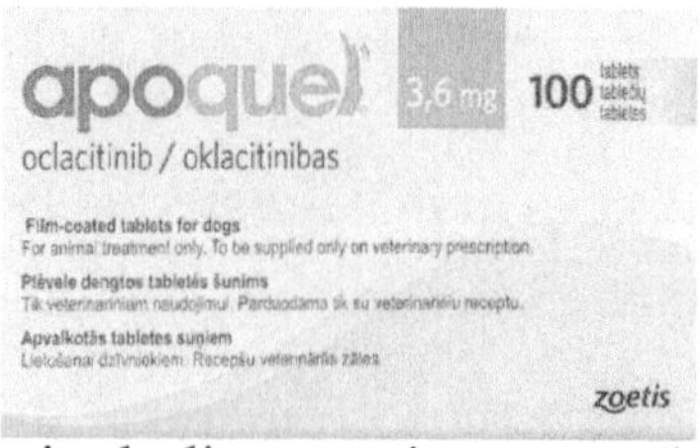

Apoquel – This prescription medicine (pictured) relieves itching by blocking the molecules that transmit the inflammation and itch signal.

Atopica – A drug used for treating skin allergies and other dermatological conditions.

Benadryl – An antihistamine used to soothe the reaction to many allergens, including environmental, parasitic, vaccine, or bee stings.

Cytopoint – Cytopoint injections have proven to be effective for the treatment of dogs against allergic and atopic dermatitis.

Dexamethasone – A steroid used for relief from allergies, the pain of arthritis, or other conditions that can cause the immune system to overreact.

Malaseb – A powerful medicated shampoo used to treat itching skin dermatitis problems, yeast, and fungal—ringworm—infections.

Piriton – A sedating antihistamine used for the relief of allergic reactions to food, insect bites, or hay fever.

Prednisone – A powerful anti-inflammatory steroid that temporarily blocks the symptoms of allergic reactions.

Triamcinolone – An anti-inflammatory steroid used to relieve itching from allergies as well as acute arthritis.

Zyrtec – An antihistamine medication prescribed for dogs with dermatitis or mild to moderate environmental allergies.

Treating Allergies Holistically

Treating allergies with traditional veterinary medications—antibiotics, antihistamines, and steroids—focuses on treating the symptoms. Although these can be very effective and provide relief to your cocker, they might also create unwanted side effects. Conversely, treating allergies holistically focuses on locating the imbalance in your dog's immune system with the goal being to resolve the cause of the allergic reaction rather than simply treating it.

Allergy symptoms in dogs tend to be dermal—skin-related—and symptoms usually display with inflamed, itchy skin that results in excessive scratching, biting, and licking. Holistic treatments focus on supporting the immune system to regain appropriate functioning and supportive care to help alleviate symptoms, so your cocker is more comfortable. Holistic therapies range from making changes in the environment, when necessary, to acupuncture, diet, and herbal supplementation. There is no simple solution that applies to all cases. Each individual dog can require different methods or a combination of methods to reach a successful outcome. Resolving allergies holistically is often a case of trial-and-error and some time will be needed to achieve results.

There are several suggestions that can be implemented as part of a holistic approach to ensure that your spaniel's overall health is maximised, and allergic reactions are minimised. These include:

- Adjust their diet to support their immune system. It is recommended that you reduce your cocker's carbohydrate intake as excessive carbs may impair their immune system. Artificial colours and flavours should also be omitted. Diets that meet these criteria and raw or cooked meat are recommended for dogs with allergies.
- Raw local honey can help support the immune system and is easy to administer since dogs can readily consume it as part of their diet. Using local honey can expose your dog to low levels of local pollen and antigens and train their immune system to not react negatively to the allergen.
- Make sure parasites such as fleas and ticks are eradicated. Commercial and natural preparations are available.
- Fleas can also be reduced by regularly hoovering your home and cleaning up your garden where they congregate. Various natural preparations can help prevent infestations.
- Remove toxic cleaning products from the home environment.
- Wipe their feet and coat to remove outdoor allergens.
- Skin-soothing baths are useful to remove irritants and biting insects. Baths and medications that soothe irritated skin, such as oatmeal ` baths, coconut oil, lavender, chamomile, and mullein preparations can ease skin lesions. Applied topically, aloe vera gel, calendula, thyme, chickweed gel, cider vinegar, witch hazel, Epsom salts, and cucumber slices can relieve irritation.

- Acupuncture treatments to restore immune system balance.
- Herbal supplementation—echinacea, ginseng, omega-3, vitamins.
- Natural anti-inflammatories—liquorice root, nettles.
- Mushrooms contain natural antihistamines that can reduce immune system reaction. Consult your vet before using to ensure appropriate dosage and type, and to be certain there are no interactions with medications.
- Supplements to aid gastrointestinal functioning such as dandelion root, probiotics, and other herbal preparations can be added to the diet.

The effectiveness of holistic treatments is largely dependent on your patience and dedication to experimenting with the trial-and-error process, which might take several weeks—or even months—to determine which treatments will provide relief from allergic reactions.

Skin Issues and Parasites

Our cocker spaniels are susceptible to numerous skin conditions that can make their life a misery. While many issues are easily treatable at home, such as external parasites, there are other more serious conditions that usually require the expertise of a qualified vet. For example, your dog might commonly suffer from rashes on the stomach caused by a simple to treat bacterial infection, or might have a far more serious underlying cause, such as Cushing's disease, which is a hormonal imbalance.

The vet will be able to determine whether the cause is genetic or hormonal, or simply an environmental or food-related allergic reaction. Once the cause has been identified, the next step is to prescribe a treatment plan to relieve the symptoms and hopefully cure the condition.

Read on to learn about some common skin conditions that can affect cocker spaniels.

Interdigital Cysts

FACT ***Interdigital cysts appear as large bumps or nodules between your cocker's toes (pictured) and are extremely painful, making it difficult for them to move or walk. Other names for them are interdigital furuncles, follicular pododermatitis, or furunculosis. Interdigital cysts are red nodules filled with blood and/or pus and are most frequently found on the front paws.***

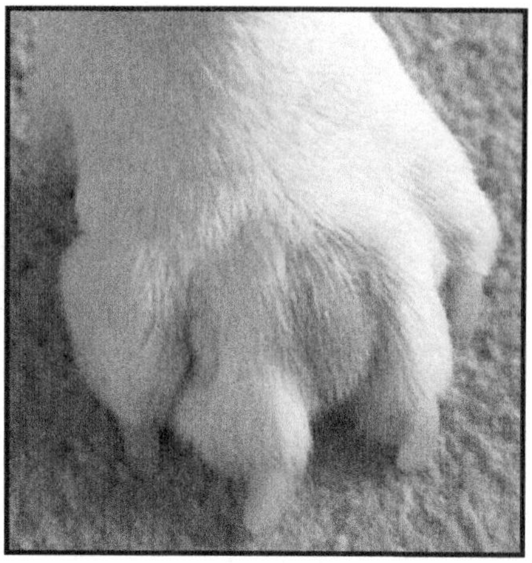

Many skin conditions can cause nodules on your cocker's paws. These include demodectic mange—from Demodex mites—atopic dermatitis, infections caused by a foreign object stuck between the toes, poor foot conformation, yeast infections, etc. This skin condition can affect any breed, including cocker spaniels.

Your dog might show signs of lameness on the foot affected when developing an interdigital furuncle. If left untreated, the problem can quickly spread to other areas, causing multiple nodules to form. Eventually, these nodules become swollen, inflamed, and painful before they burst and exude fluid. Typically, they will develop on the upper side of your dog's paw, but they can also appear on the underside. If your cocker suffers from interdigital furuncles, they will typically do the following:

- Limp from the pain, especially when walking on uneven surfaces.
- Lick and chew their paws.
- Bite at the lesion on their paws.

Diagnosing the Problem – Your veterinarian may be able to diagnose interdigital cysts based solely on their physical appearance during a routine exam. Although, further diagnostic testing might be needed to rule out other conditions—such as skin tumours—and to determine the underlying cause of your cocker's interdigital cysts.

If your vet suspects the problem is palmar or plantar follicular cysts, they will recommend a skin biopsy.

The following tests can be performed to determine a correct diagnosis:

- Skin scrapings—checks for Demodex mites.
- Impression smears.
- Fine-needle aspirates.

Treatment Options – In most instances, topical antibiotics and antibiotic ointments are enough to treat the condition. However, any type of treatment is dependent on how deep the infection has gone, which could require more intensive treatment. For the antibiotic to be effective, you must ensure your spaniel completes the recommended course. If the course of antibiotics is not completed or the doses are not accurate, your dog might develop interdigital furuncle again. A warm compress or foot soak has been found to help in treating interdigital furuncles.

A corticosteroid or a non-steroidal anti-inflammatory medication might also be recommended by your veterinarian. These medications will decrease the swelling and inflammation associated with your cocker's interdigital cysts. Not only will this decrease self-trauma that can happen if your dog licks at a painful paw, but it will also help make your dog more comfortable.

If your vet determines that the cause is a foreign object, this may need to be surgically removed, which is usually the case when the culprit is a grass seed.

Hot Spots (also known as 'Moist Dermatitis')

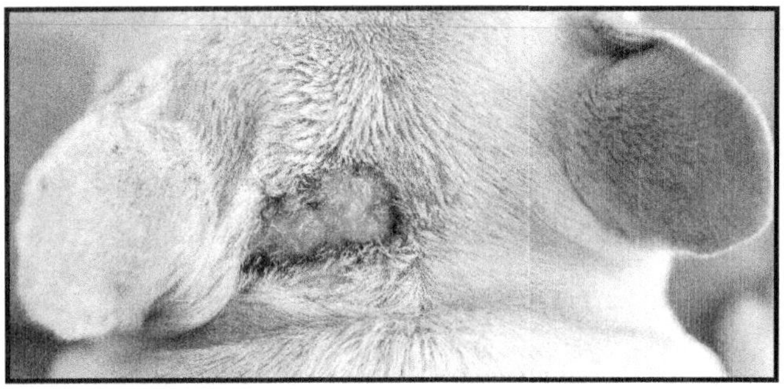

A hot spot (pictured) is an area of reddened skin that is itchy and painful. The problem can worsen if your cocker's hair is matted, and they are licking it. Typically, a hot spot appears as a large, wet scab that oozes, and is an area of skin that looks raw and inflamed. Hot spots can bleed at times and might be an allergic reaction, infection, or a lack of proper drying after your dog has been swimming.

Hot spots are more prevalent in dogs with thick coats such as cocker spaniels, golden retrievers, and German shepherds. Any breed can suffer from hot spots. One reason for hot spots is moisture becoming trapped next to your dog's skin, by matted fur, a dog collar, or simply thick fur creating an ideal spot for the infection to start. Often, chronic hot spots stem from an allergic condition. Some dogs are more prone to hot spots than others.

These spots can appear anywhere on your cocker spaniel's body, but they are usually found on the hips, limbs, and head. When bacteria build up in hot spots, they can quickly spread to other parts of the body. A dog with hot spots will suffer pain and it is often difficult for them to heal themselves naturally due to their tendency to lick, scratch, or bite at skin irritations.

A hot spot will usually dry out and begin to heal about a week after treatment begins. When it is dry and does not ooze, continue to keep the area clean and moisture free. Your cocker's fur will start growing back in about two weeks. For itching relief and hair growth, talk to your veterinarian about essential fatty acids dietary supplements.

In general, hot spots improve when they are allowed to dry, and your vet can give you advice on how to proceed. Usually, this includes one or more of the following:

- Using clippers to shave the hot spot and surrounding area—this allows air to get to it.
- Bathing the hot spot frequently with a medicated shampoo (pictured).
- Applying a small amount of an over-the-counter hydrocortisone ointment that stops itching and aids healing.
- You might be advised to use an Elizabethan collar on your dog—also known as a buster collar or a cone—to stop them from irritating the area by licking, biting, and scratching.
- Oral antibiotics or a topical solution—spray, cream, or ointment—can be prescribed to kill bacteria, and an antihistamine can help reduce itchiness.

TIP ***The best ways to prevent hot spots are to maintain good hygiene, groom your dog regularly, treat skin infections and parasites, and manage allergies. Additionally, make sure your cocker's coat is completely dry after swimming or bathing, otherwise the matted fur will trap moisture, creating ideal conditions for hot spots.***

Supplementary fatty acids can help prevent hot spots by building a healthy skin barrier and reducing inflammation. Fish oil is a great source of omega-3 fatty acids as it contains a lot of DHA and EPA. For more information on supplements and the correct dosage for your dog, contact your vet.

Harvest Mites ('Trombicula autumnalis')

These are seasonal, bright orange mites (pictured)—also known as 'chigger mites', 'scrub-itch mites, 'red bugs' and 'berry bugs'—that are active during the late summer and autumn months. They can be found in a perfectly tended garden, in the wide-open spaces of the countryside, or at the local park. Active during dry and sunny days, large numbers of these voracious mites are usually found in areas where there is matted vegetation, long grass, low lying plants and bushes, and on clumps of earth.

Whilst there is no specific breed predisposition, dogs with access to the mite's natural environment—such as areas of rough vegetation—have a greater risk of encountering the larvae than dogs who are exercised on beaches or mown parks.

A cocker running through these locations can easily pick up the mites as they prefer to congregate in areas that give them easy access to the skin, such as around the neck, margins of the ears, front legs, between the toes, armpits, stomach, and genitals. The mites will latch on to your cocker's skin with their hooked fangs and inject strong enzymes that break down and disintegrate the skin cells making them easy to suck up.

Once firmly attached to your dog's skin, these mites remain feeding on the same site for several days while they increase in size 3 to 4 times. This process causes an intense itching reaction to the mites' digestive enzymes, which could plague your dog for many weeks.

Since the mites are quite small, it is not an easy task to find them. However, if your cocker is scratching an area of their body, carefully examining the skin by spreading the hair and taking a good look will help to discover the problem before it becomes worse. If you find an irritated, crusted, or scabbed area that has a red or orange-coloured 'dust', there is a good chance your spaniel has been infected with the harvest mite.

Diagnosis will usually be through taking a skin sample at the vet's that will be examined under the microscope. Your vet might recommend a spray typically used to kill fleas, a shampoo to relieve itching, and a corticosteroid to reduce inflammation, as well as antibiotics if there is any secondary infection from the scratching.

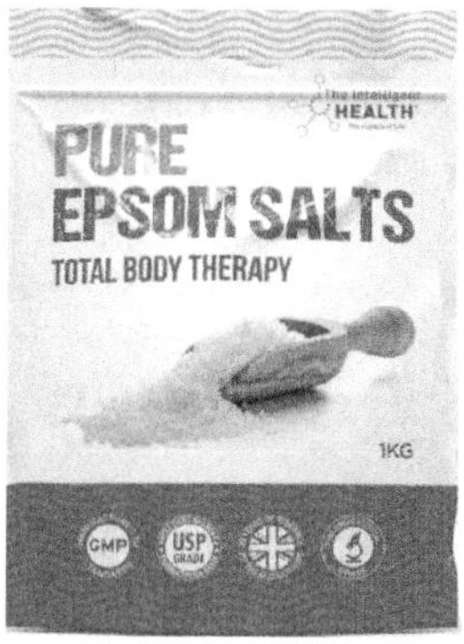

When left untreated, once the harvest mites have eaten their fill, they will drop off your cocker, and even though they may no longer be in residence, your poor dog will still suffer from the itchy sensation for many weeks.

Soothing baths with oatmeal and Epsom salts (pictured), applying calamine lotion or aloe vera to the crusted areas and adding a skin-supporting supplement can help relieve the itching.

Prevention is always better than cure. Therefore, it is best to take steps to reduce the risk of your cocker spaniel encountering the harvest mites. For instance, since the mite larvae only become active during the warmer hours of the day, walk your dog early in the morning or later in the evening and avoid areas where there are bushes, plants, long grasses, matted vegetation, or clods of earth. Also, if you have a garden where these biters can congregate, consider spraying to keep them out of your garden.

Sarcoptic Mange (also known as 'Scabies')

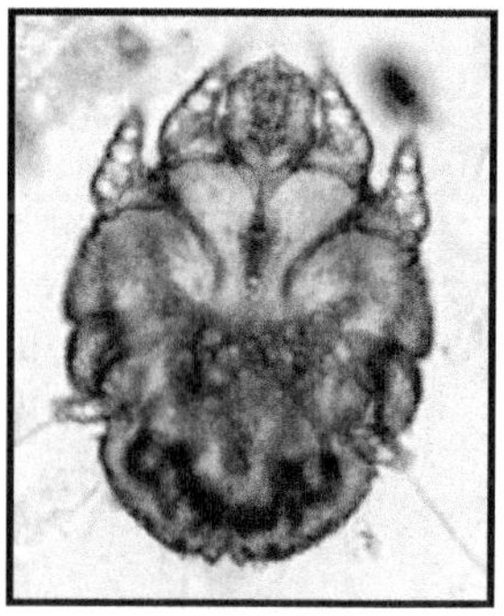

Sarcoptic mange comes from a parasitic mite—sarcoptes scabiei (pictured)—that burrow just below the skin's surface. Do not confuse sarcoptic mange with demodectic mange, which comes from a different parasitic mite. These mites bury themselves into the skin of healthy puppies and adult dogs, then feed on material in and on the skin. Another name for sarcoptic mange is scabies. It is zoonotic, meaning it is a disease transmissible from animals to humans. These mites prefer to infest hairless areas of the skin, making the abdomen, elbow, and ear flap most at risk.

According to the World Small Animal Veterinary Association World Congress Proceedings, 2004: 'There does not seem to be breed predispositions for scabies. Perhaps, Labradors, cocker spaniels and Doberman pinschers could be predisposed in North America.'

The main cause of becoming infected is exposure to another animal or person who is already infected—dog parks, groomers, kennels, shelters, day-cares—and symptoms do not usually surface until approximately two to six weeks after exposure.

When performing a skin scraping on infected dogs, it is normal not to see sarcoptic mange mites. The skin scraping is examined under the microscope to make a diagnosis. This is because the mites are tiny, burrow deep into the skin, and it only takes a few mites to create significant itching. On average, this test will confirm the presence of mites in 50% of affected dogs examined.

Because no mites are visible, does not mean your dog does not have sarcoptic mange. Therefore, a presumptive diagnosis must be made based on clinical signs. Sarcoptic mange can occur in any dog at any age.

While difficult to diagnose, and quite contagious to other animals, this condition is easy to cure with many scabicide treatments that are commonly found in flea, tick, and worming products. There are various treatments available from medicated baths and dips to oral medications and injections to resolve this infection many dogs require a combination of treatments.

TIP ***If any member of your family develops itching or a skin rash, contact your doctor immediately. Tell them you might have been exposed to sarcoptic mange or scabies. In humans, the mite is unable to complete its life cycle and dies within a few days. However, during that time, it can cause intense itching requiring medical treatment.***

Cheyletiella Mites

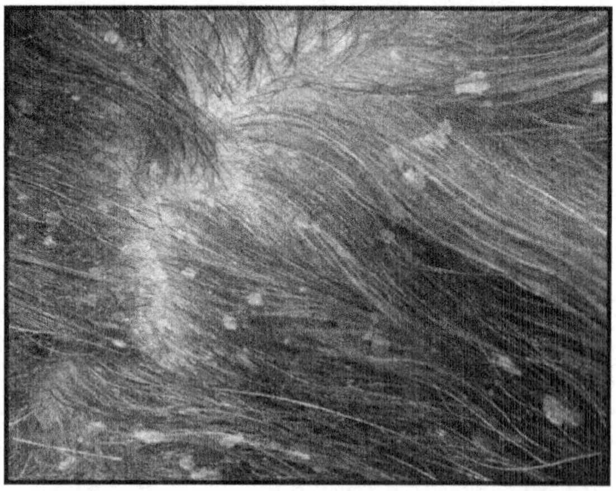

The clinical name is 'cheyletiellosis' and is sometimes referred to as 'cheyletiella mange' or 'walking dandruff' (pictured), as the mites are white and resemble dandruff as they crawl across the fur or skin. This infection is usually accompanied by large flakes of skin scaling, making it look even more like dandruff.

Cheyletiella is visible to the naked eye or with a magnifying glass. The American cocker spaniel, King Charles spaniel, and the boxer seem to be most susceptible to this mite. Although, any dog who is groomed regularly, attends a dog day-care, or frequents a place where there are other dogs can be at risk.

While considered uncommon—because of improved flea control medications—this is a highly contagious skin parasite that lives on the surface of the skin of its host as well as in the superficial skin layers. A dog can become infected with these large mites by meeting another animal that is already infected. This typically happens where multiple dogs have contact with one another, such as kennels, shelters, groomers, dog parks, breeders.

If your cocker is infected with these mites they might bite, scratch, or rub at the infected areas—often on your dog's back—and can present as swollen red skin or a red, bumpy rash followed by hair loss. Your veterinarian should be able to easily identify the infestation by taking a skin sample for microscopic examination.

Treatment recommendations will usually involve first clipping any long hair and bathing to remove scaling skin. Next will be the application of a 'miticide'—a chemical used to kill mites—that can be used as a lotion, ointment, spray, rinse, or dip. Oral medications may also be advised, such as milbemycin or ivermectin. Herding dog breeds are prone to developing 'ivermectin toxicity' and will not tolerate being treated with this anti-mite medication.

Totally eliminating the possibility of re-infestation involves quarantining, then treating all pets, and finally applying a strict cleaning protocol involving thorough cleaning of the surfaces your cocker might have encountered—bed, bedding, furniture, carpets, flooring, clothing, kennel, car. In other words, to eliminate this mite, anywhere the dog has been should be cleaned, repeating this major cleaning task at least weekly throughout your dog's treatment.

TIP ***Since these mites live in the environment for as long as ten days, complete elimination can be a long process, which could require multiple vet visits and treatment applications, and take as long as a month or more to fully resolve.***

Demodectic Mange

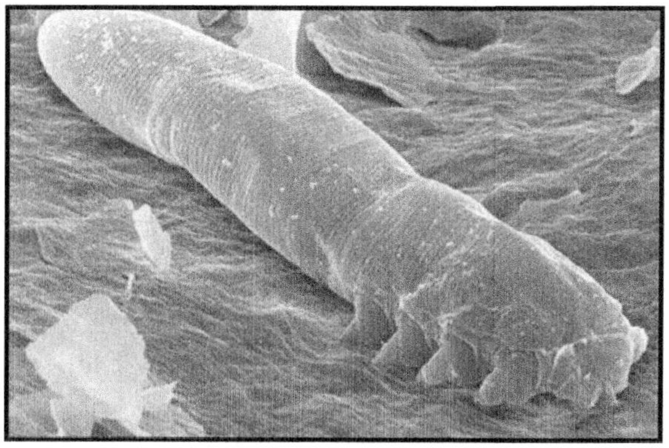

This skin disease is known by several names, 'puppy mange', 'red mange', or 'follicular mange'. It comes from one of three species of the Demodex mite (pictured)—canis, cornei, and injai—usually found in young dogs or puppies. This disease results from a weak, poorly developed or suppressed immune system that is unable to control the spread of these mites, which are passed from mother to puppy. Beagles, German shepherds, Doberman pinschers, Old English sheepdogs, collies, boxers, and shorthair brachycephalic breeds are predisposed to the generalised form of Demodex dermatitis.

FACT ***Small numbers of the Demodex mite are normally found living in harmony on the skin of every healthy dog and it is believed they are simply part of the skin's 'microfauna'. It is only when your cocker has a compromised immune system—through illness or advanced age—that the number of mites begins to rapidly multiply and inhabit your dog's skin and hair follicles, causing itching.***

Most puppies are immune to the effect of these microscopic mites and the few who are not develop hair loss, or red, crusty lesions, usually around the head. In 90% of cases, a localised problem will heal without intervention as your puppy matures and your cocker's immune system grows stronger. In persistent cases, treatment can involve the application of topical medications applied to the skin.

There are three forms of Demodectic mange, 'localised', 'generalised' and 'pododermatitis'.

The localised form involves no more than two regions of your dog's body—with no more than 4 spots in total. It will present itself as one or two scaly, bald patches that are usually isolated on your cocker's face or may include one spot on their leg. Considered common in puppyhood, treatment is not necessary or even recommended, as in most cases it will be resolved on its own.

The generalised form involves a considerably more extensive presence of large patches of your dog's skin. If left untreated, it can progress to cover the entire surface of your cocker's skin. It is mostly accompanied by a smelly, highly itchy secondary bacterial infection that requires treatment with antibiotics.

Treatment in persistent cases can involve the use of 'isoxazoline' or other flea and tick medicine and management, which might need a visit to the vet for follow-up skin scrapings.

Pododermatitis is one of the most resistant forms of mange. Found only on your dog's paws, it can be very deep and difficult to resolve. Often a biopsy of the area is necessary as bacterial and fungal cultures might be required to confirm a correct diagnosis of the infection.

There can be many causes of the inflamed area of the paws, including allergies, cancers, environmental toxins, hormonal problems, and tumours. Symptoms include red, inflamed paws and feet, itching, hair loss, constant licking, scabs, crusts, ulcerations or blisters, thickened foot pads, nodules, and darkened tissues.

Specific treatment of this form of mange is varied as there are many possible causes. Your vet will first have to determine the underlying problem before a treatment plan can be put in place. Possible treatments include foot soaks, wipes, shampoo washes, antibiotics, anti-fungal medications, and immune modulating drug therapy.

While diagnosing the cause and then managing a treatment protocol can take some time, once the underlying reason has been identified, and treatment adjustments have been made, prognosis for recovery is usually positive.

Pyoderma

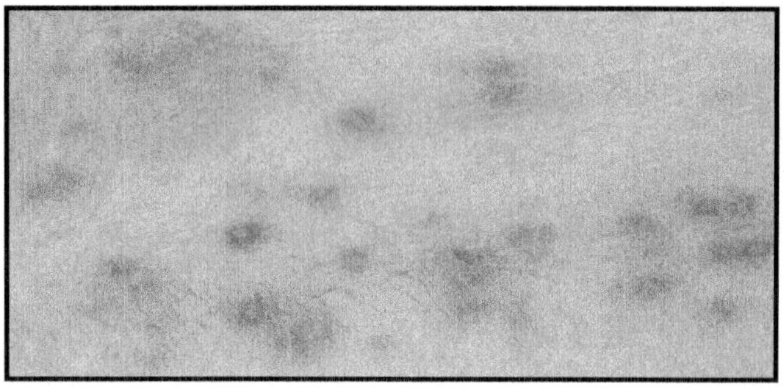

The name of this condition literally means 'pus in the skin'. This is a bacterial infection of your cocker's skin (pictured) that can arise for many different reasons and causes itching and redness that can lead to lesions on the skin that are like pimples. In young puppies, this might be referred to as 'impetigo' and commonly presents as red and raised pustules on the skin of the armpits or groin that are filled with a white pus. There can also be circular, flaky, and dry skin crusts or patches that are very itchy and cause hair loss.

As they have an excessive amount of skin folds around their lips, cocker spaniels are prone to getting pyoderma in their mouth. The folds generate a large quantity of saliva and creates a hot, humid environment, essentially making their mouth an ideal breeding ground for bacteria.

This skin infection can occur for several reasons, including the surface of the skin being broken or injured—from scratching—impaired blood flow, or a change in usual skin bacteria from a compromised immune system. Pyoderma may also be hereditary or triggered by hormone imbalances, thyroid disease, diabetes, fungal or yeast infections, parasites, some cancers, and some medications, such as, azathioprine, cyclosporine, or high steroid doses.

Frequently, pyoderma is caused by staph bacteria that can be triggered by fleas or other irritants. Certain breeds with deep skin folds that create a warm, moist environment, such as bulldogs, pugs, and Chinese shar-peis are more prone to produce bacteria.

Pyoderma can present itself as yellow pimples of ulcerated skin with a red, scaling, or crusting rash that is itchy and sensitive to touch and has a foul odour.

Diagnosis often includes skin scrapings, blood testing to determine if there is an underlying endocrine disease, and testing to determine drug sensitivity or other allergies.

Treatment usually involves routine bathing with an antibacterial shampoo two or three times a week—and then once a week—until the infection resolves, plus the application of antibiotic creams for approximately 3 to 4 weeks.

Never be tempted to pop your cocker spaniel's pimples, because doing so will expose your dog to infection, which can make the problem worse.

Fleas

FACT ***Dog fleas (pictured) are the most common parasites your cocker spaniel might encounter. In general, they are brown, measure around 1-2 mm and live for 7-14 days, dividing their time between staying on and laying eggs on your dog. Flea eggs are white, oval-shaped, and about half a millimetre in length. The eggs hatch into tiny larvae, which burrow into your dog's bedding, carpets, and upholstery and then develop into pupae.***

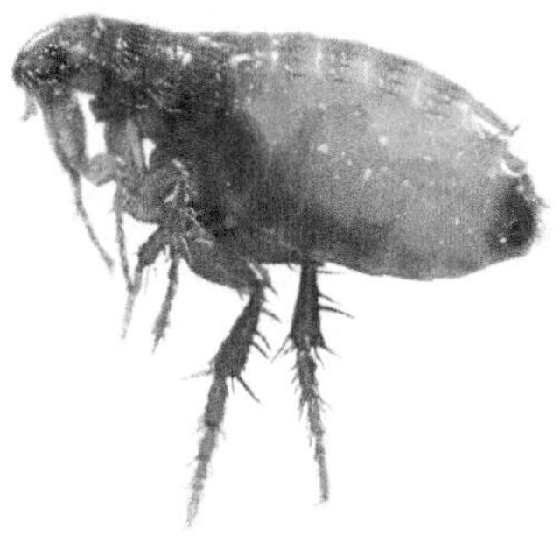

They lie silent for many months, so you will not realise they are there until they sense heat and vibration. The adult fleas then emerge and jump onto a passing 'host'—in this case, your dog—to begin the cycle all over again. No matter how clean your house is, 100 fleas could be living in your home for each one you find on your dog.

Fleas transmit diseases and are the leading cause of skin problems in dogs. All dogs are itchy after bites, and some can develop allergies, such as flea allergic dermatitis (FAD). Because of the high humidity and warm temperatures, late summer is peak season for fleas. However, a cosy central heating system in the winter means you will need to de-flea all year long.

If you cannot see them, it does not mean they are not there. Fleas can be easily detected by your cocker's persistent scratching, which can leave them with bald spots on their coat. Your dog may also develop scabs and red, sore areas of skin if they have a flea allergy. While regular dog grooming will not prevent fleas on your spaniel, it will at least alert you to any symptoms so you can get treatment sooner rather than later.

You might find them in your carpet or see flea dirt in the fur of your dog when combing it. Test these specks by placing them onto some damp tissue paper. If it is flea dirt, the specks will turn red, due to the digested blood they contain.

Always consult your vet about dog flea treatments and use only vet-approved products that have been tested for safety and effectiveness.

Powders are an old-fashioned and messy way to treat fleas on your dog, since the powder must remain on your cocker's coat to be effective and can be harmful if swallowed or inhaled.

Flea collars are not very effective in treating fleas on dogs, as they only treat the area around the neck. Additionally, they might cause irritation or hair loss. However, there is a new generation of flea collars that are much kinder to your dog's coat and skin. Your veterinarian can provide you with these, which work by dispersing the active ingredient throughout the body rather than sitting on the neck. Your cocker's collar should always have a quick release feature, otherwise your dog could become tangled or caught on something.

TIP ***A spot-on (pictured) is one of the easiest and most effective ways to prevent and treat dog fleas. In these treatments, a small amount of liquid is applied to the back of your dog's neck, killing fleas, and preventing them from developing eggs. You can find several brands, so talk to your veterinarian about which one is right for your cocker spaniel.***

Dog flea treatment also includes tablets and liquids. Essentially, these are absorbed into your dog's body, killing the fleas once they bite, or sterilising them so they cannot reproduce.

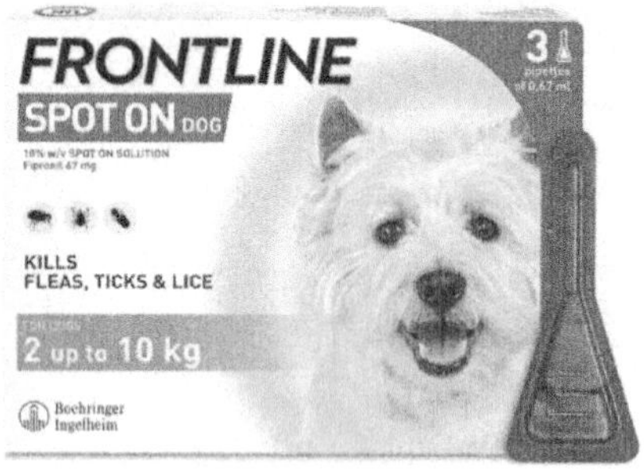

To get rid of fleas, you must treat your house as well as your pet. Use a combination of topical products to kill them, along with a treatment that prevents the eggs from becoming adults. Always follow the manufacturer's instructions when using these products. This usually means hoovering your carpet first to bring dog fleas and eggs to the surface, and then spraying your carpet thoroughly, before hoovering your carpet again after spraying.

There is no magic solution that will keep your cocker flea-free forever. Nevertheless, if you want to do your best to prevent fleas, here are some tips:

- Regularly wash their bedding.
- Reduce their contact with stray animals.
- Make sure your cocker is regularly brushed.
- Follow your veterinarian's flea control recommendations.

Ticks

Adult ticks (pictured) have eight legs and are classified as 'arachnids', which makes them relatives of mites, scorpions, and spiders. There are over 200 species of ticks, all of which survive by feeding on the blood of animals and humans.

These bloodsucking parasites have a sticky secretion and crab-like legs that help them hold onto their host before they attach themselves to the skin by the harpoon-like barbs in their mouth. Ticks are usually not a problem during colder weather, because they do not become active until the warmer spring weather when temperatures rise above 4o C (40o F).

Contrary to what some believe, ticks do not fly, jump, or drop from trees, but live on the ground in wooded areas and survive cold winter days by hiding underneath leaf litter, brush, and snow. Anyone taking their dog for walks through areas covered by leaf litter, tall grass, or wooded trails should be regularly checking their dog for ticks upon returning home.

Ticks on dogs are just large enough to be seen, especially if they have already bitten. At that point, they appear as small warts, and if you look closer, you will also see their legs. Usually, you will find them on your cocker's head and neck. To spot them, part your dog's fur and run your finger along their skin. A tick bite can also cause irritation and redness, which can be visible.

Ticks can be difficult to remove from your dog (see Care and Grooming, Chapter 9, for tick removal instructions) since you need to get the whole tick out without leaving its mouth parts buried under the skin, as this could lead to reinfection. Take your dog to the vet if you are unsure how to remove the ticks or if you are having difficulty doing so.

It is unlikely that your cocker will suffer any harm from having ticks on them. Although ticks in themselves are not dangerous, they are sometimes able to transmit diseases from another animal. For instance, they can transmit Lyme disease, which needs to be treated by a veterinarian, as well as having the ticks removed. Lyme disease can also be transmitted to humans, so if you have been bitten by a tick and feel unwell, consult your doctor.

Check with your vet if you live in an area where ticks are more common. If this is the case, you should use veterinary-approved treatments to prevent them. Various spot-on treatments, collars (pictured), and even tablets can be used to repel ticks or kill them if they attach themselves to your spaniel. Your vet can help you decide which option would be most suitable. You can obtain these preventatives from your veterinarian or, in some cases, from a pet store.

TIP ***Include checking for dog ticks in your routine. Keep an eye out for signs of ticks when grooming your dog to detect them at an early stage.***

Heartworm

The thread-like heartworm spreads only through mosquito (pictured) bites. After a growth period of approximately six months, this parasite can grow up to 30 centimetres (12 inches). As the name suggests, this worm lives in the heart and arteries that carry blood from the heart to the lungs.

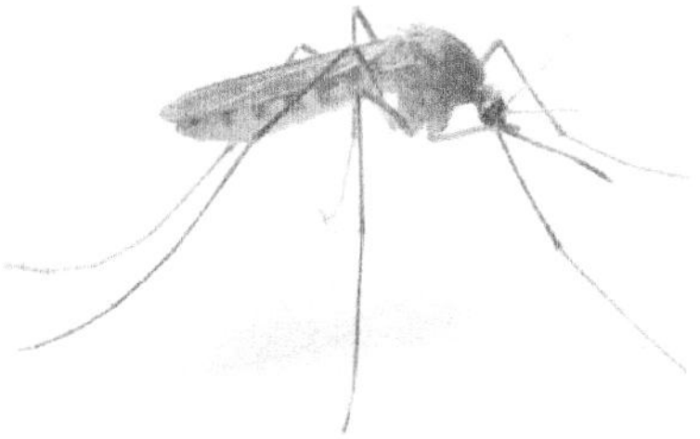

Upon maturing after six months, they can live in your cocker spaniel's body for up to seven years, reaching lengths of one foot and continuously producing offspring. It is uncommon for a dog to harbour hundreds of these parasites after a year, although the average number is 15. These worms cause inflammation and damage to the heart, arteries, and lungs. It is recommended that all dogs in the U.S. undergo an annual heartworm test, even if they are taking heartworm prevention medication.

Symptoms in an infected dog include coughing, lethargy, weakness, anaemia, high blood pressure, abnormal heart rate, difficulty breathing, and sometimes fainting.

Whilst this parasite is not found in the United Kingdom, it is common in America, Australia, Spain, Italy, and southern France. Recent climate changes have seen the parasite spread closer to the U.K., and it has recently been reported as far north as Brittany in northern France. If you take your cocker on holiday in any of these regions, they are at risk of being infected with heartworm.

There is no breed of dog particularly predisposed to heartworm. Dogs younger than six months old are unlikely to be infected as it takes approximately six months for a heartworm to develop from a microfilaria to an adult.

If left untreated, the heart will eventually fail, and death will be imminent. The only good news about the heartworm parasite is that it can only be transmitted through the bite of a mosquito. Therefore, taking steps to keep them away minimises the chance of your cocker becoming infected.

FDA-approved treatment in the U.S. is melarsomine dihydrochloride, which is sold under the brand names Immiticide and Diroban. A deep, intramuscular injection is administered to the lumbar region of the lower back of your dog, which is recommended when the disease has not progressed too far.

The treatment for heartworm is extremely painful, sometimes dangerous for your cocker, and extremely expensive. Therefore, veterinarians insist on administering yearly tests and preventative compounds—what scientists call chemoprophylaxis. Guidelines from the American Heartworm Society include the following:

- Taking a heartworm prevention medication all year round.
- Follow your veterinarian's dosage schedule strictly.
- Application of mosquito repellents approved by the FDA.
- Using environmental controls to reduce or eliminate mosquito breeding grounds—such as pools of standing water—using mosquito traps and limiting your spaniel's outdoor activities during dawn and dusk, which are mosquito feeding times.

Ringworm

Despite its name, ringworm (pictured) is not technically a worm, but a fungus.

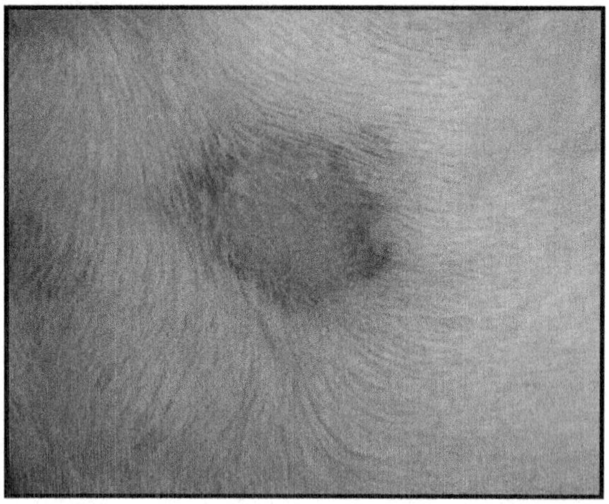

It is a common fungal infection affecting almost all domestic animals, including dogs. This fungus is called ringworm because of its round, raised, red ring appearance that is usually seen in human ringworm infections. Ringworm, scientifically called dermatophytes, is a pathogenic fungus. It is caused in 70% of cases by microsporum canis, 20% by microsporum gypseum, and just 10% by trichophyton mentagrophytes.

Dogs with weaker immune systems tend to be the ones who become infected with ringworm, such as very young or old dogs, it also includes dogs with diseases that weaken their immune systems, or dogs who have recently come from long-term stays in kennels or shelters. Genetically, Boston terriers, Yorkshire terriers, and Jack Russell terriers are more prone to ringworm infections than other breeds.

Dogs with skin conditions are also predisposed to ringworm. Normally, the skin functions as a protective barrier, but if your cocker has an open wound, fresh scratches, fleas, or a chronic skin condition they are more susceptible to an infection.

It will be in the outermost layer of your dog's skin, in the hair follicles, and occasionally in their nails. In most cases, the infection is superficial and will affect only a few parts of your cocker's body.

Ringworm is transmitted via direct contact with the fungus. Dogs get it if they meet an infected person or animal or touch something contaminated, such as a couch, comb, food bowls, bedding, or carpet. The condition usually manifests as circular areas of hair loss all over the body. The lesions may look patchy in appearance and can become inflamed or scabbed as they grow.

Ringworm does not typically itch. Hair follicles affected by the disease are brittle and easily break, which helps the disease spread throughout the home. When the fungus infects the claws, they become brittle and rough.

In most cases, your vet will recommend a topical treatment, such as cream, ointment, and/or medicated shampoo (pictured). Sometimes, oral therapy is required as well. The oral antifungal medications can help fight infection, and like topical therapy, are administered for a minimum of six weeks, but might take months for good results to happen. The spores that reside inside hair follicles remain contagious for months at a time, living on couches, grooming tools, bedding, and furniture. A part of the treatment is cleaning up all this hair, but as many dog owners know, this can be challenging.

The best way to prevent reinfection if your cocker has ringworm is to thoroughly cleanse the home and any tools and bedding they were in contact with, and to follow your veterinarian's instructions.

Canine Acne ('Canine pimples')

Canine acne is an inflammatory disorder of your dog's lips and the skin of their muzzle (pictured). If your cocker has a mild case of acne, they will often have red bumps or pustules—pimples—on their skin. In more severe cases, this can lead to generalised swelling of the lips and muzzle, scabs on the face, or bleeding wounds. When left untreated, severe cases of canine acne can result in permanent scarring.

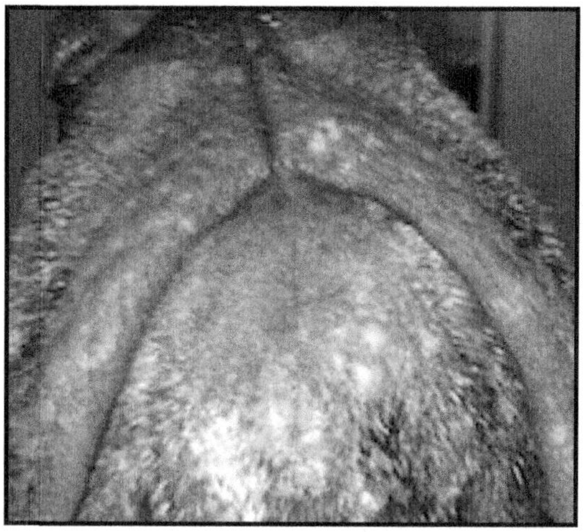

The fundamental cause of canine acne is not fully understood. Previously, canine acne was believed to be related to human acne, which is hormone induced. However, more recent evidence suggests this is not the case.

Trauma to the skin of the chin or muzzle is thought to be the trigger for many cases of canine acne. Such trauma makes the hairs break off near the surface of the skin, leading to inflammation in the hair follicle, which eventually ruptures. Once the hair follicle ruptures, it releases its contents into the surrounding skin. This instils further inflammation in the skin, as the surrounding tissues recognise the contents of the hair follicles as foreign.

There are cases where acne is associated with other underlying skin conditions and allergies. You should have your veterinarian assess your dog for possible environmental or food allergies. If your vet suspects these allergies, managing them could reduce the acne.

Genetic predisposition of the breed can also be a factor. Some breeds are more prone to acne than others, such as boxers, Doberman pinschers, English bulldogs, German shorthaired pointers, Great Danes, mastiffs and rottweilers.

Treating canine acne will involve a trip to the vet for a diagnosis that might include taking a skin scraping and various tests to rule out possible underlying causes—fungal infection, mange, parasites, allergies. Once a diagnosis is confirmed, treatment will typically include administering oral and/or topical medications.

TIP ***Topical benzoyl peroxide is the most common treatment for canine acne. This medication is often available over the counter or can be bought from your veterinarian. It reduces bacterial contamination and helps flush out the hair follicle.***

Steroids can also be prescribed to decrease inflammation in your cocker's skin. While topical steroids frequently have betamethasone or fluocinolone in them, oral steroids can include prednisolone or prednisone.

10 Skin Care Tips

Here are some additional tips to bear in mind that will help keep your cocker's skin healthy and nourished:

1. Keep your cocker's skin clean and moisturised with regular baths every 4-6 weeks.
2. Use only dog shampoo and conditioner formulated for a dog's pH and make sure to completely rinse their coat so there is no shampoo residue remaining that could cause itching.
3. Do not bathe them too regularly as this dries out the skin. Too much bathing can strip all the natural skin and coat oils and cause itching.
4. Between bath times, use moist doggy wipes designed especially for dogs before bed. This is an easy way to remove the daily dust and grime.
5. Feed them a high-quality diet that nourishes the skin. Inferior diets that comprise mostly inappropriate fillers can compromise health and create itchy skin problems.
6. Feed organic one-ingredient treats. When choosing single ingredient treats there will be no additives that can cause allergies.
7. Regularly brush and comb your cocker's coat to remove debris, shedding hair, and mats that may irritate the skin.
8. Add an omega-3, vitamin E, or salmon oil supplement to make sure that your spaniel's skin is well nourished.
9. Avoid using toxic cleaning and deodorising products that can get onto your dog's coat.
10. If you discover a problem, ask for professional help. Visit your vet, especially if you are not certain what is causing the issue.

15. Toxic Foods, Plants, and Products

'Dogs have a way of finding the people
who need them, and filling an emptiness
we didn't ever know we had.'
~ Thom Jones ~

Most owners are aware that there are certain human foods, plants, and medications that can be poisonous for their dog. However, they might not be aware of other toxic elements to be found in common plants, fertilisers, and cleaning products they use all the time. Below is a list of some of the more common products easily found in our homes and gardens that can be harmful or toxic to your cocker spaniel.

Toxic Foods

There are many foods that can be toxic to dogs, depending on their age, size, current health and how much they consume. While a good rule of thumb is to never feed your cocker human food, the following is a list of the most widespread foods that dogs should never eat and what the symptoms might be should they ingest them:

Alcohol – Even in small doses, alcohol has a huge impact on dogs. Not only does it make them intoxicated as it would a human, but it can also lead to sickness, diarrhoea, irregular heart rhythm, slowed heart rate, low body temperature, low blood sugar, and even central nervous system damage.

Avocado – Avocados are also poisonous for dogs. The avocado plant contains persin in its leaves, fruit, and seed and can cause vomiting and diarrhoea in dogs.

Bread Dough – If your cocker eats bread dough, their body heat will make the dough rise inside their stomach. As the dough expands during the rising process, alcohol is produced. Dogs who eat bread dough can experience stomach bloating, abdominal pain, vomiting, disorientation, and depression. Because bread dough can rise to many times its original size, eating only a small amount will usually cause a problem.

Broccoli – The toxic ingredient in broccoli is isothiocyanate. While it may cause stomach upset, it probably will not be harmful unless the amount eaten is more than 10% of your cocker's daily diet.

Caffeine – Beverages containing caffeine, such as soda, tea, coffee, and chocolate, act as a stimulant and can accelerate your dog's heartbeat to a dangerous level. Dogs ingesting caffeine have been known to have seizures, some of which are fatal.

Chocolate – Chocolate contains theobromine, a chemical that is toxic to dogs in large enough quantities. It also contains caffeine, which is a stimulant to be avoided.

Different kinds of chocolate contain varying amounts of theobromine and caffeine. For example, dark chocolate and baking chocolate or cocoa powder contain more of these compounds than milk chocolate. Therefore, your spaniel would need to eat more milk chocolate to become ill. However, even a few ounces of chocolate can be enough to cause illness or death in a puppy or smaller dog. No amount or type of chocolate should be considered safe for a dog to eat.

FACT ***Having eaten chocolate, your cocker could display symptoms that include diarrhoea, vomiting, increased heart rate, restless behaviour, muscle tremors, or seizures. If they have a very large quantity, they could die within 24 hours***

Cooked Bones – These can be extremely hazardous for dogs, because the bones become brittle when cooked, which will make them splinter when your dog chews on them. The splinters have sharp edges that can puncture gums and become stuck in their teeth. They can also cause choking when caught in their throat or create a rupture or puncture of the stomach lining or intestinal tract.

Especially dangerous are cooked turkey and chicken legs, pork chops, and veal bones. Symptoms of choking include pale or blue gums, dilated pupils, pawing at their face, gasping for air, or panting, unconsciousness, and collapse.

Dairy Products – Dairy products are a major source of food intolerance in dogs. Many dogs are lactose intolerant, which means they have difficulty digesting milk. Lactose intolerant dogs can have trouble drinking milk but may be all right with other dairy products such as cheese and plain yogurt, which are normally easier to digest than plain milk. Other dogs can have an adverse reaction to dairy in general.

If your dog is intolerant to dairy products, their consumption could cause stomach pain, toilet accidents, bloating, diarrhoea, excessive thirst, vomiting, dehydration, weakness, or weight loss.

Grapes and Raisins – These foods could cause acute—sudden—kidney failure in your cocker. While it is not known what the toxic agent is in this fruit, clinical signs can occur within 24 hours of eating and include vomiting, diarrhoea, and tiredness with the eventual shutdown of kidney function.

Garlic and Onions – The onion family is especially toxic to dogs and can cause irritation of the mouth, pawing at the mouth or face, stomach pain, excessive salivation, panting, weakness, refusal to exercise, rapid heart rate, pale or bluish gums, diarrhoea, vomiting, and collapse.

Mushrooms – Mushroom poisoning can be fatal if certain species of mushrooms are eaten by your cocker. The most reported severely toxic species of mushroom in both the U.K. and the U.S. is the amanita phalloides—death cap mushroom, other amanita species are also toxic. This deadly mushroom is often found growing in grassy or wooded areas near various deciduous and coniferous trees, which means you might easily come across them when out walking your cocker.

Eating them can cause severe liver disease and neurological disorders. If it is suspected that your dog has eaten these mushrooms, they will need to be immediately taken to the veterinarian. The recommended treatment is to induce vomiting straight away and give them activated charcoal. Further treatment for liver disease may also be necessary.

Pits and Seeds – Many seeds and pits found in a variety of fruits, including apples, apricots, cherries, pears, and plums, contain cyanogenic glycosides that can cause cyanide poisoning in your cocker.

The symptoms of cyanide poisoning usually occur within 15-20 minutes to a few hours after eating and can include initial excitement, followed by rapid respiration rate, salivation, or drooling, voiding of urine and faeces, vomiting, muscle spasm, staggering, and coma. Dogs suffering from cyanide poisoning that live more than 2 hours after onset of symptoms will usually recover.

Raw Salmon (pictured) – Never give your cocker spaniel raw or undercooked salmon. It could contain the neorickettsia helminthoeca parasite, which causes salmon poisoning disease, which can be fatal. Also, raw salmon contains numerous small bones. These are brittle and can lodge in their stomach or intestines or choke your dog. Whereas well-cooked, boneless salmon is absolutely on the list of safe food approved for dogs.

Macadamia nuts – This is a nut that is extremely toxic to dogs. They can cause tremors, weakness, paralysis, and severe joint inflammation. If your cocker swallows or nibbles macadamia nuts, call your vet to ask what the best course of action is.

Tomatoes – Ripe tomatoes can be fed in moderation as an occasional snack as they are considered nontoxic to dogs. On the other hand, unripe tomatoes and tomato plants should be avoided as they can cause tremors, seizures, stomach upset, and cardiac problems.

TIP ***To keep your cocker away from tomato plants, either fence off the area in your garden where they grow or supervise your dog when they are in the garden.***

Almonds, hazelnuts, walnuts – These are not technically toxic, so it is fine for your dog to eat them occasionally. However, their shape makes them a dog choking hazard. So, they are best avoided.

Xylitol – This is an artificial sweetener often found in many sweets, gums, breath mints, toothpastes, and mouthwashes. Xylitol is recognised as a poison risk to dogs.

FACT ***When puppies or dogs eat products containing xylitol, it creates a sudden release of insulin, which in turn causes low blood sugar, which can result in liver damage. Within 30 minutes, your cocker might vomit, appear lethargic, and seem uncoordinated. However, some signs of toxicity can sometimes be delayed for hours or even a few days. Xylitol toxicity in dogs can be fatal if left untreated.***

Toxic Plants

Though some plants eaten by dogs may only result in an upset stomach and mild diarrhoea for a day or two, others can cause much more serious harm that could result in liver damage or even be fatal. Plants differ in attractiveness to dogs. For example, a shrub might sit in your garden for many years without being touched by them, while a fallen conker or acorn may instantly appear enticing the moment it hits the ground. Therefore, deciding what to keep in your garden will not only depend on the toxicity of the plant, but also on how inquisitive your cocker spaniel is.

The following is an alphabetical list from The Kennel Club in the United Kingdom of the most common plants that are found in many homes and gardens and are poisonous to dogs:

- Aconitum.
- Amaryllis bulbs.
- Asparagus fern.
- Azalea.
- Bluebells.
- Cyclamen.
- Daffodil bulbs.
- Day lilies.
- Delphiniums.
- Dog's Mercury.
- Foxgloves.
- Hemlock.
- Hyacinth.
- Hydrangea.
- Ivy.
- Laburnum.
- Lily of the valley.
- Lupins.
- Morning glory.
- Nightshade.
- Oleander.
- Rhododendron.
- Rhubarb leaves.
- Sweet pea.
- Tulip bulbs.
- Umbrella plant.
- Wisteria.
- Yew.

This is not an exhaustive list of all toxic plants. The American Kennel Club (AKC) website also contains a comprehensive listing of toxic plants, vines, trees, and flowers complete with pictures to help identify them.

Safe Garden Plants

There is no reason to deny your garden a beautiful array of colour and variety of shrubs and scented flowers because you have a dog. To name just a few, the following plants are not only beautiful, colourful, and fragrant, they will attract bees and birds and are also perfectly safe for your cocker:

- Camellia.
- Coral Bells.
- Cosmos.
- Creeping thyme.
- Dill.
- Fennel.
- Fuchsia.
- Honeysuckle.
- Marigold.
- Magnolia.
- Nasturtium.
- Pineapple sage.
- Polka dot.
- Purple basil.
- Roses.
- Rosemary.
- Snapdragon.
- Sunflower.

Safe Indoor Plants

Just because you have decided to share your home with your cocker spaniel does not mean you cannot enjoy your indoor plants. The following are just a few that are known to be safe around dogs who will eat anything.

- African violet.
- Areca palm.
- Boston fern.
- Cast iron plant.
- Christmas cactus.
- Haworthia.
- Mini phalaenopsis orchid.
- Money tree.
- Moth orchid.
- Parlour palm.
- Peperomia caperata.
- Prayer plant.
- Spider plant.
- Swedish ivy.
- Wax plant.

Toxic Products

Human Medicines Toxic to Dogs

Though it goes without saying that you should always keep human medicines safely out of the reach of your cocker, some are more toxic than others, including:

- ADD/ADHD Medications.
- ACE Inhibitors.
- Acetaminophen—Tylenol, etc.
- Antidepressants—Cymbalta, Effexor, Lexapro, Prozac, etc.
- Beta Blockers.
- Birth Control Products.
- Cholesterol Lowering Agents.
- Cough and Cold Medications.

- Non-steroidal anti-inflammatory drugs.
- Sleep Aids and Benzodiazepines—Xanax, etc.
- Thyroid Medications.

Toxic Household Products

Our beloved cockers love to investigate everything with their mouth and taste it with their tongue. Since they wear no shoes, our dogs are often directly in contact with products we use to clean and moisturise ourselves, clean our homes, or use on our lawns or gardens, such as:

- All-purpose cleaners.
- Antifreeze—used in car radiators.
- Bath and kitchen cleaners.
- Carpet cleaners.
- De-icing salts—used to melt ice.
- Dishwashing detergents.
- Disinfectant wipes.
- Fertilisers—for lawns and plants.
- Petrol
- Glues and varnishes
- Grass seeds
- Herbicides.
- Insecticides—used to kill insects.
- Laundry detergent.
- Lotions and moisturisers—for people.
- Mildew removers.
- Mothballs.
- Oven cleaners.
- Paints and polishes.
- Perfume—for people.
- Rodenticides—used to kill rodents.
- Shampoo and conditioner—for people.
- Slug poison.
- Toilet cleaners.
- Weed killer.
- Window cleaners.

As you can see, there are obvious and subtly hazardous products that could seriously harm or even kill your cocker, which can be found inside and outside your home. Always keep your home dog safe, by placing all these products safely out of reach of your spaniel.

Pet Poison Control Centres and Help Lines

If you suspect that your dog has eaten something that could be toxic, immediately call a pet poison control line. These are centres for pet owners who need advice if they believe their pet has been in contact with something harmful. They should be able to tell you whether to expect any symptoms and if a visit to the vet is necessary. Where possible, you should provide them with the following information:

- Which poison your cocker has been exposed to—e.g., chocolate, ibuprofen, etc.
- How much they have consumed—e.g., 1000mg, 200ml, two tablets, even approximations could help.
- When your dog was exposed to the poison.
- Whether your dog has been unwell, and if so, what clinical signs have been observed.

TIP ***It is easier for your vet to care for your poisoned cocker if they are treated sooner rather than later. If you are in any doubt, do not wait for your dog to become unwell before calling for advice. Quick action could mean being able to save their life!***

While waiting for your vet, here is how to help your dog in the meantime:

- Never try to make your cocker vomit. Avoid using salt water as it is extremely dangerous.
- Do not attempt to medicate or treat your cocker yourself. Some human and animal medicines can be poisonous to dogs.
- To avoid cross-contamination, keep your dog away from other animals.

If your dog's skin or fur is contaminated, wash it with a mild shampoo and water, then rinse thoroughly and dry.

The Animal Poison Line is the United Kingdom's animal poison centre. This is a 24-hour, payable triage service for pet owners who need advice when they suspect their pet may have been poisoned. Call: 01202 509000

The American Society for the Prevention of Cruelty to Animals (ASPCA) Animal Poison Control Center is staffed 24 hours a day, 365 days a year and is a valuable resource for learning what can be toxic and possibly poisonous to a dog. Call: 1 (888) 426-4435.

The Pet Poison Helpline is a 24-hour payable service staffed by veterinary professionals in the U.S. Call: 0800-213-6680.

16. Keeping Your Dog Safe

'I want to work like a dog, doing what I was born

to do with joy and purpose. I want to play like a dog, with total, jolly abandon.'

~ Oprah Winfrey ~

Safe Travelling

Car Travel

Imagine you are travelling by car daily without protection from your seatbelt or airbag. Most people would not feel safe. However, not being securely restrained inside the car is a reality for many of our furry friends. Never forget to think about vehicle safety for your dog, it is quite simple to keep them safe.

Owners often ask the question, 'Is my dog safe when they are buckled into a safety harness for travel in my car?' The answer to this question is that often harnesses available in the marketplace have a significant failure rate. Also, bear in mind that if your cocker is travelling in the front passenger seat, even secured with a fully tested safety harness, they can still sustain serious injuries if the 100 kph force of the airbag strikes them.

The safest travel arrangement for your cocker spaniel is to secure them inside a kennel (pictured) bolted to the floor or secured with your vehicle's seatbelt system. A dog kennel will easily fit on the back seat of your car and be secured with the restraint system. If you plan to have your cocker travel with you, you should begin kennel training early on so your dog will calmly accept this form of travel arrangement.

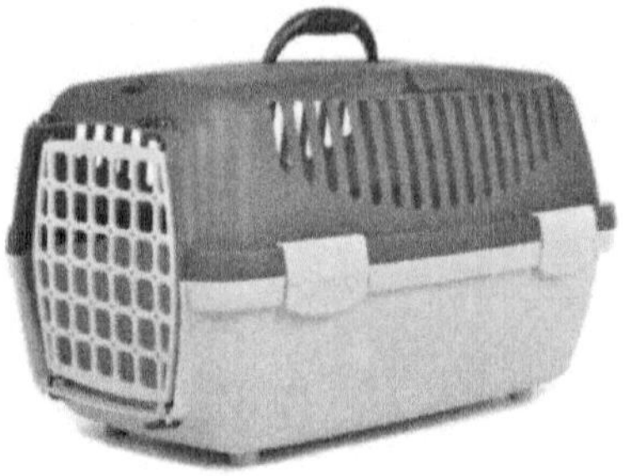

As well as providing a safe riding situation for your dog, you will avoid the fines some locations are now levying for allowing your dog to sit on your lap or roam freely inside the car. It makes sense that this is considered a distraction that could cause an accident.

Bear in mind that hot weather is very dangerous for a cocker puppy confined on a car trip for hours. Sunshades and even opening the windows for a while can help. However, make sure you never allow them to travel with their head out the window.

Air Travel

Many airlines permit small dogs to travel with their owners in the plane's cabin if the carry bag will fit under the seat. The best course of action is to call the airline in question to confirm that they will permit your dog and to also confirm the size restriction of the carrier. You might also have to book a space and pay a fee for transporting your cocker spaniel.

Most soft carriers are airline approved for the following under seat dimensions:

Window Seat: 48 cm L x 35 cm W x 21 cm H (19 ins L x 14 ins W x 8.25 ins H)

Middle Seat: 48 cm L x 48 cm W x 21 cm H (19 ins L x 19 ins W x 8.25 ins H)

Aisle Seat: 48 cm L x 35 cm W x 21 cm H (19 ins L x 14 ins W x 8.25 ins H)

While your cocker puppy might be small enough to fit into a soft carrier bag for travel inside the plane's cabin—as carry-on luggage—they will be too large when they reach their adult size. You must transport any puppies or dogs who are too large to fit comfortably inside the travel bag in a hard-sided crate or kennel in the heated cargo hold.

Bus Travel

Most public bus systems allow a small dog on board if they are contained inside a carrier bag that will fit on the owner's lap or underneath the seat, usually at no charge. Some countries—including the U.K.— permit any size dog to travel on the bus system either on lead or in a carrier unless there is some legitimate reason to refuse them.

Train Travel

Typically, every country has their specific rules and regulations regarding pets travelling on trains. The following are general rules for train travel in the United Kingdom, United States, and Canada:

National Rail, the train system in the United Kingdom, is very dog friendly. Dogs, no matter their size, can travel on lead or inside a carrier. However, if travelling on Eurostar to France, dogs are not permitted at all.

Amtrak in the U.S. only permits a total of 5 pets per train—excluding service dogs—and there is a small fee involved, so it is recommended to book well in advance of travel. They allow small dogs to travel with their owners inside passenger cars if:

- The carrier will fit underneath the seat.
- The weight of both carrier and dog is not more than 9 kilograms (20 pounds).

- The trip will not be longer than 7 hours.

Rail Canada allows small dogs to travel with their owners inside passenger cars if they remain inside an approved carrier that fits underneath the passenger seat. The weight of the carrier and pet combined must be no more than 10 kilograms (22 pounds) and there are a limited number of pets permitted on each train. You will be charged a small fee for your cocker and reserving a space well ahead of travel time is advisable.

Ferry Travel

Many ferries have an area for dogs either on lead on outside deck areas or inside the cabin if they are contained inside a pet carrier. There is not usually an extra fee for bringing your dog. However, if travelling from the U.K. to Europe on the cross-channel ferry, your cocker will need an animal health certificate—or EU or Northern Ireland-issued pet passport—a microchip, and a valid rabies vaccination, from at least 21 days before your date of travel.

Identification

Thankfully, there are several effective choices—tattooing, microchipping, pet trackers—to identify your cocker spaniel so they will be returned to you should they ever get lost.

Beware of dog theft

When your dog goes missing, it can be a very scary time. Often your dog will simply have wandered a little too far away. Sadly, we know thieves target pet dogs—either to sell them on to an unsuspecting new owner or as part of a scam to claim any reward that is offered for your dog's return.

If stolen, your cocker could easily be hidden and transported to another area, making it extremely difficult to track them down. Therefore, prevention is the key to keeping your pet safe:

- Avoid leaving your cocker spaniel unsupervised in public. Never leave your dog tied up outside a shop or alone in your car when you run an errand.
- Ensure your garden is secure. When you let your dog out, do not let them out of your sight and make certain the gates are locked and there are no gaps in your fences or walls.
- If possible, vary your walking habits by using different routes and avoid walking at the same time every day to prevent your activity from becoming predictable.
- Practise the recall command to train your cocker to come back when you call them. If you are unsure whether they will return when asked, keep them on a lead, especially in areas you or your dog do not know well.
- Keep your microchip contact details up to date so if your spaniel does go missing, they will be traced back to you. In the U.K. it is a legal requirement for all dogs aged eight weeks and over to be microchipped and registered on a compliant database.

- It is also a legal requirement for all dogs to wear a collar with an ID tag while out in public spaces. By law, it should include your name and address and add your mobile number if you wish, but avoid putting your cocker's name on the disc.

When it comes to dog theft, time is of the essence, so it is important to act immediately:

- Report your cocker spaniel missing to your local council's dog warden. You can find their contact details on your council's website.
- If you believe your dog has been stolen, contact the police and report the crime as a theft. You can call or report it online.
- So, they can record your pet as missing, contact the microchip database your dog is registered on. Then, you will be contacted if anyone tries to change the chip details.
- Ask dog walkers in your area if they have seen your dog. Put up posters where you are allowed to, and post in local social media groups.
- There are many websites in the U.K. designed to help owners report their dogs as missing, including Dog Lost, Pets Reunited and the National Pet Register. Use as many sites as possible to report your dog missing.
- Contact rescue centres in your area. If your cocker spaniel has strayed, there is every chance they will be brought to a rescue. Several organisations, such as Battersea Dogs and Cats Home, have missing and found helplines.

Licensing

TIP ***If your cocker is properly identifiable, they will be returned to you should they go missing, and this is a much happier dog than one spending who knows how long behind bars at a rescue centre. In many U.S. states, it is compulsory to have your dog licensed yearly, while in the U.K. you do not need to have a licence.***

The U. S. licence contains an identifying number and telephone number anyone can call should they find your lost dog wearing its tag. When the number is called and the tag number reported, it is identified with the owner and your dog will be returned to you.

Tattooing

Tattooing is another popular way to help identify dogs in case they are lost or stolen. Many dog owners prefer this safe, simple solution. Because a tattoo is visible, it is immediately recognisable and reported when a lost dog is found, which means this is a highly effective form of identification.

Furthermore, dog thieves are less likely to steal your cocker if it has a permanent, visible means of identification. There are several registries for tattooed dogs, including the National Dog Tattoo Registry in the United Kingdom (pictured), which has a network of accredited tattooists across the country.

In the United States, the National Dog Registry (NDR) was founded in 1966. Since that time, the NDR has supervised, directed, conducted, or overseen the tattooing of more than 6 million animals.

\chipping

A microchip (pictured) is an identification chip used to help return lost dogs to their owners.

The implant is an exceedingly small integrated circuit, approximately twice the size of a grain of rice. The chip is enclosed in glass that is implanted underneath the dog's skin with a syringe. The chip uses what is referred to as passive 'Radio Frequency Identification' (RFID) technology. This form of identification is also known as a Passive Integrated Transponder (PIT) tag.

The microchip is usually implanted without anaesthetic into the scruff of your dog's neck by a veterinarian or rescue shelter and has no internal power source. That means the chip must be read by a scanner—also known as an 'interrogator'—that energises the capacitor inside the chip, which then sends radio signals back to the scanner so the identifying number can be read. Manufacturers of microchips often donate scanners to animal shelters and veterinarian clinics and hospitals.

FACT ***If you live in the U.S., you are not obliged by law to microchip your dog. However, in the United Kingdom it has been mandatory for those owning dogs over the age of 8 weeks to have them microchipped since 2016.***

Microchipping is used by animal shelters, pounds, animal control officers, breeders, and vets to help return a higher percentage of lost canines. Some of the resistance to this idea is due to the inherent problems with the ability of certain organisations to correctly read the implants. If the scanner is not tuned to the same frequency as the implanted microchip, it will not be read, which renders the process useless.

Microchips are manufactured with different frequencies, including 125 kHz, 128 kHz and 134.2 kHz. While approximately 98% of the pet microchips in the U.S. use 125 kHz, those in Europe use 134.2 kHz. In other words, if the facility reading your cocker's microchip does not have a compatible scanner—reading at the chip's frequency—your dog will not be identified.

Pet Trackers

While there are many pet trackers in the marketplace, there are two main categories of this product:

- GPS Trackers.
- Radio Trackers.

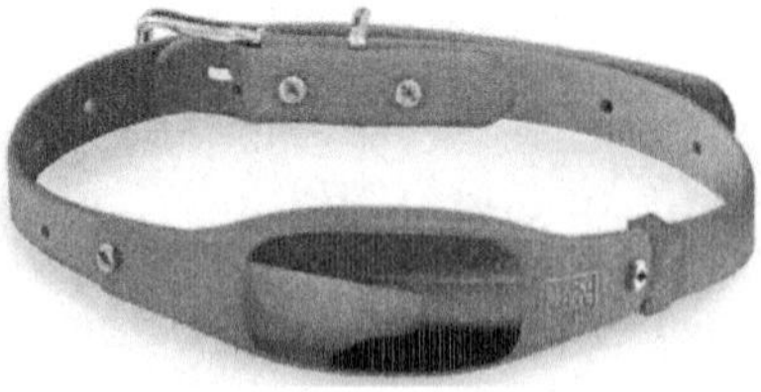

A GPS Tracker can help you locate your dog in real time by utilising cellular towers and requires the use of a SIM card or some sort of cellular service. Your dog will need to wear a collar or harness containing a tracking antenna (pictured).

There is an app available for your smart phone or device designed to go with your GPS pet tracker, so you can get detailed location data. Some produce a map of where your pet is and offer directions to help you get there as fast as possible. Some companies selling GPS pet trackers do not provide apps, but by logging onto their website you can obtain the same information.

Radio Trackers have been used for decades and are often used for hunting dogs. They function over a limited range, much like a walkie-talkie. The dog wears a collar or harness containing a tag that can be read by RF (radio) signals. These devices operate like a compass, pointing you in the direction of your dog. Unfortunately, if your cocker goes out of range, you cannot receive any information. The more you spend for a radio tracker, the greater the range is.

Where to Look

In the unlikely and unfortunate event that your cocker spaniel goes missing, if you believe they were stolen see the above section 'Beware of Dog Theft'. However, if foul play is not suspected, there are many places you can contact and things you can do to locate your lost dog, including:

- Retrace your dog's last known location.
- Contact friends and neighbours.
- Place flyers on telephone poles throughout the neighbourhood, with your contact details and your cocker's photo.
- Distribute flyers in all neighbourhood stores and businesses.
- Call all local shelters and pounds each day.
- Contact local rescue organisations.
- Contact local schools—the children might have seen your spaniel.
- Contact all businesses that deal with lost pets.
- Post a picture on social media.
- Ask the local radio station for help.
- Advertise in your local newspaper.

Dog Health Insurance

Pet owners often wonder when considering medical insurance for their dog, whether they can afford not to have it. Considering all the new treatments and medications that are now available for our dogs, which usually come with a very high price tag, an increasing number of owners are deciding to add pet insurance to their list of monthly expenses. Although, some people believe that placing money into a savings account, in case unforeseen medical treatments are required, makes more sense. Whether deciding to start a savings account or to purchase a health insurance plan, most dog owners will go to any lengths to save the life of their canine family member.

Dog insurance coverage can vary widely in cost and over the average lifespan of your cocker spaniel can be anywhere from £1 640 to £6 300 ($2 150 to $8 000 USD). These figures are based on the current average cost and are dependent on the level of coverage you have. Accident only insurance is far cheaper than full accident and illness cover. Unless your dog is involved in a serious accident or contracts a life-threatening disease, you might never need to pay out that much for treatment.

Having access to advanced technological tools and procedures means that your cocker will be offered treatment options that were once only available to people. Now, some canine conditions that were once considered fatal are being treated at considerable costs of between £820 and £5 100 ($1 000 and $6 700) or more.

TIP ***Even though you might think pet insurance will be your saviour any time your dog needs a trip to the vet, it is prudent to be careful when considering an insurance plan, because many policies contain small print excluding certain ages, hereditary and chronic conditions.***

Some people do not consider dog insurance when their dog is healthy, as they think unless their dog becomes seriously ill, they end up paying for something that might never happen. However, just like car insurance, after the accident has already happened, it is too late to buy insurance.

For example, if you take your dog to the vet who discovers your cocker has something wrong with their eyes, then you decide to purchase insurance, anything involving your dog's eye health will probably be excluded from the policy. Usually, when purchasing a pet insurance plan, you are required to provide the insuring company with a history of your spaniel's health, and in this example, the eye health issue will already be part of your dog's history. In other words, when planning to purchase health insurance for your dog, you should do so before any problems arise.

Also bear in mind that canine health insurance rates will likely increase as your dog gets older. When your dog is younger, the policy might only cost £14 ($18) per month, but it will increase considerably to as much as £140 ($180) or more per month as your dog becomes middle or senior aged, at around 8 to 10 years old.

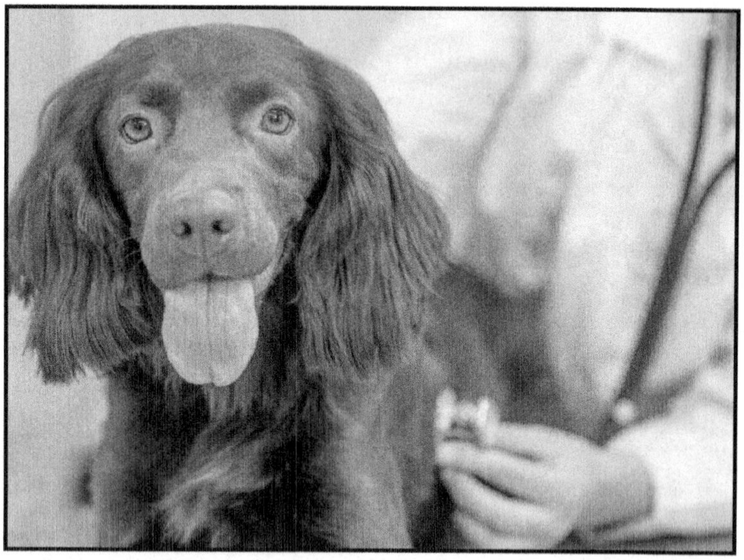

Shop around because pet insurance policies vary greatly between companies. The only way to know for certain exactly what sort of coverage you are buying is to be holding a copy of that policy so you can clearly read what will and will not be covered. Carefully read the fine print to avoid any nasty surprises, as the time to discover that a certain procedure will not be covered should not be in the middle of filing a claim.

A list of the cheapest and most expensive dog breeds to insure on accident-only policies and Lifetime policies has been compiled by MoneySuperMarket.com. The data comes from hundreds of thousands of quotes generated for real consumers. In the list of cheapest dog breeds to insure on accident-only policies, the cocker spaniel is 5th:

1. Cockerpoo—cheapest.
2. Labradoodle.
3. Beagle.
4. Patterdale terrier.
5. Cocker spaniel—most expensive.

Since many of us in today's uncertain economy might be hard pressed to pay a high veterinarian bill, the alternative of paying smaller monthly premiums can make it more affordable and provide peace of mind and improved veterinarian care for your dog.

Before choosing your dog insurance policy there are several factors you must consider, such as:

- Is your dog required to undergo a physical exam?
- Is there a waiting period before the policy becomes active?
- What percentage of the bill does the insurance company pay?
- Are payments limited or capped in any way?
- Are there excess pays—cost to the owner up-front?
- Does the plan cover pre-existing conditions?
- Does the plan cover chronic or recurring medical problems?
- Is it your choice which vet or hospital will treat your dog?
- Are prescription medications covered?
- Are you covered when travelling with your cocker?
- Does the policy pay if your dog is being treated and then dies?

TIP ***Insure your cocker spaniel when they are a young puppy, because waiting until they are older means your monthly premiums will be considerably higher.***

First Aid

First Aid Kit

Do not forget to put together a canine first aid kit (pictured) in case of emergencies, both at home and in your car. The following items should be included in the kit:

- Flannel.
- Blanket.
- Gauze bandaging.
- Styptic powder.
- Medical tape.
- Nail clippers.
- Non-stick pads for wounds.
- Scissors.
- Sterile eye wash.
- Tick twister.
- Towel.
- Tweezers.
- Antiseptic wash for wounds—hydrogen peroxide.

If you are in the United Kingdom, it would also be smart to keep a copy of the PDSA instructions on CPR for Dogs and Puppies in your first aid kit. In the States, you can find this in the American Red Cross emergency techniques called 'Saving Your Pet With CPR'. You should become familiar with the proper way to administer cardiopulmonary resuscitation (CPR) to your dog. You could also consider taking a CPR class; there are many courses being offered these days through community educational systems and veterinary practices or even online.

Of course, nobody wants to find themselves in a situation where the life of their dog is put at risk. However, the reality is that accidents do happen sometimes. Therefore, knowing a little about how to save your dog—or maybe even someone else's—is valuable time well spent.

TIP ***If your dog is injured, remember to always handle them carefully and gently. A dog who is traumatised, fearful, or in pain, even one who is usually gentle might lash out and try to bite.***

Applying CPR and Artificial Respiration

If your dog becomes unconscious, depending upon what happened to them, they could stop breathing. If they stop breathing, they will go into cardiac arrest when their heart stops beating, and your dog will die.

However, after breathing stops and before cardiac arrest, the heart can continue to beat for several minutes. This is the time window when performing CPR and artificial respiration can save your cocker's life. Ideally, one person will perform the artificial respiration, while the other performs the CPR.

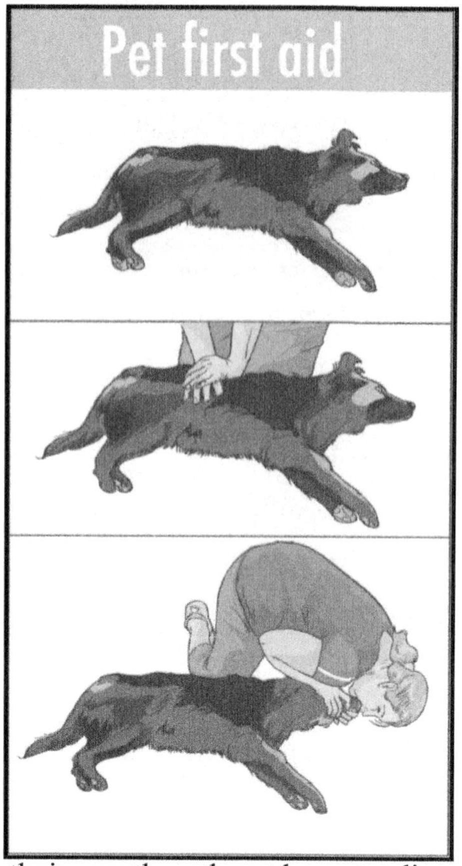

Here is how to perform CPR on your dog:

1. Put your dog on their side on a flat surface.
2. Feel for their pulse or heartbeat by placing one hand over their left side, just behind the front leg.
3. Place the palm of your hand on your spaniel's rib cage over their heart, with your other hand on top of the other hand—for puppies, put just your thumb on one side of their chest and the rest of your fingers on the other side.
4. Press down and release, compressing your dog's chest approximately 2-3 centimetres (1 inch)—squeeze and release 80 to 100 times every minute.

Here are the steps needed to perform artificial respiration on your dog:

1. Place your dog on their side on a flat surface.
2. Check to make sure your cocker has stopped breathing by watching their chest rise and fall and feeling for their breath on your hand. Check the colour of their gums, as the lack of oxygen will make them turn blue.
3. Check that your dog's airway is clear and there is nothing stuck in their mouth or throat by extending their head and neck and opening your cocker's mouth.
4. If there is an object blocking your dog's throat, pull their tongue out and use your fingers or pliers to get a firm grip on the object so you can pull it out. If you cannot reach the object, you will have to use the Heimlich manoeuvre to try to dislodge it (see below).
5. If your cocker's airway is not blocked, lift their chin to straighten out their neck and begin rescue breathing.
6. Hold your dog's muzzle and close their mouth, put your mouth over their nose and blow gently— just enough to make your dog's chest rise.
7. Wait long enough for the air you just breathed into your dog's lungs to leave before giving another breath.

8. Continue giving one gentle breath every 3 seconds while their heart is still beating and until your dog starts to breathe on their own.

Choking dog

If an object is blocking your dog's airway and you cannot reach it with your fingers to take it out, you need to take immediate action to dislodge it. As with people, you will know your dog is choking as they will retch, gag, and cough to try to expel the object. If this is the case, you might not have time to make it to your vet, so should implement the following techniques.

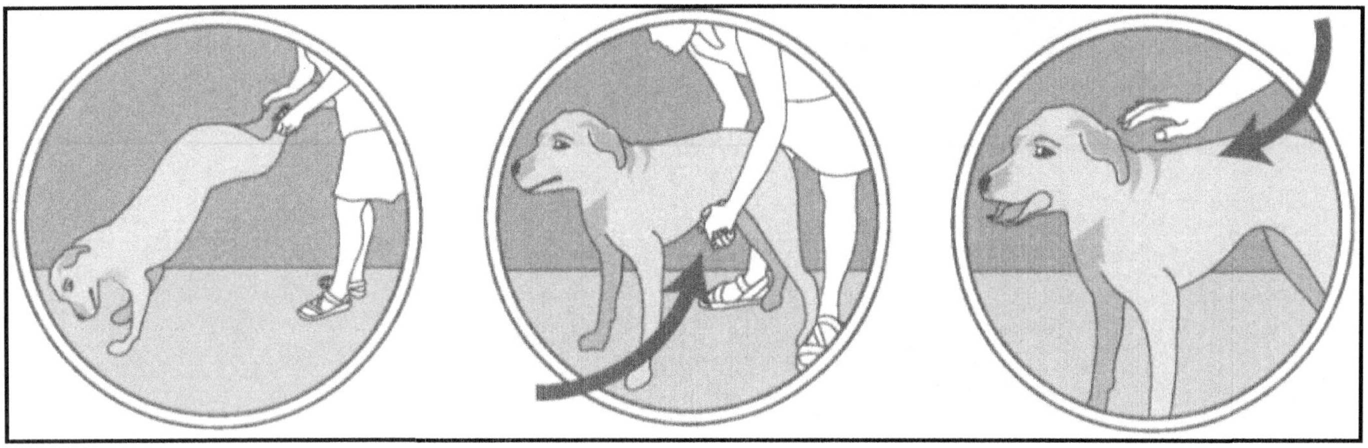

1. First, see if you can dislodge the object by opening your dog's mouth and sweeping from side to side to. Take care not to be bitten or to push the object farther into their throat.
2. To help your cocker's efforts of coughing up the object, first remove their collar. Then, lift them by their back legs and hold them vertically with their head down, like a wheelbarrow. This position might dislodge the object.
3. If the above steps do not work, try the dog Heimlich manoeuvre, as follows:
4. With you cocker spaniel standing or lying down, put your arms around their waist.
5. Close your fist and place it on the underside of their torso, where their ribs end just beneath the sternum.
6. Push up with your fist 5 times in rapid succession to compress their abdomen.
7. If your dog is not breathing, alternate this with CPR.
8. As a final solution, administer a sharp blow with the palm of your hand between your cocker's shoulder blades. Then go back to step 3 and repeat the Heimlich manoeuvre.

It is relatively rare for dogs to choke, but some objects such as golf balls or small, rubber balls can become stuck at the back of their throat. After performing the above steps, sweep your cocker's mouth for the object. Once it is dislodged, immediately seek veterinary assistance.

17. Senior Dog Care

'There is no faith which has never yet been broken, except that of a truly faithful dog.'

~ Konrad Lorenz ~

Much like humans, when our dogs reach a certain age, they begin to experience behavioural and physical changes that are all part of the life circle. The following pages offer many suggestions about how to make your senior cocker's years as pleasant as possible.

What Age is My Cocker in Human Years?

FACT ***We used to think that calculating a dog's age in human years was simple because all we had to do was take the year and multiply by 7. Even though this formula has been around for an extremely long time, the reality is not so straightforward. One explanation for the origins for this formula is that the 7:1 ratio was based on the statistic that on average people lived to about 70, and dogs lived for about 10 years.***

Small dogs tend to live longer than bigger ones, and medium-sized dogs come somewhere in the middle. As a guideline, the American Veterinary Medical Association has proposed the following to calculate your dog's life in human years:

- The first year of your dog's life is equal to15 human years.
- Year 2 for your dog is about 9 years for a human.
- After that, each human year is approximately 5 years for your dog.

We are always looking for ways to not only extend the time we have with our dogs, but to improve the quality of that time. Canine gerontology is an active field of science studying the aging process in dogs and looking to delay aging and promote healthy longevity.

Sometimes, you might not know for certain the age of your dog who has been rescued from the local RSPCA shelter or rescue and rehoming centre in the United Kingdom (SPCA or pound in the U.S.). Or perhaps your cocker was found roaming the street with no identification and they have become a family member. Should you find yourself in this situation, your dog's teeth can offer a rough idea as to what their age might be. Of course, the quality of this estimate can vary from dog to dog depending on the prior dental care they have received, but the following chart is a good starting point:

Age	Teeth Condition
8 weeks	All baby teeth are present.
6-7 months	All white and clean adult teeth are present.
1-2 years	Teeth are not so white and back molars show some yellowing.
3-5 years	Signs of tartar and some wear.
5-10 years	Signs of wear, gum disease, some teeth might be loose.
10-15 years	Teeth are worn, heavy tartar build-up, some teeth are missing.

Signs of Aging

A vet can carry out an internal examination and various tests to determine the condition of joints, bones, and organs of an elderly dog. In addition, you can further approximate that your dog is in their senior years from their appearance, if they have:

- Cloudy eyes.
- Grey hair around their muzzle.
- Loose skin.
- Stiff legs.

While many dogs retain their youthful vigour for many years, at some point they will begin to slow down. Some of the signs of aging include:

- Tiring more easily and needing shorter walks.
- Gaining weight.
- Not being so interested in playing.
- Panting more.
- Finding it difficult to jump up on a chair or sofa and being reluctant to jump back down.

- Being slower or a little unstable when climbing stairs or walking on uneven surfaces.
- Beginning to lose their hearing.
- Losing their eyesight.
- Becoming more dependent on you and not wanting to be alone.
- Sleeping for more hours during the day.
- Getting colder and shivering.
- Losing control of their bowels or bladder.
- Needing to go outside more often than usual.
- Accidentally peeing in their sleep or occasionally leaking urine.
- Showing signs of dementia or confusion and wandering aimlessly during the day or night.
- Declining appetite or becoming very picky about food.
- Refusing to eat or throwing up their food.
- Having difficulty jumping into the car.

Caring for your Senior Cocker

TIP ***The best way you can help your senior cocker spaniel when they might not be feeling their best is by giving them even more love, attention, affection, and companionship than they usually crave. They need to know you are there for them, so never leave them alone for long periods. After all, they have been relying on you for their entire life, and as they get older what they need from you is being close to them.***

There are many other things you can do to help your cocker spaniel be more comfortable and well cared for during their senior years. Read on to find out what these are.

Feeding

While the most you can do for your dog at any age is provide them with the best diet possible, sometimes, your older spaniel will begin to have less of an appetite or little interest in the food they once enjoyed. This can be because they are tired of eating the same food, or because they do not need the same amount of food as their activity level has decreased.

Often, senior dogs carry too much weight as they have a slower metabolic rate and their activity level has dropped significantly, yet they are still eating the same amount of food. Always keep an eye on your cocker's weight as they age, as overweight dogs age faster and have many more health issues than lean dogs.

If your senior cocker tends to pack on the extra kilos, help them to enjoy their healthiest years in later life. By changing to a diet lower in calories, they will not have to struggle with obesity. If your dog seems to have lost interest in their food, switching to a more flavourful and aromatic home-cooked diet or adding a tasty topper can be more enticing and reignite their love of food.

Coat Care

Keeping your senior dog comfortable, also means keeping them clean, well-groomed and parasite free. If you have your cocker's coat clipped a little shorter, they will not have to put up with such frequent brushing to prevent painful mats.

Also, make sure your dog does not have to suffer from any sort of biting parasites that cause them the misery of constant chewing and scratching. If it is bath time, adjust the water so it is not too hot and dry their coat well afterwards, as your older dog might be more sensitive to temperature changes.

Comfort, Convenience and Warmth

Just like people, older dogs can find it more difficult to maintain a comfortable body temperature. Keeping your senior cocker warm during colder winter weather, might mean a cosy coat when they go outside, or even a sweater or T-shirt when inside. Make sure their crate or bed is not in a draughty location and perhaps raise it off the floor so they will not have to suffer cold draughts.

TIP ***Though most dogs are just fine with sleeping on the floor, if they do not already have a comfy, padded bed as they enter their senior years, they might seek out more comfort. An easy way to make them more comfortable when sleeping is to provide them with a soft, cosy bed that will keep them warm while alleviating joint pain and sore spots.***

Also, if your dog is used to sleeping on a chair, sofa, or jumping up on the bed, and they are having difficulties, an easy solution is to purchase a soft set of convenient foam stairs, so they can easily get to their favourite sleeping place.

Exercise

It is likely your senior cocker will have health conditions or other problems that limit how much they can exercise. The tendency is for them to slow down a little or rest more, but it is still important to keep them active, so they stay healthy. Here are some tips that apply to almost every senior dog:

- Keep their exercise regular and gentle. This will help your senior cocker to remain active and help their muscles and joints. Little and often is better as their joints become stiffer when they have not been used for a while. There are still plenty of exercises you can do with your older dog, all you need to remember is to go at their speed and stop if they look as if they are tired or struggling.

- Do not stop walking. Your dog might be unable to go on longer walks any longer, but they still need the chance to go outdoors each day to sniff, stretch their legs, and get some fresh air. Be certain that you keep to a short route in case your cocker becomes tired.

- Take the weather conditions into consideration if you are exercising your senior dog outdoors. Older spaniels do not cope as well with high or low temperatures. You might need to walk during the cooler times of day if it is hot or buy them a dog coat for when it is cold.
- If your dog has problems with their senses, try to stick to familiar routes and places. Like people, as your cocker spaniel get older, they could start to lose their sight and hearing. Walking somewhere that is familiar to them will stop them from becoming anxious and confused.
- If your cocker's sight or hearing is deteriorating, sudden movements such as cyclists apparently coming from nowhere can take them by surprise and be extremely stressful. So, it pays to be aware of your surroundings. When you see something your dog might not have spotted, help them by petting and reassuring them.
- Always go at your cocker's pace. Never rush them or make them exercise for longer than they can. If they lie down on a walk, they need to rest.
- Your senior dog will benefit from indoor exercises. If it is too hot or cold outside, it is a good idea to provide some indoor exercise sessions until the weather is more suitable for them. Puzzle toys and indoor games are a wonderful way to keep your aging dog happy and for you to enjoy quality time together.

- If your cocker enjoys swimming, this can prove to be beneficial to them as it puts far less strain on sore joints. As soon as they come out of the water, remember to dry them thoroughly so they do not get cold and only let them swim if it is safe to do so. Be careful where you take them swimming as pools or lakes can have high or steep sides that an older dog could struggle with.
- Scent games – if their sense of smell is good, your cocker will benefit from scent games regardless of their age. It is an excellent way to keep both their body and brain in good condition.
- Playing – even though their pace might have slowed down, your spaniel will still enjoy playing. Most dogs never seem to lose their fun-loving puppy nature and will still enjoy playing with you, even when

they get older, you can still play some of their favourite games with them. Try to make the games a little gentler so they do not try to jump or twist for toys.

- Socialising – dogs are social animals. While they might not be able to keep up with younger dogs and often get frustrated by puppy antics, they will still enjoy seeing dogs their own age who they get on with, even if they do not end up playing.
- Tricks – contrary to popular belief, old dogs can still learn new tricks. Training is a marvellous way to keep your older spaniel's mind active. They will enjoy every opportunity to get their brain working.

Always check with your vet that the level of exercise they are getting is all right and is not going to cause them any problems. Ask your vet if you notice your dog having problems getting around or they do not appear to enjoy exercising anymore. There might be things your vet can do to improve their quality of life and ease any aches and pains that are preventing your cocker from getting around.

Vet Check-ups

As your cocker ages (pictured), they might begin to experience a weakened immune system, or other conditions inherent in the aging process. To know how well your dog is doing medically, it is highly recommended to increase vet visits, so any changes that might cause problems can be detected early on.

Rather than a yearly check-up at the vet's, regular health check-ups every six months or more are recommended for senior dogs. More frequent visits can help diagnose problems and provide solutions that will help your dog live their best senior life.

Toilet Breaks

As you can imagine, when your cocker spaniel enters their senior years, their ability to hold their bowels and bladder might begin to be compromised. Always be kind and do not shame them if accidents start to occur, as they will probably already be feeling bad enough about it.

Helping them could be as simple as taking them outside much more frequently—the way you did when they were a puppy—and/or if possible, providing a toilet patch for them if they cannot easily get themselves outside quickly enough when nature calls.

Dealing with Diminished Eyesight

Even though there can be several different reasons for your cocker having diminished eyesight, as they become senior-aged most dogs will suffer from cataracts, macular degeneration, and glaucoma.

The first signs that your spaniel is losing their eyesight could be so subtle that you may not notice, as dogs are used to negotiating their usual surroundings by smell alone. You might notice a reluctance to jump on or off their favourite chair under low light conditions or to be outside for the last walk at night when it is dark.

As their eyesight deteriorates, they could begin to bump into things or have difficulty finding their toys. They may even begin to act up in an uncharacteristically aggressive or defensive manner when startled by another dog or person, as their loss of eyesight is making them feel vulnerable. Most likely, they will want to stay closer to their favourite person. If your cocker seems to be stubbornly ignoring hand signals, this can be a cue that they cannot see what you are showing them.

Although dogs do adapt amazingly well to losing their eyesight, here is how you can help them continue to safely navigate their home surroundings:

- Keep all the furniture in the same place.
- Do not leave random items laying on the floor.
- Block off danger areas, such as stairs they might fall down.
- Keep all passageways where they might walk clear of debris.
- Keep their crate and/or bed in the same location.
- Remove any sharp or hazardous objects they might walk into.
- Keep their bowls in the same place.
- Use voice cues to announce your approach.
- Use a heavier step so they feel the approaching vibration.

Above all, you need to maintain patience and understanding and always try to imagine what it must be like for your dog who is losing or has lost their eyesight.

Dealing with Diminished Hearing

In an aging cocker spaniel, hearing loss is often attributable to slowly degenerating changes in the nerves inside their ears. Like failing eyesight, diminished hearing is typically a slow process that is not noticed straight away. Some of the symptoms of hearing loss include:

- Ignoring your voice commands.
- Not coming when called.
- Being unresponsive to squeaky toys.
- No longer reacting to fireworks.
- Not reacting to noisy neighbours.
- No longer responding to a dog barking in the distance.
- Sleeping more soundly.
- Not hearing the key in the door when you return.

There are some workarounds to help your cocker who is losing their hearing understand what you are asking of them. For example, if your dog still has their eyesight, communication can easily be carried out with hand signals alone.

Another alternative to get the attention of your dog with hearing loss is stamping your foot on the floor. You can also teach them to come when they hear a loud whistle, a clicker, or loud hand clapping.

Just as a dog that is losing their eyesight can be startled by other dogs or people suddenly appearing, the same can happen for a dog who has compromised hearing when someone or something suddenly appears without any sound to warn them.

TIP ***Extra caution needs to be practised when walking your dog who has lost their hearing as they will be unable to hear cyclists, vehicles, or other dangers approaching. Keep your cocker on lead when outside, so you can be certain their senior years can be as safe and stress-free as possible.***

Thankfully, when your dog begins to lose their eyesight and hearing, they usually retain their strongest sense, their smell, which they rely on to find their way and navigate their surroundings.

Dealing with Canine Dementia

As your cocker spaniel ages, they might begin to show changes in brain function, which normally display as an unsteadiness or aimless wandering—dementia. This type of behaviour often occurs during the night, especially if they are feeling pain, are confused, and disoriented. If this is happening to your dog, sit with them until they relax and fall asleep again, and make sure they cannot accidentally fall down the stairs or harm themselves in any way. Take some time to block off danger areas, so your confused dog will be safe from injury.

Mobility aids for your senior cocker

If, for any reason, your dog's activity is being affected by their mobility, it is still important to keep them as active as possible and keep a watchful eye on their quality of life.

There are plenty of things that can help so speak with your vet to see what options are available.

- To keep their minds healthy and active, give them lots of brain games.
- Ask your vet about hydrotherapy, physiotherapy, or massage techniques that could help them.
- It is often difficult to physically help a larger senior dog who is struggling because of their size. You might wish to consider buying a support harness or sling for when they go for a walk.
- To help them get up steps to and from the house/garden or into the car, you could consider using ramps around the home.
- Sometimes, tiles and wood flooring can be quite slippery for our four-legged friends, especially if they are not as steady on their feet as they used to be. To make it easier for them to walk on, you could consider putting down a rug or mat.
- If they are still able to walk but just not very far, take them on shorter, flatter walking routes to allow them to go outside and stretch their legs. You might consider driving them to a park they used to enjoy walking to so they can still sniff and walk around it.

Remember, older dogs who struggle to get around can start to grow longer nails as they are not wearing them down by walking. It is necessary to check them regularly and have them trimmed when they need it.

Euthanasia

As difficult as it can be, the final act of kindness you can offer your cocker if they are suffering from old age or debilitating injury that is seriously compromising their quality of life, is to let them pass peacefully into the next world.

FACT ***Euthanasia is a painless, peaceful, and humane way of providing a gentle death to a dog who is suffering from chronic pain, incurable illness, or the ravages of old age. While this decision can truly be one of the hardest you ever have to make, it is also the kindest thing you can do if your cocker is suffering.***

If it is unclear whether the time is right to end your cocker spaniel's suffering, it would be helpful to keep a diary or daily log where you note how much of your dog's daily life is difficult for them. Your veterinarian should also be able to help with this decision, as regular check-ups will determine whether or how much your dog is in pain.

Often, we cannot bear the thought of losing our canine friend and might delay letting them peacefully pass because we love them so much. However, you must be strong for your spaniel, and act in their best interests no matter how much it saddens you, because in the end your do not want to prolong their suffering.

Euthanasia is a procedure that is carried out by your dog's vet, either at their surgery or for those who offer house calls, in the comfort of your home. Every veterinarian will have received special training to perform euthanasia. When the time comes, this is usually a two-step process. First, your veterinarian injects your dog with a sedative to make them sleepy, calm, and comfortable. Second, a special drug is injected that will peacefully stop your cocker's heart.

These drugs work in such a way that your dog will not be aware that their life is transitioning towards a peaceful end. What they feel is very similar to what people experience when falling asleep under anaesthesia during a surgical procedure.

Once the second stage drug has been injected, the entire process takes about 10 to 20 seconds, at which time your vet will check to make certain your dog's heart has stopped.

Memorials

There are many ways to honour the passing of your cocker spaniel, as each furry friend is uniquely special to their owners. For instance, you and your family might wish to have your companion cremated and preserve their ashes in a special urn or sprinkle them along your dog's favourite walk, or across the lake where they loved to swim.

Perhaps you want to have a special marker, photo bereavement, photo engraved Rainbow Bridge poem, or wooden plaque created in honour of your passed friend. Another option would be to always keep the memory of your dog close to you by having a DNA remembrance pendant or bracelet designed.

You might also choose a beautiful set of memorial wind chimes to remind you of your beloved cocker every time you hear the chimes ring, and there are now even companies that will turn the ashes into a diamond that lasts forever.

Grieving a Lost Friend

Some people do not fully recognise the extent of the terrible grief involved in losing a beloved canine companion, especially if they have not experienced this loss themselves. While some friends might give you pitying looks and attempt to cheer you up, if they have never lost a dog, they could be secretly thinking that you are making too much fuss over 'just a dog'.

However, for many people the loss of their cherished cocker spaniel is so painful they decide never to share their lives with another dog, because they cannot bear the thought of going through the intense pain of loss again.

When your faithful furry friend has passed on, it is normal to feel terribly sad, tearful, and depressed as this kind of loss feels as acute as the loss of a human friend or life partner. The grieving process can take some time to overcome, and some people never totally recover.

After the loss of your family cocker, you need to take care of yourself by making certain you keep eating and getting regular sleep, even though you might feel a sense of loneliness. Losing your beloved dog is a serious shock to the system, which can also affect concentration and the ability to find joy or willingness to participate in other activities that are part of daily life. During this early grieving time, take extra care while driving or performing tasks that require concentration as you might often find yourself distracted.

Many people do not wait long enough before attempting to replace their lost cocker and immediately go to a shelter to rescue a deserving dog. While this might help to distract from the grieving process, it is not fair to the new member of your family. Bringing a new dog into a grieving home can create behavioural problems for the new pet, who will be faced with learning all about their new home while also dealing with the family's unstable, sad energy.

TIP ***If there are other dogs or pets in the home, they will also grieve the loss of a companion, and could display this by acting depressed, being off their food or showing little interest in play or games. You need to guide your other pets through this grieving process by keeping them busy and interested, taking them for extra walks and spending more time with them.***

It is better to take the time to properly grieve by waiting a minimum of 3 to 6 months to allow everyone in the family to feel happier and more stable before deciding on sharing your home with another dog. Of course, the grieving process is different for everyone, and each person knows when the time is right to consider another canine companion.

Rainbow Bridge

In addition, there are support groups, such as Rainbow Bridge—a grief support community, to help you and your family through this painful period of loss and grief.

Anyone who has ever felt the intense, devastating grief of losing a much-loved pet will more than likely have heard of the *Rainbow Bridge*, which is a reference to a comforting belief that there is a heaven or other worldly place that pets cross over to at the end of their life.

According to the poems that have been anonymously written about Rainbow Bridge, this is a warm, lush green meadow where there is always fresh food and water, the sun shines all day and healthy pets play with one another while they wait for their human family to join them.

While you are grieving an adored pet who spent many happy years with you, the thought that they are in a beautiful place where they are well fed, healthy, and happy while they wait for you to be reunited with them can offer much needed comfort as described in the following poem.

Just this side of heaven is a place called Rainbow Bridge.

When an animal dies that has been especially close to someone here, that pet goes to Rainbow Bridge. There are meadows and hills for all of our special friends so they can run and play together. There is plenty of food, water and sunshine, and our friends are warm and comfortable.

All the animals who had been ill and old are restored to health and vigour. Those who were hurt or maimed are made whole and strong again, just as we remember them in our dreams of days and times gone by. The animals are happy and content, except for one small thing; they each miss someone very special to them, who had to be left behind.

They all run and play together, but the day comes when one suddenly stops and looks into the distance. His bright eyes are intent. His eager body quivers. Suddenly he begins to run from the group, flying over the green grass, his legs carrying him faster and faster.

You have been spotted, and when you and your special friend finally meet, you cling together in joyous reunion, never to be parted again. The happy kisses rain upon your face; your hands again caress the beloved head, and you look once more into the trusting eyes of your pet, so long gone from your life but never absent from your heart.

Then you cross Rainbow Bridge together...

Author unknown

18. Holidays as a Dog Owner

'No matter how little money and how few possessions
you own, having a dog makes you rich.'
~ Louis Sabin ~

Taking your dog with you

Your cocker does not need to stay at home if you are going on holiday. In fact, your dog can potentially make a great travel companion. With so many dog-friendly hotels and accommodation choices in the world, it is easy to check out the basics of travelling with your dog, and the world is your oyster. The whole process is much easier if you prepare everything well in advance. Accommodation, travel arrangements, and paperwork can all be organised many months before you go, which means less stress and more fun for both of you.

Of course, you might not be planning on travelling abroad, but staying somewhere closer to home, in which case things are even easier. Keeping a few simple things in mind will really increase the ease of taking your cocker on holiday. Get your pen ready and make sure you have thought about everything in the following list:

Cover the basics – No matter how you choose to travel, there are a few essential things to always bear in mind. Your cocker can lose a considerable amount of body fluids through panting, so take a bowl and many bottles of water with you to help them stay normally hydrated. Do not forget to pack plenty of plastic bags for when your dog goes to the toilet.

Visit your vet a few months before travelling with your dog – This is especially true for holidays abroad. Make sure you discuss your travel plans with your vet around 6 months in advance to give you plenty of time to comply with any extra requirements.

TIP ***Your dog's vaccinations will need to be up to date and there can also be specific vaccination requirements for the country you are visiting. It is also likely that certificates might need to be issued, depending on where you are travelling.***

Dog insurance – Look for a policy that covers emergencies in the likelihood that your dog might need vet care on your trip abroad. Some policies even contribute to the cost of a cancelled holiday or kennel fees, if it is you who is hospitalised.

Search for the nearest vet to your holiday stay – A nearby vet might be handy and can help with many health enquiries, big or small. Make sure you note down the address and contact details of the closest veterinary practice before you travel with your dog abroad.

Consider the current life stage and health condition of your cocker spaniel – You might want to share your best times with your four-legged family member, but sometimes it is a good idea for them to skip on some of the fun stuff, especially when travelling on a plane. If your dog is under 3 months old, a senior, pregnant or ill, they are likely to have difficulties coping with a long journey. When in doubt, always check with your vet for advice.

Accommodation tips – Whether you are holidaying with your dog at home or abroad, there are many dog-friendly hotels and accommodation options to suit every taste and budget. Your dog might also enjoy dog-training holidays, which provide the opportunity to experience canine activities and sports with other dog lovers under the guidance of a qualified trainer. Be sure your accommodation is dog-friendly, and if you are staying at someone else's home, check ahead about the toilet facilities for your dog. Consider the possible presence of other pets—either during travel or at your destination—who might affect your cocker's behaviour. For example, will your dog want to chase the B&B owner's cat, or bark at the dogs they are travelling with?

Aeroplane travel (pictured) – Make sure your airline is aware you will be bringing your dog on the trip. Consult them about carrier size and requirements, which may differ according to your spaniel's height and weight. This will give you peace of mind and help you avoid a last-minute rush. Some companies will not allow dogs to travel in the cabin with you, so make sure you are prepared to be separated from your dog for the duration of the journey. It is always a good idea to include a feeding schedule note and any other relevant information just in case your dog does not make it to your destination at the same time as you.

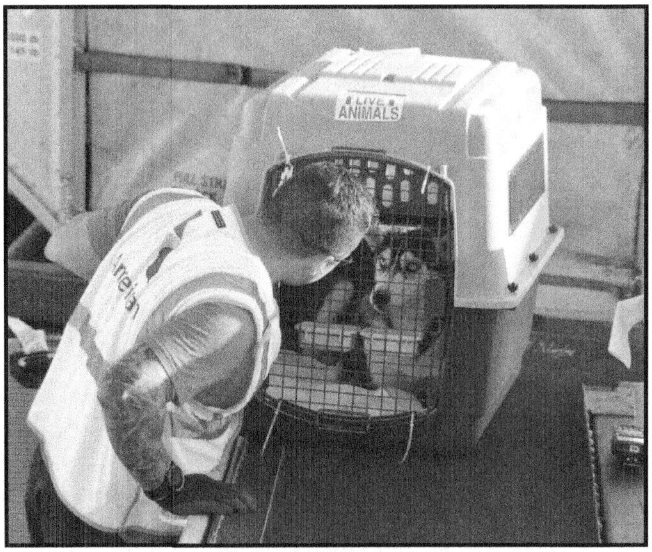

If your dog is not already used to a carrier, take several weeks to introduce them to it before your trip. Leave it open and filled with soft bedding and an occasional hidden treat. Do not forget to put a small tag on your dog's collar showing the address at your destination in case you are separated for some reason.

Leaving your cocker behind

Of course, while it would be wonderful if we could take our favourite furry friends with us on every holiday adventure, this is not always possible. Not all dogs are completely suited to travel. For example, if they are senior, ill, or have a history of anxiety during confinement or travel, you should consider leaving them at home. There are several options to consider when you cannot take your cocker on holiday with you, including:

- Find a trustworthy friend or neighbour who might agree to look after your dog. Having their owner absent or a change in their routine can be stressful for your cocker. Usually, the best option is to have a friend, relative or neighbour look after your dog in your home. This allows you to keep things as familiar and stress-free as possible for your spaniel. Also, leaving your furry friend with someone you know and trust will provide additional peace of mind while you are away.
- Locate a professional pet sitter who is available on the dates you are travelling. When you go away, a dog sitter is an alternative option to a boarding kennel. The dog sitter will either stay in your home with your dog while you are away, or some will take your dog to their home. It is a good idea to ask for recommendations from other dog owners in your area when looking for a dog sitter.
- Finding a suitable dog sitter can be a daunting task, as you need to be sure your cocker and your property are looked after properly. In the United Kingdom, the National Association of Registered Pet Sitters can give you a list of their members.

Here is a checklist of questions to ask your potential dog sitter and some things to consider:

- If you are confident they can care of your cocker's needs, meet them before employing them.
- In the U.K., you can check the criminal record of someone applying for the position. This is known as getting a Disclosure and Barring Service (DBS) check. In the U.S., you can see a copy of their police check or Criminal Records Bureau certificate to check that they have no criminal background.
- Having introductory sessions with your cocker spaniel's new carer will help them settle in ready for when you are on holiday.
- Decide whether you would prefer the dog sitter to come to your house, or whether to take your dog to their home.
- When you have found a dog sitter, make sure they are reputable by asking for reviews or references from people in your area.

- Ask them for proof of insurance, including third-party, and preferably a qualification such as dog first aid.
- If you plan to take your dog to the sitter's house, check whether they have their own dog or are looking for after other dogs. If so, it is a good idea for your cocker to meet the other dogs on neutral ground before being in the home with them.
- Ask how the dog sitter is going to ensure the security of your home.
- Be certain to exchange details regarding vets and insurance in case your dog needs medical assistance while you are away.
- Decide whether you want regular updates on your cocker, and who to contact in the event of an emergency.
- Most dog sitters will ask you to sign a contract stating what they will and will not do in your home.

Finding a certified boarding kennel that has space to accommodate your dog is another possibility.

Whichever of the above options you decide to go for, ask friends and fellow dog owners if they can recommend someone specific and do a bit of research to make sure it is the right choice for your cocker spaniel. So, call them and ask the following questions:

- How much do they charge?
- What experience do they have?
- Are they available on the dates you are travelling?
- Are they professional dog trainers?
- Will they come to you, or should your cocker spaniel go to them?

Remember, locating a professional dog sitter usually requires considerable advance notice because they are trained and trusted professionals who are often booked well ahead on major holidays.

TIP ***Normally, the least stressful situation for your dog is to have a professional live with them in their usual home so their routine is not altered, and they can enjoy walks in their familiar neighbourhood. It could be beneficial to have someone living in your home while you are away as this will deter possible break-ins.***

Whether choosing option 1 or 2, if your dog is to remain in their own home, you will need to show your friend or professional sitter around the house and tell them about any household quirks or concerns and your cocker's usual daily routines and feeding schedules. You will also need to provide the emergency veterinarian contact details so they can get in touch with them should the need arise.

Finding a certified boarding kennel that can accommodate your dog on the dates required usually requires advance booking. For peace of mind, visit the kennel to ensure it is clean, well run and that there will be the opportunity for your dog to socialise, play and interact with other dogs and go for several walks each day.

Extra Expenses – While a close friend might look after your dog for free, when opting to send your cocker to a kennel or hire a professional to care for them, there will be extra expenses involved.

Professional sitter costs vary depending on location, but on average fees for dog sitting usually range in price between £20 and £27 per night in the U.K. and $20 and $40 in the U.S.

Boarding kennel costs again vary depending on what is included and their location. On average, fees for overnight dog boarding may range in price between £15 and £20 in the U.K. and in the U.S., they range from $30 to $50.

TIP ***To avoid stressful last-minute situations, find a reliable professional or friend to care for your dog and get them acquainted well in advance of your trip.***

19. Breeding

'Once you have a wonderful dog,

a life without one is a life diminished.'

~ Dean Koontz ~

Anyone who has owned a female dog has usually considered whether to allow them to have a litter of puppies before having them spayed.

FACT ***There are many myths citing changes in personality or loss of happiness and contentment associated with not allowing a female dog to give birth. These are all untrue. Your female cocker spaniel will live just as happily without having birthed puppies, and often longer, too.***

Whatever your decision on the subject is, the following pages outline what is involved in the breeding process and what to expect.

Female Heat

Female cockers normally come into their first heat—oestrus—at approximately six months old, but this is not always the case. Depending on the dog, this can occur as late as 18 to 24 months.

Female breeding cycles

There are four periods in a female cocker's breeding cycle:

1. **Proestrus** – The first signs of heat start to appear, comprising swelling of the vulva and bloody vaginal discharge, which attracts males and lasts approximately 9 days—with a range of 2 to 22 days. Their oestrogen level rises, and their body prepares for ovulation. During this stage, the female will not permit males to breed.

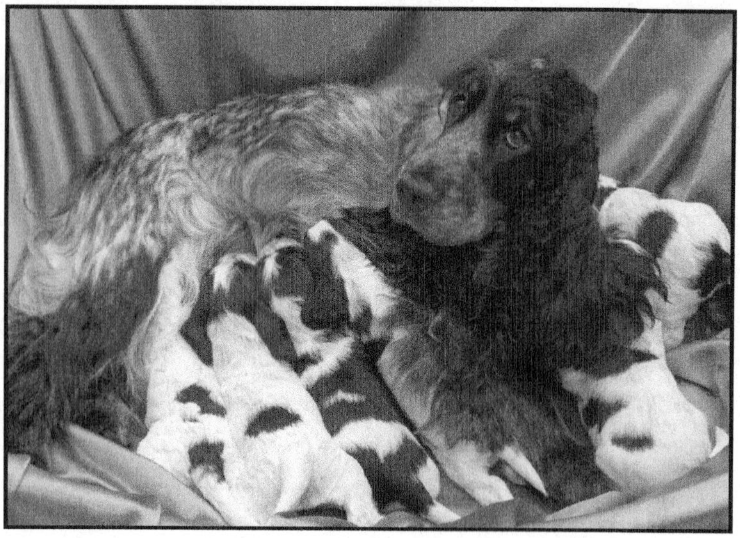

2. **Oestrus** – Lasting approximately 9 days, the female is fertile and will accept the male for breeding. This is when your cocker will become pregnant. You might see them flagging—holding their tail to the side—or showing lordosis. This is when they arch their back and raise their hind end and vulva up for the male.
3. **Dioestrus** – This is a 60 to 90-day period when the progesterone hormone takes control of your female spaniel's reproductive tract, and they aggressively prevent mating. During this time, they can show signs of a false pregnancy, even though they might not have conceived.
4. **Anoestrus** – No sexual activity takes place during this period, which lasts between 3 and 4 months. This is the inactive period until the start of the next cycle.

Behaviour during heat

If your female cocker is experiencing a heat cycle they can urinate more frequently or begin to mark objects when out on a walk or even in the home by peeing on them. This signals to prospective mates that they are ready to reproduce as their urine contains hormones and pheromones that are highly attractive to males. Other changes in behaviour might include:

- Being off their food or becoming hungrier.
- Becoming more affectionate.
- Paying more attention to male dogs.
- Tail tucking or sitting down when another dog approaches.
- Running away from male dogs.
- Becoming lazier.
- Lifting their leg when urinating or seeing a male dog.

How often?

On average, female cockers have a heat cycle twice a year. This will continue every year until your female spaniel dies or they are spayed.

Hormonal changes

During the first days of your female cocker's heat cycle there will be a significant increase in their oestrogen hormone. This causes swelling of your dog's vulva and creates the bloody discharge. Another hormonal change is the sudden surge of lutein, which is a heat-regulating hormone that causes ovulation. Finally, there is the production of corpus luteum to promote and maintain pregnancy, followed by an increase in progesterone, which makes the lining of your dog's uterus receptive for implantation.

What to be aware of during a heat cycle

While you can still take them out for their daily walks, they must always be kept securely on lead, as they might try to escape at any time and can also display aggression towards other dogs.

TIP ***If you decide not to have your female dog spayed to prevent heat cycles, you need to be extra vigilant during this time, because a dog in heat has only one thing on their mind—finding a mate. To keep the bloody mess to a minimum, your cocker will need to wear dog nappies for 1 to 3 weeks during each heat cycle.***

You might also have to fight off male dogs who have a strong urge to mate with her. The following steps can help to prevent an unwanted pregnancy:

- Always supervise your female cocker very closely.
- Remember that the urge to mate is so strong, they could do whatever it takes to make that happen.
- If you cannot watch her, place her in a secure crate.
- Keep her separated from all intact male dogs.
- Keep all windows and doors securely closed—a male dog can smell the scent of a female in heat over a mile away.

If your female cocker spaniel accidentally mates with an intact male during their heat cycle, an emergency consultation is in order with your vet who can provide a morning after injection that will terminate an unwanted pregnancy.

Pregnancy

The ideal age for a female pregnancy will depend on their size and breed and at what age they may reach sexual maturity. While they can get pregnant during their very first heat cycle (which can be anywhere between 4 and 12 months), this is not recommended, as they will still be growing herself. It is recommended that a female is not considered for producing their first litter of puppies until they have experienced their second or third heat cycle.

Is my dog pregnant?

There are several methods for determining whether your female cocker is pregnant, all of which require a visit to the veterinarian, including:

Palpation – Approximately 30 days after you suspect your female spaniel is pregnant, the veterinarian can perform an abdominal palpation. If they are pregnant, your vet will feel fluid-filled sacs surrounding the foetus the size of grapes or small golf balls. Timing of this manual test is critical, as the sacs begin to lose their distinctive shape after one month of pregnancy.

Blood test – When testing the blood at approximately 25 to 30 days after pregnancy is suspected, the hormone levels can be measured. If the female is producing the hormone 'relaxin', this indicates that they are pregnant as this hormone is only produced during pregnancy.

Ultrasound – Between 25 to 35 days of suspected pregnancy, your cocker's vet can perform an ultrasound to detect foetal heartbeats. This gives an estimate of how many puppies your female is carrying.

X-ray – Taking your cocker to the veterinarian for an x-ray is an effective way to determine if they are pregnant. It needs to be carried out at 55 or more days of suspected pregnancy, as before that time their skeletons cannot be seen on x-ray. This method gives an accurate number of expected puppies.

TIP ***To produce the healthiest offspring, you need to check that your female cocker is healthy before the breeding process begins. This is easily accomplished with a pre-natal check-up at your vet's, where they can undergo a pre-breeding examination that includes testing for parasites and ensuring vaccines are up to date.***

Though some female cockers experience morning sickness during the initial days of pregnancy and lose their appetite for a few days, there are other signs to watch for, including:

- Swollen stomach.
- Enlarged mammary glands.
- Discharge of milk.
- Increased appetite.
- Increase in weight.
- Vomiting.
- Tiredness.
- Disinterest in exercising.
- Sleeping more.
- Depression.
- Restlessness.
- Becoming more affectionate or clingy.
- Hoarding and being protective of toys.
- Moving nesting material to create a den.
- Digging to create a nest.
- Acting more aggressive or irritable.
- Possible false labour contractions.

A canine pregnancy lasts approximately 63 days, and your cocker will go into labour within 56 to 66 days of becoming pregnant. Immediately upon noticing signs of pregnancy, take your dog to their veterinarian to confirm the pregnancy and to receive instructions for their proper feeding and care.

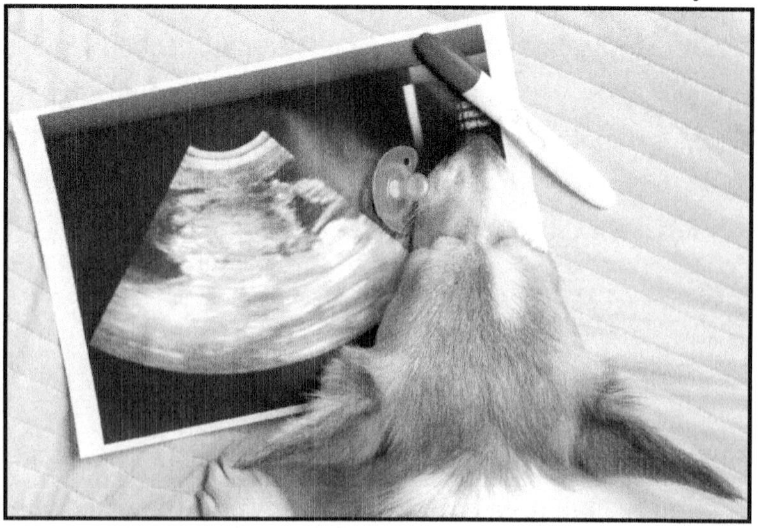

At around the 30-day mark, your vet might recommend increasing their food intake or adding an egg to your cocker spaniel's meals and switching to puppy kibble, which is higher in protein. As your dog becomes heavier with the puppies, they will lose interest in exercising and their other normal activities and need to sleep more.

When the time for birthing is drawing near, they start to display nesting characteristics, where they search for a warm and safe place to give birth. The breeder can help by providing a nesting box and your cocker will probably want to take things into the box to make it comfortable, such as towels or even a stuffed toy that they will begin to mother.

When they are close to whelping, they could completely lose their appetite and show distress by pacing, panting, and appearing uncomfortable. When the birthing time is near, their temperature needs to be checked, and should be about 37.9 to 38.2o C (100.2 to 100.8o F).

When their temperature drops to 36.7 to 37.4o C (98 to 99.4o F), the puppies will usually be born within 24 hours. If at all worried about the birthing process, you should take your mother dog immediately to their veterinarian.

If all goes well at home, within 5-6 hours of the last puppy's birth, you should take the mother and their puppies to their vet for a check-up. The vet will then make sure they have birthed all their puppies and placentas and that the puppies are all healthy.

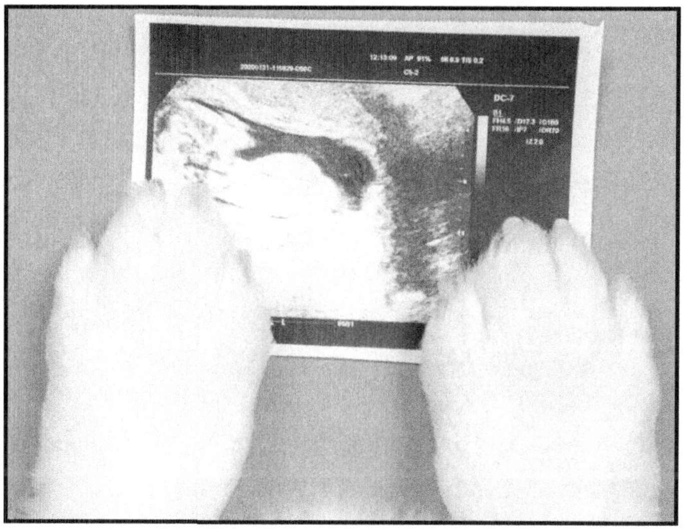

A false, pseudo or phantom pregnancy is a common condition that usually occurs between 4 and 9 weeks after a heat cycle. It simply means your non-spayed female is mimicking the behavioural and physical signs of carrying a litter of puppies as listed above.

The reason why your non-spayed cocker might experience a false pregnancy is because after your dog is old enough to be in a heat cycle, her ovaries produce hormones to prepare her body for pregnancy even if she has not been mated. These symptoms will usually subside on their own within a few weeks without any need for intervention.

Eclampsia

Eclampsia—hypocalcaemia or puerperal tetany—occurs in nursing mothers and is an emergency medical condition associated with a life-threatening drop in blood calcium levels. Mostly, eclampsia happens when the puppies are one to four weeks old, and the mother is producing the most milk.

Often, the cause of eclampsia is not found, but can be due to:

- Excessive loss of calcium from the mother to the developing foetal skeletons.
- Calcium supplementation during pregnancy.
- Producing milk after birth.
- Not receiving a balanced, premium growth and development diet while pregnant and nursing.
- A hormonal problem with the parathyroid gland.

Signs the mother could be suffering from eclampsia include:

- Panting.
- Muscle spasms with arched back and rigid legs.
- Fever.
- Increased heart rate.
- Rubbing their face on the ground.
- Agitation and whining.
- Uncoordinated gait.
- Weakness.
- Rigid muscles.
- Seizures.

Treatment frequently requires oral or intravenous calcium supplementation, anti-seizure medication, and cooling the body to reduce fever. While the mother is being treated, the puppies will need to be hand fed with a puppy formula and your vet might suggest earlier weaning to reduce the mother's stress.

FACT ***Although eclampsia is a serious condition that, if left untreated, can lead to coma and death. It can be diagnosed using a simple blood test, and with prompt veterinary intervention it can be easily cured. You must contact your veterinarian immediately if you think the mother is in trouble as eclampsia is a true medical emergency.***

When it comes to preventing eclampsia, calcium supplementation or feeding cottage cheese to pregnant and nursing dogs is normally not recommended, unless under the guidance of your vet. During pregnancy or nursing, excessive calcium intake can suppress parathyroid hormone production and increases the risk of developing low blood calcium levels or eclampsia. Your vet will advise you whether your dog needs supplementation. Your pregnant cocker should eat a high-quality diet that is rich in essential vitamins and minerals and formulated for pregnant and nursing mothers.

Pyometra

This is a serious and life-threatening infection of the uterus that occurs because of changes in your female cocker's reproductive tract during the heat cycle. The lining of the uterus thickens in preparation for becoming pregnant and if no pregnancy occurs during several cycles, the lining continues to thicken. Eventually, fluid secreting cysts can begin to form, which then create an ideal breeding ground for bacteria to grow.

When this happens—2 to 8 weeks after the last heat cycle—your female's uterus becomes inflamed and distended with bacteria and pus that can discharge—termed 'open pyometra'—from the uterus and through the vagina where it might be noticeable on their skin or hair under the tail.

If the pus is not able to drain to the outside—termed 'closed pyometra'—their abdomen will distend, and the toxins released from the bacteria will enter the bloodstream. These toxins can quickly affect your cocker and they can rapidly become very ill. If your cocker spaniel is suffering from pyometra, they will exhibit the following symptoms:

- Increased water consumption.
- Increased urination.

- Slight vaginal discharge.
- Distended and painful abdomen.
- Vomiting.
- Diarrhoea.
- Listlessness.
- Depression.

Treatment involves surgical removal of the infected uterus and ovaries by performing an ovariohysterectomy—spaying. Although hospitalisation can be required for a longer period than a routine spaying procedure, prognosis for recovery is quite high when diagnosed during the early stages. Without prompt treatment, the chances for recovery are considered very low, as the toxic effects created by the bacteria are usually fatal.

Mastitis

Canine mastitis is not a common breast infection but occurs within a few weeks of giving birth. This can be caused by puppies scratching with their claws, weaning the puppies too soon, or through some other form of bacterial or fungal infection.

If your nursing cocker suffers from painful mastitis they will present symptoms that include:

- Loss of appetite and listlessness.
- Fever.
- Refusing to allow puppies to nurse.
- Hard, almost black nipple segments.
- Red, dark, hot, or painful nipples.
- Irritation when the nipples are touched.
- Inflamed and swollen mammary glands.

Diagnosis includes blood work, and depending on the severity of the condition, antibiotics and pain medications will be prescribed. Other care includes applying warm compresses and expressing milk from the infected gland by hand every six hours to encourage blood flow and help diminish swelling and discomfort.

Early intervention can result in the affected gland returning to normal within several weeks. In other cases, the gland may be permanently damaged and unable to produce milk. Finally, should a system-wide infection take hold, even with aggressive treatment, it is possible the female will die.

Female Dog Spaying

Spaying is the common term used to describe the surgical procedure ovariohysterectomy. This is when the ovaries and uterus are completely removed to sterilise your female cocker (pictured). Some vets now perform an ovariectomy where they only remove the ovaries.

FACT ***There are many factors to consider when determining the best time to spay your cocker puppy, including health and behavioural factors, together with your dog's environment. Consult your vet to determine the optimal time to spay your dog.***

What's Involved?

Your veterinarian will examine your cocker and usually perform pre-anaesthetic blood tests. If everything is all right, your dog will be anaesthetised. Most dogs need an intravenous catheter to administer the anaesthetic and provide fluid therapy during the surgery. After your spaniel has been anaesthetised, a breathing tube is placed in their trachea—windpipe. This allows oxygen and gas anaesthetic to be delivered directly into their lungs. The surgery comprises making an incision just below the umbilicus—belly button—before removing the ovaries and uterus, or just the ovaries, depending on your vet's technique. Most vets use absorbable sutures, which means you do not have to return to have them removed.

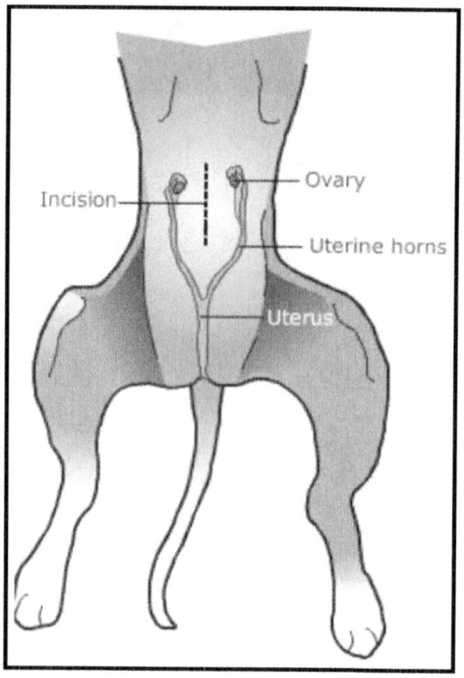

If all goes well, your cocker will usually be able to return home the same day or the following day.

While the spaying process for a female dog is more invasive than neutering a male dog and takes a little longer to heal, the after-surgery protocol is much the same as it is for a male dog (see 'After Surgery' below).

Pros and Cons

There are both advantages and disadvantages to be considered when thinking about spaying your cocker spaniel.

Potential advantages of the operation include:

- Prevents accidental pregnancies.
- Reduces aggression or irritability.
- Eliminates the desire to search for a mate.
- Reduces the risk of mammary cancer.
- Eliminates the hormone fluctuations that cause false pregnancies after the heat cycle.
- Dogs spayed before their first heat have less than 0.5 % chance of developing mammary tumours.
- Reduces the risk of pyometra.
- Eradicates the need to protect the female from males.
- Dispenses with the mess and odour involved in the heat cycle.

Potential disadvantages for choosing to not have your female dog spayed include:

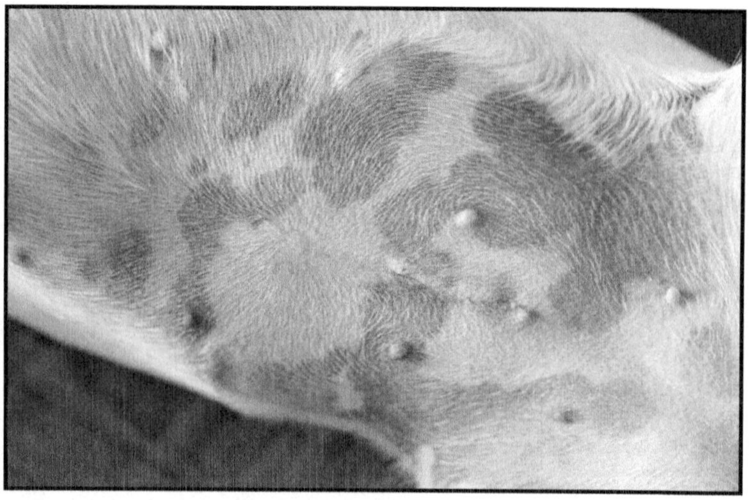

- Increases their lifespan.
- Spaying before maturity is associated with increased risk of certain behaviour, such as noise phobia.
- Increased risk of hemangiosarcoma.
- Possible weight gain due to metabolism rate reduction.
- Increased risk of hypothyroidism.

Note: Spaying does not create a change in personality, intelligence, playfulness, or affection.

Male Dog Neutering

It is always important to discuss the decision with your vet because exact timings are based on several distinct factors, such as weight, behaviour, health conditions, size, etc.

FACT ***Male dog neutering—or castration—is an operation to remove your cocker's testicles, after which your dog will no longer be able to father puppies. Dogs should not be neutered until they are at least 6-9 months old.***

What is Involved

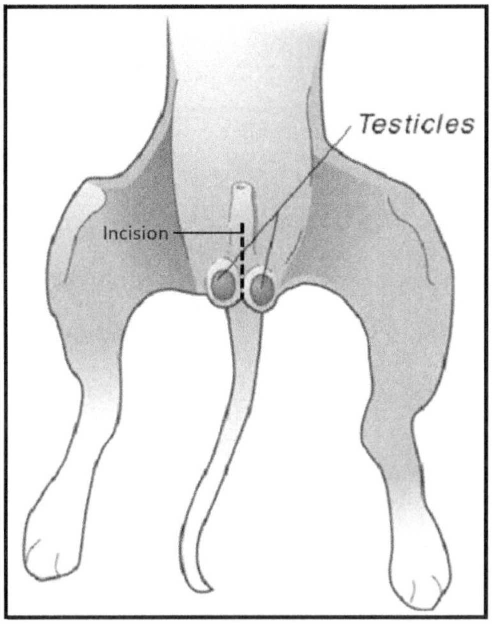

This simple, routine surgical procedure is conducted by your vet. Before surgery, your cocker will usually undergo a health check, which typically includes bloodwork.

The vet makes a small incision in front of your cocker's scrotum to allow access to the stalks of the testicles. These are severed and the testicles removed through the incision, then your vet will stitch the incision (pictured). The entire surgery usually takes 5 to 20 minutes.

In most cases, your dog cannot eat for at least 8 hours before the scheduled surgery, as anaesthesia often causes vomiting. The operation is performed under anaesthetic and the procedure is usually as follows:

- Intravenous fluids and/or medications are injected to support circulation and blood pressure.
- An endotracheal tube is inserted into the trachea—windpipe—to deliver the anaesthetic gas and provide oxygen to the lungs.
- Pulse oximetry is initiated to measure the oxygenation of the blood.
- Blood pressure and temperature monitoring commenced.
- Warming blankets are used to prevent hypothermia.
- Electrocardiography is used to monitor their heart.

After Surgery

Many dogs are fine to go home later the same day. When your cocker spaniel wakes up from their surgery, they will be in a crate where they are kept warm and monitored for any problems. When you go to pick up your dog, they will probably still feel groggy and might whine when they first come home, as they will still feel disoriented. Keep them quiet and warm, as it could take a little while for them to regain their normal temperature.

FACT ***It is likely your cocker will need to wear an Elizabethan collar or a cloud collar—a soft inflatable collar—to prevent them from licking the healing area.***

The vet will usually recommend that your spaniel should not engage in vigorous exercise during the 10-day healing period, after which they should return to their normal activities. Note that it can be difficult to curtail your young cocker's urge to run and play if they recover quicker than ten days.

Pros and Cons

There are both pros and cons you might want to consider when thinking about neutering your cocker spaniel.

Pros or reasons to book an appointment at the vet's include:

- Prevents accidental, unwanted pregnancies.
- Reduces the risk of prostate disorders.
- Prevents testicular cancer.
- Eliminates the urge to wander in search of a female to mate with.
- They are less likely to engage in aggressive conflicts with other male dogs.
- Reduces leg lifting or marking territory.
- Reduces sexual behaviour—humping other dogs, pillows, legs.
- Reduces the risk of being attacked by another dog.
- Your cocker spaniel will often be calmer, more focused, and loving with people.

Cons or reasons associated with deciding against the surgical procedure include:

- Possible weight gain.
- Increased risk of hemangiosarcoma.
- Increased risk of hypothyroidism.
- Increased risk of cognitive impairment during geriatric years.
- Concerns about possible complications during surgery.

Other Sterilisation Techniques

Zeutering is a new, non-surgical procedure designed to sterilise male dogs. Rather than removing your cocker's testicles, the chemical 'zeuterin' is injected into the testicles to render them sterile. This procedure is 99% effective, but as it is quite new, long-term effects have yet to be identified.

Furthermore, as this procedure does not remove the testicles, testosterone remains, which can cause aggressive tendencies towards other male dogs. This type of sterilisation will not protect your male cocker from some health risks that neutering can eliminate, such as certain cancers. Make sure to thoroughly research the subject and discuss it with your veterinarian before proceeding.

A vasectomy procedure for your cocker involves removing a portion of the tube that carries sperm from the testicle to impregnate the female dog. While this surgical procedure will render your dog infertile, they will still produce testosterone. Along with their testicles, they still have an interest in females, marking territory, being aggressive towards other males, and can still develop the cancers that neutering prevents.

Should I Breed My Cocker Spaniel?

Whatever your reason, there are important considerations to think about before embarking on a breeding programme.

FACT ***Most owners find their cocker's companionship so rewarding they wish to breed from their dog to continue the bloodline and/or keep a puppy. Others, particularly first-time owners, buy a female cocker with the intent to breed them when they are old enough.***

Below are the questions you need to ask yourself:

- Why do I want to breed my cocker? Perhaps, you just wish to continue the bloodline of your wonderful dog and keep one of the puppies who will be just like their mother. Bear in mind that the odds are against this type of outcome, as it is rare that any puppies are like their mother. If you want a dog with similar characteristics as your previous companion, it is a far better idea to contact the breeder or organisation where you obtained your dog. There is a possibility they might have a similar dog who would make an excellent addition to your family.
- Will I be able to find homes for the puppies? As the owner of the female cocker spaniel, you are responsible for finding homes for the puppies you do not wish to keep. Unfortunately, due to the number of unwanted dogs in animal shelters this is not always easy.
- I want to breed my dog to reduce their sexual activity. Does this work? Mating your cocker can make such behaviour worse. If your intent is to control or curtail your dog's sexual behaviour or proclivities, breeding them will not solve the problem.
- Will I be passing on any genetic defects or health concerns that could affect the offspring and weaken the breed? This possibility is always likely, but on the other hand, good breeders always make sure that no undesirable characteristics are being passed on during their breeding programme.
- Do I have the knowledge, time, and commitment required for successfully breeding my female? Dog breeding takes a lot of work, research, and knowledge. Ethical and responsible breeders work with a mentor who would have taught them about breeding dogs and helped them through breeding their first litter. Also, they will have done hours of research and know all the proper information needed before even deciding to mate their dog.
- Can I afford all the extra costs involved in breeding my female cocker (see section below)?

Breeding your female spaniel is far more complicated than letting them freely roam among intact males you come across at the park and then sitting back to wait for the puppies to emerge. Beyond the initial expense of purchasing a purebred female, the costs involved in breeding them can be as much as £2 700 in the United Kingdom—based on a litter of four puppies. In the U.S. it can be as much as $4 500 or more. The sort of expenses you might expect include:

- Pre and post-natal visits to the vet.
- Health tests and clearance.

- Stud-service fee.
- Progesterone tests.
- Ultrasound and x-rays.
- Food.
- Supplements.
- Whelping box.
- Whelping kit.
- Deworming—for multiple puppies.
- Vaccinations—for multiple puppies.
- Puppy food.
- Microchips.
- Possible C-section birth.
- Registration of the litter.

TIP ***Breeding your dog is not something you should enter into lightly. It is a huge responsibility, and you need to be certain you are doing the best for your cocker and their puppies. It is not just about putting two dogs together to create the perfect litter of puppies. Breeding requires knowledge and expertise that all responsible breeders possess.***

Of course, the final decision is up to you. But once you consider the aforementioned factors and expenses involved in the breeding process, you might decide that breeding is not something you wish to embark on.

20. Rescue Dogs

'Petting, scratching, and cuddling a dog could be as soothing to the mind and heart as deep meditation, and almost as good for the soul as prayer.'

~ Dean Koontz ~

If you have decided to share your home with a cocker spaniel, it is not always necessary to get your puppy from a breeder. There is always the option to adopt from various rescue shelters in the United Kingdom, such as the RSPCA—SPCA facilities in the U.S. While this means the dog or puppy you adopt will usually be older, there are many who make their way into shelters at a young age.

There are rescue and adoption facilities with almost every breed in most major cities around the globe. This means if you have decided to adopt a cocker spaniel, all you need to do is enter a search in Google that includes your location, the name of the breed and the words 'rescue' or 'adoption'.

Also, many breeders can connect you with a dog who needs to be rehomed, and various social networking groups are very willing to point you in the right direction.

Should I Adopt?

While deciding to adopt or rescue a cocker who needs to be rehomed is a very personal decision. There are several factors to consider when deciding if this is right for you.

FACT ***Many dogs end up at a rescue facility or shelter during the adolescent time in their life between six months and a year old.***

Beyond becoming lost and separated from their family, there are many other reasons why a dog has been turned over to a rescue or shelter. For instance, shelters are overflowing with dogs who have not been properly house-trained, socialised, or taught basic obedience. Due to that, they could have developed behavioural issues their owner found too hard to overcome. Other reasons that lead owners to surrender their dog to a shelter facility include:

Insufficient Research – Sometimes, deciding to get a dog is spontaneous, rather than a well thought out and thoroughly researched decision. Careful research when deciding to add a dog to your family ensures this will be a lifelong choice that makes everyone happy.

Energy Incompatibility – First-time owners might not be aware how important it is to choose a dog who fits well with their lifestyle and energy level. For example, choosing a high-energy dog for a family who spend their leisure time in front of the TV can spell disaster for everyone.

Training Inexperience – The amount of training involved in raising a dog to be a well-behaved family member is not always apparent to the prospective dog owners. When this becomes clear after a few months, many owners decide to take their dog to a shelter.

Cost of Dog Ownership – Sometimes, people are not aware of the exact costs involved to properly care for a dog until they get one. Food, toys, clothing, grooming, pet sitting, and vet bills can represent a significant cost, especially if your cocker has added health issues.

Unforeseen Life Changes – Life happens and often our circumstances can change dramatically. This can mean encountering health issues that prevent properly caring for your dog, moving to a new home that does not allow dogs, a new job or baby who leaves little time for the dog.

Time Commitment – The amount of time you have available to care for your dog can change as you become busier and other areas of your life begin to take precedence. Sometimes, children beg for a dog and promise to care for their every need, and then their interests change, and the dog's requirements are neglected.

Allergies – The family might not have been initially aware that someone in the home has an allergy to dogs, or a new baby or roommate could be allergic.

Unruly Behaviour – Though a dog's unruly behaviour might simply be during their adolescent phase, when they are biting or exhibiting other dangerous or aggressive tendencies, this is often when they find their way into a rescue shelter.

Health Problems – Sometimes, when a dog is injured or has chronic or age-related health issues, they could be surrendered to a shelter, because their owner can no longer afford medications, or does not have the time or patience to care for them.

FACT ***In the United Kingdom it is estimated that at any given time there are over 600 000 homeless dogs in over 1 000 shelters. In the United States there are over 10,000 shelter and rescue groups alone, sheltering over 3.1 million dogs each year.***

Mostly, adopted dogs are physically healthy and might already be neutered, vaccinated, microchipped, and often house-trained. All this reduces the initial cost of purchasing your cocker spaniel, while giving a deserving dog a second chance.

Rescued dogs can lack life experience and come with some behavioural problems that need to be addressed. However, if you are patient, fair and consistent with their training programme, most dogs are eager to become an affectionate and loyal family member. Rescuing a dog also means that you will have helped to control the overflow of dogs who have been abandoned to various organisations, which makes the choice to rescue a win-win for both the dog and you.

Due to bad press and publicity, shelter dogs have often had an unearned bad rap. When people—mostly non-animal lovers—think of shelter dogs, they picture a vicious, volatile animal who has been surrendered to a shelter because it bit its owner. Nevertheless, this couldn't be further from the reality. Here are some shelter dog facts that should finally dispel any doubts you might have.

- Not every shelter dog is a mutt – People believe the only way they will ever find a purebred cocker is through a breeder, but that is not the case. On the contrary, in the United States DoSomething.org notes that a staggering 25 percent of all dogs in animal shelters are purebred.
- A huge problem is overpopulation – Adorable as puppies are, the world simply has too many of them—at least compared to the current demand for dogs. Not only are most dogs not neutered, on average a fertile dog produces one litter a year, each litter consisting of between four to six pups. When these puppies cannot find homes, they end up in shelters, creating a high demand for the small number of shelters.

- No neutering or spaying costs – Having your dog neutered or spayed is expensive, but it is not an expense you have to worry about if you adopt a shelter dog. Most shelters cover the cost of the procedure while the dog is in their care. These costs are included in the fee you pay when adopting your new four-legged friend.
- Supporting a good cause – By adopting, you are fighting against the puppy mills, where dogs are kept in overcrowded, soiled cages, unable to socialise or roam.
- Shelter dogs are unique – If you want a dog who is one of a kind, the shelter is the place to go. According to a study of over 900 puppies published in PLOS ONE, the average shelter dog is a mix of three different breeds!
- Shelter dogs love humans – A recent study published in the Journal of Veterinary Behaviour: Clinical Applications and Research found that, compared to pet dogs, shelter dogs are 'more socially driven to gaze and interact with humans'. If you adopt instead of buying through a breeder, you should be ready to receive all the affection in the world.
- Pit bulls are extremely misunderstood – Pit bulls are the most common breed found in animal shelters, but that could be because they are misunderstood. While most people consider the breed to be aggressive and vicious, one study conducted by the website Dognition has found out of 35 common breeds the pit bull was ranked as one of the least aggressive.

- There are more homeless animals than people – Dogs suffer from vagrancy as much as people do. According to the DoSomething.org website, for every homeless human there are five homeless animals on the street.
- You can live longer – If you adopt a dog from the shelter it is a win-win situation. According to one study published in Scientific Reports, out of 3.4 million individuals, single dog owners were 33 percent less likely to die compared to their pet-free friends.
- Dogs provide children with a better home environment – What they say about shelter dogs is true: You not only save them, but they save you, too. A University of Florida study found that having a dog around helps children to cope better with stress, preparing them for success in the future.
- People still buy dogs from breeders instead of adopting them – Although people are aware how many dogs there are in shelters, the ASPCA stated that 34 percent of dogs are obtained from breeders, whereas only 23 percent are adopted from humane societies or animal shelters.
- All shelter dogs are carefully evaluated – One thing stopping people from adopting a dog from a shelter is the worry that the dog will have hidden health or behavioural issues. However, according to vice president of companion animals at the Humane Society of the United States, Kenny Lamberti, 'the vast majority of dogs that would come from a shelter are evaluated for behaviour

and health'. Not only do shelters analyse every animal that comes into their care, but they do so in a more thorough manner than most breeders and pet shops.

- Most shelter dogs are euthanised – It is sad but true. According to the PetFinder pet adoption website, nationwide approximately 60 percent of shelter dogs nationwide are put to sleep every year because they cannot find a home.
- Most dogs do not find their forever home – If you are still unsure about adopting a shelter dog, then consider this: According to the Mosby Foundation, a non-profit organisation that helps care for abused and injured animals, only 1 in every 10 dogs born is ever placed in a permanent, loving home.

If you decide adopting a rescue dog is a journey you wish to embark on, you can find a list of the main U.K. and U.S. rescue organisations following this chapter.

What to Expect When Adopting a Dog

Even though you might wish to save a cocker from a shelter or a rescue organisation, it is possible you are not a suitable candidate. Whilst it is true that there are countless puppies waiting for an owner, it is essential for dog shelters to thoroughly check people before giving them a dog to take home. Their goal is to ensure each dog up for adoption goes to a happy, loving family who will be a good match for their personality, so they do not end up back in the shelter.

When it comes to the adoption process, most dog shelters have the same rules:

- Submit an adoption application.
- Have an interview with one of the shelter's counsellors.
- Meet the rescue cocker spaniel you have chosen.
- If the interview is successful and the spaniel you chose is the right fit for you and your family, you will be required to pay a small adoption fee before taking them home.

By following these steps, shelters try to ensure people who adopt dogs are not doing it on a whim and re capable of providing love, care, and a long-term home for their would-be four-legged companion.

Although, beforehand it is important to be aware that shelter interview questions will be personal and intrusive for some people. Each shelter has their own specific interview procedure, but most tend to structure them like an informal, honest conversation instead of an exam you need to pass. Once you understand all those questions are only there to ensure your future canine family member is in the right hands, you will have no problem answering them.

When it comes to the dog adoption interview, below are some of the questions you should expect:

- **What is your family situation?** How many children are in your family and how many adults? Does everyone in the household want to adopt a dog?
- **What is your housing situation?** Do you live in your own home or are you renting? What type of property do you have? Are you planning to move soon?
- **What is your previous experience with pets, and do you own any animals right now?** The number of pets, history of having pets, and what happened to each of them? Do you know how to socialise a cocker into their new family?
- **What is your work situation?** Can you afford to own and look after your new cocker? How long are your work hours and do you have to commute? Will you leave your dog alone for hours due to your work?

These are questions to determine if you are suitable to take on the responsibility of owning a dog. Although, they might seem a bit too much, they are essential. When you understand that moving away is one reason dogs are abandoned, followed by strict property owners, financial issues, and lack of time due to work responsibilities, these personal questions make far more sense.

The next two questions are area aimed at helping the counsellor understand whether you are the right personality match for the cocker you want to adopt and vice versa:

- **What lifestyle do you lead?** Are you an active, outdoorsy person or will you take your dog with you on holiday, to social events, etc? Are you in a relationship and how would your dog fit into it?
- **Do you have any knowledge about rescue dogs?** Will you train and socialise your dog? Are you aware that dogs sometimes end up in a shelter because of abuse and neglect and never fully recover? What is your reason for adopting this dog?

Being honest when answering these questions is an absolute must. Be truthful with yourself and do not agree to something you are unsure you will be able to see it through. Nobody wants the adopted cocker spaniel to be unhappy or experience abandonment again.

Rescue Dog Special Needs

Unless a rescue dog has some form of medical or physical impediment, they will have no needs that are considered special, beyond giving them time to get used to their new home. Often, people who rescue dogs can end up creating behavioural issues for their dog, because they feel sorry for their previous treatment.

A *feeling sorry* type of energy is not what a rescue dog requires, as they could already be feeling nervous, confused, and uncertain. What will help them to acclimate to new people and surroundings is a kind, yet strong and confident leader who they can learn to trust and follow, so they can relax in their new home.

Plan to give your rescued cocker spaniel time to adjust to their new home and family. Dogs can take anywhere from a few hours to several months to become used to living in a new home. During their adjustment period, do what you can to make your new cocker feel safe and comfortable. While they adjust, be patient and try to keep things consistent and predictable in their unfamiliar environment.

A cocker who has spent several weeks or more in a shelter might be stressed because their life has become so unpredictable. By establishing a feeding routine, with regular walks, playtime, and bedtime you can provide them with some stability. Normally, this will significantly help your spaniel to adjust to their new home.

TIP ***Treat your shelter dog the same way you would any new puppy coming into your home. Assume they have never had any training. Even if your cocker had obedience training in the past, they could need a refresher after all they have been through.***

Your best option is to expect your dog to know nothing. That way you will be pleasantly surprised if they know some basic commands or are house-trained already. Nevertheless, it means you will not be setting your cocker puppy up for failure by having expectations that are too high. Be certain you train your new spaniel using positive reinforcement. Training sessions should be upbeat and stress-free.

Socialisation can be a challenge with adopted dogs. As with training, it is important to get your cocker spaniel used to their environment, people, and other animals they may encounter in their new life with you. This should be done slowly and within your cocker's comfort level.

Assuming too much, or too little about your dog's past is one of the most common mistakes new owners make with their rescue dog. Not every dog in the shelter has had a traumatic past. Also, not all of them have been properly trained or socialised. With every aspect of your cocker's care, take the approach that it is a blank canvas waiting for your direction, training, and love.

Remember, training starts the day your new spaniel comes home. It is tempting to coddle them for the first week or so to try to make up for their time spent in the shelter.

However, if you allow your shelter dog to engage in certain behaviour when you first bring them home, you might find it harder to train them to stop doing those things later. This includes things such as jumping on the sofa, eliminating on the carpet, or chewing table legs. You need to establish your cocker's boundaries early on and ensure the entire family enforces them.

As with a new puppy, it is important to introduce your shelter dog to crate training as soon as possible. That way, you can work on house-training and be comfortable your cocker spaniel will not get into mischief when left unsupervised.

A crate is helpful as it gives your shelter dog a place of their own. Between living in a shelter and coming to their new home, your cocker might feel extremely stressed. Having a place to retreat to when they feel overwhelmed will go a long way towards helping your spaniel settle in.

Crates can be difficult for some dogs, especially if their previous owner used it as a place of punishment or they spent too much time in one. To turn their crate training into a positive experience, never force them in if they are reluctant.

While your cocker is adjusting to their new home, be sure to always supervise them, especially when outside. Even if you have a fenced-in garden, your dog could become curious about or startled by noises, sights, and smells outside the boundary. If they get loose, your cocker will have a hard time finding their way back to their new home as they are unfamiliar with the area.

It is highly recommended that you enrol your rescue dog in an obedience class. Regular training sessions are helpful for getting your dog into a routine. Starting a training programme also helps to establish boundaries for your dog from the offset. An obedience class will set your cocker up for good behaviour and make it easier for them to become a happy and healthy member of your family. Remember, dogs are most at ease if they know the rules. Training your new dog properly from the start is one of the best things you can do for them as dogs crave structure and predictability.

How to Choose a Rescue Dog

It can be difficult to choose the right dog for your family. Each dog has their own personality, so it is essential to find a dog who fits in with your own character.

One of the biggest mistakes you can make is to fall in love with a dog just because of their looks. Yes, they might have the cutest puppy eyes you ever saw, but can you commit to taking care of all their needs? Will the dog you want get on well with your other pets or children? If you choose a cocker for adoption whose activity level and personality do not match yours, you are bound to have some trouble.

When you choose a rescue dog from your local shelter, bear in mind there are some dogs who have little chance of being adopted.

For some people, deciding which dog to take home can be something of a roller coaster. Seeing all those pleading eyes and so many loving puppies and dogs it can make you feel guilty you are not taking them all with you.

The best thing you can do is help as much as you can, whether by volunteering your time, donating, or spreading the word about adoptable dogs and shelters that take them in.

Final Thoughts

Without question, regardless of whether they are from a shelter or a breeder, all dogs are loyal and loving. If you decide to adopt a dog, you will be saving their life. For a shelter dog, you might be their last chance for happiness. To be totally honest, there is nothing quite like the bond rescue dogs make with their families. They never forget their human is the one who gave them a second chance.

Although you cannot change a dog's past, you can help shape their future!

Helpful Links

Associations and Services

- Association for Pet Obesity Prevention: www.petobesityprevention.org
- Dog TV: https://www.dogtv.com
- Canine Journal: www.caninejournal.com
- International Boarding and Pet Services Association: www.ibpsa.com

Societies & Clubs

- American Kennel Club: www.akc.org
- American Spaniel Club: www.americanSpanielclub.org
- Cockers Online: www.Cockersonline.co.uk
- English Cocker Spaniel Club of America: www.englishCocker.org
- Royal Society for the Prevention of Cruelty to Animals: www.rspca.org.uk
- The Cocker Spaniel Club: www.theCockerSpanielclub.co.uk
- The London Cocker Spaniel Society: www.londonCockersociety.co.uk
- United Kennel Club: www.ukcdogs.com

Breed Forums

- Cockers Online Forum: www.Cockersonline.co.uk
- Dog Forums: www.dogforums.com
- My Cocker Spaniel Forum: www.myCockerSpaniel.com
- Pet Forums: www.petforums.co.uk

Cocker Spaniel Breeders

- Acadia's Cockers: https://www.acadiascockers.net/
- Aisza English Cocker Spaniels: www.CockerSpanielpuppy.co.uk
- Candy's Cockers: www.candysCockers.com
- Carmelfair Cocker Spaniels: www.carmelfair.co.uk
- Honey Tree Cocker Spaniels: www.CockerSpanieldogs.co.uk
- Shadool's Cockers: www.shadoolsCockers.com
- Shenmore Cocker Spaniels: www.shenmore-Cockers.co.uk
- Soundview Cockers: www.webbcockers.com/
- Tru-Luv Cockers: https://www.truluvcockers.com/
- Toybox Cockers: www.toyboxCockers.com

Dog Trainers & Psychologists

- Assistance Dogs International: https://assistancedogsinternational.org/

- Dognition: www.dognition.com

Poison Control

- Animal Poison Line: www.animalpoisonline.co.uk
- Pet Poison Helpline: www.petpoisonhelpline.com
- American Society for Prevention of Cruelty to Animals: https://www.aspca.org/pet-care/animal-poison-control

Rescues

- Angels Under Our Wings: www.angelsunderourwings.com
- Camp Cocker Rescue: www.campCocker.com
- CAESSR: www.caessr.org.uk
- Cocker Spaniel Rescue Network: www.CockerSpanielrescue.org
- DIBS Rescue: www.dibsrescue.com
- Preloved: www.preloved.co.uk
- Saveour Spaniels: www.saveourSpaniels.org.uk
- Second Chance Cocker Rescue: www.secondchanceCockerrescue.org
- Spaniel Aid UK: https://spanielaid.co.uk/
- The Cocker Spaniel Club Rescue Scheme: www.theCockerSpanielclub.co.uk

Resources (Informational)

- Canine to Five: www.caninetofive.com
- Dog Food Advisor: www.dogfoodadvisor.com
- Dogs Naturally Magazine: www.dogsnaturallymagazine.com
- Fairmount Pet Service: https://fairmountpetservice.com/Blog/index/
- Plato Pet Treats: www.platopettreats.com
- Purina: www.purina.com
- The Farmer's Dog: www.thefarmersdog.com
- Truth About Pet Food: www.truthaboutpetfood.com

Canine Care Log

Vet's Details	Groomer's Details	Sitter's Details
Name: Tel: Address:	Name: Tel: Address:	Name: Tel: Address:

Dog's Name	Date	Vet or Groomer?	Treatment	Cost	Comments

Published by Alex Lloyd 2022

Disclaimer and Legal Notice: This product is not medical or legal advice and should not be interpreted in that manner. You need to do your own due diligence to determine if the content of this product is right for you. The authors and the affiliates of this product are not liable for any damages or losses associated with the content in this product.

While every attempt has been made to verify the information shared in this publication, neither the author nor the affiliates assume any responsibility for errors, omissions, or contrary interpretation of the subject matter herein. Any perceived slights to any specific person(s) or organisation(s) are purely unintentional. We have no control over the nature, content and availability of the web sites listed in this book.

The accuracy and completeness of information provided herein, and opinions stated herein are not guaranteed or warranted to produce any specific results, and the advice and strategies, contained herein may not be suitable for every dog or individual. The author shall not be liable for any loss incurred because of the use and application, directly or indirectly, of any information presented in this work. This publication is designed to provide information regarding the subject matter covered.

The information included in this book has been compiled to give as thorough an overview of the subject as possible and detail some of the symptoms, treatments etc. that are available. It is not intended to give medical advice. For a firm diagnosis of any health condition, and for a treatment plan suitable for you and your dog, you should consult your veterinarian or health care consultant.

The writer of this book and the publisher are not responsible for any damages or negative consequences that may arise because of following any of the treatments, suggestions or methods highlighted in this book.

The writer of this book understands and respects the many differing opinions regarding what may be considered appropriate choices when caring for any dog. Any identified products, suggestions, opinions, methods, or recommendations that may be noted here are simply based on professional experience, which may or may not agree with every reader and nothing written here is intended to be in any way adversarial or confrontational.

Printed in Great Britain
by Amazon

83037427R00210